THE OCCUPIED CLINIC

The Occupied Clinic

Militarism and Care in Kashmir   ⚘   SAIBA VARMA

DUKE UNIVERSITY PRESS   DURHAM AND LONDON   2020

© 2020 Duke University Press
All rights reserved
Printed in the United States of America on acid-free paper ∞
Text design by Amy Ruth Buchanan
Cover design by Courtney Leigh Richardson
Typeset in Portrait by Copperline Book Services

Library of Congress Cataloging-in-Publication Data
Names: Varma, Saiba, [date] author.
Title: The occupied clinic : militarism and care in Kashmir /
Saiba Varma.
Description: Durham : Duke University Press, 2020. |
Includes bibliographical references and index.
Identifiers: LCCN 2019058232 (print) |
LCCN 2019058233 (ebook)
ISBN 9781478009924 (hardcover)
ISBN 9781478010982 (paperback)
ISBN 9781478012511 (ebook)
Subjects: LCSH: Psychiatric clinics—India—Jammu and
Kashmir. | War victims—Mental health—India—Jammu
and Kashmir. | War victims—Mental health services—
India—Jammu and Kashmir. | Civil-military relations—
India—Jammu and Kashmir. | Military occupation—
Psychological aspects.
Classification: LCC RC451.I42 J36 2020 (print) |
LCC RC451.I42 (ebook) | DDC 362.2/109546—dc23
LC record available at https://lccn.loc.gov/2019058232
ISBN ebook record available at
https://lccn.loc.gov/2019058233

Duke University Press gratefully acknowledges the Office
of Vice Chancellor for Research at the University of
California, San Diego, which provided funds toward the
publication of this book.

Cover art: Untitled, from *The Depth of a Scar* series.
© Faisal Magray. Courtesy of the artist.

For Nani,

who always knew how to put the world back

together

CONTENTS

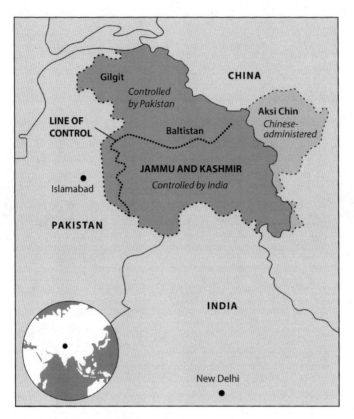

FIGURE P.I. Map of Kashmir

In translating spoken Urdu and Kashmiri in this text, I have provided diacritical markings only for long vowels (for example, *āzādī*) in order to ease pronunciation for non-native speakers. In so doing, I have departed from a technically precise transliteration. I have avoided all diacritical markings on names, however, and followed convention.

ACKNOWLEDGMENTS

Grace Lee Boggs reminds us that everything we know of ourselves and the world comes through conversation. Every idea here was born with someone: in cars, cafés, couches, conferences, and classrooms. My deepest thanks to all those named and unnamed who co-journeyed with me.

Professional journeys and book writing are long and tenuous processes, especially in academia today. Like many academic books, this one began as a PhD dissertation and with a writing group. I am deeply grateful for almost fifteen years of thinking, communing, and togetherness with Chika Watanabe and Gökçe Günel. Thank you for being my touchstones on this crazy journey. With Melissa Rosario, Aftab Jassal, and Courtney Work, we made an unflappable writing community that set the tone for years to come. My dissertation committee supported and challenged me in all the right ways. Annelise Riles provided a bedrock of enthusiasm, while demanding courage, originality, and disciplinary care. Lucinda Ramberg made me kin, inviting me into her home and life, and taught me how to blur the personal, ethical, affective, and intellectual with the most joyous results. My studies with Stacey Langwick were intellectually transformative, exciting, and full of mirth. Durba Ghosh always asked the big questions, reminding me of the unsaid and what's at stake. Her tenacity and curiosity continue to inspire me. I also thank the teachers who forged an intellectual path for me early in life: Misty Bastian, Michael Billig, Anjuli Kaul, and Pramod Menon.

For those who have read, listened, commented, and invited me to present this work, enriching it in countless ways, I thank: Can Aciksoz, Tuva Beyer Broch, Paul Brodwin, Mara Buchbinder, Jocelyn Chua, Ellen Corin, Talia Dan-Cohen, Chris Dole, Nadia El-Shaarawi, Daena Funahashi, Cristiana Giordano, Eric Greene, Akhil Gupta, Sherine Hamdy, Chris Hanssmann, Ayesha Jalal, Erica C. James, Zeynep Korkman, Rebecca Lester, Purnima Mankekar, Kate Martineau, Tomas Matza, Mark Micale, Towns Middleton, Jecca Namakkal, Shanti Parikh, Sarah Pinto, Hans Pols, Peter Redfield, Annemarie Samuels, stef schuster, Lotte Buch Segal, Merav Shohet, Esa Syeed, Jennifer Terry, Allen Tran, Andrew Willford, and Asli Zengin. My writing group, Hanna Garth, Lee Cabatingan, and Minu Tankha, provided a steadying hand and laser-sharp focus, and I thank them for their constant, collaborative care. Alexia Arani offered brilliant comments on the final manuscript and organized an incredibly thoughtful index that helped me see the stakes of this project in a fresh way. I have also learned so much from fellow medical anthropologists of South Asia: Dwai Banerjee, Jocelyn Chua, Lawrence Cohen, Veena Das, Sushrut Jadhav, Sumeet Jain, Jocelyn Marrow, Sarah Pinto, Lucinda Ramberg, Aidan Seale-Feldman, Harris Solomon, Cecilia van Hollen, Emma Varley, Bharat Venkat, Kalindi Vora, and many more—thank you for your amazing work. Kaushik Sunder Rajan, Sarah Pinto, and Peter Redfield raised the bar for what reviewers can do—and be. Thank you for incredibly thoughtful and insightful comments that saw through and beyond the words on the page. My editor, Courtney Berger, believed in this project when it desperately needed a champion. She and Sandra Korn have been a dream team.

I'm deeply grateful for a social, political, and intellectual life in southern California that is in equal parts stimulating and fun: Maud Arnal, Tarik Benmarhnia, Amy Cimini, Denise Demetriou, Claire Edington, Yến Lê Espiritu, Hanna Garth, Cathy Gere, Joe Hankins, Todd Henry, Ari Heinrich, Lilly Irani, Bonnie Kaiser, Dredge Kang, Simeon Man, Lorena Gómez Mostajo, Dan Navon, David Pederson, Nancy Postero, Leslie Quintilla, Matt Vitz, Kalindi Vora, Rihan Yeh, and Sal Zarate have been wonderful friends and coconspirators. The UCHRI Feminist Science Studies collective hatched brilliant, nefarious plans in a hot tub: Chris, Leslie, Lilly, Kalindi, and Sal—I am so grateful to be able to learn from you. Amy, Claire, Lilly, and Kalindi generously commented on chapters, inspired many ideas, and kept my soul full and happy. In the Department of Anthropology, I thank Steve Parish for his faith in my work and his generous mentorship. Thanks to Tom Csordas and Jan Jenkins for their collegiality. My UCSD undergraduates never fail to sparkle in dark times. My "Living in an Emotional World" graduate seminar offered helpful comments on chapter 5. Many writing sessions were fueled by the lovely staff and coffee at Subterranean coffee shop.

It is no accident that this book ends with reflections on Kashmiri hospitality. The Mehta family, particularly Anita Mehta, created a web of kinship, warmth, and strength that I will always cherish. I remain ever grateful for the friendship of Hemi Mehta and Sonali Mehta. Yasir Zahgeer and Asiya also provided a generous and welcoming home base and fed me many delicious meals. Yasir has been an incredibly resourceful friend, interlocutor, and research assistant. My first visits to Kashmir were possible thanks to the remarkable kindness of the Khan family—Khan Sahab, Sami, and Ishfaq in particular—who welcomed two strangers into their home with no questions, just open arms.

I navigated the complex landscape of Kashmiri public and mental health care thanks to many psychiatrists, clinical psychologists, social workers, counselors, and patients. Visitors to mental health settings—patients and caregivers alike—stopped their lives and risked exposure by talking to me, and then went beyond by inviting me into their homes and sharing aspirations, fears, and anxieties. Although many must remain unnamed, my gratitude to them is beyond measure. In particular, I want to thank "Mauna" and her family for their kindness and openness in the midst of extraordinary pain. My foremost thanks also to Dr. Arshad Hussain, whose dazzling intellect continually challenges preconceived critiques of psychiatry and who continues to be a dream interlocutor for any anthropologist. Dr. Muzzafar Khan was always a welcoming presence and offered me fieldwork access that would change the course of my intellectual project. My thanks also to Dr. Zaid Wani, Dr. Mushtaq Margoob, Dr. Mudasir Firdosi, Dr. Sadaqat, and Dr. Huda Mushtaq (who shared countless lunches with me in her office), Dr. Wiqar Bashir, Dr. "Abdullah," Dr. Arif, and many others. I have also learned an immense amount from humanitarian organizations, including MSF and Action Aid, that allowed me to follow their projects, their successes and challenges. Arnaud Meffre has been a generous friend since the beginning of this project. Justine Hardy and Prerna Sud have been amazing guides, friends, and unpaid therapists on this journey. I heartily thank them and the Kashmir LifeLine staff for letting me into their world.

This project has also been deeply enriched by friends and Kashmir studies scholars who live and breathe decolonization. Aaliya Anjum has been a joy to think with and always knows how to make me laugh. Aijaz Hussain offered innumerable thought-jewels, many of which are reflected in the pages that follow. Wajahat Ahmed read, engaged, and infinitely improved several chapters, corrected historical and historiographic wrongs, and shared jokes, insights, and poetry across long distances. On a fateful trip to Makhdoom sahib, Feroz Rather became a fellow *musafir*. Over the years, I have learned so much from Showkat Ahmed, Nosheen Ali, Mona Bhan, Parvaiz Bukhari, Sanobar Durrani, Haley Duschinski, Naushad Gayoor, Zulfikar Hussain, Mohamad Junaid, Sanjay Kak, Hafsa Kanjwal, Suvir Kaul, Seema Kazi, Inshah Malik, Freny Manecksha, Sanna Irshad Mattoo, Cabeiri deBergh Robinson, Aditi Saraf, and Ather Zia. Nishita Trisal and I spent many days cowriting and cothinking, and without her sharp editing and unfailing generosity, I would still be spinning my wheels. Emma Varley is a joy to collaborate with, a precious friend who has forever reshaped how I think about medicine. Faisal Magray lent his beautiful photograph for the book's cover.

Given and chosen families have been patient, supportive, and offered plenty of welcome distraction. Brenda Baletti and Alvaro Reyes, political wayfinders and lifegivers, thank you for being our family in the United States and for doing—not just showing—a beautiful otherwise. Even though they are far away, the deep and abiding friendship of Yeshwant Holkar, Sidhant Khanna, Noemi Y. Molitor, Jill Ranson, and Anita Trehan means the world to me. Seerat Bhalla, Smita Tewari Jassal, Tanu and Samir Kukreja, Deepa Lal, Namrita Puri, Ravi Inder Singh, Gaurav and Sumaya Singh, Abhai Varma, and many others have encouraged me. Meher, my sister, is always here, in every word I write. Thank you for making me laugh like no one else, for your understanding, love, and those cozy evenings talking about everything under the *razai* that we will never outgrow. My parents, Manju and Krishan, have showered me with boundless love. Thank you for teaching me how to love fiercely and openly, giving me plenty of space to flourish, for nurturing a love of reading and writing, and for showing me how to struggle with grace. Aftab Singh Jassal, moon in my sky, my dream conversational partner—thank you for your wildness, your love, and for encouraging me to leave the ground behind.

Letter to No One

My dear Na-cheez,[1]

You warned me something was coming. "Something big," you said, in an elusive text message before the blackout began. Hours later, I woke to a persistent, loud knocking.[2] As my eyes opened, I saw the sky had turned—from the depths of blackness, it was now an inky blue.

Aunty was at my door. Immediately, I felt something was wrong, because she had climbed the steep staircase up to my room with her bad knees.

"My cell phone is dead," she said calmly. "Can you check yours?"

I put on my glasses and stared at my phone's screen. The Indian telecommunication company's imprint, "Airtel" was gone. A message— "No Service"—had taken its place. The Wi-Fi symbol, still optimistically blooming on the screen, turned out to be just that, a symbol. A symbol that now stood for nothing. When I picked up the landline, the dial tone had disappeared. There was an eerie silence on the other end.

Aunty and I went out into the alleyway, concealing our nightclothes with voluminous shawls. Neighbors had also gathered, and we collectively mused why our communications had disappeared. For days, there had been ominous warnings: all tourists and Hindu pilgrims had been ordered to leave the state of Jammu and Kashmir overnight; helicopters, planes, and drones were zigzagging the sky, crackling drumrolls of war; 35,000 extra troops had landed in the valley, adding to the more than 400,000 troops already here; people were nervously stocking up on food and basic essentials, as if anticipating the arrival of a massive storm.

At the same time, the well of sardonic humor was deep: *the certainty of uncertainty*, people joked, *in a zone of occupation*. People had learned to doubt themselves. Maybe it was all in our heads? Maybe it was to stir panic out of thin air? But deep down, we knew. Eight million soothsayers registered ethereal transmissions of affect, feeling, and familiar dread in their bones. Meanwhile, the state government publicly scolded Kashmiris for "rumor mongering" and insisted that everything was normal.

This was a message telling you to mistrust your own senses. This was how your body was taken away, how it was made not-yours, bit by bit.

6 a.m. Muffled sounds from a patrolling paramilitary jeep announced the start of curfew. They ordered everyone back inside their homes until further notice. For hours, we sat and waited for our sentencing—the punishment, apparently, has to come first. The Indian government had made two historic decisions, designed to bring the "troubled" and "terror-ridden" (their language) state of Jammu and Kashmir under greater central Indian government control. The last vestiges of Kashmir's autonomy were revoked, and the state was broken up into two union territories.

On television, we watched the government's PR machine churn. The decisions were sold to the Indian public as necessary for Kashmir's greater integration with India, to end terrorism, facilitate economic development, and invigorate the tourism industry. Though the decision was articulated in the language of care and development, those most affected by it were not consulted. The 8 million residents of the state were put under a total, indefinite communication blackout and curfew. *To prevent any untoward incident*, an amphibious bureaucrat croaked on TV. In the days that followed, the TV, now our only connection to the outside world, became a funhouse mirror. We watched as distorted images of the reality on the ground were fed back to us.

At first, everyone tried to keep the tone light. The Indian government had done things like this before: curfews, communication blackouts (more than 180 have been imposed on Jammu and Kashmir since 2012), and many other decisions made without consulting Kashmiris still felt unsavory, but they were not new. Kashmiris had learned that to live in a zone of perpetual instability is to live in a state of constant vigilance, to recognize that yesterday's unimaginable and impossible can become today's reality.

But then, things started to fall apart. First slowly, and then faster. A few isolated incidents leaked out: an elderly man's wife had died in Delhi, but because of the blackout, no one had been able to reach him. A friend's mother, and countless, nameless others, were running out of chemotherapy drugs, which had to be ordered online. As the days of curfew, blackout, and infrastructural war continued, salaries and savings evaporated. I heard stories of middle-class families breaking their children's piggybanks to stay afloat.

After the first month, which people only survived thanks to their premonition, careful planning, and execution, the catastrophes cascaded. As the blackout stretched on, I was haunted by your words. Back in the summer of 2014, after the Hindu supremacist BJP government led by Narendra Modi had first swept to national victory, you had said, "Modi has come to finish us. He has come to destroy Kashmir." I had dismissed your words as hyperbolic. But now I understood. You did not mean genocide in a spectacular sense, although, as you know, Modi has that, too, in his-story. Rather, the game now was slow violence in the form of demographic changes and settlements, the influx of financial capital, from whose spoils Kashmiris will be excluded, changes to land ownership laws, the detention and criminalization of young people, the prohibition of expression and dissent, weaponizing all aspects of civilian life.

"If the government had to do this, fine! But why did they have to do it like *this*?" someone asked. Others found a silver lining: perhaps now, we had finally reached a limit—the government's decision to take direct control of the state clarified the true nature of Indian rule: "How can anyone now deny that this is an occupation?" I heard, over and over again. Maybe the ruse of democratic rule was finally up. Without the distraction of screens, only novels to keep me company, my dreams became more vivid.

Though you've lived through many blockades before, this time must feel different. This siege was harder to see, harder to measure. While in previous periods it was possible to count casualties and injuries, now the siege was being invisibilized across many scales thanks to the communication blackout. Indian state officials flatly denied that there were any casualties since the blackout began, despite many reports to the contrary. Hospital administrators were prevented from admitting injured protestors (all patients were suspected protestors and therefore "criminals") so as to avoid counting those bodies. Every morning, there were fresh reports of boys disappearing from their beds, snatched by the police in the middle of the night. One evening, while walking in the neighborhood, I saw family members gathered outside the police station, bound together through unspeakable loss. They would spend the night there, squatting on the cold concrete pavement, waiting for news of their kidnapped children's whereabouts.

A siege with no body counts. The absence of body counts did not mean the absence of harm. You saw how, on television, one BJP spokesperson described the siege as "not a big deal. Kashmiris have been through sieges before." Practices of survival and coping were turned into tactics of war. Like water squeezed out of a dishrag, life was wrung out, quietly, slowly, determinedly. The siege's effects became more pernicious. They were psychological, not just physiological—wearing people down, testing their willfulness, eroding their dignity. Capturing these harms was difficult because the siege's effects were ordinary and subtle, death by a thousand cuts. In a metric-obsessed world, Kashmir disappeared from view. This was precisely the point.

ॐ

While some international news stories reported on the siege, most governments applauded India's efforts or stayed neutral (neutrality, too, is a position, Na-cheez). A market of a billion consuming humans, a prize too great to jeopardize. Nonetheless, the Indian government did not like Kashmir receiving so much attention, nor did it want its own actions scrutinized.

Another PR offensive was launched, and it required a new repertoire of images from Kashmir to match the rhetoric that everything was "normal" and that Kashmiris were "happy" with the revocation of their autonomy and the institution of settler colonial policies. Yet, when the government tried returning things to "normal"—removing the (official) curfew, reopening schools, colleges, and government offices —no one was in the mood to comply. Things were *not* normal, people insisted. Without any direction, people again knew what to do. They refused "normalcy" and began collective civil disobedience. Overnight, the siege transformed into a voluntary strike. No one sent their children to school. No one opened their shops. No one, except government employees who were forced, went to work, forgoing salaries and stability. People exercised restraint and patience, fully knowing that a politics of refusal would mean inflicting further suffering on themselves.

Somehow, they resisted the script of bare life. Bakr-Id, the biggest annual Muslim holiday, came and went, without any celebrations, with locks on the city's largest mosques. *Too dangerous to let people gather,* another bureaucrat had barked another excuse. Instead of the conventional "Eid Mubarak" greeting, people joked, "Qaid Mubarak!" Congratulations to our imprisonment! I consoled myself that the communication blackout had also cut off the state's own eyes and ears. It could no longer eavesdrop on conversations; it had no idea what people were thinking.

Without 4G and Whatsapp and landlines, people created counter-infrastructures. We wrote notes and letters and created safe drop-offs across the city. We theorized collectively because each of us had access to only shards of information. Grace and hospitality flowed, like a cool summer breeze, keeping life and relations circulating. Neighbors visited each other, carrying news and gifts, checking on everyone's well-being (*khairiyat*). They sent rice pudding. We sent apples and plums from the garden. We heard stories of other sieges, in other times. "During Sikh rule in the nineteenth century, all the mosques were turned into horse stables," you reassured me. "Don't worry. We've been through much worse." These centuries-old wounds were recalled with the mixed emotions one has when remembering a scar from an innocent childhood game.

꩜

Na-cheez, I am ashamed I left before the siege was over. My month of fieldwork had run out and stuffy faculty meetings and empty course syllabi appeared on the horizon. I promise you, I did not want to leave. I wanted to refuse the political economy of knowledge and the global order that allowed for my departure, while forcing others to remain, and to remain obscured. And besides, the siege had held the rest of the world in abeyance. That was worth clinging onto.

I never fully arrived in California. Questions about Kashmir, a combination of genuine concern and naivete, produced a strange feeling in me. Each time I narrated something of the siege, I felt emptier. Or, more accurately, I felt myself in a cave of echoes. I had lost the origin. Well-meaning friends asked if I might want to see a therapist. I refused. I did not want to do any more translating. I wanted to hold onto my anger a little longer, to feel its pointed edge against the obscenely abundant jacaranda blossoms that were inciting me to forget.

Meanwhile, the funhouse mirror continued producing distorted figures of you and your captors. It made violence palatable. This, you taught me, is an old strategy of colonial rule. It was tried before. But I am still trying to understand what kind of care leaves people in pieces, Na-cheez? And what forms of life escape?

It seems absurd to ask how you are, to hope for your good health in these conditions. In any case, I have no way of getting this letter to you. So I'll simply say: Till soon.

[T]here is a sense of holding together in one's grasp what cannot be held . . . of trying to make the body do more than it can do—of making connection[s] while knowing that they are not completely subsumed within [one's] experience of them.

—Marilyn Strathern, *Partial Connections*

IT IS GETTING SO DARK
It is getting so dark that I can scarcely go on writing;
and my brush is all worn out.
Yet I should like to add a few things before I end.
I wrote these notes at home,
when I had a good deal of time to myself
and thought no one would notice what I was doing.
Everything that I have seen and felt is included.
Since much of it might appear malicious and even harmful to other people,
I was careful to keep my book hidden.
But now it has become public,
which is the last thing I expected . . .
Whatever people may think of my book,
I still regret that it ever came to light.

—Sei Shonagan, *The Pillow Book*, c. AD 1000

FIGURE INTRO.I. Kāthī Darwāzā. Courtesy Nishita Trisal

Care

In Srinagar, Kashmir:

A network of narrow, dusty roads takes me to Kāthi Darwāzā, an imposing gateway into the once-splendid, medieval city of Nagar Nagar. Nagar Nagar, with its palaces, ateliers, and gardens, is long gone. But the military encampment that protected it, perched on one of Srinagar's most sacred hills, Koh-e-Marān or Hari Parbat, remains. From this mountainous perch, over centuries, one military garrison has replaced another.

Kāthi Darwāzā, graffitied and weathered, is still a boundary marker. It offers an entryway into the Old City from shiny, new Srinagar, with its gaudy, concrete structures, bustling avenues, and chaotic traffic. Runaway chickens from the nearby Animal Husbandry Department dart back and forth through the gateway, pecking at crumbs and litter on the road. For me, the archway is a different kind of threshold, an opening between home life and fieldwork.

I disembark from my auto-rickshaw outside Kāthi Darwāzā. Others, too, descend from rickety and colorful public buses. A motley crew, we walk through the doorway together, past imperial debris, open sewers, chemist (pharmacy) shops, and fruit sellers. After a ten-minute walk, we arrive at another gate. This one is newer. In bright blue letters, it announces itself in English: the Government Psychiatric Diseases Hospital, Kashmir's only public psychiatric hospital for a population of 8 million people.[1] A fort within a fort, secrets folded within.

It's a busy Saturday morning in early November.[2] I make my way to the hospital's crowded outpatient department (OPD), where Dr. Manzoor,[3] a psychiatrist, is on duty. It's only been a few weeks since I started fieldwork, and I'm still unfamiliar with the rhythm of the OPD. I'm here to learn about an unfolding "epidemic of trauma," a product of a long-standing conflict between Kashmiris' unfulfilled demands for political self-determination set against competing claims by both India and Pakistan over the region.[4]

In response to Kashmir's struggle for self-determination—which became an armed movement in 1988—the central Indian government heavily securitized the region, making it the most densely militarized in the world; dissolved the Jammu and Kashmir state assembly; and imposed stringent anti-terrorism and emergency laws that transformed everyday life.[5] Because some armed groups received assistance from Pakistan, the Indian state glossed the movement as Pakistani-sponsored "cross-border terrorism," while erasing its own extralegal actions in the region. By the turn of the century, the armed movement was largely defeated, but the approximately 400,000 Indian armed forces deployed—including military, paramilitary, and militarized police forces—were never withdrawn. "Anti-terror" emergency laws have remained in place, criminalizing Kashmiri Muslims as potential terrorists. The (mis)reading of Kashmir's struggle for self-determination as a movement fomented by "terrorists" gained greater force with the United States' "war on terror," which sanctioned racial profiling and policing of Muslim communities worldwide.

Meanwhile, the indefinite imposition of emergency-like conditions exemplify a new modality of warfare, which deliberately blurs lines between civilians and combatants. Despite the fact that there are only a few hundred fighters in a population of 8 million people, and that most Kashmiris have turned toward civil disobedience and peaceful protest, they continue to live in a state of perpetual war—what many describe as a colonial and military occupation (*jabri qabzeh*).[6] More than seventy thousand Kashmiris have been killed and more than eight thousand are unaccounted for since the armed conflict began.[7]

The movement for Kashmiri self-determination has come at an extraordinarily high social, political, and psychological cost. Kashmiris say that no family is untouched by the conflict. In 1993, soon after the conflict began, Kashmiri psychiatrists noticed an alarming increase in "disorders directly related to traumatic events," including spikes in "depression, anxiety, dissociation, post-traumatic stress disorder (PTSD), and acute stress reactions" among civilians.[8] By the early 2000s, as rates of violence ebbed, incidence of psychological trauma soared. Psychological trauma replaced mortality as the defining public health concern in the region.[9]

Psychiatry, a historically neglected and marginalized part of India's public health system, burst out of obscurity. In the wry words of one psychiatrist, until then, "people had been too worried about life and death to pay attention to trauma." Rates of trauma and PTSD further increased after a devastating earthquake hit the region in 2005, killing more than eighty thousand people in both Indian- and Pakistani-controlled Kashmir. By 2006, epidemiological surveys showed that more than 60 percent of Kashmiris were suffering from high levels of anxiety, nervousness, tension, extensive worrying, and trauma that persists through their lifetimes.[10] Unlike earlier cases of trauma or PTSD, which were specific to populations such as refugees, now an entire civilian population was diagnosed as traumatized.[11]

Articles with titles like "800,000 Kashmiris Haunted by Horror" and "Kashmir's Trauma Generation" appeared in the local, national, and international press.[12] Many featured the psychiatric hospital as the epicenter of a crisis. The hospital went from a sleepy backwater with an annual patient load of about a thousand visitors per year in 1989, to over eighty thousand patients per year by 1999, without any corresponding increases in the number of psychiatrists. The exponential increase in people suffering from psychological distress led several local and international humanitarian organizations, including Doctors Without Borders (Médecins sans Frontières, or MSF) and Action Aid International, to start providing mental health services. When I began fieldwork in 2009, mental health experts were still desperately trying to keep up with the deluge of patients, many of whom were repeat visitors.

Back in the crowded OPD, meaning slips through my fingers like water. Patient after patient—or more precisely, one kin group after another—enters. The flow is relentless. A doorman attempts to maintain order. He guards the door, a thick stack of medical cards on a stool in front of him. Every time the door cracks open, more faces peer inside, hoping for their turn. He calls out names, *Ashraf Hussain! Irfana Maqbool!* Another family shuffles to the front and edges inside. The doorman hands them their white medical cards, many of them worn and palimpsestic. The door slams shut.

Inside, I watch Dr. Manzoor, patients, and kin engage in rapid-fire exchanges in Kashmiri and Urdu.[13] There are a dozen people in the small room at any given time—one family being attended to, the next on standby. Their presence lingers long after they depart. I smell a warm, musky hearth, pine trees, rose water—an earthy, smoky, and floral bouquet—signaling winter's approach. Some exchanges are wordless, consisting only of scrawls of "CST"—continue same treatment—which will be exchanged for psychiatric drugs (if available) at the hospital's pharmacy or from one of the more expensive pharmacies that opportunistically exist outside the hospital's gates.[14] Most patients know pharmaceuticals cannot cure them, but something is better than nothing.

The psychiatric hospital is almost 70 years old, and it would soon be upgraded to a National Institute of Mental Health, giving psychiatrists ac-

FIGURE INTRO.2.
Waiting outside the OPD.
Photo by author

cess to resources and prestige. Yet this transformation would largely be lost on visitors, who will still see it as the *pāgal khānā*, the asylum. Patients are haunted by the knowledge that, until very recently, patients living in the long-term wards were chained to their beds.[15] For these reasons, they still worry about being "locked up" here. Most want their prescriptions filled and their most adverse symptoms alleviated. A short, quick exchange. Unfortunately, the long lines mean that a quick hospital visit remains a fantasy.

A woman—perhaps in her forties—enters with her daughter and son-in-law. She tells Dr. Manzoor that three of her sons are dead. One, who was thirteen months old, died after a fall. Another died of pneumonia. She is vague about how the third died, but it sounds like he was a "militant," the name given to those who took up arms against the Indian state. Three of her daughters are alive. She says her husband doesn't believe she is sick and did not let her come to the clinic for two weeks because it is the harvesting season. She has been experiencing *dag*, a Kashmiri word meaning restless pain, for the past eleven years. She's been on Fludac—a generic version of Prozac—and another generic antidepressant for most of that time. Like most patients at the hospital, she does not know her diagnosis and does not ask. She's here because she's out of medication.

During their interaction, Dr. Manzoor turns to me and says in English, "Her multiple somatic features are characteristic of trauma victims."[16] He emphasizes the word "characteristic," making it crackle. He occasionally translates these encounters for me, especially those related to trauma and PTSD. His explanations are terse, the result of years of giving case presentations as an intern and junior doctor. His statement contains a twofold translation: a physiological sign, dag, is converted into an English-language psychiatric diagnosis. Psychiatrists like Dr. Manzoor believe that Kashmiri patients lack knowledge of the psyche and express psychiatric symptoms as physical symptoms because these are more culturally acceptable and less stigmatizing. In other words, Dr. Manzoor is saying that, though this woman *thinks* she is suffering from dag (physical pain), she is *actually* suffering from psychological trauma. Psychiatrists call this process "somatization." However, Dr. Manzoor does not have the time nor the inclination to explain any of this to his patient. He scribbles another round of Fludac, and she's gone.

Next, an elderly woman enters. She has come alone, which is unusual. She's wearing a face-covering veil (*burqā*), but it is casually tossed over her head, in the unfussy way many elderly women wear it. Dr. Manzoor asks how long she's been ill. She's on the verge of tears. She says she has been coming since "the English lady" was here. She is referring to Erna Hoch, a Swiss psychiatrist who was a professor of psychiatry and served for some time as the head of the department (HOD) of psychiatry in Kashmir.[17] Hoch retired in 1980, so this woman's distress is also chronic. She speaks rapidly, trying to maximize her time with Dr. Manzoor. In the middle of her soliloquy, Dr. Manzoor's phone beeps a loud and obnoxious melody, a text message received. She pauses, midsentence, while he clumsily punches a response. A precious moment slips by.

When he's done sending his text, Dr. Manzoor looks up and, to my surprise, asks if she will switch to Urdu so I can better follow her story. Her eyes dart in my direction; she seems uncomfortable but reluctantly agrees. She has been coming to the hospital for a long time, she repeats. She has one son. Two of her brothers were killed by "unidentified gunmen." This term is a code word for *ikhwāns*, Kashmiri armed fighters who were turned into counterinsurgents by the Indian military and who committed some of the worst atrocities during the conflict. She is a widow, she says. She lives with a persistent body ache. Dr. Manzoor tells me, in English, that she hasn't come to terms with any of these deaths. "She's unlikely to improve," he says. "Another typical trauma case." He prescribes a benzodiazepine, another illegible scribble.

As she's about to leave, Dr. Manzoor suddenly asks if I want to ask a question. Caught off guard, I struggle to formulate something. I ask if she prays. She says she tries, but she can't. In a patronizing tone, Dr. Manzoor encourages her to pray. I am annoyed at myself for asking this question, but also at Dr. Manzoor for turning my question into a critique of her behavior.

The next few hours pass like this, smudges of anguish, blurs of medical cards, and muted grief, like a steel-gray ocean registering the coming of a storm. Soon, my field notebooks will be filled with similar, fleeting, dreamlike encounters between doctors and patients, aid workers, and recipients. This fragmentary archive both frustrated and fascinated me.[18] Too much left unsaid, festering disputes glimpsed through flashes of life.

Abruptly, at 3 p.m., the hospital empties out. Many patients are from rural areas and must start on their journeys so they can be home by dusk. The habitus of military occupation dictates that people do not stay out after dark, though there is no official nighttime curfew. Dr. Manzoor gathers his belongings. He will now go to his private clinic, where he consults with patients until 8 p.m. almost every day. Although Dr. Manzoor and other public-sector employees are technically forbidden from private practice, he tells me it is a necessity: the salary from the public hospital is a "pittance." When I ask when he takes time off, he chuckles, "every other Sunday."

He offers me a ride in his well-used Hyundai I-10, and I ask him to drop me off at Dal Gate, the city's tourist and transportation hub. Driving through the Old City, we pass the Martyr's Graveyard, where more than a thousand Kashmiri protestors who have died at the hands of Indian armed forces are buried, past the remnants of nineteenth-century wooden homes, and stately, intricately carved shrines (dargāh), influenced by the architectural shapes of Buddhist stūpas.[19] The Old City's narrow alleyways invite disorientation. Looming mountains, suddenly visible in a gap between two structures, stare back as if rudely awakened after a long sleep. Past the tar road, a small stream gurgles and then disappears, reminding you that once upon a time, before occupation, before haphazard construction, the cities of Kashmir were once connected and entirely navigable by water.

As we get to the new city, the streets and boulevards widen and the vista opens, the mountains now bold and unobstructed. Along Dal Lake, one of Srinagar's best-known tourist attractions, rows of ornamented tourist houseboats with romantic names like Fairy Land and Queen of Sheeba stand nonplussed above the green slush and plastic that dot the lake's surface. In recent years, the lake's decrepitude has become a social and political flashpoint—

nature, too, has been ravaged by the conflict.[20] *"People were too worried about life and death. . . ."*

Dr. Manzoor drops me off. After sitting in the OPD all day, I want to stretch my legs. Moreover, fall is in the air, Kashmir's most spectacular season. As I walk, the cool air washes over me. My fieldwork bag and aluminum water bottle clink against each other. I pass the tourist shops, flaunting their identical wares—silver jewelry, colorful papier mâché boxes, woolen shawls with intricate embroidery, and hand-knotted carpets. The shopkeepers beckon me in their practiced English, *"Hello, Madam, come and look, no problem!"* Just as casually as I am called, I am released. I cross Abdullah Bridge, the traffic buzzing past. Like the new and old Srinagar, Abdullah Bridge is also haunted by a more beautiful and older twin. To its east lies the dilapidated but delicate wooden Old Zero Bridge, currently under a tourist makeover. Tourism and war, side by side, just one of the many ironies of life here.

Two soldiers and one military bunker greet me at this end of the bridge. Another bunker awaits on the other end, along with some unruly spirals of concertina wire, the leftover of some counterinsurgency operation from long ago. The spirals, which snag your clothes and nick you if you do not contort your body just so, slow down movement. Rem(a)inders: things are not what they seem.

ONE BUNKER, ONE BUNKER, TWO

Safely over the wire, I'm now in Rajbagh, my neighborhood. I pass the bakery, shuttered now, but a bustling hub at 6 a.m., when young men from every household queue for warm, fresh bread, even during curfews. I pass the elementary school, where the squeals of children wake me every morning. Then I'm in the lane of my guest house. *One more to cross, a big one.* The Central Reserve Police Force (CRPF), a paramilitary force, has occupied an entire block across from my guest house. Behind us rises an abandoned mansion, the site of a fierce battle between the CRPF and an armed group in the early 1990s. The mansion still holds this history—broken windows, licks of smoke discoloring the walls, the attic now a bird sanctuary.

A soldier is always perched in the bunker overlooking the street. He has a perfect view of who comes and goes. I never meet his gaze, though I feel it penetrating my clothes. The back of my neck bristles as I walk by, even though my identity as a non-Kashmiri protects me from harm. Sometimes the soldier will belt out a melancholic Bollywood song when women pass by, flirtations designed to float in the realm of the harmless. Other times I see a few of them playing a vigorous game of volleyball or their uniforms, freshly laundered, drying on clotheslines. For them, too, this stands in for normal life. When the conflict began in 1988, the soldiers deployed were told that they would be in Kashmir for a week to help facilitate an election. They've now been here for thirty years.

High above the paramilitary encampment, the leaves of the towering *chinār* tree are changing color. The evening call to prayer crackles to life from the mosque. The *āzān*'s plaintive melody, soon echoed by dozens of other mosques throughout the city, rises and floats in the space between day and night. The smoke from burning leaves stings my eyes. I knock on the large, steel gate. The elderly groundskeeper, a migrant worker from Nepal, opens the side door and greets me. I'm home.

ψ

For the past three decades, Kashmiris have been living through multiple crises—an indefinite, legally enforced state of emergency, unparalleled militarization and securitization, unfulfilled demands for independence, and enormous psychological and emotional suffering. As I visited different sites of mental health care around the city to study Kashmir's "epidemic of trauma," Indian armed forces, guns, and bunkers were ubiquitous. Sometimes, their presence was menacing, and at other times, because of their disproportionality against mundane urban life, comical. At first, I considered the military presence background noise and kept my gaze fixed on the foreground: the clinic. Militarism was part of the general unsettled nature of things, something to write about in a "context" chapter, I thought. Though they troubled me, as a medical anthropologist, my notes were dominated by the clinic's daily bustle, not its military outsides. I thought of medicine as a mode of redress where the harms of militarism and violence were being responded to and reckoned with.

As my fieldwork progressed, however, the boundaries I had unconsciously drawn between medicine and militarism dissolved. External crises were unfolding *inside* the clinic. Curfews and strikes disrupted flows of drugs, equipment, personnel, and professional opportunities; hospitals, medical professionals, and ambulances were attacked and threatened; and the culture of impunity unleashed by unfettered emergency powers had spread to medicine, breeding corruption, mistrust, and malpractice. Clinicians struggled, day after day, to shore up the clinic's therapeutic boundaries against violence.

Together, these entanglements revealed that medicine was not just a remedy for violence but part of its repertoire. This complicated my work as an anthropologist trying to "study medicine." What was my ethnographic material and what was the context or background?[21] Conventional modes of anthropological categorization and ordering—violence as background and medicine as foreground—failed.

☙

TWO MODES OF PRESENCE: A RELATIONAL APPROACH TO OCCUPATION

Eventually, I realized I had it inside out. I had been trying to tell a story of medicine *in* violence. But I had to tell a story of violence *through* medicine. Rather than see medicine nested in a context of violence, in a state of occupation, military and medical infrastructures were co-imbricated, physically and symbolically. Rather than medicine and war, humanitarianism and militarism, or care and violence, as opposites, they were related. How did militarism and care become so inextricably linked, and with what effect? In what ways is care not always, and not necessarily, an antidote to violence?

This book attends to the critical junctures—the moments, practices, and techniques—when medicine and militarism merge. The chapters show how routine, therapeutic encounters are reshaped by military and counterinsurgency logics —from identifying bodies in distress (chapter 1) to who is doing the treating (chapter 2) to how treatment is brought to a close (chapter 3) to the ways that care is evaluated after the fact (chapter 4). In the final chapter (chapter 5), militarized care comes to a sudden and unceremonious end and forms of relatedness and care that exist and thrive beyond military and humanitarian logics. Each chapter title is named after a critical juncture that shows how military and counterinsurgency practices and discourses infiltrate the clinic, everyday life, and experiences of distress, producing disorienting and overlapping worlds. These uncanny resonances across clinical and military spheres reveal the political stakes of mental distress in Kashmir.

Back at Kāthi Darwāzā, more secrets of empire await. People in Kashmir see contemporary entanglements of care and militarism as deeply historically rooted. The region has been under direct or indirect colonial rule since

FIGURE INTRO.3. Caring for Kashmir. Courtesy Elayne McCabe

1586, when the Mughal emperor Akbar's forces invaded Kashmir and the last Kashmiri ruler was deposed. Kashmiris left their agricultural activities en masse to fight the Mughal invasion, but a year later, the Kashmiri peasantry was devastated, facing colonial rule and famine. To help mitigate the famine, and to "win the hearts and minds" of the colonized population, Akbar instituted a labor program in which he hired thousands of peasants to build a wall around the imperial city. Today an inscription on Kāthi Darwāzā still reads: "No one was forced to work on the construction of the wall and all were paid."[22] The inscription tells of Akbar's humanitarian assistance program from centuries ago, made to a place and population he "loved."[23]

Some 450 years later, Kashmir remains under foreign rule (India, Pakistan, and China), and, according to its current rulers, it is still deeply cared for. Poised against an azure sky, another military infrastructure, newer than Kāthi Darwāzā, also professes love. This proclamation goes a step further than Akbar's: the military's overflowing capacity for care extends *even* to birds.

These twin proclamations of imperial love are separated by centuries, but they resonate nonetheless. For the last three decades, the architecture of Indian occupation has combined militarism and care. These are occupation's two "modes of presence."[24] Today, militarism and care continue to exist in close proximity—spatially, materially, epistemologically, and ontologically—and explicitly borrow from one another. For example, the military mandate to eviscerate terrorists and defeat insurgency exists alongside mandates to care, guarantee life, and heal suffering through public health and humanitarianism. The psychiatric hospital shares a wall with the central jail; one of the few inpatient substance abuse treatment centers to treat approximately 11 percent of the adult male population addicted to benzodiazepines is located inside the militarized police headquarters; the Indian military uses psychological and psychiatric techniques, such as counseling and psychotherapy, to heal Kashmiris from their "misguided" politics; and clinical and everyday language—such as the word *encounter*—refer to both biomedical encounters and police violence. At face value, most Kashmiris do not see civil institutions such as public health as overly repressive, yet medicine plays a critical role not just in responding to, but in refracting and transforming violence's forms and effects. A relational approach to occupation thus reveals how Indian rule is not characterized by total domination or necropolitics, but through recombining the necropolitical and biopolitical, humanitarian, and carceral, violence and care, nervousness and calculation.[25]

Conquests justified in the name of care are not particular to Kashmir nor to the Indian state. These are increasingly evident in global governance—from transnational humanitarianism, legal regimes around asylum seekers and refugees, corporations embracing "corporate social," and counterinsurgency campaigns designed to "win back hearts and minds." In other words, both militarism and humanitarianism—processes often considered opposites—are connected through the sign of *care*. As Miriam Ticktin has asked in a different context, "What does it mean to have care do the work of the government," and in this case the military?[26] While many scholars have described the increasingly intimate connections between militarism and care post-9/11, there are some key differences in my analysis. First, medicine, and more specifically psychiatry and psychology, are central to this story. "Terror" and "compassion" economies collide with most tragic effect in the clinic. Subjects who have been torn apart by state violence find themselves turning to those same institutions for redress.[27] Second, while much work on military-humanitarian interventions has focused on the *explicit* borrowing of humanitarian justifications and technologies for military interventions, there are many subtle ways that military and emergency logics suffuse clinical and humanitarian practices and everyday life. Third, while the rise of military-humanitarian interventions is often read as a sign of a "new transnational world order" based on a growing "desire to intervene" on the part of industrialized countries, humanitarianism is also used to fulfill nationalist goals.[28] Rather than evidence of growing internationalism, this book locates humanitarianism and care within the grammar of rising xenophobia in the Global South.

A NOTE ON CARE

What is possible—clinically, ethically, socially, and politically—under occupation? What forms of care? What forms of life? In the pages that follow, care emerges as a fraught sphere of effort that is never quite what it seems.

In Kashmir, care has become a catchall for vastly different actions, desires, and practices—from counterinsurgency operations to psychosocial counseling by humanitarian NGOs to public health. To differentiate between these multiple meanings and uses of care, I use different terms. I understand *militarized care* as discourses and practices conducted by the Indian state, military, or police officials to further an imperialist project, which are articulated in the language of "protection" and "national security." When describing the practices of nonmilitary actors, such as humanitarian NGOs and public health actors, I describe them as *humanitarian care*, *NGO humanitarianism*, or *clinical care*. These included electroshock therapy, prescribing medications, counseling, talk therapy, and ethical listening. Though these efforts are meant to be apolitical and neutral, they become distorted by violence and militarism. Finally, I describe *everyday care* as noninstitutional forms of care, including hospitality, feeding, attending to hospitalized kin, and remembering loved ones through dreams and reveries. During my fieldwork, all these forms of care were copresent, with radically different affective valences, effects, and outcomes.

Nonetheless, the entanglement of care with nationalist and militaristic projects reveals the need to unmoor care from associations with the "good"—attachment, protection, redemption, or happiness. The traditional binary between care and suffering—with care representing the alleviation of distress—no longer holds.[29] Rather, we must unsettle and "vex" militarized and humanitarian care through feminist and decolonial framings.[30]

Scholars of humanitarian and biopolitical care have persuasively shown how efforts to care can have unintentional, even harmful effects.[31] For example, in the aftermath of natural disasters or crises, determinations of which bodies, persons, and communities deserve care are based on subjective and politically expedient calculations that are racialized, classed, and gendered. Further, given that capacities to care are finite, processes of giving care can be uneven. By caring for some, others might be excluded. Thus, humanitarian and clinical care can offer succor, but can also produce inequality or create exclusions. Scholars have described this as the "violence of humani-tarianism" or the "violence of care."[32] While these critiques are important for attending to humanitarianism's unintended effects, they do not always consider how care is an embodied and relational practice.

For this, we have to turn to feminist scholars of gendered labor, who have shown how care work is deeply affective, unrecognized, undervalued, mar-ginal, and labor-intensive.[33] In my fieldwork, I was drawn to how care work produced ambivalences and challenges for experts and nonexperts alike, in-cluding kin, nurses, doctors, aid workers, and bureaucrats operating in con-strained circumstances.[34] Attending to the embodied and relational thick-ness of care reveals how care's opposites—refusal, neglect, disinterest, and harm—emerge *in* and *through* practices of care, not outside them. Relatedly, suffering or abandonment are not merely the results of care's absence, but are folded into processes of care.

Because of care's imbrications with violence, unlike other ethnographies of violence, this work does not call for more care in response to social suf-fering. Instead, it shows how care does not necessarily lead to succor, and indifference does not necessarily lead to neglect. These simplistic opposi-tions and their moral mappings are inadequate to capturing the dynamics of Kashmir's colonial past and present.[35]

ψ

While we now know that military and imperial projects explicitly borrow humanitarian rhetoric, and have done so for a long time, my ethnography demanded an accounting of militarism's many indirect, discreet, and unin-tentional effects.

In Kashmir, militarism and care are related at three different registers. First, gendered *rhetorics* and *discourses* of love and care—such as "we even protect birds"—ground and justify continued Indian military presence in Kashmir.[36] The Indian state has consistently imagined its relationship to Kashmir as based on care and humanitarianism, despite its consistent and overwhelming reliance on repressive military force. The strategic use of hu-manitarian discourses became particularly salient after 1998, when the In-dian military shifted from kinetic operations—operations involving active warfare—to counterinsurgency.[37]

Counterinsurgency, a military doctrine that includes the use of siege war-fare, cultivating networks of local collaborators and informants, and using development and humanitarianism as tools to win the hearts and minds of civilian populations, is often described as a kinder, gentler form of warfare. Unlike conventional war, which aims to "cow enemy populations through displays of shocking, awesome force," counterinsurgency attempts to cow them by love, care, and restraint.[38] As Jennifer Terry notes, counterinsurgency strategies often use biomedical logics—such as "surgical strikes" or analogizing an insurgency to a "tumor"—that mask how military operations "actually undermine the health and security of the very people the operations are claiming to liberate."[39] Rather than brute force, these "softer" tactics—always gendered female—attempt to reorient civilian sympathies away from insurgents and instill feelings of cooperation, trust, and loyalty for the military.[40] In Kashmir and elsewhere, however, counterinsurgency has always been combined with more punishing military strategies, including widespread arrests, torture, and other methods designed to produce "shock and awe" in colonized or occupied populations.

Second, like other militaries, Indian armed forces use humanitarian, medical, and psychological technologies as instruments of warcraft.[41] While scholars of Kashmir have attended to the necropolitical harms caused by Indian military occupation, less attention has been paid to the state's "biopolitical" presence, including how medicine and psychiatry have become tied to counterinsurgency.[42] Yet, in recent years, occupation and state violence have taken a distinctively biomedical and therapeutic turn. *Militarized care* interventions, including police-run substance abuse clinics, counseling, rehabilitation programs for stone throwers, free medical and mental health camps, and post-disaster relief, use medicine and psychiatry to claim Indian armed forces are healing a traumatized population. These interventions conveniently ignore the fact that most Kashmiris see Indian security forces as the primary cause of trauma, rather than its antidote.

Third, and most important, spaces and logics of care are also unintentionally affected by militarism and a culture of impunity. This is evident in neutral and apolitical spaces, such as NGO humanitarianism or public health. Violence and militarism seep into the clinic at several different levels. At the level of the body, experiences of loss and unlivability in the personal subjective mirror Kashmir's "knotted" colonial and neocolonial geopolitics (see chapter 1).[43] Many patients and experts who encounter humanitarian care have themselves experienced political violence or may become politicized through encounters with injurious health systems (chapter 2).[44] Over and over again in my fieldwork I heard: "No one is healthy in Kashmir." At the level of interpersonal or intersubjective relations, the co-imbrication of military and humanitarian care wreaks havoc on kin relations, often leading to frayed trust and intimacy. Miscommunications in medical encounters are symptomatic of the uncertainties and instabilities unleashed by counterinsurgency and other military operations, such as the state's pervasive use of political collaborators, informers, and spies. Finally, at a systemic level, medicine becomes an exemplary site to witness the tentacular reach of militarism, rather than its counterpoint. Both doctors and patients struggle against the culture of impunity in public health, which they see as a direct result of unfettered militarism and emergency powers (see chapter 2). For example, in addition to being the most densely militarized region in India, Kashmir has also earned the dubious distinction of being the most corrupt. Precisely because medicine is meant to be palliative, its corruptibility is seen as particularly egregious. Not only is medicine unprotected from the logic of disruption; it spawns its own forms of instability. In other words, medicine and psychiatry do not just respond to, but reinterpret and transform the ontological instabilities produced by violence.

These scales of imbrication show that despite militarism being imagined as rational, controlled, and circumscribed—characterized by "surgical strikes," "containing the insurgency," or establishing "tight control" over an area or population—it exerts immense social, temporal, phenomenological, and material force on everyday life. Militarism is both "sticky" and diffuse—it is saturated with affect and infiltrates spaces and worlds without recognizing that it does so.[45] Rather than temporally delimited, its effects linger long after operations have ended. To understand these traces, we need to dive into Kashmir's history.

♨

HISTORIES OF CARE

The contemporary crisis in Kashmir derives from *overinvestments* in care rather than long-standing neglect. Since 1586, Kashmir has been directly or indirectly ruled by foreign empires: Mughal (1586–1753), Afghan (1751–1819), Sikh (1819–46), Dogra (1846–1947), and India, Pakistan, and China (1947 on). My interlocutors consistently pointed to two politically and psychically resonant signposts in this long history: 1586, when the last Kashmiri ruler was deposed, and 1931, when the first organized mobilization for Kashmiri independence occurred and twenty-one Kashmiris were massacred by the police. This *longue durée* historical consciousness resists dominant Indian and Pakistani nationalist imaginaries of the region, which privilege the 1947 Partition or the 1988 uprisings as the origins of the Kashmir conflict (see chapter 1).[46]

In 1846, after the Anglo-Sikh war, the Kashmir Valley was sold to the Dogra empire. It joined the Tibetan Buddhist–majority region of Ladakh, Hindu-majority Jammu, and Muslim-majority Gilgit and Baltistan to form the princely state of Jammu and Kashmir, a geographic territory that continues to ground a collective Kashmiri identity and demands for decolonization.[47] Kashmiri Muslims remember (Hindu) Dogra rule as a particularly oppressive historical period marked by exploitation, discrimination, and neglect. Muslim tillers were denied land rights and were heavily taxed; all land belonged to the maharaja or to Kashmir's Hindu (Pandit or Dogra) minority.[48]

During Dogra rule, the region became a coveted destination for foreign mountaineers, photographers, travelers, and other adventurers. Its stunning mountainous landscape figured prominently in naturalist travelogues and was featured in the work of photographers who won major prizes in Europe. As Ananya Kabir describes, as "the *idea* of Kashmir became important to different constituencies, its resonance multiplied"; the region became a "territory of desire."[49]

In the 1920s and 1930s, Kashmiri Muslims, inspired by anti-imperialist social movements erupting across the subcontinent, began demanding social and political rights. In 1946, a politician named Sheikh Abdullah launched the "Quit Kashmir" movement, mirroring the "Quit India" movement against British rule. Abdullah, along with a few communist intellectuals, drafted a manifesto called "*Naya* [new] Kashmir," which promised, among other things, land-to-tiller rights and the right to equal pay. After Abdullah's National Conference government came to power in 1948, he reversed centuries of exploitation that Muslim tillers had faced through Afghan, Sikh, and Dogra rule. These land reforms were the most radical anywhere in the world outside the Soviet bloc and lionized Sheikh Abdullah in the minds of Kashmiri Muslims (indeed, he became known as Sher-e-Kashmir, the Lion of Kashmir).

Meanwhile, the region's political future remained unsettled. On the eve of India's and Pakistan's independence from British rule in 1947, the fate of over five hundred princely states was left undetermined. While most acceded to either Pakistan or India, Kashmir's maharaja was undecided.[50] Under contentious circumstances, he acceded to India, defying the aspirations of an overwhelming majority of his subjects.[51] In what many Kashmiris view as an act of betrayal, Sheikh Abdullah endorsed the maharaja's decision. These events eventually led to the first of three wars between India and Pakistan.

FIGURE INTRO.4. Kashmir Baramula, view down the river. Source: Museum of Photographic Arts

After the 1947–48 war, India and Pakistan divided the former princely state along a ceasefire line, known today as the Line of Control (LoC), effectively engendering a state of "permanent liminality."[52] The territory under Indian control was named Jammu and Kashmir, while the areas under Pakistani control were named Gilgit-Baltistan and *Azad'* [free] Jammu and Kashmir (AJK).[53] The UN recommended that India and Pakistan "bring about a cessation of fighting and create proper conditions for a free and impartial plebiscite to decide whether the state of Jammu and Kashmir is to accede to India or Pakistan."[54] India initially agreed to the plebiscite, but later withdrew.[55] These events helped create an image of Kashmir as a "border dispute" between India and Pakistan, rather than a region with a unique social history and heterogenous regional identity. Today, pro-independence activists in Kashmir call for reunifying and decolonizing both Indian- and Pakistani-held Kashmir.[56]

In the following decades, Indian sovereignty over territory under its control was cemented through military and humanitarian overinvestments.

FIGURE INTRO.5. Satirizing the postcolonial. Artist: Mir Suhail.
Source: Rising Kashmir

These were done in the name of caring for the secular nation and its minoritized populations, but were used to stifle the political aspirations of Kashmiris. Borrowing and extending techniques from British colonial rule, the Indian state enacted one of the world's "most established, sophisticated, and pervasive systems of emergency rule and legislation" and repeatedly criminalized pro-independence demands as "conspiracies" and "antinational."[57] The Indian state's global image as the "world's largest democracy," a generous aid donor, and noninterventionist actor have helped disguise its military excesses in Kashmir and other border regions.[58]

Meanwhile, aid to Kashmir was also used to produce psychic, social, and political-economic dependence on the Indian state—a classically neocolonial arrangement.[59] In the 1960s, Kashmir had India's "highest per capita central aid, highest per capita plan and lowest per capita taxes among the states of India . . . [while lagging] behind the rest of the country in its economic growth and productivity."[60] By the 1970s, more than 50 percent of the state's expenditure consisted of debt and interest repayments. The debt servicing liability on loans given by the central to the state government today is staggering: 5.35 rupees for every rupee borrowed; in other words, resources required for productive investments are being diverted to debt repayments.

Kashmiri pro-independence activists have cited these facts to claim that "India is guilty of treating Kashmir as a colony."[61]

For decades, Kashmiri intellectuals and politicians have been concerned about the effects of the Indian overinvestments and fostering client–patron relationships on Kashmiri political subjectivity. Pro-independence Kashmiri political leaders, such as Maqbool Bhat, one of the founders of the Jammu Kashmir National Liberation Front (NLF), who was hanged by the Indian government in 1984, offered a potent critique of the corrosive effects of Indian aid and dependency and how it may sediment in psyches and habitus. As Bhat once said, "the war of liberation cannot be fought by those who seek aid from others."[62]

In contrast, in the Indian imagination, Kashmir has been showered with magnanimous love and aid to the detriment of other regions. While this overinvestment is justified because of Kashmir's territorial importance to the Indian state—Kashmir is described as an "indivisible limb" (atoot ang) and the "crown jewel" of the Indian nation—Kashmiris living within it are invisibilized or problematized. Mainstream Indian publics struggle to understand why Kashmiris would seek independence from India. In the Indian nationalist imaginary, losing Kashmir would mean reliving the trauma of Partition, which for many remains an unassimilated loss. Today, the litmus test of Indian patriotism is the question, "Do you believe Kashmir is an integral part of India?" With the ascent of the right-wing Bharatiya Janata Party (BJP) government, there is little space for debate; the answer must be, unequivocally, "yes." Unlike other "marginal" places that struggle against abandonment or neglect, Kashmir is loved—too loved—by India and Pakistan.

But why is this love necessary? Loving Kashmir is critical to how Indian nationalism attains perfectibility.[63] Images of Kashmir's topographical beauty, honed during British/Dogra rule, also shaped postcolonial Indian libidinal overinvestments in the region. These images circulate in postcards, posters, and Bollywood films, producing a virulent libidinal economy and a favored honeymoon destination.[64] Through these acts of circulation and consumption, Kashmir's beauty becomes synecdochally linked to the Indian nation-state; its beauty is something that Indians can possess. Second, by loving the only Muslim-majority state in the country, India can claim that it has perfected a secular, liberal, multicultural identity, particularly against an Islamic Pakistani state. Third, and paradoxically, loving and caring for Kashmir is a thinly disguised and converted form of Islamophobia. Rather than "hating" Pakistan or Kashmiri Muslims, Indians can bond over "loving"

Kashmir.[65] In this libidinal logic, Kashmiri Muslims are injured and killed not because of discrimination, but for "the psychic health and well-being" of the Indian (Hindu) nation.[66] However, as we will see, this libidinal attachment is insatiable. Currents of resentment and anger from donor to recipient unsettle. After all they have been given, why are Kashmiris still dissatisfied?

Despite India's claims of magnanimity, Indian love and care for Kashmir has always been laden with expectations, despite its claims of magnanimity. In exchange, Kashmiris must give up aspirations for independence and self-determination. However, this bargain became increasingly fraught as decades of Indian rule progressed. During the 1970s, when Indian state control over the region was cemented, a vibrant culture of political satire simultaneously erupted, critiquing and mocking Sheikh Abdullah and the Indian government.[67] Several underground pro-independence revolutionary groups emerged during this period, including the JKLF, which would spearhead the armed struggle in the 1980s.[68] The 1970s and 1980s also saw major shifts in the Indian political mainstream, including the collapse of the Nehruvian compact, intensifying regional conflicts and demands for greater social and political rights across India.[69] In several Indian states, including Punjab, Manipur, and Nagaland, movements for self-determination flared up. Intellectuals, activists, and civil society actors were killed, arrested, censored, and silenced. While many of these states were also heavily militarized—and some, like Manipur and Nagaland, remain so today—they do not prompt the same affective intensity from Indian nationalists as Kashmir because they lack its particular history of overinvestment.

In 1987, reports that a Jammu and Kashmir state assembly election was rigged in favor of the pro–Indian National Conference sparked a mass movement against Indian rule. As one doctor I interviewed told me, the 1987 elections were the first and last in which he voted. Indeed, for many Kashmiris, 1987 represented the final crack in India's democratic apparatus, proving once and for all that Indian love had merely been a disguised iron fist. In 1988, the JKLF, an organization with secular, leftist roots, waged a guerrilla war against Indian armed forces with the slogan *Kashmir banega khudmukhtar* (Kashmir will be independent). Other organizations, such as the Jama'at Islami and Hizbul Mujahideen (HM), supported merging with Pakistan. In 1988, Kashmiris began an armed struggle to overthrow Indian rule. Because some armed groups received assistance from Pakistan, the Indian state glossed the movement as Pakistani-sponsored "cross-border terrorism," while erasing its own extralegal actions in the region. Part of India's claim over Kashmir rests on its self-image as a pluralistic, democratic, and secular country. However, many Kashmiris feel they have never enjoyed the fruits of Indian democracy, as draconian laws have been in place for decades. Further, many see Indian rule as the latest in a long line of foreign colonial occupations.

Meanwhile, Pakistan, flush with arms and militants it was recruiting and training for the American-sponsored Afghani resistance against the Soviet Union, increased its support for the HM and provided weapons and ammunitions training in Pakistan-controlled Kashmir.[70] Thousands of Kashmiri youth crossed the treacherous Pir Panjal mountains into Pakistani-controlled Kashmir to train against the Indian army. The Afghan mujahideen's successful war against the Soviet Union also had a huge emotional effect on Kashmiris. If the Soviet army could be defeated, then why not India's? Many described the first months of the armed struggle as *junoon*—a collective state of passion, excitement, even madness. Slogans chanted during protests, which at times drew hundreds of thousands of people, emphasized that Kashmiri self-determination (*āzādī*) could not be bought through gifts of roads, economic relief or other humanitarian or development assistance: "No roads! Āzādī! No relief! Āzādī!"[71]

As the transnational circuit of militants, weapons, and training became clear, relations between India and Pakistan deteriorated further. As Seema Kazi notes, Pakistan's participation in the Kashmir uprising allowed the Indian military to collapse the goals of militarization for external defense and use the military for domestic repression.[72] India labeled the Kashmir armed uprising "cross-border terrorism," rather than a pro-independence movement. Both countries scaled up their military presence along the border. Between 1990 and 1994, 400,000 Indian troops were deployed to the region. In 1998, both India and Pakistan became nuclear powers, escalating the stakes of the Kashmir conflict. By 2015, India was the world's fourth largest defense spender, buying 50 percent of all Israeli weapons exports, many of which are "field tested," that is, were used to kill or maim Palestinians.[73] Many of these weapons are implicitly or explicitly imagined as necessary for Kashmir's protection. Kashmir keeps India's military-industrial-surveillance complex—worth US$62 billion in 2019—ticking.

In addition to sending half a million soldiers to fight the armed movement, the Indian army also deployed paramilitary troops and militarized the Jammu and Kashmir police. All these forces operate under the umbrella term *armed forces*. They include the Assam Rifles (a paramilitary force raised by the British colonial administration for policing northeastern India), the Border Security Force (BSF), the Central Reserve Police Force (CRPF), Rashtriya

Rifles (RR), Indian Reserve Police Force, and paramilitary forces like the Special Task Force (STF, later renamed the Special Operations Group [SOG]), ikhwāns (former militants recruited as counterinsurgents), and armed members of Village Defense Committees. Everyone in Kashmir is familiar with these acronyms—BSF, CRPF, SOG, RR. They roll off tongues.

Using mechanisms in the Indian constitution, Kashmir was declared—and remains today—in a "state of emergency." This categorization allows Indian armed forces to operate with extraordinary powers—such as "catch and kill" and shoot on suspicion—and be granted immunity from prosecution. These powers are seen as necessary for maintaining India's "national security" in the face of terrorism. Yet, extraordinary powers have also caused widespread human rights violations, including extrajudicial killings, rape, unlawful detention, torture, and enforced disappearances. Many Kashmiris call Indian armed forces "insecurity forces" because of their deplorable human rights record and the fact that state violence is overwhelmingly directed toward civilians, not armed fighters. The term *insecurity forces* reveals the ontological gulf that exists between Indian and Kashmiri perspectives on the conflict.

In the mid-1990s, the armed struggle fragmented along pro-independence and pro-Pakistan lines, a split in Kashmiri political subjectivity that has still not been reconciled.[74] Many Kashmiris critiqued the usurpation of their independence struggle by Pakistan, as the HM and other pro-Pakistan armed groups killed prominent independence activists, politicians, religious figures, and religious minorities. In 1990, thousands of Kashmiri Hindu (Pandit) families fled the region under duress, and many still live in refugee camps and have not returned. At the same time, many Kashmiris remained sympathetic to Pakistan's efforts to support Kashmiris against Indian aggression. These developments, often described as the "Islamicization" of the armed struggle, also worked in India's national self-interest by reducing Kashmir to a dispute between a secular, tolerant India and an intolerant and fundamentalist Pakistan.[75] Although most Kashmiri Muslims did not support violence against religious minorities, the exodus of Kashmiri Pandits (who are Hindus) and their unresolved status continues to be a pain often "weaponized" by the Indian state to cast Kashmiris Muslims as Islamic radicals.[76]

By the mid-2000s, the Indian military had mostly rooted out the armed insurgency by exploiting internal divisions in the movement between pro-Pakistan and pro-independence groups. Despite significant reductions in violent incidents and in the numbers of armed fighters, the Indian state has maintained its troop presence in Kashmir at approximately 500,000—an extraordinary ratio of a thousand troops for each insurgent. The Indian military has also significantly reduced "infiltration"—the flow of armed fighters, weapons, and ammunition—from Pakistan. However, despite these changes, none of the emergency laws put in place in 1990 has been revoked. Emergency powers, typically conceptualized as temporary and reactive, have become part of a larger, more permanent "methodology of governance."[77] Kashmiris continue to live in a thoroughly militarized landscape, as if they are still in the depths of war. Everyday life remains structured by security checkpoints, soldiers, and bunkers in streets and neighborhoods; curfews block movement and regulate the times of travel; frequent and unpredictable internet and cell phone communication blackouts; cordon-and-search operations in homes, neighborhoods, and villages; highly regulated and securitized borders; and blocked roads and highways to prevent flows of food, medicine, essential goods, and trade.

Military victories did not root out desires for independence, although the movement changed form. While Pakistan continues to publicize human rights abuses in Indian-controlled Kashmir to the international community, the struggle has indigenized. Armed fighters remain a small, though psychically important part of the struggle, Kashmiris have developed a range of nonviolent and creative tactics of civil disobedience to protest militarization, including strikes (*hartāl*); shutdowns (*bandh*); mass, unarmed protests; and stone throwing (*sangbāz*) targeted at military infrastructures. As Sanjay Kak describes, the shift from armed to unarmed protest has been "nothing short of tectonic."[78] Political writings, journalism, art, poetry, graffiti, and online activism counter state violence in all its forms—from enforced disappearances to corruption in the public health system. As Mohamad Junaid notes, these tactics should not be considered "adaptation" or "resistance," which assume that subjects are merely reacting to state power. Instead, they "constitute Kashmiri youth as political subjects in their own right."[79]

The turn to nonviolent resistance has not improved the lives of Kashmiris, however. Rather, militarization and systematic human rights violations continue; India and Pakistan remain in a political stalemate, unwilling to give Kashmiris a seat at the table; and xenophobic, anti-Muslim, Hindu nationalism following the BJP's electoral victories in 2014 and 2019 has only gained virulence. These developments have solidified the Indian state's status as a "foreign occupier"—an occupier on which, given the few sources of stability in the region, many are forced to depend for material survival.

Meanwhile, the Indian state has responded to these developments with even more violence and care. Political agitations are (mis)read as disguised desires for aid. For example, after mass pro-independence protests broke

FIGURE INTRO.6.
Stencil graffiti of stone thrower
in Srinagar. Photo by author

FIGURE INTRO.7. Line of No Control. Artist: Sandeep Adhwaryu.
Source: *Times of India*

out in 2016 (chapter 5), Indian Prime Minister Narendra Modi argued that Kashmiris needed "laptops, not stones," in their hands.[80] Similarly, after the region's autonomy was revoked in August 2019, Modi called for Indians to "hug each Kashmiri" to create "a new paradise."[81] Despite calls to care for Kashmiris, they have been met with gunfire, lead-coated pellets, and tear gas in every major protest since 2008, resulting in large numbers of deaths and injuries.[82] Figure Intro.7 shows a Kashmiri protestor's body ravaged by lead-coated pellets, satirizing how state violence toward Kashmiris is represented as love.

In recent years, Indian love for Kashmir has grown even more forceful. Kashmir's mental health crisis offered an opportunity to reestablish the Indian state's legitimacy. Trauma was rivaling terrorism as the most pressing governance concern.[83]

ॐ

OCCUPYING THE CLINIC

What does it mean for trauma and mental health to emerge as "matters of care" in this moment and within this colonial genealogy?[84] Why would a militarized state assume responsibility for restoring the health of a war-weary population, and what does this commitment mean for medicine's assumed neutrality?

The Indian state's humanitarian impulses have taken increasingly medical, psychological, and therapeutic form since the turn of the century. In 2001, the Indian military launched "Operation Sadbhavana [goodwill]" to legitimize the military's role in governance and civil society by adopting development and humanitarian goals.[85] Today, militarized care efforts include mental health interventions by Indian armed forces and post-disaster emergency relief. For example, the Jammu and Kashmir police have set up inpatient and outpatient clinics across the state to address a burgeoning substance abuse epidemic. The police also regularly hire civilian mental health professionals, including child psychologists, to conduct workshops and camps on mental health in schools and communities, targeting, in the words of the inspector general, "young minds" to understand "why youth are resorting to violent means of protest [i.e., stone pelting]."[86]

While these explicit uses of humanitarianism are limited relative to the Indian military's overall budget, their effects on public health and medicine are significant. Through them, the clinic has gradually become a "zone of mutual provocation" between military and humanitarian logics.[87] In addition to becoming an object of militarized care, mental health care has also become a priority for public health and for local and international NGOs (henceforth "NGO humanitarianism"). In NGO humanitarianism, subjects of care are seen as carrying a "capacity for ideological disposition that has to be cultivated in a particular direction," but these directions can be quite different.[88] For example, humanitarian NGOs encourage Kashmiris to imagine themselves as "patients" and "victims," rather than as political subjects (chapter 4). Meanwhile, sites of militarized care cultivate affective dispositions such as gratitude and obeisance in patients, which are closely linked to the state's counterinsurgency aims (chapter 5). While militarized care is a form of "political humanitarianism,"[89] NGO humanitarianism and public health interventions try to be neutral and apolitical.

Medicine and psychiatry have become sites of contestation, in which radically different social, political, and ideological projects intermingle. The effect is like a latticed window (*pinjakārī*)—an architectural feature still visible in Srinagar's Old City, where it adorns nineteenth-century wooden homes—where light mixes with dark and vegetal forms with empty space.

Similarly, the clinic becomes a latticed space where multiple projects and histories intersect: public mental health care, transnational psychiatric humanitarianism, counterinsurgency, and militarized care. The clinic—in the broad sense of the discourses, practices, and spaces of humanitarian, medical, psychiatric, and psychosocial care—thus becomes a critical site for witnessing the peculiar admixture of military and humanitarian aims. Cure converges with the violence it would seem to address.

One critical disruption of combining humanitarian, military-humanitarian, public health, and counterinsurgency aims—which can work at cross-purposes—is the steady erosion of international humanitarian tenets around neutrality, impartiality, and immunity. Typically, in war contexts, the clinic is a protected space. International humanitarian laws decree that the wounded must be treated regardless of their political affiliations, and health workers and the clinic should be shielded from the dangers of battle.[90] This is because medicine and humanitarianism are supposedly forms of ethical care distinct and apart from politics.[91] For example, when James Orbinski accepted the Nobel Peace Prize for MSF in 1999, he described the role of medical humanitarian organizations thus: "Humanitarian action is more than simple generosity, simple charity. *It aims to build spaces of normalcy in the midst of what is abnormal*" (emphasis mine). As Orbinski noted, humanitarian care does

FIGURE INTRO.8. Latticed windows in the old city. Courtesy Sanna Irshad Mattoo

not try to change the "abnormal," which is the work of politics, but provides a humane counterpoint to it: a refugee camp, a counseling office, a mobile clinic.

However, the clinic has been shown to be vulnerable to attack in politically unstable contexts, and providers routinely become embroiled in political struggles.[92] Despite commitments to neutrality, Kashmiri psychiatrists like Dr. Manzoor, with whom I began this introduction, worked in and against long histories of occupations, insurgency and counterinsurgency, intermediate crises such as chronic resource shortages, and immediate, short-term crises such as natural disasters and periods of political unrest. These political crises and their differing temporalities were not external to medicine, but were actively present *in* the clinic, unsettling "neutral" humanitarian care.

During my fieldwork, I noticed how care workers and patients (and anthropologist) expended much labor and energy trying to disentangle the "abnormal" (militarism or violence) from the "normal" (the humanitarianism and caring). Yet the best efforts of individual providers were sometimes overwhelmed by the broader milieu of mistrust and corruption that had encroached upon medicine as a result of military and counterinsurgency practices. For example, though Kashmiri psychiatrists tried to introduce more ethical forms of psychiatric care into their practice, such as outpatient treatment rather than long hospitalizations, they could only achieve these goals through the "counter-protocol" use of electric shock, which was also a form of state torture (chapter 3).[93] Rather than the clean line separating the "abnormal" and "normal" in Orbinski's humanitarian fantasy, these conditions were frequently blurred in everyday clinical practices, presenting ambivalences and contradictions for experts and patients alike.

ψ

CONTESTATIONS

The clinic was also a contested space in another sense. While critiques of global medicine and humanitarianism often foreground their modes of systematic exclusion, the occupied clinic was a space where normative biomedical ethics were remade and subjectivities, relations, and hierarchies disrupted or overturned.[94] Contestations in medicine often derive from and respond to coloniality, but they also exceed it. Although psychiatry was not a significant "tool of empire" in British India, India's relation to Kashmir and the global rise of humanitarianism suggests a different dynamic.[95] In Kashmir, care in all its guises—militarized care, public health care, and NGO humanitarianism—was contested, both because of the infectious nature of militarism and because the forms of institutionalized care offered were meager.

Mental health care is particularly prone to contention because it is an unusual form of humanitarian relief. It is not curative, offering only temporary, and often politically compromised, relief. For example, affordable substance abuse treatment was available to patients, but only from the police; public health care consisted of limited access to psychopharmaceuticals; and NGO humanitarianism offered, at best, psychosocial counseling or emergency relief kits (a few kilos of rice, lentils, and cooking oil) after a traumatic event. Unlike access to clean water, food, or residency permits, none of these gifts made the difference between life and death for victims of trauma. They were "bare gifts" accompanying minimal biopolitics.[96] For many, these bare gifts were symptomatic of the state's anemic commitments to its humanitarian presence as compared with its military presence. This political economy of care made such gifts easier to refuse (chapter 5).[97]

Despite many efforts by the state and international organizations to transform Kashmir's political crisis into a public health crisis, in other words, to "medicalize" the occupation, these attempts were ultimately unsuccessful.

While trauma does important political work for Kashmiris, its significance lies not in the clinical and humanitarian notion of trauma as exception—as an unusual event that overtakes people's psychological capacities—but rather as a nebulous, constant disturbance that has spread through the social, impinging on people's capacities to dream, imagine, and act (chapter 1). Despite psychiatric and humanitarian attempts to localize trauma within specific incidents, Kashmiris understand violence as both a traumatic event *and* traumatic environment, "the atmosphere that shape[s] one's capacities to attach to the world" (chapter 1).[98] Instead of locating distress in individual bodies or specific events, Kashmiris semiologically locate trauma both externally and internally, through English words like *turmoil* and Kashmiri words like *mahaul* (atmosphere) and *hālāt* (situation), which connect bodily symptoms with social and political etiologies, casting the longue durée of colonial violence and the *moyen durée* of military occupation as deeply disrupted.[99]

While Kashmiris use discourses of trauma and PTSD toward certain political ends, there are ongoing debates about the extent to which Kashmiris should embrace an identity of collective victimhood. As medical anthropologists have shown, certain clinical diagnoses can be used to shore up racialized inequalities or other forms of structural or political violence.[100] Some see the label of "traumatized" as a continuation of discourses representing Kashmiri Muslims as mad, irrational, fundamentalist, and radical because they belong to a political community that seeks independence from a supposedly benevolent, secular, and tolerant nation-state. While humanitarian discourses of trauma might be well intentioned, they can establish Kashmiris as helpless victims unable to govern and care for themselves.

Rather than seeing Kashmir's "epidemic of trauma" as the product of some internal failing—whether religious identity or neurobiological malfunctioning—Kashmiris argue that mental illnesses and collective trauma have "political etiologies," that they are a direct product of colonial, social, economic, and political violence.[101] As Fanon similarly noted, the production of madness on a mass scale in colonial Algeria was "a *direct* product of oppression."[102] In this sense, Kashmiris insist that an epidemic of trauma is not merely a public health crisis, but a political crisis. This move resonates with how other communities that have suffered racism, colonization, and violence understand their distress. Indigenous scholars and activists, for example, have demanded greater attention to centuries of settler colonialism as a determinant of ill health among native populations today.[103]

How does a community then contest characterizations of collective disturbance and madness? How do they not only unsettle coloniality's negations, but create and cultivate "modes of life, existence, being and thought *otherwise?*"[104] There are flourishing counter-imaginaries of health and well-being in Kashmir, articulated through a decolonial lens that exceeds and precedes Kashmir's colonization (see the poem, "Before," chapter 1, and chapter 5). In some cases, the contestations are linguistic and overt—in language, protests, graffiti, and affectively charged encounters between aid workers and recipients. Many Kashmiris have proudly reclaimed the word "madness" (*mot*) as an ironic commentary on their own resistance movement, which confronts one of the largest armies in the world with little outside support. They place hope in what may seem to be an abstract futurity, even if it is read as "mad." Many told me, "We're in this for the long term. It may take 100, 150 years to get our freedom, but we don't mind." In Kashmir, embracing this long historical consciousness allows a person to remain patient, strong, and courageous—markers of a different kind of well-being and moral rectitude than what biomedical psychiatry or humanitarianism offer (chapters 1 and 5). Rather than the depoliticized term *mental health care*, they and I use the tropes of *madness* and *disturbance* to show how some social and political conditions are, indeed, maddening.

At other moments, contestations live beneath surfaces, behind language. This should not be surprising, given that existential, ethical, and social suffering are not fully graspable, knowable, or translatable experiences.[105] Beyond the irreducibility of pain and suffering, regimes of care and severe mental illness can both actively produce (il)legibility and (in)expressibility. Communication breakdowns in humanitarian and clinical encounters are intrinsic to knowledge-gathering processes, not incidental to them (chapter 4). This is not as simple as a dichotomy between speech and silence, but a more nuanced relation between individuals or groups who are not necessarily silent, but systematically *not heard* in that those hearing them "often can't bear to be changed by what they hear."[106] Modes of unintelligibility in the clinic must be nested in a political history of erasing Kashmiri voices and aspirations.

Yet there are modes of relating that exceed both militaristic and humanitarian impulses that bend care toward something other than indifference or displays of deservingness. Counterpoints to militarized care are found in poetry, art, and literature, as well as everyday practices such as hospitality (*mehmān nawāzī*) and duty. For these reasons, poems (both my own and others') pollinate this book. Unlike military or humanitarian care, hospitality and duty are meant to be given without expectation of return. While ephemeral, they reveal how Kashmiris are actively forging a poetics of self-determination in the present.

One of the most surprising aspects of militarization is that it produces its own undoing. Since occupation disrupts everyday life, communication, and temporality, it allows for in-between, liminal spaces and shadow sides to arise. Disturbance produces time and occasion for stories, reveries, and jokes that challenge it. Attending to these contestations required reaching beyond the conventional ethnographic tool kit and normative linguistic register. I oriented myself to poetry, disordered speech, embodiment, lamentation, dreams, and other elliptical communications that invited a different "politics of hearing."[107] These bridged somatic and existential pain and everyday traumas and spectacular violence. They resisted dominant anthropological impulses to capture reality and instead offered ethical and epistemological openings that help us see how violence makes its own sociality.

CHAPTER 1

Siege

No flower here, nor bulbul, nor garden, not even one . . .

We went to the doctor,[1] brought medicine, took it properly
Even after discipline, no disease is cured, not even one

Cities are choked, villages silent
No war epics, no Gulrezs,[2] are read, not even one

. . .

Easy to put a shoulder to a hill and shift its location
But very difficult to change a mind, not even one

For a long while, I have been pained by a passion
No healer for this disease, not even one

—*Ghazal* by Ghulam Hassan "Ghamgeen"

A late March afternoon, a Thursday.[3] Most psychiatrists at the hospital have left for the day. The remaining staff turn their attention to those who do not—cannot—leave, patients who have been living in the hospital's "closed" (long-term) wards for weeks, months, years. Life here moves more cautiously than in the OPD. Some are here because their level of distress warrants long-term hospitalization; others have stabilized but cannot return home because their families feel ill-equipped to care for them or, in some cases, have abandoned them. I have been spending my afternoons in the women's closed ward, trying to develop a rapport with the dozen or so patients and the two "wardens," Asmaji and Haleemaji, in charge of them. Despite the hospital's commitment to outpatient, community-based mental health care, its past as an asylum still lingers. *Prisoners and wardens*, not *patients and caregivers* inhabit wards that feel more carceral than caring.

Every day, we carousel through the same routine. Lunch at 11 a.m. It is one of only two times each day that patients are allowed out of the ward. Some-

FIGURE 1.1. Closed ward. Photo by author

times, if the weather is nice, the wardens will let them sit on the grassy knoll outside and soak in the sun for a few minutes, a small relief from the dank inside, where the sour smell of cheap disinfectant and mothballed blankets hangs in the air. By 12:05, everyone is back in their beds, awaiting their medications. MSF counselors sometimes lead recreational activities for the patients, but these happen erratically. Days fold into each other, only occasional creases marking time's passing.

Today, everyone is murmuring about how one of the patients tried to run away, but she was caught outside the hospital's gates. I don't know how she was brought—dragged?—back. I can't help but look at her now, wonder what she's feeling. Everyone is sneaking glances at her. Her purple-printed *salwar kameez* is matted with sweat and dirt. She was beautiful in a past life.

An elderly male nurse calls out names from a hand-written list, while Asmaji and Haleemaji dole out doses from a medicine tray. Several women plead for an injection when their name is called. "Why are they asking for an injection?" I ask Nusrat, the ward's oldest resident, who has befriended me, and whose bed I am sitting on.

"They have all become weak [*kamzor*]," Nusrat says. "Injections give them strength." I note the tense Nusrat uses, the present perfect: the women *have become*, not they *are* kamzor. This means that something has changed, something has happened since they were hospitalized. Maybe it's just me, but the demand for injections seem particularly vociferous today. Maybe they need something to steel themselves against news of the capture.

ॐ

Another Thursday, this time late June. I was accompanying Action Aid International, a psychosocial organization, on a routine visit to their beneficiaries' homes.[4] On this day, Action Aid's team of counselors consisted of five men and one woman. We drove an hour north from Srinagar on the Srinagar–Leh highway to Ganderbal district, the heat of the city behind us. After weaving up mountain roads, the air changed. It was spiked with a chill; the bitter and refreshing scent of pines wafted in through the windows.

We arrived in a village that everyone called "Gujarpati"—an informal name given to settlements where Kashmir's minority Gujar community live.[5] The village looked different from others we had visited, the houses made with natural materials rather than cement. In one household, we met a woman in her thirties named Shakeela. Like many Gujars, she was fluent in Urdu, so I could follow the conversation between her and the counselors. Her brother-in-law was killed, she said. She didn't name the perpetrators, though she likely knew who they were. The family saw him being arrested, and then never saw him again. One of the male counselors brusquely probed, "Arrested, yes, and what else?" He was trying to assess the level of trauma the family had suffered to establish that they were truly in need of Action Aid's assistance (there are so many vulnerable families to choose from). Shakeela said her husband was assaulted during the incident. Now he was hearing-impaired and was suffering from insomnia.

I asked Shakeela what the situation was like in their village during the 1990s, during the height of the armed conflict. She said, "Back then, there were lots of 'crackdowns' [military sieges or cordon-and-search operations]. We used to run away because the army used to come at night and force us out of our homes. But now, it doesn't happen so often. We're not afraid anymore." She told me she still has nightmares when remembering the past. "I have taken lots of medicine for this," she said, and showed me a brown glass bottle on the shelf, covered in layers of dust, mostly emptied of its liquid contents. The bottle, a tonic, a brand of Unani medicine,[6] claims to improve bodily vitality and strength. As I examined the bottle, Shakeela explained, "Too much worrying [*pareshānī*] makes a person weak [kamzor]."

✼

Spilling out of these two scenes of care was a singular complaint or symptom called *kamzorī* in Urdu (or in Kashmiri, *kamzōrī*). Generally translated as a persistent feeling of fatigue, loss of vital energy or substances like semen or blood, or the weakening of physical and psychological capacities due to aging or mental illness, kamzorī was by far the most ubiquitous complaint in mental health care settings across Kashmir. While central to local experience and ideology, and present in almost every psychiatric encounter I witnessed, kamzorī never appeared in globally circulated epidemiological reports on Kashmir's mental health crisis. Its absence was not merely because it was translated into an English-language psychiatric diagnosis, such as depression, traumatic stress, or PTSD, but because it was rendered illegitimate in comparison to them. This chapter spotlights kamzorī, not merely in a familiar anthropological scalar move from 'global' to 'local' knowledge, but because kamzorī demands acknowledging the presence of multiple bodily and health ontologies inside the clinic.

Kamzorī raised a different set of political, moral, and relational stakes than other psychiatric complaints and disorders. For example, Shakeela said her persistent fear of sieges had led to a loss of strength and vitality. Although she had received counseling from Action Aid, she described her treatment as incomplete and was using Unani supplements.[7] Relatedly, by demanding injections instead of pharmaceuticals, patients in the closed ward signaled that hospitalization was having detrimental effects on their health. In both scenes, complaints of kamzorī persisted *despite* access to care. What does it mean that kamzorī was not a mark of care's absence, but its presence? And why was kamzorī ubiquitous in occupied Kashmir?

Medical anthropologists argue that symptoms or complaints are more than biological signs. They may also materialize or represent social and economic realities—such as gendered, racialized, classed, or caste inequities and precarities.[8] As Margaret Lock and Vinh-Kim Nguyen write, the body and the social world are mutually constitutive; what happens in the body "is informed by social worlds and the social world is in turn informed by the reality of physical experience."[9] Symptoms of distress can be saturated with meaning and can be an indirect way of expressing inconvenient or difficult truths. For example, in Iran, heart distress is both literally and symbolically important to the sufferer. At the literal level, heart distress connotes palpitations and heart flutters and requires the intervention of a cardiologist. At a metaphorical level, however, heart distress can index difficult personal and social circumstances, feelings of loss or grief, and worries about health and financial affairs.[10]

These insights offer a starting point for understanding kamzorī as a meaningful expression of distress, but they rely on an understanding of symptoms as being representations or translations of something else. My ethnography suggests, on the contrary, that kamzorī requires attention on its own terms. For one, kamzorī has more expansive meanings than the English word *weakness*.[11] Kamzorī describes a mode of embodiment that is not individual, but is social and relational. For example, Lawrence Cohen shows how low-caste (Chamar) communities used discourses of kamzorī to explain how centuries of caste-based discrimination, inequality, and violence had produced debility, both in individual bodies and in their community as a whole. In other words, kamzorī articulated the debilitated singular body with the debilitated body politic; complaints of kamzorī "glided" from "the personal subjective to the collective."[12] Kamzorī was also a moral discourse: it registered the effects of caste discrimination, while preserving the moral integrity of the "weakened" at the hands of the "weakeners."[13]

In Kashmir, too, the kamzor body was also a relational body. Kamzorī never just indexed an individual condition; it was always used to describe social conditions. For example, Shakeela's kamzorī was a product of her being a subject of occupation. Her kamzorī was tied to collective experiences of physical and structural violence that Kashmiris had suffered, which manifested themselves in bodily attenuations. Second, kamzorī was not triggered by a particular incident of violence, but was linked to living in a traumatic *environment*, which led to, in her words, "too much worrying." Shakeela described kamzorī as the cumulative effect of living through decades of military and counterinsurgency operations. Although the "crackdowns" (sieges) had largely stopped, kamzorī remained. Kamzorī was thus the siege sedimented and memorialized in bodies. In making this point, Shakeela offered a powerful critique of logics of militarized care, in which sieges and "crackdowns" are justified as necessary to protect civilians from dangerous "insurgents." Instead, Shakeela felt overwhelmed, besieged, and inundated by these technologies and their potent traces. Meanwhile, although sieges are designed to stop time, to contain and isolate territories and populations, their effect was the opposite. Kamzorī flowed out into the social, from one person to another.

For these reasons, kamzorī broadens the scope of what counts as wartime injury. Kamzorī showed that war's effects were not just physical or psychological, but existential, moral, and spiritual. Spiritual and moral vitality not only were critical dimensions of health and well-being for Kashmiris, but also were necessary to combat occupation. Thus, as a mode of embodiment, kamzorī's presence and persistence signaled more than a "body totally imprinted by history."[14] Kamzorī offered a "biomoral" critique of occupation.[15] In other words, kamzorī described a body whose materiality contained the possibility of an *otherwise*. The body that "mattered"—the body that Shakeela and the women in the closed wards called for—was not just physically fit, but also had moral and political "strength" (*tāqat*), nourished by meaningful and intact social relations, restraint, forbearance, and patience—qualities essential for surviving colonization. In other words, kamzorī denoted a different body than the somatic or physical body treated by biological psychiatry. It registered the siege's effects on bodies, psyches, and the body politic, but it also offered a line of escape.

Given kamzorī's social usefulness and its semantic richness, why, then, was it invisibilized in the clinic?

ॐ

Like kamzorī, which accumulates through time, this story, too, builds, one twig at a time, on a mound of kindling. The first twig describes how and why kamzorī was rendered an insignificant complaint in the clinic.

A slow day in the OPD.
Slow enough to know when things are heard
and not heard.
Another woman, another complaint of kamzorī.
It's not a leftover, she insists,
it was always there:
a wound that will not go away,
a disease without a healer.[16]

(*Depression*, the doctor insists.)
Be positive, he says.
She is much better now, isn't she?
The pills (all those pills).

She can't look at him.
Her body speaks to her, she says,
it shudders with weakness,
heavy legs.

Weights
holding her down.
Drowned if you do,
drowned if you don't.

The doctor doesn't like being
a healer with no disease.
This is not why he spent
seven-plus years accumulating
expertise, training, skills, techniques.

Her:
it was always there.

Him:
separating thing from thing.
Wrong thing in,
wrong thing out,
like barbed wire.

It ends like all clinical dramaturgies:
kaenh chhyun parvai,
nothing to worry about.

ψ

This poem describes an encounter I witnessed between Dr. Manzoor, a psychiatrist, and a patient named Ruksana, who came to the psychiatric hospital's OPD with complaints of chronic kamzorī.[17] The poem tries to convey
the mistranslations and miscommunications that are not incidental to, but
constitutive of, processes of translation in both psychiatry and anthropology
(what else was *I* missing from her story?). Though Dr. Manzoor attempted to
bridge this divide, and Ruksana attempted to communicate her pain to him,
they were only partially perceptible to each other. Kamzorī existed at the
disjuncture of their different truths, where the "somatic" body of biomedicine and patients' "biomoral" bodies diverged, becoming *two different bodies*.

The encounter between Dr. Manzoor and Ruksana typifies the epistemological and ontological gulfs that can exist between biomedically trained
psychiatrists and their patients. Psychiatrists read symptoms like kamzorī
as pathophysiological or neuropathological phenomena. For Dr. Manzoor,
kamzorī was not a complaint of significance because it lacked a physiologi-

cal basis, specific etiology, and because it could not be seen through imaging technologies.[18] As the French physician and philosopher of science Georges Canguilhem famously noted, disease prestige is conferred based on the extent to which symptoms can—or cannot—be readily localized in the body.[19] Further, when complaints of kamzorī could not be attached to *specific* instances of loss or violence, they could not be readily subsumed into the framework of traumatic stress or PTSD, which were far more recognizable and legitimate than kamzorī.[20]

Psychiatrists like Dr. Manzoor did not consider disorders of fatigue like kamzorī as stand-alone concerns, because vitalism is not considered a marker of health in biomedical logics. As Arthur Kleinman has argued, in biomedicine, disorders of fatigue have to be secondary to something else.[21] This is despite the fact that unexplained fatigue is the most common "unspecified complaint" in Euro-American clinical settings—appearing in up to a third of all doctors' visits. By contrast, in the world's other major medical systems, including Chinese medicine, Ayurveda, or Unani, fatigue is not only a legitimate complaint, but a legitimate diagnosis.

In some cases, psychiatrists explained away kamzorī as psychogenic: as real but subjective. They argued it was a form of "somatization" or "conversion"—unconscious processes by which patients turn psychological problems into more culturally acceptable physiological ones.[22] In other words, they felt that patients' bodily complaints were disguised expressions of depression or other psychiatric conditions. Yet, identifying kamzorī as "somatized" depression or trauma did not necessarily make psychiatrists more empathetic. Many, like Dr. Manzoor, felt their patients were using kamzorī to receive "secondary gains," such as staying on medication, time off work or reproductive labor, or receiving extra care and attention from kin. Women who complained of kamzorī—as they most often did—were particularly suspect. As Jocelyn Chua has astutely noted, psychiatrists in South Asia, who are overwhelmingly male, tend to judge female patients more harshly than their male counterparts, *especially* when they appear with "low-prestige" ailments like kamzorī.[23] Rather than locate patients' concerns in a framework of demanding domestic labor and patriarchal kinship structures, psychiatrists described them as "spoiled" women who were failing to perform their gendered roles adequately. As one psychiatrist told me, "Nowadays, patients want treatment [*eilāj*] for all kinds of aches and pains. 'The nail on my pinky finger hurts, so give me something for it,' they'll say."

Yet, the ubiquity of kamzorī meant it was not easy to dismiss entirely. It presented an obstacle for psychiatrists, who were themselves desperate to establish their efficacy as healers in a competitive therapeutic environment ("Be positive," Dr. Manzoor insisted).[24] To paraphrase the poem with which I began this chapter, kamzorī threatened to render Dr. Manzoor useless, *a healer with no disease*. To guard against this, psychiatrists occasionally prescribed iron tablets, vitamins, or Unani and Ayurvedic tonics—solutions they considered placebos. However, as we saw with Shakeela, patients saw these solutions as only *partially* satisfying. For them, kamzorī was not a cultural signifier—it did not stand in for something else. Neither was it only about regaining physiological strength. Rather, kamzorī indexed the collective integrity of the body—and health's—material, spiritual, moral, and political dimensions. Given Dr. Manzoor's lack of acknowledgment of this bodily ontology, Ruksana felt kamzorī was *a disease with no healer*.

Clinicians were also caught in a global "political economy of trauma"[25] that made it difficult—if not impossible—to focus on kamzorī. Kamzorī took time, resources, and attention away from what many felt was the *real* mental health crisis in Kashmir: the "epidemic" of trauma and PTSD. Trauma and PTSD offered important social, economic, and research opportunities for humanitarians and psychiatrists. Since the 2000s, humanitarian aid workers and Kashmiri psychiatrists have published papers on trauma and PTSD in prestigious scientific journals, given interviews to the local and international press, and traveled to international conferences.[26] These actions, alongside media, public health, and humanitarian efforts, put Kashmiri psychiatry on the map. One 2009 article described Kashmir as "one of the most traumatized places on earth."[27] Accompanying the article were photographs of men's faces, etched with worry. The photograph's frame was exceeded, conveying deluge, a hospital *besieged* by trauma. Epidemiological studies of trauma and PTSD in Kashmir affirmed the prevalence of PTSD among civilians, and unlike previous studies of war veterans or refugees, who were removed from the site of trauma, they offered an understanding of what happens when people continue to live in traumatic environments.

Just as kamzorī offered a moral framework for patients, psychiatrists were drawn to PTSD because it, too, was morally exculpatory. Unlike other diagnoses of psychological disorder, sufferers of PTSD are unique in that they "are seen as innocent victims and treated with patience and respect—a huge and valuable digression from the sense of suspicion and distrust that formerly pervaded the clinical phenomena associated with trauma."[28] In Kashmir, pro-independence and human rights activists used epidemiological reports on PTSD to argue that Indian militarization was inherently pathogenic, and that militarization and sustained human rights violations had led to culturally specific forms of distress such as "midnight knock syndrome"—people getting panic attacks at night as they imagine security forces or militants searching for them. Because PTSD confers innocence on sufferers, the moral underpinnings of these studies were useful for Kashmiris trying to counter Indian state discourses about Kashmiri Muslims as "terrorists." Beyond being clinical diagnoses, trauma and PTSD emerged as critical ethical and political languages through which Kashmiris could point to their victimization as occupied subjects.

However, as I described in the introduction, the Indian state and military also used trauma and PTSD for political purposes that were far from liberatory. Further, as the conflict distended into a third decade, a diagnostic category that hinged on people experiencing *specific* incidents of violence—such as bombings, killings, or sexual violence—proved limited. Instead, like Shakeela, many located their pain in the longue durée and in a generalized milieu of unease. Dr. Abdul, who became a close interlocutor, described the dangers of the "traumatization of psychiatry," i.e., what he felt was an overemphasis on trauma and PTSD at the expense of other ailments. Yet he simultaneously recognized the difficulty of moving away from trauma and PTSD, since these had become "*the* language of suffering in Kashmir," fusing with Kashmir's independence struggle.[29]

ψ

Nonetheless, my ethnographic observations showed that, by 2009, patients were much more likely to suffer from kamzorī than PTSD, and that kamzorī usually outlasted other psychiatric symptoms. For example, in Ruksana and Shakeela's cases, as well as the women in the closed ward, kamzorī marked a remainder, a body incomplete. Where did this feeling of being besieged come from, and why was it so resilient?

A second twig. Kashmiris have also been subjected to a number of sieges across different periods of colonial rule. Under Indian military occupation (1990 to the present), sieges or crackdowns have been a significant counterinsurgency strategy. Throughout the 1990s, sieges occurred regularly in dense civilian settings. Although rarer today, they still happen in rural areas. Like other counterinsurgency strategies, sieges require civilian participation, which demonstrates civilian-military cooperation against an "insurgent" or "terrorist" Other. Military officials describe sieges as "population-centric": rather than eliminate the civilian population, they flush out "insurgents" or "terrorists" who may be hiding among them, thus saving lives. The counter-

FIGURE 1.2. Patients seeking care at the psychiatric hospital.
Courtesy Robert Nickelsberg

insurgency imagination posits that these acts of counterinsurgency care will remake civil-military relations: turning civilians away from (negative) attachments to militants toward (positive) attachments to Indian armed forces.

Before a siege begins, security forces first cordon off or surround a given area so that no insurgents can escape. Then, the beginning of the siege is announced over loudspeakers from the village mosque or from patrolling paramilitary jeeps. All village residents must leave their homes with their identity cards. Men are often asked to assemble in the village square (*maedān*), while women gather in a separate area. Men, young and old, must walk toward the square with their "arms held high and pointing toward the sky," the universal hands-up-don't-shoot gesture.[30] The gendering of space, ostensibly done in the name of care, is a source of great social anxiety: it allows soldiers unfettered access to women's bodies without the protection of male kin and prevents women from protesting if men are arrested or taken away for interrogation. Identity cards are matched to faces and each house is thoroughly searched for any signs of militants or weapons. In other cases, when sieges are spurred by information gleaned from an "informer" or "collaborator," residents have to line up in front of the collaborator—whose face and identity are always hidden. The collaborator examines each civilian carefully and may name one as a militant or sympathizer.[31] This process can take hours or days, and the men must remain outdoors for the duration of the siege, even in the depths of winter.

In contrast to the benign image of the siege as a form of militarized care, in reality, sieges are highly charged experiences. Anthropologist Wajahat Ahmad describes a siege he experienced one freezing January morning in 1994. People's sentiments ranged from anger to fear, "as they tr[ied] to come to terms with a routine humiliation."[32] Other scholars have similarly argued that so-called population-centric counterinsurgency strategies in fact target and instrumentalize civilians in war.[33] Sieges disrupt everyday life, stall movement and time, and enable extrajudicial actions and deaths to occur. Contrary to their purpose, sieges can actually heighten tensions between military forces and civilians. For example, in 2008, a village in Kupwara district was kept under siege for eight days continuously, one of the longest in recent Kashmiri history. As one newspaper described, the military kept turning the electricity on and off throughout the siege. People complained that the sick and elderly could not access medicine. Under pressure, the troops temporarily lifted the siege, and some villagers fled to a neighboring village. By the eighth day, relations between the troops and villagers had completely deteriorated. Villagers refused food offered by the troops. Eventually, the troops withdrew without finding any insurgents, arms, or ammunition in the area.[34] This incident reveals how, rather than improving relations between armed forces and civilians, counterinsurgency can result in their unmaking.

Sieges are not isolated incidents. They leave marks in village landscapes and on the subjectivities and memories of Kashmiris who have lived through them. Ahmad describes how his village's clinic was used as a torture chamber during the siege in 1994.[35] Villagers still remember the eerie cries of torture floating through the air. People gave new names to spaces touched by the siege—the hospital became the "crackdown hospital," the high school "crackdown high school," and the Eid prayer ground, "crackdown Eidgah."[36] These new signifiers convey the siege's capacity to infiltrate all aspects of village life and public space, and they offer a powerful counternarrative to military narratives of sieges as limited, contained, and care-full.

Sieges have a deep history in Kashmir. Many describe the history of colonization since 1586 as one long siege.

Away from the world, away even from the monsoon rains of India, one might have expected that Kashmir would have been left to itself, but its beauty and rumored wealth allured the Mughals, and from the end of the 16th century, the Kashmiri people have groaned under a foreign yoke. . . . Tyrant after tyrant tortured and degraded them, while at awful interludes came fires, floods, earthquakes, famines and cholera.

—Walter R. Lawrence, Kashmir's land settlement commissioner, in a speech made at London's Westminster Town Hall on December 13, 1895

Shakeela plotted chronic kamzorī within a lived history of counterinsurgency. She used kamzorī to make "historical sense" of her changing bodily experience.[37] Yet kamzorī was also tied to the violence of prior occupations. In the nineteenth century, British missionaries observed kamzorī as a bodily symptom with a "political etiology," produced by Kashmir's political and economic subjugation under Dogra rule.[38] Through their commentaries, missionaries revealed how medicine in Kashmir was never purely humanitarian, but always political.

In the 1860s, British missionaries were keen to establish medical missions in the empire's North-West Frontier, including in the princely state of Jammu and Kashmir, which was under indirect rule.[39] During this period, dual narratives of Kashmir proliferated in the colonial imagination. On the one hand, Europeans saw Kashmir as a respite from the dusty, hot plains and gave it derivative nicknames like "Switzerland of the East." On the other hand, racialized descriptions of Kashmiri Muslims as "apathetic and fatalistic"[40] painted the population as spiritually corrupt and in need of Christianization.[41] These racist, colonial imaginaries of Kashmiris as overly accommodating, lazy, and weak—in a word, kamzor—persist today.

Medical missionaries faced severe constraints in their goal, however. Foreigners were not allowed to reside in the princely state beyond the summer months, and there were deep currents of mistrust between the Dogras and the British.[42] Dogra rulers were nervous about increased British intervention in their territory, possible foreign invasions, and the presence of spies. Such suspicions were not entirely unfounded. As Christopher Snedden notes, this was the time of the "Great Game" (or what the Russians evocatively called the "Tournament of Shadows"). The British and Russian empires competed for dominance in buffer states in Central Asia, as well as Afghanistan and Jammu and Kashmir. Both the British and Russian empires indulged in "vari-

FIGURE 1.3. Subdistrict hospital in Seer, Kashmir. Courtesy Wajahad Ahmad

ous unobtrusive, or underhanded, tactics," including sending European men disguised as locals or explorers making "scientific" or shooting trips. Russian and British spies maneuvered in each other's territory.[43]

Despite these political intrigues, thanks to a fund of fourteen thousand rupees raised by the Church Missionary Society, the Kashmir Medical Mission was established in 1865. The Dogra Maharaja Ranbir Singh strictly delimited the mission's scope, including prohibiting all missionizing activities. He also refused to relax the prohibition on foreigners remaining in Kashmir during the winter. Thus, missionaries had to make the treacherous journey down to the plains every year as winter set in and restart their mission anew every spring. The Kashmir Medical Mission was nonetheless a success.[44] In one summer, Dr. William Elmslie, the mission head, reported treating two thousand patients. The mission was tinged with the affects of a savior project: care was accomplished with an upbeat tone and marked with furious activity and progress. For example, Arthur Neve, another mission head, described the bustling mission hospital: "It is scarcely the busiest season, but already 135 beds are occupied," "everything is once more in full swing," "by 4 p.m. over 350 patients had been seen."[45] The gaze of medical missionaries spotlighted medicine's efficiencies, its works completed.

These affects of care were staged in contrast to the violence and repression of the Dogra regime. In their memoirs, missionaries bemoaned the Dogra state and the maharaja's regular interference over the clinic, even though much of this interference came after Elmslie was found to have been proselytizing patients—betraying the terms of the agreement with the sovereign. After this, the maharaja used "coercive measures . . . to prevent patients attending the Mission dispensary." Police spies were sent in the guise of patients to report on all the clinic's happenings, and soldiers cordoned off the clinic and recorded the names of all visiting patients.[46] These events uncannily resonate with the next phase of Kashmir's occupation, when the clinic was again turned into a site of surveillance.

Although medical missionaries were strongly discouraged from making political statements against the Dogra regime, many described the effects of oppressive policies on the Muslim-majority population. For example, in his memoir, Elmslie wrote:

> But what is this oppression that I have spoken of? It is this—that at one swoop half of every man's produce goes to the Government treasury. Half of everything, not merely of his grain, but even of the produce of his cattle, or whatever he has. . . . More than this even, his very fruit trees are watched by Government and taken half for the Maharajah. *A poor Kashmiri can call nothing his own.* But, in reality, it is not only half a man loses, for at least another quarter is taken by the rapacious government officials who have to collect the nominal half. . . . *The wonder is, how the people exist at all.* Of course I am a credulous missionary, and believed every story I heard, but I should like to find the man in Kashmir who could deny these facts. But it is not only the poor peasants who suffer; perhaps the condition of the shawl weavers is worse still. . . . These shawl weavers are a *lean wan race, recognizable at once from their sallow complexion, thin cheeks and despondent look* [emphasis mine].[47]

Oppression, according to Elmslie, had given "the whole country a look of poverty," creating an epidemic of kamzorī, embodied as "sallow complexion[s], thin cheeks and despondent look." Kamzorī materialized not just the physical toll of exploitation, but the immoral cruelty of Dogra colonialism. Critiquing Dogra policies and violating medical neutrality came at a high cost. Some later attributed Elmslie's "suspicious" death to poison, "for he had made many enemies by his outspoken condemnation of the then prevailing tyranny."[48]

The situation deteriorated further, when Kashmir was ravaged by a terrible famine from 1877 to 1879. Dr. Arthur Neve, then head of the Kashmir Medical Mission, heard "terrible stories . . . of the suffering." He described the "very scanty ragged garments" worn by weavers, the "emaciated bodies of many of the poorer classes," and "half-naked corpses that . . . [were] lying by the roadside even in the European quarter." The famine, according to him, was not a "natural" disaster, but was caused by "malignant forces"—i.e., Dogra policies which had left peasants in penury. Rather than provide aid to those suffering, the Dogra regime made attempts to hide the effects of the famine. Neve chronicled one "sinister rumor" that "some hundreds of starving people had been purposely drowned in Wular Lake, to which colour was lent by the sudden death of an eye-witness and informer within a few hours of making the report." Though Neve questioned the story's authenticity, its traction indexed "an alienation of sympathy, and . . . an intensity of sinister suspicion which boded ill for the relation of the poor Mohammedan [Muslim] cultivators and weavers with their rulers."[49]

In fact, Kashmiris did fight back against Dogra oppression. Lawrence described seeing a protest in which peasants "fl[u]ng off their clothes and smear[ed] themselves with wet mud," marking their destitution and animal-like existence at the hands of the Dogra government.[50] Such descriptions show how the weak, laboring Kashmiri Muslim body not only passively registered suffering and harm, but also was a site of resistant political subjectivities. These accounts show how kamzorī—the sense of being besieged by external forces—persists through time. To make a deliberately paradoxical statement: kamzorī, weakness, is historically resilient.

The effects of Dogra colonialism produced more than physical debility, however. Kamzorī was also used to ascribe a moral weakening that had beset Kashmiris as a result of being colonized subjects. British colonizers had much to say about the way colonialism had shaped the collective "personality" of Kashmiris. For example, Walter Lawrence, a land settlement officer, described how turning Kashmir and the North-West Frontier Province into a battleground between the Dogra, British, and Russian empires had had a detrimental effect on the Kashmiri "national character."[51] According to him, the "terrible system . . . of espionage and blackmailing" practiced by each of the colonial powers had forced Kashmiris to become "treacherous" and distrustful of each other and of outsiders. While such generalizations are racist and essentializing, they posited a relation between political conditions and capacities for morality. This topic produced heated discussions in contemporary Kashmir.

✤

Summer 2013: I'm in Kashmir, my first return since completing my dissertation. Friends and acquaintances tease me: *So, when is the book coming out?* Flustered, I tell them it's going to take years. But before I know it, my shame gives way to the thickness of social relations. All over Rajbagh, my old stomping ground, people somehow remember me: the sharp-tongued woman who lives next door; the dried fruit seller in the back alley (always well stocked with bitter walnuts, buttery almonds, and tart apricots); the avuncular autorickshaw driver with the salt-and-pepper beard who has ferried me across the city many times, his gray *kurta* flapping in the breeze; the grumpy shopkeeper with red-rimmed eyes who doled out change to me for two years without so much as a smile, but whose eyes light up when he sees me now. *Kab aaye?*—when did you arrive?—he seems to genuinely want to know.

I'm here with only the vaguest to-do list because I know, in Kashmir, you don't need to search for projects. They are in plain sight, like soldiers in grenade-proof bunkers. During long, lazy afternoons embellished with tea (Lipton for me, *nun chai* for everyone else), biscuits, and *girdas* from the bakery, in living rooms where newspapers are scattered about, a series of headlines grabs my attention:

Spurious Drugs in Kashmir Hospitals
Tablet with "0% Antibiotic" Is at Heart of Drug Scandal in J&K
Fake Drugs Supplied to Hospitals in Jammu and Kashmir as Pharma
    Company Denies Involvement
Spurious Drugs: Doctors, Society Claim J&K Govt. Playing with Lives

A corruption scandal is afoot. It centers on the supply and subsequent cover-up of between 100,000 and 200,000 tablets of fake amoxicillin trihydrate, a first-line antibiotic, to Kashmir's public hospitals. The pharmaceuticals, sold under the brand names Maximizen-625 and Curesef, were supposed to contain five hundred milligrams of amoxicillin each, but contained zero milligrams. Medical experts estimate that the supply of fake amoxicillin, which went unreported for three years, contributed to the deaths of hundreds of people, including three hundred children.[52] News spreads fast. A *New York Times* article titled "Medicines Made in India Set Off Safety Worries" uses the scandal to discredit India's generic pharmaceutical industry, which has supplied amoxicillin to US hospitals as well.[53]

What shocks people is not the fake drugs—stories of fake drugs are an unfortunate but common phenomenon across the Global South. Nor is it the fact that there's corruption in the public health system. According to a study by Transparency International, Jammu and Kashmir is India's second most corrupt state, after Bihar. More than eight hundred corruption cases against politicians and bureaucrats are registered with the State Vigilance Commission and the crime branch of the Jammu and Kashmir police department, with little or no resolution. With Kashmir's extraordinary corruption already widely known, the amoxicillin scandal still erupts as a scandal because children's lives have been staked.[54] As one civil society organizer described, "this is not about amassing wealth through corrupt means, but about playing with human lives."[55] Everywhere I go, people are outraged—from autorickshaw drivers to doctors to university students. The amoxicillin scandal is on everyone's lips. For many, it affirms long-standing fears about the quality of medicine and care in a dilapidated public health system. The scandal is evidence of how, far from being an apolitical, neutral, biopolitical good, public medicine can perpetuate harm.

※

Unlike the sense of resignation that sometimes accompanies news of endemic corruption in South Asia, this scandal galvanized the public. After the scandal first broke, in May 2013, pro-independence political parties called a one-day, citywide strike (bandh). Medical professionals, civil society, religious leaders, and politicians marched through the streets wearing black armbands, calling for implicated politicians and public health officials to resign. One poster from the protest read: "Sack and hang those involved in drug scam." The Doctors Association of Kashmir (DAK), a civil society organization, filed a public interest litigation (PIL) petition in the High Court, calling for the crime branch to take over the investigation and issue summonses for the former health minister and four other accused public health officials. Syed Ali Shah Geelani, one of Kashmir's most important politicians, described the supply of fake drugs as an act of "genocide" by the Indian state against Kashmiris.[56] Although the fake drugs had spread outside Kashmir, the scandal and the explanatory logics that followed rendered the region, once again, a zone of exception.

Like all protests in Kashmir, the amoxicillin protests were carefully monitored and surveilled by the Indian state and its security agencies. Those seen as being "too vocal" were arrested and censured. The whistleblower, Dr. Nisar ul Hasan, who also happened to be the president of the Doctors Association of Kashmir, was a prime target. In June 2013, he was arrested while on duty at Sri Maharaja Hari Singh (SMHS) hospital, one of Kashmir's largest public hospitals. During his shift, he was called to a nearby police station under the pretense that a senior officer needed medical attention; however, on reaching the station, he was arrested.[57] Doctors and paramedics at SMHS immediately protested for his immediate release. In an interview, an anesthesiologist stated unequivocally that Dr. Hasan's arrest was retribution for his anti-corruption activism.[58] Dr. Hasan's arrest revealed how easily the state's biopolitical aspirations to care could be subsumed by its impulse to punish. Medicine was, not for the first time, overrun by militarism.

After spending several weeks in jail, Dr. Hasan was released. I arranged an interview with him through a journalist friend. The three of us met briefly in a restaurant in Srinagar, and then Dr. Hasan invited me to his office for a more in-depth interview. I met him in his relatively plush and quiet chambers in SMHS, the hospital's cacophony reduced to a hum. The interview, which unfolded over several hours, was more of a monologue than a dialogue. Throughout the interview, a man—perhaps an assistant (I don't know because he was never introduced to me)—sat next to me, a disquieting and silent presence. This unknown person, as well as Hasan's domineering personality, made the interview an uneasy experience. Dr. Hasan, however, was oblivious to my discomfort. I barely had to ask a question before he launched into a soliloquy.

"Slaves cannot tell the truth," he began dramatically. Over the course of the interview, Dr. Hasan unpacked this elliptical statement. For him, the tragedy of the amoxicillin scandal was not in the supply of fake drugs, but in the cover-up. Hasan described how a senior public health official had approached him with the incriminating laboratory results, but the official had lacked the courage to publicize the results himself. Instead, he asked Dr. Hasan to do it and begged to remain anonymous. Despite pressure from fellow doctors and his own family not to publicize the report, Dr. Hasan had called a press conference. However, he honored the official's wishes and never revealed his identity.

For Dr. Hasan, the scandal was not an isolated incident, but a symptom of the collective moral kamzorī that had beset Kashmiris. Unlike many people with whom I spoke, who delimited kamzorī to the period of Indian military occupation, Dr. Hasan recalled the longue durée—more than four hundred years—of colonialization: "What do these centuries of colonization do? What they do is that they make it impossible for anyone to have the courage to tell the truth. They have made Kashmiris totally morally kamzor. Kashmiris no longer have courage." According to him, centuries of colonization, including Indian humanitarian and militaristic overinvestments trying to "buy Kashmiris loyalty," had caused endemic corruption, which had eroded people's capacities to make sound moral judgments. While mainstream Indian political discourses pointed to Jammu and Kashmir's exceptional corruption as evidence of its chronic inability to govern itself, a counter-discourse, from Kashmiris themselves, argued that the Indian government had deliberately cultivated a culture of corruption to dilute claims to self-determination. This situation had been further aggravated by the armed struggle, for which unaccounted money from Pakistan and the Gulf states had flowed into Kashmir.[59]

According to Dr. Hasan, centuries of collective humiliation as colonized subjects had led to a loss of collective morality.[60] Colonialism had led to multiple kinds of kamzorī: diluted demands for political self-determination, ill-health, and moral and spiritual corruption. "If people are being fed poison instead of medicine and no one cares, then where are we?" His voice soared in anger. "This level of corruption has destroyed the movement [tehreek]," he continued, referring to Kashmir's movement for self-determination. "The Indian state no longer has to kill Kashmiris"—he rolled his office chair from side to side—"I mean, yes, they might kill one or two here and there, but only if they are real threats. But what's happening now is that Kashmiris are killing Kashmiris." Contrary to statements that the amoxicillin scandal was a genocide by the Indian state, or that the Indian state was enacting necropolitical power over Kashmiris by making determinations of who can live and who must die, Dr. Hasan described the more subtle and indirect effects of colonialism on the colonized. By stating that "Kashmiris are killing Kashmiris," he linked the amoxicillin crisis with other forms of violence committed by Kashmiris *against* Kashmiris during the armed conflict.[61] These were examples of moral kamzorī—of misdirection, weakening social bonds, and a lack of accountability.

While I frequently heard critiques of Indian occupation, such stinging critiques of Kashmiri society—even if emplaced within a history of colonization—were rare. They suggested that deeper forms of disorder lay below the surface, much like the invasive weeds that damage the Dal Lake's ecosystem. People in Kashmir worried about these forms of slow violence, but much like environmental crises, could not prioritize them until they erupted (*too busy worrying about life and death*).

As an Indian researcher, it was also challenging for me to access these critiques. After all, Kashmiris are well aware of the established cottage industry of Indian scholars, bureaucrats, and intellectuals who publicly decry and delegitimize the Kashmiri movement for self-determination—not unlike what British colonizers once did to independence-minded Indians. Given this history, people I did not know well found it necessary to defend and explain their politics to me. They were eager to explain and justify the histories of Indian state violence (*your government*) that had led them to a pro-independence position.

It took years of building trust and intimacy to hear internal critiques of the movement, which, in the wrong hands, could be dangerous. A close friend, a law professor, once remarked that occupation doesn't allow you to hold up a mirror to your own society because you are too busy pointing to the oppression being meted out by the occupier: "Only when it's over, after fifty or a hundred years, you see the tumors that have been festering, the things you couldn't see before." She continued, "It's easy to kick things like corruption down the road, because they don't seem as important as other things, like life itself. But at what cost?" Like many Kashmiris, she worried about the less visible effects of occupation. What happens when people are too kamzor to fight back, as Dr. Hasan put it?

Dr. Hasan became a whistleblower to counter the moral kamzorī that had beset Kashmiris. Demanding accountability was a way of doing something otherwise. As Elizabeth Povinelli notes: "every arrangement installs its own possible derangements and rearrangements. The otherwise is these immanent derangements and rearrangements."[62] Dr. Hasan's family and colleagues read his decision as a "derangement"—a break in the logic of survival—and as madness. He said, "*They* think I am mad," referring to how his friends and family had responded to his activism, "but *I* think 99 percent of *them* are mad." Meanwhile, he viewed the logic of survival—of bearing occupation's routine humiliations, participating in corruption, not speaking freely for fear of repercussions, and keeping to oneself—as *actually* deranged. Here, Dr. Hasan made ironic use of the register of "madness" or "derangement." Centuries-long occupations had turned everything inside out, he argued, including people's most basic sense of right and wrong, rationality and irrationality.

Other medical professionals also felt similarly betrayed by collective moral kamzorī. As one angry commentator wrote in response to the crisis: "Dr.

Nisar ul Hasan is a victim of corrupt govt. bootlickers. He has spent months in jail for the common masses . . . these [doctors are] *gaddār* [treacherous] and *munāfik* [hypocritical]. . . . This doctor body [DAK] is full of murderers, rapists and criminals."[63] The writer used highly charged language—as we've seen, terms like treachery and duplicity have a long history in a society anxious about collaborators and informers—and leveled these accusations against doctors, who are supposed to embody the highest ethical ideals. This accusation revealed how, far from being neutral or palliative, medicine had become complicit in processes of social and political violence.

The philosopher Alain Badiou describes how there are particular moments or events in a person's life that open them up "to a radically different composition of the self, *a switch* that has a lasting effect and involves the most significant . . . ways in which that person conceives of her or himself [emphasis mine]."[64] For Dr. Hasan, calling the press conference, publicizing the scandal, and owning the risks and repercussions that would inevitably follow, were that "switch." As expected, this choice came at enormous personal and social cost. In May 2014, Dr. Hasan was suspended from DAK, but he continued publishing his critical online newsletter. Though he was later reinstated, he has had more public quarrels with the media, government, and the DAK and has been arrested several times. Disrupting the social and ethical norms of occupation—being otherwise—meant aligning himself against his social milieu, embracing an existence others would deem "mad."

According to Hasan, "99 percent" of Kashmiri society was mad (kamzor), because they had attuned themselves to a profoundly disordered everyday reality. In Kashmir and northern India, the word *kamzorī* signifies a weakening of the brain's capacities for rational speech, reason, and sense making. Labeling someone kamzor diminishes their opinions or perspectives. However, as Lawrence Cohen points out, "the line between productive wisdom" and "*bak-bak* [nonsensical speech]"—the speech of a kamzor mind—is thin. The difference "depends not only on the content of the productive voice but frequently on the politics of hearing."[65] In mainstream biological psychiatry, kamzor, mad, or disordered speech is seen as irrational, out of control, irresponsible, or something to be managed.[66] But a different politics of hearing might be more open to the "productive wisdom" inherent in the speech of those deemed kamzor or mad. Embodying a different politics of hearing can also disrupt the notion that those suffering from mental or psychological distress are passive victims. Instead, it can help us recognize how kamzorī can be an eloquent mode of distress, one that uncovers how medical and political harms interweave.

Another twig, the fire is lit.

Inayat—a young man I met at a police-run inpatient substance abuse center called the De-Addiction Centre (DDC) in 2011—exemplified the necessity of hearing kamzorī in a new way. Located in the heavily fortified, militarized police headquarters called the Police Control Room, the DDC was on the ground floor of a two-story building, nestled next to a cricket oval used for anti-riot drills. When the police were practicing their drills, they looked almost like cricketers, with puffy leg pads and face helmets, only one wargame was far more dangerous than the other. The police's media and publicity department was on the building's upper level, as well as a small gymnasium, occasionally used by patients during their daily exercise hour. Police jeeps were always parked outside the DDC, and they frequently zoomed up and down the Control Room, leaving mushroom dust clouds in their wake. Against this bustling traffic, the DDC was usually a subdued space. Patients were disallowed from venturing beyond the parking lot, but unlike other substance abuse treatment centers, they were not chained to their beds and were allowed kin visits. They were acutely aware that their thirty-day treatment was taking place in a deeply militarized space.

The DDC was the culmination of years of effort by senior police officials to restore the image of the police after it carried out brutal counterinsurgency campaigns in the 1990s. Because of this, as well as its historical association with the Dogra regime, the Jammu and Kashmir police force is one of the least trustworthy public institutions in the region.[67] Today, the DDC and other mental health programs are part of the police's effort to "win back hearts and minds." Kashmir's burgeoning substance abuse epidemic proved the perfect opportunity because of the urgent need for services. One study found that 31.3 percent of college-age Kashmiri men abuse drugs; the vast majority use benzodiazepines, such as Alprax (alprazolam) or diazepam (Valium), or opioid analgesics such as codeine (codeine phosphate), while approximately 53 percent use cannabis (charas). In recent years, there has also been a sharp rise in heroin use.[68] Since its beginning in 2008, the DDC has treated more than 13,972 male patients, including 1,266 inpatients. Despite families having strong apprehensions about turning in their loved ones to the police for care, the DDC was attractive because it was highly subsidized. Families only had to pay for the cost of food and medications, approximately Rs. 3,000 per month, compared with ten times as much in private centers.

FIGURE 1.4. The police De-Addiction Centre. Photo by author

I was told that the police administration had gone to great lengths to hire qualified mental health professionals to run the DDC; this demonstrated the seriousness with which they took their humanitarian project. One clinician told me, "Addicts are outcasts in our society—no one respects them. But here we take them in and restore their dignity." Dr. Sajad, the clinical psychologist directing the center, and other staff—a psychiatrist, social worker, and pharmacist—were promised little interference from the police in everyday clinical affairs. Clinicians told me that they tried their best to maintain global ethical standards of confidentiality, professionalism, and inpatient care, despite their location and funding.

Yet there were "tensions of practice" between the police's humanitarian and military imperatives. For one, the Police Control Room was where people were jailed, tortured, and interrogated, and patients were haunted by specters of military violence. Some patients themselves had histories of political protest and were nervous about the potential conflicts of interest between the DDC and police. Given histories of mistrust between the police and civilians, they had trouble believing that the police's motives were purely humanitarian and feared they would be recruited as police informers or collaborators after their treatment was complete. After all, they reasoned, clinicians and, by extension, the police establishment had access to intimate details about their substance use—which many of their kin did not. Many worried this information could easily be used against them. Despite efforts to follow global standards of substance abuse treatment, military logics seeped in. Clinicians' authority was frequently enforced by the presence of two police personnel, who provided twenty-four-hour security cover. Violence—and the threat of violence—were used occasionally when patients violated the clinic's rules. For these reasons, treatment was a highly charged, stressful, and ambivalent experience.[69] For clinicians too, these dynamics produced some discomfort. In informal conversations, clinicians described being torn between their role as police employees and caregivers, sometimes privately disagreeing with the police's counterinsurgency efforts.

These uneasy overlaps infected my work as well. I felt the "tensions of practice." While clinicians and police staff warmly welcomed me as part of the DDC team, police and paramilitary personnel violently clashed with unarmed protestors out in the streets. As an anthropologist, I found myself both dependent on and critical of the police infrastructure. I, too, was caught between collaboration and resistance.[70]

ψ

Inayat was seeking treatment at the DDC for substance use disorder and schizophrenia, the latter being one of the most telltale forms of kamzorī. Like many people diagnosed with schizophrenia, Inayat's behaviors and language were cryptic. His way of communicating was nonlinear and fragmentary.[71] I have tried to fill in what I could through memoir, ethnography, and social history. Yet rather than create a concrete whole, my account recalls Sarah Pinto's method of a "hermeneutics of discord"—an account of contradictory stories that offer insight into the cracks between normative ethics, law, and medicine.[72] Inayat's story exemplifies the psychic discord that happens when opposing state imperatives—humanitarianism and militarism, care and harm—collide in people's lives. The combination of counterinsurgency and medicine were not merely background details of his life, but had shaped him in profound ways.

At first, I only knew *of* Inayat, in a casual, secondhand way. The other patients described him pejoratively as "different" and "other" (*alag*). Inayat had a habit of picking up other people's discarded cigarette butts and smoking them down to the filter. Patients at the DDC were allowed to smoke cigarettes during treatment, but their consumption was monitored. "Disgusting [*chhēe*]!" I heard Rafiq, a teenage patient from an upwardly mobile, middle-class family yell after Inayat picked up one of his discarded butts. "He has habits like an animal," he muttered as he walked away. I understood Rafiq's statement not only as a critique of Inayat's behavior, but also as a way to distance himself from Inayat's more severe mental illness. Although Rafiq and the other patients did not know Inayat's diagnosis, they knew he was suffering from something more than substance abuse. Inayat had a weak (kamzor) or mad (*pāgal*) brain, the signs of which were evident in his strange habits, emotional volatility, and elliptical speech.

Inayat was petite and wiry, his hair buzzed short, military style. The first time we talked, Inayat told me a story—which he had told many others at the DDC —about a broken love affair he had with a young woman he called Rosy. Inayat had carved Rosy's name with a knife on both his biceps and had once written her a letter in his blood to demonstrate his love. She had apparently torn the letter up in front of him, an act which Inayat described as "the deepest betrayal." Rafiq asked me what I thought of Inayat's story. "*Zyādā filmī nahīn hai?*" (isn't it a little too melodramatic?) he had said, smirking. Although melodramatic love stories were ubiquitous in the clinic, Inayat's had apparently exceeded the bounds of the socially acceptable.[73]

Clinicians were also puzzled by Inayat. Dr. Sajad encouraged me to talk to him, describing him as an "interesting case," a young man suffering from a "bizarre delusion." I found evidence of the bizarre delusion in Inayat's medical file, which I read with his permission one day while waiting for him to finish group therapy. The file stated that Inayat thought the psychotropic medications he was being given at the DDC had turned into a land mine inside his body. The clinicians' treatment plan was to disprove Inayat's irrational belief through the use of a rational, medical technology—ultrasound—which would prove there was no land mine inside him. I didn't know how to broach this topic with Inayat, so I waited for him to bring it up.

ψ

One day, while Inayat and I were chatting in the DDC's front room, a small, narrow, carpeted area where patients ate and received guests, and where I occasionally conducted interviews, Inayat described his light green eyes as "cat eyes" (*billī ke ānkhen*). They were penetrating, even frightening; I had trouble holding eye contact. However, it took me a minute to register what he meant. *Cat eyes.* Inayat's speech contained more than disorder; in it were buried histories. *Cat* is a code word that describes collaborators and counterinsurgents—many of them former insurgents—recruited by the Indian state to destroy Kashmir's movement for self-determination. As I described earlier, during sieges and crackdowns, cats were brought to villages to identify insurgents hiding among civilians. In these operations, the cat's identity remained concealed. In *The Collaborator*, novelist Mirza Waheed describes them: "The men wore dark green uniforms, overalls, and had tied their black scarves in a way that made the fabric form tight skullcaps on their heads, as the rest of the material flew about behind their backs. From a distance, from the angle we were looking from, they looked like a pack of animals—creatures different from ordinary people. At last I understood the name they had been given: *black cats*."[74]

Since the armed conflict began, two classes of political collaborators or counterinsurgents emerged in Kashmir: ikhwāns (literally, "brothers") and *mukhbīrs* (collaborators). From about 1994 on, Indian armed forces began systematically using captured or surrendered former militants, many of them Kashmiri, in counterinsurgency operations. These former militants, ikhwāns, were recruited to fight against their former organizations or other armed groups. Between 1996 and 2003, ikhwāns committed extrajudicial killings, abductions, and assaults on militant groups, journalists, human rights activists, and medical workers, at times with orders from armed forces, but also independently. By outsourcing human rights violations to ikhwāns, Indian armed forces cleverly deflected attention away from themselves. In addition to helping suppress the insurgency, Indian security officials credit ikhwāns with successfully facilitating the 1996 Assembly elections in Jammu and Kashmir—an important symbol for the Indian state to show that democracy had been "restored" after six years of armed conflict.[75] In 2003, it was estimated that between 350 and 500 ikhwāns still remained on active duty with the Jammu and Kashmir police and army and were being paid a regular stipend; many others were absorbed into the armed forces and police. For many Kashmiris, the word *ikhwān* conjures terrible memories, bitter betrayals of "Kashmiris killing Kashmiris," as Dr. Hasan put it. Many live in social isolation.

The second category of collaborators, called mukhbīrs, signifies a more general culture of betrayal caused by occupation. Mukhbīrs constitute a looser, broader, more hidden, and more heterogenous network than ikhwāns.[76] Journalists estimate that approximately 100,000 mukhbīrs are on the payrolls of the police, intelligence agencies, and armed forces. Like ikhwāns, mukhbīrs are characterized by doubleness: some are former militants who betrayed the cause of independence and now feed information to the occupiers, while others were forced to instrumentalize their social relationships to survive. Unlike ikhwāns, whose identities are known, mukhbīrs must remain duplicitous. Their efficacy depends on being "one of us": their identities must remain concealed. As Begoña Aretxaga has argued in the context of the *cipayo*, a word used by radical nationalists to describe members of the Basque police force, the collaborator's betrayal is qualitatively different from violence committed by an oppressor: "Unlike the invader, or the stranger, the traitor retains a trace of us . . . the image of the cipayo contains the traumatic residue of an imaginary unity that has not been given up, while it signals the fact that it no longer exists."[77] In other words, much like Dr. Hasan's discussion of the conflict's implosion, Inayat, too, pointed to a betrayal within.

ৠ

Inayat's "betrayals within" were multiply enfolded in his life history. In our conversations, he spoke at length about his father. "He never acted decently," he said. "He didn't fulfill his obligations to us." Inayat's father was physically abusive and an alcoholic. Once when he was a child, his father hit his mother on the head with a lead bucket. Without skipping a beat, Inayat told me, "Many years later, I also beat her up in the same way. They put me in the mental hospital." This was just one of the many repetitions and mirrorings between his father and himself that structured Inayat's story. His father worked for the police, and the family eventually went to his commanding officer and complained about his violent behavior. Eventually, Inayat's father was transferred to another department because of the family's repeated complaints.

About two and a half years earlier, Inayat's father had remarried. Inayat, his siblings, and his mother went to live with his maternal uncle (*māmā*) in his mother's natal home. His mother did embroidery work to help make ends meet, but the family was dependent on Inayat's māmā. Inayat was bitter about his father's remarriage because *he* was the one who was supposed to get married. He had asked his maternal uncle's daughter to marry him (a cross-cousin marriage common in Kashmiri Muslim families), but she said she would only marry him if they moved in with Inayat's father. Inayat had refused. "How can I leave my mother?" he asked me, exasperated.

Inayat said he started using hashish (charas) after his father abandoned the family. He smoked between five and ten hashish "cigarettes" a day.[78] He also sometimes mixed cannabis with whiteout fluid, which he described as "the most powerful intoxication [*nashā*] in the world." I asked Inayat how the drugs made him feel. He said, "with charas I feel total blindness. I feel like charas sucks the blood, that there will be nothing left inside of me." For the next few years, Inayat was in and out of the psychiatric hospital. He was institutionalized at least three times. The first time, he was admitted after he tried to commit suicide. The second and third times, he was physically violent toward his family. Meanwhile, his drug use also escalated. All of his hospital admissions were involuntary: "they gave me a diazepam injection and I passed out." I asked him about his experiences in the closed wards:

> Everyone there was crazy. But *I* wasn't crazy. Just because I hit them [my family members] doesn't mean that I was crazy. We had a fight because I told them straight up, "yes, I smoke charas." The first time I was institutionalized, I stayed in the family ward [a short-term, open ward] and it was not bad. I stayed there, I was well behaved, even though I had to spend one night [in the closed ward] with the *mentals*. The second time, I got into a fight with my mother because she told me to go to work even though I wasn't getting a salary. I hit her. I thought, *why should I go to work when they don't respect me?* . . .
>
> I used to feel so bored in there. I tried to talk to the other patients, but they were all crazy. If someone had one cigarette, everyone would go running after it! About two or three months ago, in March or April, I slipped on a broken tile in the bathroom and cut my foot really badly. I lost about three or four pints of blood. They sent me home in an ambulance the next day. That's how I got out.[79]

Just as Rafiq had distanced himself from Inayat, Inayat too distanced himself from those bearing the "real" marks of kamzorī.

ψ

One day while Inayat and I were chatting, he said something that surprised me. "Everyone has their own story of drug use," he was saying philosophically, "some do it for a girl, some lie, some tell the truth. I have nothing to say about that. My father was the first person to betray me, then Rosy, then my brother disappeared. Now, I just think about my brother."

I was not sure if I heard right, so I asked him to clarify.

"My younger brother is missing [*lāpatā*]," he said nonchalantly, as if he had told me this a thousand times before. "He's been missing for the past five years." According to Inayat, the Border Security Force (BSF), a paramilitary organization, had approached Inayat's brother, Yousuf, and asked him to become a mukhbīr. Yousuf told Inayat and their father that he had refused, but they suspected he was working for the Criminal Investigation Department (CID), a branch of the Jammu and Kashmir police. Their father became suspicious of Yousuf's activities and stopped him from going to school. At some point, Inayat said, "my father thought even I was a mukhbīr."

After being stopped from studying, Yousuf worked as a day laborer (mazdōr). Then, "one day, he left for mazdōrī and never came back. I think maybe he's locked up in Cargo," Inayat said. While Inayat had been loquacious in his description of his love affair with Rosy, his brother's disappearance was condensed in these two, pithy sentences. I struggled to understand them. Inayat's brother had been gone almost five years, and yet he believed he was waiting to be found in "Cargo." "Cargo" is one of the most notorious interrogation and detention centers in Kashmir, run by the Special Operations Group (SOG), the counterinsurgency wing of the Jammu and Kashmir police.[80] In the last few years, Cargo was converted into the police's information technology department—from one kind of information gathering to another. According to leaked WikiLeaks cables between International Committee of the Red Cross (ICRC) aid workers and US diplomats, the ICRC had failed to gain access to Cargo for many years to work with prisoners. I did not know if the Cargo Inayat was imagining even existed anymore, but I did not say anything.

Soon after Yousuf's disappearance, the family had submitted a first information report (FIR), the minimum standard documentation required to initiate police investigations in India. However, in a common strategy of deferral to discourage families from pursuing these cases, the police "lost" the FIR, so the family had to file a new one. Then, one day, the Border Security Force again came "knocking on their door" and tried recruiting Inayat as a mukhbīr. He refused.

The family tried to resume normal life as much as possible. But Inayat's parents' marriage dissolved, a process undoubtedly accelerated by the strain of their son's disappearance. Then, when Inayat was a first-year college student, the police asked him and a friend to do counterinsurgency work. Inayat's friend refused, and without his friend, Inayat felt he would not be useful. But he agreed. I could not tell if Inayat felt forced, whether a part of him wanted to be a mukhbīr like his brother, or maybe he thought becoming a mukhbīr would help him find his brother.

He said, "When I remember my brother now, all I do is cry."

Inayat was vague about what he did for the police. Instead, he focused on how he was "disrespected." Despite working for the police for five years, he never got a formal appointment or a promotion. There were long stretches of time when he did not get paid. He said bitterly, "If I had joined the Task Force [the police counterinsurgency wing], I would have participated in an encounter, a promotion list would have been drafted, and my name would have been on it." Military or police "encounters" consist of armed—sometimes staged—confrontations between law enforcement personnel and terrorists, insurgents, or other criminals. In Jammu and Kashmir and other militarized states in India, killing suspected militants and terrorists is incentivized and rewarded. For each dead militant, law enforcement officials earn between Rs. 35,000 and 50,000, as well as out-of-turn promotions. Scholars and human rights experts have argued that these incentives, along with the structure of emergency laws that protect extrajudicial killings from persecution, create a perverse system in which Kashmiri civilians are routinely disappeared and then killed and passed off as Pakistani terrorists.

On my way home from the clinic that day, I felt queasy—not so much at Inayat's compulsion to violence and retribution, but at the way different worlds were collapsing into each other. Questions raced through my mind: Why does Inayat want (need?) to participate in the disappearance of others, while mourning the disappearance of his own brother? What does it mean that the very same organization (the police) that destroyed Inayat's family was now in charge of treating him? What connected collaboration and schizophrenia? And finally, what did Inayat's statement—that medicine had turned into a land mine inside his body—have to do with these predicaments?

ψ

To respond to these questions, we must approach Inayat's kamzorī, his madness, and disordered speech as capturing potentially uncomfortable truths about the entanglements of military and humanitarian apparatuses at the level of the body and kin relations. But where do we start unpacking a phrase—a pill has become a land mine inside my body—so allusive and aphoristic?

Gregory Bateson theorized schizophrenic speech as a problem of communication, in which the schizophrenic may use metaphor—sometimes literally—to avoid confronting the contradictions of inhabiting two irreconcilable positions (the "double bind") simultaneously. According to Bateson, by using metaphors—such as "a pill is like a land mine"—patients can point to problematic situations without directly confronting the situation or person responsible for them. This is particularly useful when that person is in a relationship of greater power to them—a therapist, parent, or authority figure of some kind.[81] Through Bateson, we could say that Inayat's allusive statement condenses his fear and anger toward the police while protecting him from the repercussions of making that claim outright. The pill as land mine indirectly expresses the double bind of being both cared for and harmed by the police.

Yet, Inayat's is a life of double binds. It is not an exceptional occurrence, as it is in Bateson's analysis. Inayat has spent his adulthood as a mukhbīr. According to Bateson, in chronic double bind situations such as Inayat's, a person's "metacommunicative system—the communications about communication—are broken down." This can lead to Inayat's mind, like "any self-correcting system which has lost its governor," spiraling into "never-ending, but always systematic distortions."[82] Inayat did experience a profound breakdown in his communicative and metacommunicative capacities; he was inhabiting a world without sense. It *does not* make sense that the same institution that disappeared his brother was now his employer and caregiver. It *does not* make sense that he thought his brother was still alive. It *does not* make sense that he fantasized about profiting from disappearing others. While Bateson's analysis offers a window into Inayat's speech, it offers only a metaphorical reading. Much like translations of kamzorī we encountered earlier in this chapter, I found this explanation ultimately unsatisfying. My time with Inayat was so much more material than metaphorical.

To attend to the more concrete dimensions of Inayat's experience, and kamzorī more generally, I turn to the work of feminist phenomenologists. According to Ellen Corin, the experience of schizophrenia is suffused with alienation: alienation from oneself and from the outside world. Being a mukhbīr heightens this state of alienation, producing what Sarah Pinto beautifully calls "layered dissolutions."[83] Unlike Bateson, who would read Inayat's statement—the pill is a land mine—as *confusing* two semantic orders, a feminist and phenomenological reading understands this expression as *crystallizing* multiple existential, clinical, and kinship crises: his father's suspicion that Yousuf was a counterinsurgent, Inayat replacing/becoming his brother, Inayat working for the police who may have disappeared his brother, and Inayat wanting to disappear others.

Through kamzorī, the mukhbīr undoes himself and, in so doing, tells us about the condition of life in occupied Kashmir. His so-called delusion tells us that *all mukhbīrs are ticking time bombs.* Rather than violence as something external to him, Inayat's body has itself become a militarized landscape. With a land mine inside him, Inayat becomes a "fractal person" to the extreme, a person with relationships enfolded within his body, a person simultaneously internal and external, known and unknown, himself and not himself, his brother and not, his father and not, collaborator and not, Kashmiri and not.[84] The pill embodies what is inarticulable or unrepresentable, *l'actuel* in him; it refers to what the psyche has to work upon or against in order to construct meaning.[85] "The pill has become a land mine" describes what the intermingling of counterinsurgency and care, collaboration and schizophrenia, the state and kinship, can do to a person. Pills and bombs, the technés of militarized care, address the aporia within him.

For clinicians and many others, Inayat's words were taken as the ravings of a madman (*pāgal*). Yet his life history reveals the emotional and psychic dissonance that can occur when people's lives are torn apart by militarism and when militarized care is the only available mode of redressal. Sometimes the contradictions were too much to bear. But much like the protesting, mud-smeared, kamzor bodies that nineteenth-century missionaries described, Inayat's words also contained defiance: a world become indigestible.

ψ

Inayat's experience and the others I have chronicled reveal how symptoms like kamzorī are more than just "cultural signifiers"—locally appropriate and resonant terms—through which people grapple with otherwise unspeakable existential, social, and political experiences. They cannot be straightforwardly read as "texts" or as signs of disease, transparent things that can be packed and unpacked. The kamzor body does more than simply "express" a given cultural order. Kamzorī insisted that the body mattered and that it was moral and irreducible. Through kamzorī, people undid, redid, and aspired to new orders and ways of being.

❀

One last twig.

Some sieges do end. Some even end well. In "A Victorious Campaign,"
a satirical short story by the Kashmiri writer Arif Ayaz Parrey, the story's
protagonist is an old, mentally ill (kamzor) man named Āzād, someone who
today might be diagnosed with schizophrenia.[86] Not accidentally, the word
Āzād means freedom; thus Parrey cheekily equates the quest for freedom as
madness. Like Inayat, Āzād has strange habits: he talks to himself, is aloof,
and speaks uncanny truths. The villagers keep their distance from him, but
they also respect him, seeking out his advice and healing powers (another
politics of hearing).

One July morning, the *mintry* (the Kashmiri way of saying the English
word *military*) arrives in Āzād's village. The villagers are startled by the sudden presence of soldiers in their midst. The officer in charge tells the village headman that the mintry is here to stay, and they set up camp outside
the village, on top of a hill, which also happens to be one of Āzād's favorite
contemplation spots. The village is put under an indefinite siege. Soon, relations between the villagers and the military deteriorate. Teenage boys get
into skirmishes with the soldiers. Āzād, too, gets in their way. He is locked
up and tortured for five days. At the height of tensions, a nasty fight breaks
out, resulting in four boys from the village being shot and killed.

Following these incidents, strange things start happening inside the
camp. Soldiers who fall asleep inside their barracks wake up to find themselves outdoors. The poplar trees around the camp mysteriously start fall-
ing, injuring many soldiers. A chinar tree, which has a barrack built around
it, opens up its branches, tossing up bricks and corrugated tin sheets. The
military eventually decides to withdraw from the camp, but refuses to admit
that the withdrawal has anything to do with the supernatural events. But the
villagers are convinced this is why they are leaving. They know the mystical
events have everything to do with Āzād's strange power. The military leaves
and the fragrance of freedom is released in the air, "an idea has been planted,
the idea of victory."[87]

The hierarchies of madness and civilization, power and helplessness, have
been inverted. Madness—kamzorī—unseats supposedly civilizing, rational
power. *Strangeness*—not force, not cunning, not liberal human rights—is what
ultimately undoes the siege.

BEFORE

A story was told:
remember a time
when it was not this way.
Before disease, affliction, kamzorī.
You have to go back all the way to 1589:
when the padshah Akbar the Great
took Kashmir.
He crossed the Pir Panjal
on horseback.
But his head was throbbing—
an empire-sized headache.
Peasants were tilling fields of saffron:
(sidebar—so we know they were near Pampore)
bold, purple flowers, did you know?
Not the orange threads you use in your bouillabaisse.
He asked them for a cure.
They responded:
But what is a headache?

CHAPTER 2

A Disturbed Area

In exercise of the powers conferred under . . . the Armed Forces (Jammu and Kashmir) Special Powers Ordinance, 1990, the Governor of Jammu and Kashmir *hereby notifies the areas given in this notification as Disturbed Areas.*
—Jammu and Kashmir Government, December 6–7, 1990

Ethical agency is neither fully determined nor radically free. Its struggle or primary dilemma is to be produced by a world, even as one must produce oneself in some way.
—Judith Butler, *Giving an Account of Oneself*

Dr. Manzoor was alone in the psychiatric hospital's outpatient department (OPD), in a bad mood.[1] The day before, his back spasmed while replacing a flat tire. He was in a lot of pain. To make matters worse, it was October 27, a strike (hartāl) day. None of the junior residents or interns had come. He was the only psychiatrist who had shown up for "duty," the English-language term used to describe a work shift or posting.

October 27 commemorates the day in 1947 when Indian troops first landed in Kashmir to crush a rebellion aimed at overthrowing Dogra rule.[2] These events eventually led to an all-out war between India and Pakistan. Raiders from Pakistan who joined the fight looted and destroyed the Baramullah Medical Mission, abducted Sikh girls and women en masse, and razed homes and businesses to the ground.[3] Medicine became a casualty of political violence. Decades later, this was still true.

Dr. Manzoor was alone despite the fact that the health sector—doctors, ambulances, and pharmacies—is granted exemption during curfews and strikes and allowed to operate freely.[4] In practice, however, safety is not always guaranteed. Health professionals have been attacked or harassed by armed forces personnel, militants, and stone pelters, many a car windshield shattered despite the clear display of a red "+" symbol. On this day, like many others, the fear of losing life or property had kept medical professionals home.

Dr. Manzoor's cell phone rang frequently, the shrill ringtone piercing the silence. I imagined the junior doctors and postgraduates on the other end nervously explaining their absence in a register of regret and helplessness. Meanwhile, Dr. Manzoor loudly aired his frustration: "The other day, there were six doctors and today I am supposed to handle the entire OPD *and* the EEG [electroencephalogram] machine alone? There is no one here. *No one* is here," he repeated. Throughout his shift, I watched him dash back and forth from the OPD to the hospital's laboratory, looking harried. There were far fewer patients than normal—the hartāl had kept them away too—but more than enough to keep Dr. Manzoor occupied.

Depopulated, the hospital felt strange. Not a good day for fieldwork, I decided. I kept my distance from Dr. Manzoor, lest I incur his wrath by asking too many questions. Both ethnographic and psychiatric knowledge were overcome by the strike. I wandered the empty halls of the hospital, taking photographs of *disturbed medicine*, feeling ghostly.

ψ

This chapter appropriates the Indian state's language of "disturbance" as a provocation, to unsettle a normative politico-legal technology. When the Indian parliament designated the state of Jammu and Kashmir a disturbed area in 1990 through the Jammu and Kashmir Disturbed Areas Act (DAA, 1990–2015) and the Armed Forces (Jammu and Kashmir) Special Powers Act (AFSPA, 1990–present), it not only signaled that the region was "disturbed" by insurgency; it also triggered emergency legal provisions, giving sweeping search, arrest, and preventive detention powers to security forces, authorized and provided legal cover for them to shoot suspected terrorists or insurgents or commit other extrajudicial actions, and suspended the fundamental civil rights of Kashmiris in the name of "national security."[5] Thus designating a region a "state of disturbance" is not merely a locutionary act, but an illocutionary act that does things in the world. "Disturbance" subverted civil authority in favor of military rule, but it also unleashed a slew of other unintended effects on social and political life.

Kashmir's "disturbed area" designation was meant to be short-term and temporary, to address an acute situation of insurgency. However, Kashmir's disturbed condition has stretched into a chronic, long-term crisis, lasting more than thirty years.[6] Because of its durability, disturbance glosses both

FIGURE 2.1. Hartāl day at the hospital. Photo by author

immediate situations, such as emergencies or flare-ups of protests or disaster (what Ilana Feldman describes as the "humanitarian situation"), as well as the *chronic* problem of Kashmiri subjugation and colonization (the "humanitarian condition").[7] "Disturbance" thus combines the temporal logic of both permanent exception *and* periodic disruptions. Despite significant changes in the nature of Kashmir's movement for independence—from violent to nonviolent form—Kashmir's disturbed status has not been lifted. Since 2010, the armed insurgency has waned to just three hundred militants against 400,000 troops, yet Indian military and state officials refuse to remove emergency laws, arguing that Kashmir would slide back into disorder if they did. Emergency laws, they argue, are "necessary evils," needed to restore order and normalcy.[8] Any sign of protest against Indian rule, including peaceful nonviolent resistance, is seen as abnormal and as justifying emergency provisions. Normalcy, in other words, is asymptotic in this military imaginary.

In contrast, Kashmiris define disturbance very differently. For them, the continued presence of armed forces, the culture of impunity produced by emergency laws, and the paralyzing temporalities of crisis and emergency constitute the true disturbances.[9] While there is a broad literature in law and anthropology on legal exceptionalism, many of these works focus on

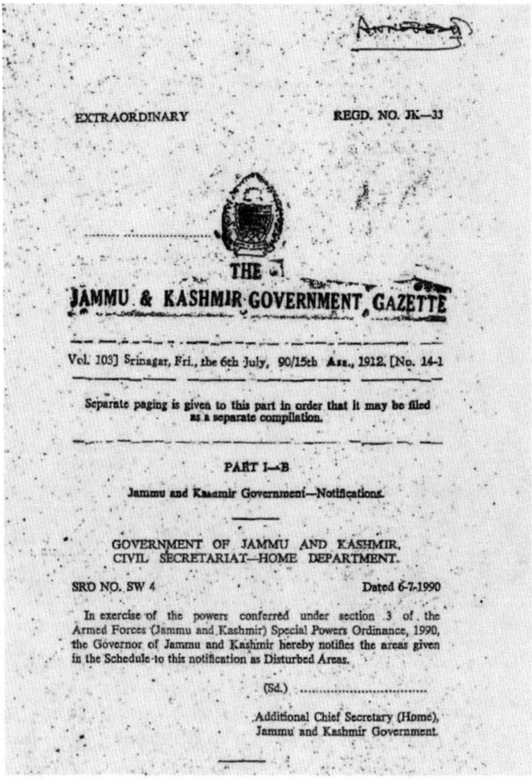

EXTRAORDINARY REGD. NO. JK—33

THE

JAMMU & KASHMIR GOVERNMENT GAZETTE

Vol. 103] Srinagar, Fri., the 6th July, 90/15th Asa., 1912. [No. 14-1

Separate paging is given to this part in order that it may be filed as a separate compilation.

PART I—B

Jammu and Kashmir Government—Notifications.

GOVERNMENT OF JAMMU AND KASHMIR,
CIVIL SECRETARIAT—HOME DEPARTMENT.

SRO NO. SW 4 Dated 6-7-1990

In exercise of the powers conferred under section 3 of the Armed Forces (Jammu and Kashmir) Special Powers Ordinance, 1990, the Governor of Jammu and Kashmir hereby notifies the areas given in the Schedule to this notification as Disturbed Areas.

(Sd.) ....

Additional Chief Secretary (Home),
Jammu and Kashmir Government.

FIGURE 2.2. Disturbed Areas Act. Source: Jammu and Kashmir state government

the legal subjects and subjectivities produced by emergency laws—the figure of the "abject" refugee, for example.[10] Yet, in Kashmir, exceptionalism and impunity were unmoored from law and had spilled into everyday life, producing existential uncertainty and disrupting space and temporality, people's ethical capacities, their sense of what was possible and sayable, and an eroding trust and reliability in state institutions and experts. Far from being limited to civilian-military encounters—as counterinsurgency doctrines alleged—disturbance was leaky, infectious, and penetrating.

Medical providers and patients alike felt that disturbances had glided from the legal-political to medicine. Although medicine had not witnessed the same physical devastation as other zones of conflict—the Gaza Strip, occupied Palestinian territories, Syria, or Iraq, for example—there was a pervasive sense that disruptions had permeated these supposedly neutral biopolitical spaces. In Kashmir, some medical practitioners theorized disturbance as something beyond their control that impinged on their ethics and practices, making medicine itself diseased. Like Dr. Hasan in the previous chapter, they described their colleagues' professional and personal ethics as compromised by currents of political instability and social disorder. Despite doing the humanitarian, caring work of the state, sometimes at great personal cost to themselves, public health workers felt undervalued, poorly compensated, and at risk—in short, victimized. They viewed medical professionals and the health system as pawns in the larger political conflict.[11]

At other times, however, doctors' narratives exceeded narratives of victimhood. While disturbance had entered medicine through militarism, it now fully suffused their practices, sensibilities, habits, and performances. Returning to an era before disturbance was impossible. The question was, rather, how ethical subjectivities and expertise could be forged *in* and *through* disturbance. Some embraced a sense of humor about "disturbed" medicine and public health, joking that it was a "miracle" that Kashmir's public health system was functioning at all. Yet they acknowledged the difficulty of maintaining any sense of pride or security in this system.

While living and working in a disturbed area produced contradictions for all occupied subjects, the contradictions were particularly acute for care providers.[12] Providers did not have clear-cut or consistent tactics for navigating disturbance.[13] Their self-representations often shifted between being victims and agents, between being responsive *to* and being responsible *for* disturbed medicine—in other words, being both inside and outside disturbance.

When we think of health systems in conflict, we tend to think of incidents of spectacular violence, such as aerial bombings, gunfights, or drone attacks. However, disturbances also exist as quiet, subtle chaos. Less discernible but potent traces of disturbance linger in health infrastructures and subjectivities and can fester into virulent form—as miscommunication, doctor–patient mistrust, or iatrogenic violence.[14] Rather than bombed-out hospitals, disturbances can sediment as stillness, slowness, a hollowing-out of spaces and ethics of care. *One lonely psychiatrist, in a bad mood, running an entire hospital.*

༈

Soon after Jammu and Kashmir became a disturbed area in 1990, the change registered in the landscape. Armed forces occupied protected forests, temples, orchards, and gardens. Cricket grounds became desiccated ovals in the middle of the city. Historical sites became interrogation centers; cinemas became military bunkers. Counterinsurgency tactics, such as sieges, crackdowns, and cordon-and-search operations, transformed village after village. Checkpoints, roadblocks, and identity checks became everyday realities. One person reminded me of the injustice of having to carry around his identity card at all times: "Why does an eighty-year-old Kashmiri elder have to show his identity card to a solider, but the soldier, who is not *from here*, never has to show his card to us?" Curfews and shutdowns became more frequent: places you could and could not go; times when you could and could not go outside. Over time, extended kin networks fragmented as a result of restricted movement (although, according an outsider, those bonds still appeared remarkably strong). Those who could afford it built high walls around their properties, turned homes into mini-fortresses, hoping they would deter military and paramilitary cordon operations. Women stopped gathering by communal wells, streams, and rivers (*yārbal*) to catch up on gossip or take a break from the drudgery of household chores. Whispers of women being raped, violated, and "mistreated" (*bezati*) by armed forces spread.[15] Ghost stories, staples of village sociality, stopped being told. Why tell ghost stories when there is something real and immediate to fear? Life was reduced to necessity.

To protest the effects of the emergency laws imposed on them, Kashmiris had no choice but to produce their own disturbance. Striking, voluntarily stopping all commercial activity—shops, colleges, schools, transportation— became the most common form of nonviolent resistance and civil disobedience, strategies that were used by Indians against British rule.[16] Every Wednesday, Kashmir's pro-independence political leadership issues a "protest calendar," which includes information about the duration and intensity of upcoming days of protests, marches, or other acts of resistance. The state government usually responds to or anticipates the protest calendar by issuing its own calendar of curfews, intended to stop people from gathering and protesting.[17] Internet and telecommunications shutdowns—Jammu and Kashmir has experienced more than 180 shutdowns since 2012, the most of any Indian state—often accompany the strikes and curfews. The effect is, from both sides, frozen time.

Everyday life oscillates between suspension and anticipation: *suspension* because emergency laws stretch out the present emergency indefinitely, preventing a future from erupting; *anticipation* because disturbed time is about uncertainty: waiting for the next incident of violence and the corresponding halting of life.[18]

Because disturbance encompasses both crisis *and* emergency time, disturbances infiltrate moments where there is no declared curfew or strike.

Nonemergency days are endowed with newfound urgency; everyone jams errands into a crack in the calendar, because no one knows when it will come again. One day in the summer of 2010, the first day the curfew was lifted after ten days, more than two hundred people descended onto Pick 'n' Choose, a small, upscale grocery store in central Srinagar. The line stretched out the door, people sweating in the suffocating space, loading up on chocolate, Lizol, Marie biscuits, and shampoo, the essential and the frivolous. *All the better to survive curfew with, dear.* People from across the street watched amusedly as the line snaked out the door. One of my Marxist friends complained that disturbance has heightened consumerism in Kashmir, because an everyday act like shopping is one of the few ways to cling onto normalcy. The same observation holds true in other periods of unrest; after 9/11, President Bush told US citizens it was their patriotic duty to shop.

As an outsider, the temporality of disturbance was difficult to inhabit. It *was* a habitus, I realized, a way of being in your body, occupying a particular spatiotemporal order. People did not learn these skills overnight, but of course, with thirty years of practice, everyone else was much better at managing disturbed time. Disturbed time means slow time. You need to know how to stretch out a cup of nun chai, slurping its half-solid, half-liquid contents for an hour, as if sucking minutes off the clock. Conversations and interviews that begin in the morning stretch out till late afternoon. Lunch invitations seamlessly turn into tea and then dinner. I beg my hosts to release me—surely I have exhausted their hospitality. But every time, I'm met with the same response: "What's the rush? Stay the night, we'll take you home tomorrow." Occupation time is elastic and loose, both a boon and a hindrance for fieldwork. No one is in a rush to do anything (including be interviewed), but on the other hand, they have all the time in the world to talk.

ψ

Though disturbed time affected everyone, how did care providers like Dr. Manzoor understand the effects of political disturbance—inadequate resources, strikes, curfews, and other social and legal irregularities—on their practices?[19] What kinds of affects, ethics, and expert subjectivities were possible in these conditions?

Kashmir's disturbed area status quickly registered in medicine. In a memoir, *Kashmir: In Sickness and in Health*, Dr. Gulzar Mufti, an expatriate Kashmiri doctor, described his political awakening at the nexus of public health and the politics of occupation in the early 1990s. One day, while in his car and on the way to Sri Maharaja Hari Singh (SMHS) hospital, Mufti witnessed a scene that later haunted him:

> Four heavily armed men belonging to the [paramilitary] Border Security Force . . . stopped a bus overloaded with Kashmiri men and women. All passengers were ordered to line up; men were separated from women, and the leader of the four men looked into the faces of each passenger one by one. . . . So far so bad, but worse was to follow. The guy picked a man in his late fifties, who had a *karakuri* (a cap made from the skin of a lamb reared in the mountains of Karakoram) [signifying a humble and rural person] on his head and had a grey but trimmed beard. The [soldier] slapped him hard, yelled and swore at him. The shaky victim passed out and fell down. . . . Each woman was looked at closely. Finally, the driver of the bus got a verbal thrashing from two of the armed men. . . . [Eventually] the passengers were allowed to embark, and the bus left.[20]

While the Indian state defined "disturbance" as Kashmir's insurrection, many Kashmiris began seeing events like these—the casual yet extraordinary violence of military occupation and the impunity enjoyed by soldiers under emergency laws—as the *real* disturbance. Kashmiris describe this as *"zulm"* (oppression).

Mufti, an outsider, is shocked. His chauffeur, a local, is not. He offers Mufti some advice: "*lekh scha-haz thok laerith gacchi* [abuse is not spit that will leave a stain]; *aki kane bozun, bei kane trawun* [in one ear, out the other]."[21] The chauffeur suggests that coping with zulm requires the capacity to forget daily humiliations and traumas. Mufti, however, sees his chauffer's response as an example of how inured (kamzor) Kashmiris have become in the face of oppression.

On reaching SMHS, Mufti finds another crisis brewing: "I did not expect it to be like the British hospital where I worked, but the appalling scenes of insult to human dignity, displayed in an amalgam of dirt, despair, and overcrowding, also overwhelmed me. I thought of the *genz* (leather dealers) living in *genz-khod* (the locality where animal skin dealers in downtown Srinagar used to reside)—the local healthcare administrators and the government of the day being the genz and the hospital the genz-khod. Kashmiris call it *genz-nus* (a leather dealer's nose) that cannot smell the stench."[22]

Mufti's description is laden with colonial, classed, and casteist assumptions about professions like leather work as dirty, unsanitary, and backward. For Mufti, scenes both inside and outside the clinic—which exemplify, in different ways, "appalling scenes of insult to human dignity"—show how

Kashmiris have become routinized to humiliation and degradation. Like leather dealers who can no longer smell the stench of leather, they live in a state of moral, spiritual, and political corruption without resisting it (see chapter 1). While this representation was far from the truth—Kashmiris *were* responding to state violence and oppression in many different ways—it nonetheless shows how the clinic was imagined not as a space outside of or apart from violence, but as a *casualty* of violence. However, while Mufti could openly critique Kashmir's health and political systems as an expatriate, future generations of doctors found their voices stymied.

From the 1990s on, the boundaries between the clinic's insides and outsides further dissolved. Doctors, almost daily, found evidence of torture on patients' bodies, in addition to treating high numbers of civilian casualties— between 1990 and 1994, 5,119 people were killed and thousands more injured. Kashmiri health professionals were frequently detained, assaulted, and harassed while attempting to perform their duties. Security forces deliberately prevented ambulance drivers from transporting injured persons to hospitals for emergency care, and had beaten, shot, or strafed ambulance drivers attempting to provide care to the wounded and had shot one driver while he was on duty. Others were caught between the armed forces and militant groups and were attacked and threatened for treating, or failing to treat, injured parties from both sides. They were forced to perform surgery at gunpoint, with masked gunmen looking over their shoulders. Hospitals were (and still are) periodically teargassed and turned into theaters of state surveillance.[23] Despite threats to their own lives, many served as expert witnesses in human rights reports.

Aside from these overt attacks on the clinic, a supposedly protected and neutral space, medicine also became disturbed in more subtle ways. Doctors everywhere in the Global South have to undergo long and expensive training, are paid low salaries, and endure physical risks. But after Kashmir was declared disturbed, medical examinations were delayed for seven consecutive years and job openings and promotions frozen. Disturbance added even more uncertainty to an already arduous professional path. Waves of qualified Kashmiri professionals emigrated abroad or to Indian cities.[24]

Meanwhile, the insurgency's early years saw a volatile security situation, with the Indian government losing control over the region. Initially, armed groups seemed to have the upper hand over Indian armed forces.[25] In 1991, the Kashmir Valley was described as overcome by "hordes of young, Kalashnikov-wielding men roam[ing] the streets and neighborhoods of Srinagar, the capital, and the valley's other towns like Baramulla, Anantnag, and Sopore. The sound of gunfire and explosions mingled with chants of 'azādi' [freedom] emanating from demonstrations large and small. People from all strata of society took part in protests against Indian rule."[26] Millions of dreams of freedom floated into the air, the effervescent collective feeling that it would be here soon. The ground was shifting under their feet.

Many in Kashmir viewed the fragility of Indian state institutions as one of the armed struggle's early successes and described how being in open rebellion against Indian rule unleashed a collective euphoria. People believed they were on the cusp of a new social order. On one occasion, even Kashmiri police officers went on strike, a move that eventually led to their disbanding (they were later resurrected). The Criminal Investigation Department (CID), an intelligence agency that the central Indian government had relied on for decades to suppress dissent, also stopped cooperating.

Doctors, too, eschewed their commitments of neutrality and many became staunch supporters of the armed movement. Hospitals served as hiding places for militants. Many well-known physicians, such as Dr. Mehrajdin, a cardiologist, served on the pro-independence Jammu and Kashmir Liberation Front's (JKLF) Executive Council.[27] These developments reflected a social order in flux, a topsy-turvy reality. In this milieu, ordinary people began doing extraordinary things, including upending social and professional hierarchies. Power structures shifted as militant organizations gained footing over state apparatuses.

Yet the feeling was not all exuberance; one Kashmiri psychiatrist, Dr. Mudasir, described this as a period of "upheaval," which directly affected public health:

> In medical schools or colleges or hospitals, there used to be a senior doctor and then subordinates, *there was a clear hierarchy* . . . but suddenly when the conflict started, the structure was lost. Respect for the social structure was gone. . . . When I was in medical college, I remember one day the Consultant [senior physician] told the peon to do something, and he responded, "I'm not doing it, go and do it yourself. Who the hell are you?" This normally would not happen in a society which is stable and where everyone knows their place. . . . But *suddenly everybody was rebellious and everyone was afraid of each other*. I don't think that helped the system. . . . Hospital orderlies, peons, even sweepers opened their own private clinics! Nobody checked on them. Because it was dangerous. Because if someone said, "Oh, you should not do that," they could say, "I can get you killed, I know x person." I think this happened a lot in the 1990s. . . .

Nobody listened to each other and suddenly some people mysteriously got rich. So, the doctor would come in a small car and his peon would come in a big car! [Laughs] It's true. I've seen examples. There were so many strikes and you couldn't say anything to anybody. Hospital staff and employees would close down the medical college at a moment's notice. It happened many times. And then, because everyone was so anxious, whenever something happened, people would just shout at each other, instead of listening. . . .

You know, there's the concept of survival of the fittest—if you are in prison, and you don't fight back, people take advantage of you. So, in Kashmir, everyone became aggressive, rebellious, *everyone was fighting for him or herself*, which ultimately led to more negative than positive things. And the health system suffered because of that.[28]

As Dr. Mudasir described, the sense of possibility of a new order soon darkened. Faustian alliances with militant groups and ikhwāns allowed people to short-circuit existing systems of merit and professional hierarchies. As a result, Dr. Mudasir argued, people lost faith in public institutions and developed a lack of respect for authority and hierarchy. These churnings made people bolder, ruder, and more aggressive (*tez*) than before.

While some took advantage of the disorder, those who did not suffered. Dr. Uzma Chishti, a physician, told me that despite doing extremely well in the state medical exams in the early 1990s, the Public Service Commission had not confirmed her for a job because her father had refused to pay a bribe. She described how, since the disturbance began, gaining public-sector employment was no longer based on merit, but on personal networks, connections, and corruption. When I suggested that such practices might be true outside Kashmir too, Chishti reminded me that Kashmir was exceptionally corrupt. Echoing the words of Dr. Hasan in the previous chapter, Uzma said that disturbance had produced in Kashmiris, including those in medicine, a "habit of corruption." Disturbed habits soon congealed as modes of survival—just habits.

ψ

By the mid-2000s, life in Kashmir had returned to a glacial crisis state, with fewer emergencies on the horizon.[29] However, as a disturbed area, the state's biopolitical functions—such as educating its populace or keeping people healthy—remained subservient to its militaristic goals. As Dr. Mudasir put it: "I think the central government only has one priority: to maintain law and order, or perhaps, to make law and order worse! There is no emphasis on anything else—education, health, anything. There is so much money that comes from the central government [to the state government], there are so many government policies, but all the money just goes to corruption. There is no actual plan. There's no health policy, there's no mental health policy, there's no way forward. It's all just random! This is how you start believing in God [Laughs]."[30]

Dr. Mudasir used humor to reflect on how the state's militaristic aims of mitigating "disturbance" had overwhelmed its other responsibilities, including its humanitarian functions. While the "harmful" apparatus of the state was thriving, its "caring" apparatus was flailing. That the health system was functioning at all was an act of God, he joked. Rather than a carefully calculated policy, Dr. Mudasir described this arrangement as the working of a nervous, paranoid, and irrational state.

Meanwhile, people found that the dissipation of armed conflict did not lead to the ebbing of other disturbances. Disturbances remained, like salt lines left on the seashore. What Dr. Mudasir described as "randomness" was felt in everyday clinical encounters and realities. One October day, I was sitting with Dr. Manzoor in his office in the psychiatric hospital.[31] Patients were waiting to be seen, but Dr. Manzoor had put the postgraduates in charge, even though he was the most senior psychiatrist on duty and was supposed to supervise them. He seemed in the midst of his own personal rebellion. He had turned off all the lights in his office and bolted the door, with both of us inside. *Do not disturb* bat signals. Whether his rebellion was a product of laziness, resignation, or fatigue, I wasn't sure.

Inside, we busied ourselves killing time. I was writing up field notes, he was playing FarmVille on his computer. The room was thick and stuffy with the heady chemical scent of Gold Flake cigarettes. He smoked with one hand, while his other hand clicked away on his computer mouse. I suddenly remembered to ask him about the elusive head of department (HOD) of psychiatry, who was rarely at the hospital.

"What about him?" he asked.

"Well, I rarely see him . . . ," I said.

"You probably *won't* see him," he said.

"So, if the HOD's absent, who's running the show?"

He smiled and looked up from the screen. "The show runs itself," he said enigmatically. Then he leaned back in his chair, resting his head in his interlaced hands. After a dramatic pause, he said: "A man goes to three countries.

First he goes to America. Then he goes to Russia. Finally, he comes to India. After he comes to India, he says, 'Now I know there's a God because he's the only one running this country.'" He laughed loudly.

Like Dr. Mudasir, Dr. Manzoor described the public health system as disorganized, running without order or planning. However, unlike Dr. Mudasir, who historicized these events within Kashmir's disturbed area status, Dr. Manzoor described a generalized postcolonial disorder.

Despite Dr. Manzoor's humor, chronic dysfunction had burrowed itself in the public health system, leading to deleterious effects for both doctors and patients. On another occasion, I accompanied a local humanitarian organization called Kashmir LifeLine to a trauma hospital in a town called Kangan in Ganderbal district.[32] When we visited, the subdistrict hospital was brand new and was one of the few specialized trauma hospitals in Jammu and Kashmir. Kashmir LifeLine specializes in delivering nonpharmaceutical psychosocial care, often unavailable in India's public health system. The organization was running a counseling office at the hospital twice a week. The counselors allowed me to hang out at the hospital, but I was not permitted to sit in on any counseling sessions.

With raised expectations of what a specialty trauma hospital would look like, my heart sank upon arrival. The halls of the subdistrict hospital, which is meant to serve 500,000 people, were empty. After a while, a handful of patients trickled in for counseling, and Kashmir LifeLine's counselors split into pairs in adjacent rooms. One of the rooms was completely bare except for a single bed with a navy cushion that looked as if it had been slashed with a knife. As the sessions got underway, I wandered the eerily barren halls. Metal chairs, bolted to the floor, looked odd with no bodies in them. I poked my head into one of the deserted inpatient wards. All the beds were unoccupied except one, around which a family was gathered, tending to a sick relative hooked up to an IV. During my wanderings, I did not see a single doctor. Everything was covered in dust; piles of rubbish accumulated in the corners of rooms and hallways, and all the bathrooms were dysfunctional.

Two hours later, after the sessions were over, one of Kashmir LifeLine's administrators and I finally managed to track down a doctor. He was the hospital's only surgeon, and we tried to keep pace with his brisk strides down the hallway. He said that over forty doctors' posts in the hospital had not been filled since the hospital's construction was completed. I was puzzled: the unfilled posts could not be the result of a lack of qualified personnel. In 2010 alone, over 1,500 qualified doctors were unemployed in the Kashmir Valley.[33] The surgeon clarified: "The posts have simply not been advertised." Since all public-service job openings must be advertised in newspapers before people can apply, this meant that no one had applied, let alone interviewed, for over forty available posts. Even staff and janitorial positions had not been advertised. The surgeon was working thirty-six-hour shifts at the hospital. He recently conducted two operations simultaneously, moving back and forth between two anesthetized bodies. "Last night, there was only one doctor on duty who had to deal with 150 patients, twenty-five of whom were [new] admissions," he said. I asked why the posts had not been advertised. The surgeon shrugged his shoulders and said, "Political reasons," but did not elaborate.

Before journeying back to Srinagar, the Kashmir LifeLine team and I ate lunch together ("take lunch" is how Kashmiris say it) on the stony banks of a mountain stream, a few hundred feet away from the hospital. Someone laid out a sheet for everyone to sit on. The afternoon sun was warm, but the stream sprayed a light, cooling mist into the air. The scene was idyllic, a universe away from what we had just experienced. Everyone shared their lunch: short-grained, sticky white rice, sautéed vegetables, and, my favorite, *hāk*, spinach leaves boiled with mustard oil, garlic, and red chilies. There were several varieties of chicken (no Kashmiri meal is complete without meat). I was teased, for the umpteenth time, for being a vegetarian. Choosing to be vegetarian was unfathomable and drew incredulous laughter. Afterward, everyone washed their hands and dipped their toes in the stream's glacial waters, and we climbed back into the Tata Sumo for the return trip home.

On the bumpy ride back, the surgeon's mysterious response of "political reasons" echoed in my mind. I asked one of the counselors about what the surgeon said. He explained that Kangan used to be a "hotbed" of militancy. The privations we saw were no accident: "The hospital is deliberately being kept understaffed and underequipped by the state government. This is collective punishment against the local population who sheltered and supported militants during the armed struggle," the counselor said matter-of-factly. In other words, the counselor offered a "political etiology" for the hospital's decrepit condition.[34] In this perpetual war between the state and its citizens, medicine was collateral damage.

However, not everyone agreed that such infrastructural degradations were the result of specific political calculations. When I told Dr. Mudasir about the trauma hospital, he disagreed with the counselor's analysis: "I have a different theory about this. If you go anywhere in Kashmir, you see huge constructions. District Hospital Anantnag is so big! The reason for these trauma hospitals and such—it's just for the money. Whenever you're building anything, it involves contractors, politicians, engineers—everyone gets a cut." Constructing Kangan's trauma hospital had probably been an extremely lucrative project, he said, and now there were few incentives to recruit doctors and hospital staff. Hospitals like this were designed to be "dead ends." These failed infrastructural projects were not caused by political disturbance, according to him, but were the effects of more widespread financial corruption: "You know, we have medical tourism in India," he said, referring to India's US$3 billion industry, which offers high-end medical care to foreign patients, "but we have no emergency services."

"You know the Domino's theory?" he asked.

I didn't.

"Now, in any major city in India, you can get a pizza in half an hour or less, but you can't get an ambulance, even in Delhi, the *capital*. At *any* time!"

Although we laughed at the absurdity of pizzas being more accessible than ambulances, Dr. Mudasir's Domino's theory sharply critiqued the stark inequities in the Indian public health system. While Dr. Mudasir did not deny that corruption within the public health sector had a political etiology, he simply offered a *different* political etiology for the crisis, one in which Kashmir was not an exception, but was part of a corrupt national—or global south—imaginary. However, there was an added irony to the absence of emergency services in a region designated a permanent zone of emergency. There were gaping infrastructural holes that humanitarian medicine— despite all its expertise in emergency medicine—could not fix and which militarism aggravated. This potholed landscape of care—characterized by economic boondoggles for some and obscene neglect and failure for others—was not a product of incompetence, but constituted the structural logic of militarization and occupation, which kept places like Kashmir disturbed.[35]

Despite their differences, both Dr. Mudasir and the counselor agreed that public health infrastructures in Kashmir were deeply dysfunctional. *Disturbance* was more than medicine becoming politicized or its neutrality undermined. Rather, disturbances had unleased strange irregularities and "randomness" into the atmosphere. These conditions required medical providers to respond. Some, like Dr. Manzoor and Dr. Mudasir, used humor. Others expressed their disgust and anger and forged subjectivities as politicized experts against disturbance.

FIGURE 2.3. Junior doctors on strike. Photo by author

Since its founding in 1959, the Government Medical College (GMC), the teaching arm of SMHS hospital, has been the site of periodic strikes, protests, and shutdowns, including a strike by medical students that ousted the first principal of the college in the 1960s.[36] Decades later, in 2009, seven hundred junior doctors—trainees, junior residents, and registrars—members of the Junior Doctors' Association (JDA), went on strike.[37] These junior doctors were younger than doctors like Dr. Mudasir and Dr. Manzoor, who graduated from university in the 1990s and whose contemporaries had joined the armed struggle (henceforth the "rebel generation"). Instead, most junior doctors were children when the fighting erupted. They had lived their whole lives in a disturbed area, but had not witnessed the junoon (passion) of the insurgency's early years like the rebel generation had. They had only seen militarization and receding economic possibilities.

In October 2009, the JDA's strike protested the combined effects of Kashmir's exceptionalism and the neoliberalization of the public health system. While junior doctors in other states received monthly salaries of Rs. 60,000 (about US$1,000), junior doctors in Jammu and Kashmir received only Rs.

16,000 per month (about US$240). The state government had repeatedly failed to implement salary increases mandated by the central government's pay commission. Meanwhile, as elsewhere, the state government was relying increasingly on contract labor, rather than paying salaried employees full benefits and pensions. The state government had been unresponsive to months of lobbying by doctors, so the JDA decided to go on indefinite strike. Because junior doctors provide the bulk of hospital care, many patient services ground to a standstill. Rather than continue to be buffers against disturbance, doctors themselves produced disturbance, an ethical stance that seemed ambiguous. When I asked one doctor about disrupting patient care because of the strike, he said, "Of course it's a dilemma. Patients end up suffering the most. But emergency services are still on."[38] Despite the reassuring statement, he sounded guilty.

Outside the Government Medical College's canteen, a poster with an image of a bandaged stethoscope read, "Wounded Healers: Support Resident Doctors." When I visited the medical college on the thirteenth day of the strike, it was still going strong. The lawns of the medical college were packed with hundreds of physicians listening to speeches, making posters, sitting in clusters, and chatting. Though not strictly enforced, the crowd tended toward gender separation: women on one side, men on the other.

In their speeches, members of the JDA emphasized doctors' steadfastness through the conflict, despite political, economic, and social disruption. The air was electric. Some of the slogans received thunderous applause from the audience:

"Doctors are not demigods. We are crippled by our workload!"

"We sacrifice our health for their health!"

"During the 2005 earthquake, in other parts of the state, people were running for their lives. But we did not run. We stayed with our patients!"

"We have reduced the number of graves in Kashmir!"

"Let any politician or bureaucrat sit with us for just one night in Lal Ded [a public maternity] hospital."

"We didn't do an MBBS [Bachelor of Medicine, Bachelor of Surgery] degree to become street hawkers, begging outside the homes of bureaucrats!"

The doctor's strike helped constitute doctors as an ethical professional community. The speeches emphasized the critical yet thankless role doctors had played throughout the conflict. Reminiscent of James Orbinski's Nobel speech, doctors described themselves as panaceas against the multiple harms that had beset Kashmiri society—from political violence to financial corruption. Not only were doctors on the front lines of war, tending to casualties and injuries; they also had to contend with an increasingly fragile and ill-equipped public health system, as services, trainings, postings, opportunities, and resources stagnated or were siphoned off due to disturbance. At the same time, the speeches established doctors' bodies and subjectivities as "wounded," as repeatedly and exceptionally victimized at the hands of a corrupt government ("we sacrifice our health for their health"). The speeches oscillated between emphasizing the moral agency of doctors and marking their helplessness in the face of political and structural violence.

I was eager to know how these ideas were circulating beyond the prepared speeches, so I joined a group of three women physicians, who were sitting together. I introduced myself.

"I remember you," one said. She wore her hair in a long, single braid and pushed her glasses up her nose.

I had forgotten her name. Shit.

"We met last year in the psychiatry OPD," she reminded me. "I did my residency there. Now I'm in pediatrics."

"Ambar," she said, after a few seconds, relieving me of my embarrassment.

"Ambar!" I exclaimed. "You didn't like psychiatry?" I asked, in what I hoped was a light, teasing tone. The question landed badly. She was quiet for a while, then bombarded me with questions about living in the United States, living in Delhi, where my family is, whether they have visited me in Kashmir, why I have lived alone for so long, am I married, do I pay for everything myself. It went on. My answers made me sound lonely and uncared for. I was reminded of Sarah Pinto's powerful observation that the line between abandonment and freedom can be fuzzy.[39] But maybe because they took pity on me, I spent the afternoon with Ambar, Nazima, and Heena and learned their perspectives on medicine in crisis.

All three felt that medicine in Kashmir had been profoundly tainted by violence and that doctors' bodies had been made vulnerable. However, rather than danger emanating from political violence—fears of being attacked, bombed, or kidnapped, for example—they identified danger in the social. According to them, the affect of rebelliousness that Dr. Mudasir had described had sedimented in the behaviors and attitudes of patients and their families. Heena explained: "A while ago, I was working at SMHS, the patient was a ten-year-old with pancreatitis. *Sixteen* doctors and nurses were working on this child, but he died. The child's relatives ambushed the doctors, or tried to, and we narrowly escaped through the back door." According to Heena, despite their best efforts—having sixteen attendants was unheard of in an under-resourced setting—doctors had become easy targets for a public frustrated by decades of disturbance and upturned social hierarchies and norms.

Heena's narrative also conveyed how disturbance had produced a gulf between doctors and patients. In contrast to the slogans at the strike, which emphasized solidarity between doctors and patients, Heena's narrative perpetuated a notion that doctors and patients occupied incompatible worlds and ethical dispositions. Patients—the "public"—had become dangerous and unruly, the very embodiment of disturbance, while doctors had maintained their rectitude, affective neutrality, and civility. According to them, doctors had become scapegoats for patients' anger because they represented the state's humanitarian "mode of presence," which was within reach, whereas the militarized state was not. Meanwhile, although patients could unleash their anger, doctors themselves were hamstrung. They had to remain both politically *and* affectively neutral due to professional norms. As public-sector employees, they could not overtly critique the state without facing serious repercussions. Despite efforts to maintain neutrality, according to Ambar, Heena, and Nazima, humanitarian norms granting protection to medical professionals and health spaces had failed. Heena marveled at the ability of doctors to work in these conditions: "When doctors come from outside Kashmir, they are shocked [*hairān*] at the conditions in which we work." "We are handicapped, but we still work," Ambar added.

Though junior doctors shared a common vision of themselves as "wounded healers," they had different ideas about how to contest disturbance. When I asked about the reasons for the strike, Ambar responded first. Rather than point to the most publicized issue—that of pay equity with other "non-disturbed" states—Ambar said: "This is a corrupt state. From the CM to the MS." From the chief minister—the highest government official in the state—to the medical superintendent. Her statement was punchy, like a bumper sticker. Her big eyes shimmered with rage. Ambar said the strike was a necessity. Doctors had to become "political" if they wanted to bring about a more equitable system and root out disturbances. Also, by restoring justice within the medical system, other parts of Kashmiri society might be positively affected. The term *justice* was telling; for Ambar, pay inequities were symptomatic of a deeper, systemic rot. In making this argument, Ambar echoed decades of women's organizing efforts in Kashmir, which have articulated and demanded freedom from corruption, political persecution, and militarization.[40] At this point, however, Nazima interjected: "But think: if we were in positions of power, wouldn't we be corrupt too? Because we wouldn't become corrupt for ourselves, right? We would be doing it for our families. That's why I don't think the system can change—because we would all try to benefit our families!"

We all laughed at her blunt perspective. For Nazima, the strike was not about disrupting systemic corruption, but about earning an equitable salary. Nazima argued that doctors were already part of a corrupt system; their use of power to better their families was a socially acceptable response to disturbance. By contrast, Ambar asserted the need for doctors to maintain a higher ethical standard and push back against corruption. Despite their differences, both felt that medicine in a disturbed area could not be neutral or apolitical—either it had to hold the state accountable or it had to harness disturbance.

Many patients had a different understanding of the effects of disturbance on medicine. While both doctors and patients agreed that disturbance had limited people's capacities to relate to one another, many patients disagreed with the moral high ground that doctors took, pointing to how doctors had benefited from the conflict economy. Doctors had sacrificed patient care for their own economic benefit, they noted, and there was an absence of demands for structural reform or better patient services in the JDA's platform. This echoed other forms of unethical practices that patients described— doctors being motivated by financial rather than ethical motives, the absence of accountability for inadequate care, poor quality of pharmaceuticals and public health care (reinforced by the amoxicillin scandal), earning and the deteriorating skill set of doctors, who relied more on technologies than embodied knowledge. While doctors felt they were unjustly victimized, patients felt their skepticism of public medicine was well founded.

For example, one patient I met in the waiting room of an Unani clinic, Bashir Iqbal, described the mistrust he felt toward doctors. He noted that wealthy Kashmiris traveled to Delhi or other Indian cities to access good medical care because it was impossible to find reliable care in Kashmir. "Why do they go to Delhi or Bombay? Don't we have doctors and hospitals here? This is because the system we have here is ruined [kharāb]," Bashir said, "even if there are some good doctors." He continued, "Here, in Kashmir, I have no faith if I go to the doctor, because how would I even know if he prescribed poison or if he prescribed medicine?" Bashir limited his critique of providers to spaces of disturbance. For him, that doctors might prescribe poison and call it medicine was not hypothetical. As we saw in the previous chapter, patients in Kashmir's public hospitals were given spurious antibiotics for years. Bashir described the proliferation of fake and spurious medicines as "poison." His words emphasized how medicine's soteriological capacities had turned harmful. Endemic corruption had turned medicine into a vector of violence.

I heard many stories of medical malfeasance that correlated with Bashir's concerns. I heard rumors of women being misdiagnosed and tricked into getting expensive hysterectomies for ordinary psychological and psychiatric complaints. Doctors themselves often circulated these stories, but always described malpractice in second- or third-person terms, as the work of corrupt others, never themselves.[41] The veracity of these stories notwithstanding, their circulation reinforced how medicine, much like politics, law, or the military, had become a space of impunity and corruptibility. Emergency powers had not only granted military personnel protection from prosecution; impunity had spread, like a virus, through civil institutions and everyday life. These narratives produced skepticism around medicine's claims of cure and made medical encounters deeply ambivalent for patients. They led many patients to self-medicate, micro-dose, or reject biomedicine entirely, as Bashir had done. Occupation has taught Kashmiris that survival requires being polite, friendly, and keeping a distance. These feelings were heightened in doctor–patient interactions, because as Bashir said, "after all, the doctor has our life in his hands."

Rather than disturbance creating a shared reality, it further fragmented social relations. The two-way mistrust between doctors and patients crystallized anxieties about the effects of disturbance on interpersonal, intimate relations. During fieldwork, I was often given friendly warnings, like "you never know who anyone is in Kashmir," a statement meant to warn me not to trust too easily, given the long-standing history of informers, spies, and collaborators in Kashmir. Several times after I interviewed someone, I learned of their "other" identity—as a former militant, collaborator, or someone with high-up state connections. This knowledge, a virtual map overlaid on everyday sociality, always came after the fact, and it unnerved me. *How would I ever grasp these subterranean histories?* I also worried about the virtual map circulating about me: *Who was I spying for? Did people trust me?* Over time, these multiple ontologies taught me to remain open to surprise. I learned how unraveling and unlearning is a critical part of fieldwork.

ψ

The positivist method of approaching disturbance as an object of ethnographic knowledge outside of oneself, something to be analyzed, problematized, and mastered, failed me. Living in a disturbed area had a temporal and phenomenological pull. The frequency of interruptions, bouncing from anticipation to suspension, "caught" me. Jeanne Favret-Saada uses the term *caught* to capture the sense of submitting to something to gain access to it, and of losing control, or losing mastery over one's subject matter.[42] After initially trying to claw my way out of suspension—by insisting on going out, day after day, only to find empty clinics and sullen hospital staff—soon, I gave in to disturbance. Like drifting into jet-lagged sleep, my hesitation give way to an intense pleasure. There were still some strike days when I felt restless, agitating to do something, aware of fieldwork time slipping away. But, as the days and months deepened, I was lulled into its orbit. My body felt slower, heavier. *Was I becoming kamzor too?* I let myself fall into lugubriousness, and during days of continuous strikes and curfews, I stopped trying to do anything. Instead, I spent days reading novels beneath the blossoming apple tree outside my room. I watched an absurd amount of television—old Hindi films from the 1970s and 1980s—strangely comforting in their sepia tones, with their thunderous, violin-filled soundtracks. I played gin rummy for hours with Aunty. When "normal" days returned, I resisted them. My muscles felt sore, they begged me to rest a little longer.

♉

While all medical professionals were affected by disturbance, psychiatrists felt particularly victimized. They saw themselves as doubly exceptional, because they belonged to the most stigmatized branch of medicine *and* because they felt their work was most directly impacted by political disturbance, in the form of widespread psychological distress they were seeing in their patients. They had two different, but not mutually exclusive, strategies for dealing with disturbance. On the one hand, psychiatrists tried to shore up the clinic's boundaries *against* disturbance by advancing psychiatry as a scientific and technical enterprise. Through investing in advanced technologies such as diagnostic and laboratory tests, better training for psychiatrists and other mental health staff, and focusing on their own research and publication outputs, they sought to catapult Kashmiri psychiatry beyond the context-specific milieu of Kashmir to become an internationally recognizable brand. To do this, they forged professional ties and relations with mental health institutes and professional organizations across India and globally. In contrast, others drew legitimacy from working in disturbed conditions as efficiently and ethically as possible. Rather than aspire to a national or global standard, they felt obligated to make Kashmiri psychiatry more responsive to the specific needs of Kashmiri patients. These strategies enacted very different political possibilities and uses for medicine and science in disturbance.[43]

The first approach of standardizing and modernizing psychiatry beyond disturbance was the most visible. During my dissertation fieldwork, the psychiatric hospital underwent a dramatic transformation. Thanks to a US$4.5 million grant to the central government's Ministry of Health and Family Welfare, the hospital was chosen to become a "Centre of Excellence," a national research and training institute for mental health expertise: psychiatrists, clinical psychologists, psychiatric social workers, and nurses. As Kashmiri psychiatrists proudly told me, only eleven of thirty-seven public mental hospitals from across India were chosen.[44] The transformation of the hospital into a Centre of Excellence was part of a transnational discourse and management strategy spearheaded by institutions such as the World Health Organization (WHO) and the Movement for Global Mental Health (MGMH) to build mental health expertise in developing countries in a cost-effective way.

News of the successful Centre of Excellence grant infused Kashmiri psychiatrists with hope and energy.[45] The grant signaled a future of technical advancement, a final cut from the hospital's shameful past as an asylum and the failures of public health care under disturbance. Dr. Manzoor described the hospital's past as Tora Bora, the mountainous Taliban stronghold in Afghanistan, which signified backwardness and isolation, the nadir of disturbance. Dr. Mudasir similarly described the hospital's bleak state when he was an intern in 2003:

> I think it was early winter, there was a chill in the air and the sky was invisible under a shroud of clouds. . . . Patients were seen in two small rooms. In one room, there was a consultant psychiatrist and his registrar, and in the other room a few postgraduate trainees and SHOs [station house officers]. The corridor was full of patients. . . . Each room had a small table, a few chairs, and a coal heater in the center. There was no room to move around, and one could see people in a range of moods, holding their hospital cards in trembling hands waiting for their turn. There was no privacy and I was surprised how the psychiatrists were able to listen to personal stories and make sense of it all.[46]

Not only was the hospital's infrastructure pitiful and patients desperate; Dr. Mudasir's description also conveys the inability of doctors to guarantee basic ethical guidelines—such as confidentiality—in these conditions. At the time, psychiatrists were almost exclusively treating severely mentally ill patients, many of whom required hospitalization. Custodial logics—including chaining patients to their beds—were still de rigueur.

FIGURE 2.4. The former government psychiatric diseases hospital. Photo by author

Many psychiatrists desired to forget this shameful past, and the Centre of Excellence grant provided a makeover opportunity—not only a facelift but a shift in the hospital's identity. By 2013, the hospital looked very different. A new gate bore the hospital's new tongue-twister name: the Institute of Mental Health and Neurosciences (IMHANS), Kashmir. Outside the medical field, this change barely registered. For most Kashmiris, the hospital was—and will always be—the asylum. But for psychiatrists, the name change indexed the hospital's structural, ontological, and epistemological transformation, its passport out of disturbance. Even the signage— transformed from bilingual, rusty, and dilapidated to English-only, colorful, and modern—marked this shift.

When I visited in 2013, I was greeted by the cacophonous sounds of construction—drumming, drilling, banging. A new, multistoried academic block and library for faculty and postgraduates, a laboratory for genetic testing, and dormitories to house future postgraduate mental health professionals were being built. The Centre of Excellence scheme was all future-oriented— new diagnostic tests, training the next generation of experts, and treating patients in the community rather than in the hospital. Futurity counteracted the suspended time of disturbance.

The hospital's transformation was not merely a scientific or technical exercise, however. The Centre of Excellence grant also offered new affec-

FIGURE 2.5. Institute of Mental Health and Neurosciences, Kashmir.
Photo by author

tive and moral possibilities for psychiatry. It separated past and present and separated those who were chronically ill from those who could be treated through psychiatry's "modern" methods. Few, if any, resources from the grant were dedicated to improving inpatient care. Instead, the grant enabled Kashmiri psychiatrists to integrate themselves with Indian psychiatry, much as the strikers demanded. As Dr. Manzoor put it, postgraduates in Jammu and Kashmir could now get training and educational opportunities on par with other postgraduates (PGs) across India: "Now the PGs have an EEG machine, they have seminars. It's thanks to us. We didn't have a single class when we were PGs, but now, look how many classes they get!" he told me proudly. While the grant flooded the mental health sector with resources and brought prestige to Kashmiri psychiatry, the project was divorced from the specificities of Kashmir's mental health crisis. Instead, it folded the hospital and Kashmiri psychiatry into non- or less-disturbed national and global health imaginaries.

Despite these efforts, disturbance oozed into the clinic. Some psychiatrists complained about the infrastructural changes, arguing that the hospital had been turned into a "concrete jungle" instead of a welcoming space for patients. Another complained that his chambers had become "a bureaucrat's office." Expensive walnut wood and carved paneling was installed along the hallways ("Who asked for this?" one psychiatrist asked rhetorically, implying, "Where did the money come from?"). Funds were siphoned off for people's pet projects, I was told, rather than the grant's original goals. I heard rumors of new faculty posts that should have been created but were not. As with the Kangan trauma hospital I described earlier, many felt that the Centre of Excellence was merely an excuse for hospital administrators to make money through construction projects. Rather than improve psychiatry, the grant had bred harm as money flowed without accountability.

I learned these things in snatches and whispers. On entering psychiatrists' offices, animated conversations in superfast Kashmiri would abruptly stop. Some told me they were sickened by the lies and affirmed the impossibility of medicine apart from and outside of disturbance. The grant had failed in its goal of transforming the hospital into something "new," they argued. "So many people have bad memories of the hospital," Dr. Mudasir told me. "We should have used the grant to find land elsewhere . . . we could have started from scratch, created a space where patients could walk around, breathe fresh air, not be locked up all day." He noted that the hospital's transformation into an "institute" made little difference to the population it was meant to serve. Others, however, held out hope that the new infrastructure could offer a blank slate, a chance for Kashmiri psychiatry to undo the wrongs of the past.

ॐ

Psychiatrists also had another way of dealing with disturbance: making Kashmiri psychiatry more responsive to the specific psychological distress caused by occupation. Some described their decision to join psychiatry as an ethical and political calling. One day, I spoke with thirty-nine-year-old Dr. Malik, a psychiatrist at Sher-i-Kashmir Institute of Medical Sciences (SKIMS) hospital, where he worked in outpatient services. It was late afternoon and Dr. Malik had just finished seeing patients. The hospital was relatively quiet; outpatient services, like household water supplies, end abruptly. We sat in his office at the end of a long, shiny hallway and spoke for more than an hour. Like other psychiatrists, Dr. Malik traced his interest in psychiatry to a painful personal memory of violence. He described how, one night in 1998, "unidentified gunmen"—possibly ikhwāns—killed four of his neighbors. One of the few survivors was a three-year-old girl whose father and grandfather had both been killed in the attack. "Her name was Khushboo," he told me quietly. "She developed mania. Years later, she was still suffering." This experience made Dr. Malik realize how psychiatric care could be lifesaving. Dr. Malik excelled in the state medical examinations and found himself in the fortunate position to choose any specialization he wanted. He chose psychiatry, despite resistance from his family and the lure of more prestigious and lucrative specializations. Emphasizing his agency—he had willingly chosen psychiatry—marked an important shift in medical expertise because of a negative perception that previous generations of psychiatrists had failed to qualify for "better" specializations.

Nonetheless, Dr. Malik still felt the weight of stigma in his days as an intern: "We would crack jokes and laugh at patients because we did not understand their suffering. Initially, we had a sense of humor about their problems. But later, the issue would trouble us: "Why are they here? Why can't we do anything for them?" Despite Dr. Malik's good intentions, empathizing with chronically ill patients was not automatic or seamless. Rather, as Jason Throop has argued, empathy is a process constituted by "moments of connection to moments of disconnection, from feelings of mutual understanding, attunement, and compassion to feelings of confusion, misalignment, and singularity."[47] It took years, Dr. Malik said, to develop empathy for *all* his patients. Since I did not see him interacting with patients, I was unable to gauge whether and how his ideals translated into practice; however, he endeavored to make psychiatry responsive to Kashmiri victims of violence.

Humanitarian NGOs were also trying to make mental health care more locally responsive, attentive, and culturally appropriate. They critiqued the public mental health system, in which patients had hardly any time with the doctor yet were often diagnosed with chronic conditions and almost always prescribed a pharmaceutical cocktail. Instead, these organizations promised nonpharmaceutical, holistic, and interactive care through psychotherapy and counseling. They positioned themselves as humanitarian exceptions to the militarized state and an ineffectual public health system (see chapter 4).[48]

This form of ethical care became clear to me one December morning, when I attended an Action Aid counselor training workshop.[49] The workshop was convened in a hotel on the banks of the Jhelum River. As I walked in the chilly morning air, I noticed dense fog skimming the surface of the river, winter unfurling its thick blanket. I was still trying to get used to the flickering, low-voltage electricity, the frequent but unpredictable power cuts, and the heady, nauseating gas heaters that mark the onset of Chilai Kalan, the forty harshest days of winter.

The workshop was run by a Kashmiri psychiatrist, Dr. Abdul, who primarily worked at the psychiatric hospital but also consulted for NGOs, thanks to his sharp intelligence, earnestness, and surplus energy. As the workshop began, we made our way to large, circular tables, each of which seated about eight to ten people. Most of Action Aid's staff—about forty men and women in their twenties and early thirties—were present. The workshop began with a male counselor leading a group exercise called progressive muscle relaxation (PMR). As we tried out the exercises—flexing arms and thumbs, bending arms at the elbow in imaginary bicep curls—a few giggles and chatter erupted in the room. When the young man finished, everyone applauded vigorously. The next item on the agenda was a case demonstration. Two female staff acted out a mock counseling session. Afterward, a spirited discussion broke out in which the audience critiqued the counselor's handling of the session. The participants were reminded of a three-step approach: establish empathy, identify emotions, and make empathetic statements. The focus on empathy distinguished the counselors from practitioners in public health settings, who often did not have the time or, in their words, the "luxury" to engage patients in conversation, or those like Dr. Malik, who had learned empathy on their own.

After the empathy activity, we broke for lunch. The hot buffet was a simple but welcome respite from the cold banquet hall. After lunch, Dr. Abdul began his lecture. Though his talk was about diagnostic criteria and guidelines, Dr. Abdul began by telling the counselors to worry less about "what DSM IV [the *Diagnostics and Statistical Manual* of the American Psychiatric Association] has to say about depression," and focus more on "what *people say*." He asked the audience: "What complaints do people with depression bring to you?"

People threw out answers: "Aches and pains!" "Palpitations!" "Headaches!" "Loss of interest!" "Loss of appetite!" "Isolation!" Dr. Abdul wrote each down on the whiteboard. "So," he said:

> Looking at this list, it's clear that no one comes to you with a DSM version of depression. . . . People talk about *somatic* symptoms; they describe themselves as *physically* ill. The question for us really is, how do we explain the somatization of mental health? *Why* do people talk in somatic symptoms? . . . The language of distress in our culture *is* somatic. Let's take a death ritual, for example . . . the person who cries the loudest, who cries the most, is automatically assumed to be the closest relative, am I right? [Giggles from the audience]. . . .

A person may have done twenty ECGs [electrocardiograms], but their pain may not be addressed. That's because we are not talking about a heart's physiological capacity to pump blood, but about the heart that feels, that same heart that jumps when a young man sees a beautiful woman. . . .

The most important thing in terms of patient care is *the patient's perspective.* We should accept that all biological problems do not have biological solutions. It's not just about the words people speak, but about their whole body. Depression speaks for itself, you feel it. . . .

By the time a patient comes to you, he or she already has an economy of illness. What's happening in the world is that pharmaceutical companies and others are entering the mental health space and are trying to make us as sick as possible. We have to be very, very ethical. In fact, I would like Action Aid mental health workers to stay away from formal models of mental illness, because I believe that *less knowledge makes you more empathetic . . .* you *feel* schizophrenia or depression. You learn the language of distress from the patient's mouth.

In sharp contrast to the Centre of Excellence model, Dr. Abdul espoused a counterhegemonic approach to psychiatric and psychological care, emphasizing its relational and empathetic capacities. Dr. Abdul wanted counselors to stop medicalizing, diagnosing, and treating people according to the norms of biological psychiatry and a capitalistic health system.[50] Instead, he argued, "*less* knowledge makes you *more* empathetic," because it allowed counselors to remain linguistically, epistemologically, and phenomenologically close to the patient. According to him, psychiatry was less about textbook knowledge and more about listening to the patient, prioritizing their perspective, and "feeling" your way through their distress. For Dr. Abdul, if mental health care was beholden to the language and subjectivities of patients, it could counter disturbance. This principle was central to Dr. Abdul's clinical work and research objectives.

On another occasion, Dr. Abdul described another strategy for making psychiatry more responsive to the needs of Kashmiris. He imagined a new diagnostic category in the DSM, one accompanying the diagnosis of "complicated grief," but which more specifically captured the experiences of families of the disappeared.[51] Approximately eight thousand people have been disappeared in Kashmir and there are thousands of unmarked graves strewn across the landscape, particularly near the Line of Control. Enforced disappearances demand a different kind of grieving, Dr. Abdul argued, because when people are disappeared, families cannot experience closure. No death rituals can take place, no gravestone can be visited and tended. In Kashmir, disappearances have been particularly difficult for married women, who live in a liminal state, unable to recover and unable to mourn, garnering them the name *half-widows*.[52]

Dr. Abdul described this new diagnostic category on another cold December afternoon in the canteen of the psychiatric hospital. I warmed my hands around a cup of tea, unwilling to drink the archipelago of over-boiled milk that had formed on top. "In psychiatry," Dr. Abdul said, "complicated grief is a condition in which symptoms of grief and loss may linger or become debilitating with time. Complicated grief features some symptoms common to depression and PTSD, including intrusive thoughts, images of the deceased person, and a painful yearning for his or her presence. But maybe these symptoms vary for families who had experienced forced disappearances? Perhaps families of disappeared persons experience a different kind of complicated grief, which requires a new, or at least an amended, diagnostic category?" he asked, leaning forward in his chair. "Imagine if this diagnosis, based on the experiences of Kashmiri families, made its way into the DSM."

At first I wasn't sure how to interpret Dr. Abdul's idea. Was he instrumentalizing the suffering of Kashmiri victims to advance his own career? Would his idea alienate Kashmiris from their own experiences by translating their distress into a technical, medicalized vocabulary, which he had lectured the Action Aid counselors *not* to do?[53] Perhaps. But I understood Dr. Abdul's effort differently. He was trying to use globalized psychiatry as a tool for his own ends. In contrast to the Centre of Excellence approach, which injected global and national expertise, resources, and technology into the psychiatric hospital to flatten its local particularities, Dr. Abdul saw the DSM as an imperfect technology that could be perfected with more detailed, precise, and culturally specific experiences. Notably, Dr. Abdul did not claim that complicated grief produced by enforced disappearances was a "culture-bound syndrome."[54] Rather, he argued that the experiences of Kashmiri families should be recognized as universally valid, just like depression or schizophrenia. By translating Kashmiri grief into a universal, as opposed to "culture-bound" syndrome, he both recognized and contested the claims of globalized psychiatry.[55] Rather than disavow disturbance through global technical mastery, Dr. Abdul envisioned psychiatry's global relevance as hinging on cultural specificity.

Other medical providers, including psychiatrists, also exceeded humanitarian accounts of themselves as victims of violence or as neutral and impartial observers. Their life histories elaborated still more complex entanglements between medicine and militarism.

Many doctors belonging to the "rebel generation" were influenced by the life history of Afzal Guru—one of Kashmir's most famous martyrs—who had been studying to be a doctor when he decided to join the armed struggle.[56] Members of the rebel generation gave complex and ambivalent accounts of disturbance. Those who had graduated from medical school at the cusp of the insurgency often found themselves in uncertain and intriguing circumstances, in the topsy-turvy world Dr. Mudasir had described. They had interesting stories to tell: many were forced to collaborate with militants or the armed forces, had written fake autopsy reports (the hallmark of involuntary or enforced disappearances), and some had even been kidnapped and threatened by armed forces, militants, or counterinsurgents. Many were drawn to and sympathized with those who had taken up arms on their behalf. Doctors of the rebel generation, unlike the junior doctors, shared stories of an ambiguously charged reality, one in which disturbance was not only negative.

One afternoon in the summer of 2016, I met Dr. Abdullah, a pediatric surgeon in his late forties whom I had come to know well, for a quick lunch of vegetable fried rice in the dental college canteen ("the best food on the SMHS campus," I was told) along with some of his colleagues. Enormous flies buzzed around us while we ate, competing for the greasy but tasty food. Afterward, Dr. Abdullah took us to see his office in a brand-new, multistoried hospital building. Like the Kangan hospital, this brand-new building was also abandoned. Someone mumbled something about the failure to get "permissions" to move departments from their current locations into this new building. It took Dr. Abdullah a few minutes to find the keys to his office on the fifth floor. "I never come here," he chuckled apologetically. "But it's more private." We entered Dr. Abdullah's small, modern-looking chambers. It was immediately obvious that a lot of money had been spent on outfitting the doctors' rooms. Because the room hadn't been opened up in a long time, it was stuffy. To air it out, Dr. Abdullah put on the ceiling fan and kept the door open. With no one else around, we still had privacy. He passed around a box of *mithai*—sweets—from a patient's family. In this late-August stupor, exemplifying the stillness of disturbance, he told a story.

During the height of the insurgency, Dr. Abdullah was posted to a clinic near the Line of Control. It was his first posting out of medical school. One evening, some militants entered the hospital and kidnapped Dr. Abdullah at gunpoint, saying they needed the operating theater. He quickly understood that the militants belonged to a Pakistani armed group, "quite radical and jihādist" in their views, he said. Although he did not mention its name, based on his description, it was likely the Lashkar-e-Taiba (LeT).[57]

Dr. Abdullah was not afraid of the militants, even though the men were armed. Instead, he saw the kidnapping as an opportunity to get to know the militants better and understand their aims and motivations. He described the group's young leader as an "intelligent and thoughtful fellow, someone you could have a discussion with." They proceeded to chat and discuss politics all night long, including debating the long-term strategy of the LeT. Dr. Abdullah pressed the young militant to rethink their approach:

> I asked him, "Okay, so say you win Kashmir, then what?" "Then we will start our jihād in India," the leader responded. "How will you start your jihād in India?" I challenged him. "India has a population of 1 billion people, and only 15 percent of the population is Muslim. How will you change every single Indian, with their own religion, their own practices, and their own beliefs? Are you going to convert each and every person to Islam? Could you stomach what it would take to do that? And even if you *did* successfully convert each person to Islam, then what? Are you going to go around the whole world doing that?"

Dr. Abdullah and the militant leader had a vigorous and stimulating conversation that lasted until the early hours of the morning. The militant listened patiently to Dr. Abdullah's challenges about waging global jihād.[58] Although he disagreed with the organization's political ideology, Dr. Abdullah found the young man thoughtful and sincere.

Unlike dominant narratives of disturbance—in which militancy and state violence had unleashed corruption, disorder, and chaos into the body politic—Dr. Abdullah's encounter with disturbance was the opposite. The militant treated Dr. Abdullah not as a captive, but as a mentor who could sharpen his analytical skills. Rather than a scene of violence, the encounter exemplified each performing their social roles perfectly: Dr. Abdullah dutifully questioned the militant and he dutifully defended his stance. In contrast to popular portrayals of Islamist "jihādi militants" and "terrorists" as rebellious and violent, the young man was polite and nondogmatic. The narrative showed that militancy and violent rebellion, labeled Other/excessive/outside, could be absorbed into the social, under the right conditions.[59]

The next morning, the militants let Dr. Abdullah go.

Dr. Abdullah told the story with some bravado—this was a war story, after all—but also tenderly. Had this event been documented in media or human rights accounts, it would have been recorded as yet another story of medicine violated by the unruly forces of violence. However, Dr. Abdullah resisted telling that kind of story. Instead, he revealed more complex relational and emotional entanglements between himself, a medical practitioner, and agents of disturbance. Rather than antagonism—medicine versus militarism—the two connected.

Other rebel generation doctors had also experienced the ethical agency of militants, troubling the commonsensical notion that violence had harmed medicine.[60] For example, one Friday afternoon when everyone else in the clinic had gone for Friday prayers, Dr. Sajad, the head of the police-run De-Addiction Centre (DDC), told me about a near-death experience he had at the hands of the Border Security Force in the early 1990s:

> One day, there was a BSF raid in our area. . . . The raid occurred because a militant was found in Safarpora with a loaded gun. They made everyone come out of their houses, as usual. Hours went by while we waited outside, but the BSF couldn't find anyone. But they were convinced that there was a militant hiding somewhere. Then one of the BSF soldiers pointed his gun at me and two other men from our neighborhood and told us to come up in front of the crowd. We had to stand as human shields between the security forces and everyone else. The BSF soldiers had their guns pointed at us, and they made an announcement through their megaphones that they would fire on us if the militant did not come out. I closed my eyes. I imagined the guns pointed at us from both sides—from the BSF, but also from inside, wherever the militant was hiding. We were in caught the middle. . . . Then, suddenly, I don't know from where, a militant ran through the crowd, pushed us aside and came to the front, right in the line of fire. He said, "Spare these three, you can kill me."

Like Dr. Abdullah's story, Dr. Sajad's narrative problematized characterizations of militants as vectors of disturbance. By telling this story in the belly of the police headquarters, Dr. Sajad also engaged in his own small act of rebellion. Although Dr. Sajad's job was to provide substance abuse treatment for the police's "winning hearts and minds" campaign, he too revealed a more complicated relationship toward disturbance, without jeopardizing his position as a police employee.

✤

Walter Benjamin describes how the logic of disturbance is transmitted from law into everyday life. For Benjamin, extraordinary laws come into being so that law enforcement and the military can intervene "for security reasons"— in the name of care—while creating a "brutal encumbrance through a life regulated by ordinances."[61] The "brutal encumbrance" of ordinances resonates with how Kashmiris imagine the effects of emergency laws as releasing generalized disorder and disarray in people's subjectivities, ethical capacities, and professional visions. Though designed to isolate insurgents from civilians, disturbances do much more, and something other, than this. Like a squid's sprayed ink, disturbances feel leaky, uncontained, and sometimes dangerous.

Both Dr. Abdullah's and Dr. Sajad's narratives reveal how the infiltration of disturbance into medicine—the militarization of medicine—was not totalizing. Though medicine became the preeminent site to witness disturbance, medicine was more than a ledger of violence; it multiplied and refracted militarism's effects. Occupation had made the clinic less a standalone institution and more a space contiguous and symbiotic with violence, neglect, and harm. At the same time, disturbance did not necessarily make doctors victims. They were not entirely co-opted by state logics, despite being embedded in them. While disturbance is a technology of militarism, it also disrupted militarism—through irregular working hours, inadequate staff, curfews, and empty afternoons. These allowed for respite and reflection, for *other* stories of disturbance to burst forth.

THE DISAPPEARED

DOPDI

In Western India's
dusty plains,
bright sunshine strikes like an unending bolt of lightning.
A renegade, a Naxalite[1] fighter on the run.
A woman is named after a famous figure in Hindu
mythology—Draupadi—
but because she is Adivasi,[2] she is Dopdi instead.
If you know the myth, you might guess what fate awaits her.
The back of your neck might tingle.

After committing a major action against the police,
Dopdi goes underground.
After many months of running and hiding,
after her husband has been caught and killed,
after exhausting hideouts and secret networks,
after villagers on the brink of starvation can no longer resist
the lure of rice, lentils, cooking oil, and salt,
after threats from the police close in,
after it is inevitable she will be caught,
after emergence becomes being,
Dopdi is found.

Imagine the worst.
The worst happens to her.
She should be dead, but somehow, she survives.

Somehow, she stumbles out of the shed
where she's been kept
and confronts
the men, those men of the police

who violated her.
Now, she demands that they "counter" her.
Do an encounter killing, she directs them,
finish me off.

En-count-er.
To meet as an adversary.
To be against.
To undo.

In demanding an encounter,
in anticipating her fate,
she takes control,
makes the encounter hers.

What are we doing here? you might ask.
Dopdi is not a Kashmiri.
Dopdi belongs
in dusty villages—
West Bengal
or Bihar or Jharkhand
or Chhattisgarh.

*

We're in Kashmir now,
placid lakes and neon paddy stalks.
People here also know encounters.
Done in the name of order and safety,
encounters have made
not one, not two, but many Dopdis.

In slipping and sliding from Naxalbari to Kashmir,
We defy the logic of the encounter, which cuts persons
and places from each other.
We'll sniff out its odorless, traceless presence,
the disappearance of the disappearance
like Dopdi sniffs out the desperation of those holding her captive.

   (A rerendering of the short story "Dopdi" by Mahasweta Devi,
   translated by Gayatri Chakravorty Spivak)[3]

> It will surely kill, or it will possibly kill, or perhaps it merely hangs over the being it can kill at any and every moment . . . it turns man into stone. From the power of transforming a man into a thing precedes another power, otherwise prodigious, the power of turning a man into a thing while he is still alive. He is alive, he has a soul; and yet, he is a thing. . . . Still breathing, he is nothing but matter, still thinking he can think nothing.
>
> —Simone Weil, *The Iliad, or, The Poem of Force*

Springtime in Kashmir.[4] Tepid sunshine, torrential rain, tulips blooming on the foothills of the Zabarwan mountains like neat rows of soldiers, mustard fields bursting with gold, snow still visible on the tallest mountain peaks. I'm halfway through my fieldwork. Artifacts— notebooks, NGO brochures, pamphlets, medical journal articles, mental health reports—pile up modestly in my room. I grow attached to these paper towers, their tangibility reassuring against nebulous conversation, the backbone of ethnography.

I finally feel I'm getting the hang of things in the psychiatric hospital's crowded OPD. My arrival in the hospital is no longer met with quizzical looks; I can interpret most diagnostic codes scrawled on medical cards; doctors invite me to events they think I might be interested in; and we share jokes and gossip during in-between moments. My field notes are becoming more structured and, a little disturbingly, are mimicking the pithiness of medical records. Pithy, yet bursting with millions of tiny betrayals and heartaches, like invisible paper cuts:

Shameena—a woman in her mid-thirties who I meet at the back of the packed OPD. Her cream and green dupatta is wrapped gracefully around her head. She says she hasn't felt good for four years, since she got married. She complains about her mother-in-law and tells me her husband is a doctor. He doesn't believe she's ill, so she always comes to the hospital alone. This is extremely unusual; patients are generally accompanied by a bevy of kin. She describes her husband as tez (belligerent) and says that as soon as she hears him opening the gate when he's home from work, her heart starts beating fast. She cries herself to sleep about 4–5 times a week and has a hard time getting out of bed in the morning. She tells me all this softly, although even if she shouted, no one would be able to hear her because of the din. It's a very

intimate moment in a very public setting. Dr. Manzoor is busy with an elabo-
rate kin drama in front of Shameena. When it's her turn to see him, she sits
down on the patient's stool and surprises me by removing her shoes. She tells
him that her feet hurt and that she has pain in her chest. I whisper to her,
"Tell him about your throbbing heart . . . about the gate." Red flags are going
off in my head about a potential domestic violence situation. But Shameena
doesn't say anything. She nods at me once, a pact of silence established be-
tween us. Dr. Manzoor diagnoses her with a "recurrent depressive disorder,"
and she leaves.

I understood why Shameena withheld these intimate details from Dr. Manzoor. I had heard gendered accusations emanating from both male and female mental health experts. Female patients were often told that their complaints were illegitimate or that the cure for them was to better perform their domestic labor. Women bore the responsi-bility for making sure their emotions remained in check and that the household was a friction-less, well-functioning place.[5]

The hospital was no place for secrets. Shrines (*dargāh*), such as Makhdoom Sahab, the shrine of the Sufi saint Hamza Makhdoom Kashmiri (c. 1494–1576), located at the peak of Hari Parbat, accessible by 127 large stone steps, were better places to whisper the unsayable. From the dargāh, the psychiatric hospital was a tiny dot below.

Rereading my field notes, I was caught by the realization that both doctors and patients approach care encounters with desires, hopes, dis-appointments, and fears. Just like fieldwork. You pursue leads, some go somewhere, others don't, and most others, I just don't know yet.

ψ

Absorbed in fieldwork rhythms, I barely registered the storm brewing on the horizon. A few days after my encounter with Shameena, on April 30, 2010, headlines declared that the Indian army killed three Pakistani militants who tried to cross the border from Pakistan into Indian-controlled Kashmir. According to the army's press release, the three militants attacked patrolling troops, exchanged fire, and were killed in an "encounter." Afterward, a "thorough search [of the area] was conducted," but no further arrests were made.[6]

Reports of the incident stated that the three militants were killed near the Line of Control (LoC), the heavily militarized border sep-

FIGURE INTER.1. Shah Hamdani shrine. Courtesy Robert Nickelsberg

arating Indian- and Pakistan-controlled Kashmir.[7] Since the start of the conflict, fighters from Pakistan, Afghanistan, and even as far away as Chechnya have crossed the LoC to participate in Kashmir's armed struggle, a feat that requires climbing to an elevation of five thousand meters and successfully avoiding security patrols, treacherous cliffs, and avalanches.[8] Over the last two decades, the Indian state has militarized and fenced 550 of 740 kilometers of the border: coils of razor-sharp concertina wire are piled two meters above the ground; thermal imaging systems and surveillance radars detecting human movement have been installed; and regular patrols have reduced the number of "illegal" crossings by 80 percent.[9] As with other militarized, high-tech borders, such as the US–Mexico border, crossings can never be completely stopped and often become justifications for more militarism. Though the majority of armed fighters today come from within Indian-controlled Kashmir, rather than from across the LoC, in the popular imagination, the LoC remains a dangerous gateway from which terrorists, drugs, arms, and all threats to the Indian nation-state originate. Meanwhile, for Kashmiris, the LoC is an "open wound," representing an "ongoing Partition" that has separated families, neighborhoods, villages, and land for decades.[10]

A month after the infiltration, spring had deepened into summer. There were rumblings about three missing Kashmiri men who disappeared around the time the army reported the LoC infiltration. Pressure was mounting for the state government to find them. Their families feared the worst—that the three young men had been forcibly disappeared.[11] In most forced disappearances, the disappeared do not return alive.[12] If and when they do reappear, they do so as suspected gangsters, Naxalites, or terrorists whose deaths can be justified in the calculus of national security. In the novel *The Collaborator,* Mirza Waheed describes Indian state practices of staging the deaths of young Kashmiri men, displaying their dead bodies along with weapons, ammunitions, Pakistani rupees, and fake identity cards, which disguise the person's true identity and establish him as a Pakistani national.[13] Through these morbid displays, the military justifies its presence as a benevolent force protecting the border from "foreign infiltration," and for this, officers and soldiers receive significant benefits and rewards.[14] This pattern of representation and concealment—the "disappearance of a disappearance"—leaves families desperately searching for loved ones.[15]

Families of the disappeared can also be criminalized and censured for searching for missing kin. As we saw in Inayat's case, the police and courts regularly obstruct families from registering first information reports and may delay or erase missing persons and habeas corpus petitions.[16] One of the most violent aspects of encounters and disappearances is their suddenness. There is a razor-thin line and universe separating the "before" and "after" someone is disappeared. For example, Begum Jaan, a fifty-two-year-old woman interviewed in a human rights report, describes how her husband left home for evening prayers at the village mosque one day and never returned.[17] On a most ordinary day, her life was transformed forever.

The families of the disappeared suspected that the three "Pakistani militants" killed on the Line of Control were not militants at all. After mounting public pressure, the chief minister, Omar Abdullah, ordered the three bodies to be exhumed.[18] The exhumation was meant to bridge the ontological gulf between the military's version of history and people's political consciousness.[19] On May 29, 2010, the exhumations revealed that the bodies belonged to the three missing Kashmiris. The event became known as the "Machil fake encounter," an emblem of how militarized care is experienced as direct and debilitating violence.

Another version of history emerged. Perhaps Shazad, Shafi, and Riyaz had left their villages in the back of a military jeep before the sun came up that morning in April. Maybe they had felt optimistic because they had been promised jobs as army porters. Maybe they had woken bleary-eyed. Maybe the icy water with which they had washed their faces still stung. Maybe their mothers had insistently thrust warm rotis with knobs of butter into their hands. Even though it was still dark outside, maybe their mothers had insisted on waking up with them. Maybe they had been taken from their villages in Baramulla to Machil, a border town on the LoC. Maybe they were killed there, on April 29, 2010. Maybe their bodies had been photographed, then labeled as Pakistani militants. Maybe the soldiers who committed the deed had received bonuses, stars, and promotions for having foiled an infiltration attempt and producing three dead Pakistanis.

However, as in other places where enforced disappearances are rampant, people counter state demands to forget. In Kashmir, these acts are gendered—women determine grammars of remembrance. As Ather Zia notes, from the 1980s on, mothers and sisters participated in *dharnas* (sit-ins) in public squares, in front of army bunkers or camps every time a person was arrested, beaten, disappeared, or killed.[20] The most well-known Kashmiri activist against enforced disappearances is Parveena Ahangar. Ahangar's son disappeared in August 1990 after which she subsequently founded the Association of the Parents of Disappeared Persons (APDP), a civil society organization that today has hundreds of families in its membership. Once a month, members of the APDP, most of whom are women, gather in Pratap Park in central Srinagar and sit for hours armed with posters, photos, and images of their loved ones, in subdued but insistent protest. This repetitive act is not about recalling what happened, but about imbuing public spaces with private memories.[21] These rituals remind us that death, disappearance, and loss are not isolated incidents, but social and relational.

Although people know that "fake" encounters happen all the time, the Machil exhumation report sent shudders across Kashmir, particularly because it coincided with the peak of the military's "winning hearts and minds" campaign.[22] Senior military officials were publicly asserting the army's "zero tolerance" policy for human rights violations and were calling for strict punishment for crimes committed. Initially, the Indian army tried to reconcile its rhetoric with the reality of the Machil fake encounter. It turned over Major Rehman

Hussain—the commanding officer in the Machil case—to the Jammu and Kashmir police and dismissed him from service. The three victims' families were compensated with Rs. 300,000 (US$4,387) each. Later, the army personnel indicted were given life sentences, the first and only case in Kashmir in which this has happened. Yet, despite these initial gestures toward justice, they later unraveled when the soldiers argued in their appeal that the Kashmiri civilians were wearing Pathan suits, a Pakistani style of clothing. This mere sartorial association with Pakistan—and by extension with terror—legitimized their suspicion of the three men. The connection to "terrorism" was enough to undo the life sentences. The officers were later released on bail.[23]

Yet even before the case unraveled, Machil led to questions about more Machils. How many more innocents were strewn across the landscape, mislabeled, and reclaimed as military victories?

Then, things accelerated. On June 2, the Jammu and Kashmir police stated that they would investigate other suspected fake encounters by the Indian army. On June 3, residents of Rafiabad staged mass protests seeking the whereabouts of five youths who went missing five years ago. On June 4, a Kashmiri independence leader, Yasin Malik, went on a hunger strike to protest the Machil encounter. On June 7, Indian Prime Minister Manmohan Singh was scheduled to visit Kashmir; he gave a muddled message calling for dialogue—"shun violence, let's meet on table"—and in the same breath espoused the logic of collateral damage—asserting that in situations like these, sometimes "innocent people have to suffer." Sporadic protests continued. On June 10, a student in the eleventh grade was assaulted by the Central Reserve Police Force (CRPF). Then, on June 11, Tufail Ahmed Mattoo, a twelfth-grade student, was killed by a tear gas canister fired from close range, while he was walking home from his tuition class. His backpack, containing half-filled notebooks with math problems, preparations for upcoming medical school entrance exams, was found near his body. On June 12, Tufail's body was buried in the Martyr's Graveyard. During the funeral procession, sixty people were injured in clashes with paramilitary and police forces.

On Saturday, June 13, a full shutdown (bandh) marked Tufail's death. Angry protestors in the Old City attacked a CRPF bunker and razed it to the ground. On Monday, June 14, the headline in *Greater Kashmir* read, "Srinagar on the Boil." Small-scale protests continued amid an undeclared curfew. Then, for a moment, things seemed to dissipate. On Wednesday, June 16, the headline read, "Life Back to Normal in Valley."

Over the weekend, the situation deteriorated again (*halāt kharāb*, the situation has spoiled, people said). On June 20, a day newspapers called "Bloody Sunday," the CRPF opened fire on a funeral procession, killing a teenager and critically injuring four others. Over the next few days, the police and paramilitary fired live ammunition on more unarmed protestors and stone throwers. The cycle seemed unrelenting and unfathomable. By the end of June, ten civilians have lost their lives. A twenty-four-hour curfew was enacted.

My fieldwork routine, which felt so solid just days earlier, crumbled. Every day there was news of more clashes, more injuries, more lives unconscionably cut short. Other than recording "body counts," the life-and-death events of the day, I could barely write. One field entry read, "How does this immediate pain and suffering translate into cultural practices of mourning, remembering, counting?" but it trailed off. This was no ordinary disturbance. Soon, the Old City was cordoned off. Even ambulances struggled to get in and out. This meant the psychiatric hospital was out of bounds. However, the police-run De-Addiction Centre (DDC), which was closer to home, was sometimes still accessible by foot. Yasir, the DDC's social worker, called or texted to tell me whether it was safe for me to come. He signaled using the language of temperature: "hot" (not safe) or "cool" (safe). For a while, clinical routines ambled along in the midst of disturbance.

☙

Tuesday, July 6, 2010: A frustrating morning. A five-minute meeting with Dr. Wani, the director of health services, despite waiting for more than two hours. It's not his fault. The state health department is a hot mess. A sea of frustrated doctors is trying to get information about their new postings—information that has been delayed because of the Machil unrest. They are frustrated, agitated, sharp-tongued. Disturbance breeds rebelliousness. A besieged Dr. Wani asks for more time.

After watching this bureaucratic drama for some time, I walk from the Directorate of Health Services to the De-Addiction Centre to start the day's fieldwork. It's only a fifteen-minute walk, I tell myself reassuringly. But immediately upon stepping onto one of Srinagar's larg-

FIGURE INTER.2. Shutdown and curfew. Photo by author

est avenues, I realize my mistake. The street is deserted at 11 o'clock in the morning. A few other civilians, matters out of place like me, pick up their pace, as do I.

At the main gate of the Police Control Room, a gate I have crossed dozens of times, always with the requisite pat-down and too-interested look inside my fieldwork bag by the female police officers, a police-man tells me I can't enter. I show him my identity card and he tosses it back in my face, "So what? I have forty of these." There's a disdain in his voice that I've rarely heard in Kashmir. Eventually, I call Dr. Sa-jad, who asks Farooq, the DDC's security guard, to come and get me. After Farooq takes me through security, I complain about the guards, but he reminds me how the police are also on edge: "Do you see what's happening out there?" his voice soars, referring to the street clashes be-tween protestors and the police. "We're getting badly beaten. Of course we're angry!" Of the many things I have learned from living in distur-bance, one of the most important is this: we are each alone in our feel-ings of victimization.

When I enter the DDC, the clinicians and the eight inpatients are already in a session with Dr. Kishwar, a former professor of Dr. Sajad's, who is visiting from Dharamsala, a hill station in northern India. Dr.

Kishwar guides us through a relaxation exercise. We close our eyes and do a series of visualizations: imagine smooth pools of water, focus on each of the problems in your life, one at a time, put them all in a basket and throw them away. With my eyes closed, the space between inside and outside dissolves.

The session ends. The patients return to their large, dormitory-style room. Some lie on their beds, others gather in front of the television to resume watching the 1970s Amitabh Bachchan classic, *Amar, Akbar, Anthony*. Meanwhile, Dr. Sajad, Dr. Kishwar, and I chat in the counseling room. Farooq magically procures snacks—pistachio-almond milk boxes and Marie biscuits—from the police canteen. Magically, because absolutely nothing is open today.

I am still feeling a little raw after the incident at the gate and the exercise, which has agitated, rather than relaxed me. I ask Dr. Kishwar about people's practices of self-medication, which I have been thinking about lately. She tells me that Kashmiris' desire to self-medicate might have something to do with social alienation, with people's sense that they have lost control over their own lives and fates. She suggests a book on trauma by Peter Levine called *Waking the Tiger*. As she's describing the book, Farooq bursts in and tells us we all must leave the Police Control Room right away. In the distance, I hear loud firecrackers or exploding bombs. In fact, they are neither. Actually, more trained ears tell me, tear gas shells. The next few moments are fuzzy. We jump out of our seats, gather our things, divide up. Dr. Sajad ferries me home. It is my first brush with "active" conflict in this long, slow, simmering war.

At night, I learn that four people died today. One—twenty-five-year-old Fancy Jan—was standing near a window in her house, near where we were eating biscuits. A stray police bullet hit her in the chest. Her last words were: "There is a fire in my heart."[24]

ॐ

Within a few weeks, we found ourselves at sixty-two—sixty-two lives lost. Any moment now, another would fall. My journalist friend, Dilnaz, sent me an Excel spreadsheet named "Body Count," that she was updating daily. I was grateful for the orderliness of it—the way she had highlighted the names of the deceased, assembled order and facts out of the burning rubble. The spreadsheet made the dead countable and grievable.[25] In the absence of reliable information from the news media, friends phoned each other anxiously, checking news and government reports against each other, twice, sometimes thrice. Our cell phones became umbilical cords, Facebook an artery. In the eerie quiet of the unrelenting curfew—no screeching cars, no honking buses, no raucous schoolchildren next door—all I could hear were the pleasant sounds of nature in the afternoon.

But even our lifelines were not stress-free. Everyone worried about Facebook being full of fake accounts, cops posing as protestors. Be careful what you post, people warned. The solace of communicating was laced with fear. Then, I heard that the internet was going to be banned. Something which had seemed unthinkable was not only possible, but became real. This is what Taussig once described as "paranoia as social theory."[26] In addition to the curfews, communications blackouts—no internet, SMS, and mobile phone connectivity—became frequent, justified by the state to "secure law and order" and prevent protests. All the private telecommunications companies followed the government's orders. Capitalism, a deflated balloon in front of national security. These blackouts revealed that war was not being waged only against those labeled "miscreants" and "antinational elements," but against an entire civilian population.[27]

During this time, and much later, I asked myself: What does psychiatry even matter? It felt trivial to be writing a dissertation when innocent lives were being lost, when the state's necropolitical powers were on full display. At the same time, I recognized this imaginary itself signified the power of emergency: to make anything other than life in extremis seem irrelevant and trivial. As news of the protests—later given the name *intifada* by pro-independence activists—filtered into the media, family and friends encouraged me to return to Delhi.[28] In response, I half joked: I feel safer in Srinagar than Delhi. Though every day there were more deaths, I was never endangered, protected both by Kashmiri hospitality, which flowed even in emergencies, and militarized care, which is made for Indians like me. Every evening and at the smallest sign of unrest, Kashmiri friends reached out, checking to make sure I was safe. This care reminded me of the bodily and social difference between me, a non-native anthropologist, and those putting their bodies on the line.

Despite my initial feelings of disconnection between my research and the protests, it became clear that medicine and militarism did not occupy separate worlds, even though their stakes were different. Militarism encroached on the clinic in obvious and less obvious, intentional and less intentional, ways. The DDC was ensconced in the logic of militarized care, the strategic co-optation of humanitarianism by the Indian military. But militarism also seeped into the clinic indirectly: sounds (shelling, firing, shouting), sensations (panic), and affects (anger, outrage, fear) disrupted routine enactments of care. The state's own humanitarian efforts were enmeshed in, and over-determined by, violence and militarism.

CHAPTER 3

Shock

How can this inequality be maintained if not through jolts of electric shock?
—Eduardo Galeano, *Days and Nights of Love and War*

In India the problem in accessing mental healthcare is not so much due to stigma as it is due to illiteracy, ignorance, and lack of knowledge, myths, and supernatural beliefs.
—Anirudh Kalra, director of a psychiatric hospital in Ludhiana, India

"*Karant* [current]?" Sohaib, a male patient in his twenties, asked one afternoon, as the OPD fizzled down to its unceremonious end.[1] Only a handful of patients, the end of a long line, still waited to be seen at the psychiatric hospital.

"Mmm, not exactly," Dr. Farooq, a resident psychiatrist, demurred. "It's not karant. Not in the way you think. . . . It's a surge. It's only for a moment, to your brain."

"Surge?" Sohaib repeated, growing more concerned.

All South Asians have been burned by electric surges. Singed sockets, blown circuits, sparks flying through your veins, electronic corpses. What would a surge do to a person's brain? Dr. Farooq tried several more times to convince Sohaib that his brain receiving an electric "current"—in the form of electroconvulsive therapy (ECT), known colloquially as karant or "shock"[2]—would be a good thing for his long-standing depression.

Sohaib firmly and politely responded: "No, Doctor Sahab, I don't want this treatment." Dr. Farooq, exasperated, knew the cause was lost. As Sohaib left the OPD, his shoulders relaxed, his frown unfurled, a sense of relief coursed through his body.

After Sohaib was gone, the OPD filled with laughter.[3] Multiple psychiatrists work simultaneously in the OPD, so the fraught negotiation had occurred in front of Dr. Farooq's senior colleagues. The other doctors cracked jokes at his expense. I sometimes forgot that the OPD was a vulnerable space not just for patients, but also for physicians, some of whom are still interns or residents, standing on jello-like expertise. The encounter between Sohaib and Dr. Farooq amused the others because it overturned social hierarchies in the clinic, in which doctors are supposed to give orders and patients are supposed to obey. Sohaib's refusal to obey was rare in a context in which psychiatrists were used to being treated deferentially. Gifts of rosy apples from orchards in Sopore and kisses of thanks delivered on the back of their hands were the expected responses to doctors' orders. Patients asserting themselves—even politely—made psychiatric expertise appear a little too wobbly for comfort.[4]

Dr. Farooq was an easy target; his cheeks grew redder as the teasing soared. But behind the laughter was a sense of relief. Everyone had failed to convince a patient to undergo ECT at some point. Once the joking petered out, a more serious discussion about ECT began. Everyone agreed Dr. Farooq's failure was rhetorical: a failure to persuade, convince, and effectively communicate.[5] Everyone agreed that ECT was the most difficult psychiatric treatment to convince patients to undergo. The psychiatrists felt the problem was translational.[6] How to express ECT in Kashmiri? The surge analogy was clearly failing.

"What about the analogy of cardiac arrest?" someone offered. "Doctors have to give the heart a jolt of electricity when it fails, don't they?"

"We should tell them ECT is just like defibrillation!" another said.

The psychiatrists nodded and agreed enthusiastically. What they forgot to mention is that, unlike defibrillation, most if not all patients given ECT were fully conscious and sentient.

ψ

According to psychiatrists, patients like Sohaib were reluctant to undergo ECT because their understanding was clouded by superstitions and myths. Bollywood films had spread fallacies about ECT and reinforced stigmatized images of custodial care and asylum abuse, they argued, occluding evidence-based studies of ECT's efficacy. This widespread "ignorance" of ECT was frustrating for psychiatrists, who argued that for a "resource-scarce" country like India—the language often used in global health reports—ECT was one of the cheapest, safest, and most effective treatments for severe mental illnesses. Given that psychiatrists in Kashmir were confronting a mental health crisis and chronic resource shortages, ECT was invaluable in their care tool kit.

This made the rhetorical work around ECT all the more frustrating. Psychiatrists often said: if only we didn't have to bother with all this talk, we could get so much further. For them, the analogy of ECT to defibrillation was not just a linguistic translation, but was metalinguistic. It captured a fantasy in which psychiatry was equivalent to surgery, in which a patient, instead of talking back, was silent, unconscious, and acquiescent. This fantasy existed in friction with the fantasy of nonjudgmental, empathetic, and listening-centered care promoted by Dr. Abdul and Action Aid (chapter 2). While some psychiatrists *sometimes* saw the rhetorical work of psychiatry—taking medical histories from patients and kin, convincing patients to comply with treatment regimens and stopping treatments from religious healers (pīrs) in favor of ECT and other treatments—as its most exciting element, others saw rhetorical work as cumbersome. While they felt this "educative" labor was necessary to help overcome patients' "lack of knowledge" about mental health care, many wanted to fast-forward to treatment.

Patients had very different reasons for hesitating over karant, or shock, reasons that went beyond a lack of knowledge.[7] Instead, patients were hyper-attuned to karant's multiple valences. In Kashmir, karant did not just signify electroconvulsive therapy; it was also associated with electric shock, a technology of state torture that has been used extensively and systematically on Kashmiri bodies. In other words, shock was not just a medical technology, but a technology designed to bring about social and political compliance and control. Rather than a therapeutic (humanitarian) form, patients associated shock with harm (militarism). Circulations of shock between military and medical logics and spaces were more than just associational; they transformed karant's meanings and possibilities beyond its clinical and therapeutic functions.[8] By finding and feeling resonances between therapeutic uses of shock in clinical settings with punitive uses of shock in military settings, Kashmiris were commenting on occupation as an assemblage of both military and humanitarian presences.[9]

To capture the resonances between different shock(s) and their accruing meanings, we will zigzag between military and humanitarian spaces, criss-crossing moral imaginaries of national security and militarism in the interrogation center and commitments to more humane, modern community-based care in the family ward in the public psychiatric hospital. In the family ward, where patients reside ideally for a maximum of thirty days, admitted patients must be accompanied by kin ("attendants" in the hospital's language), who provide food, medicine, and basic nursing care during hospitalization because of chronic shortages in mental health expertise and resources. As Renu Addlakha notes, in South Asian hospital settings, families play multiple roles as legal guardians, reliable informants, nursing aides, and agents of surveillance, giving rise to a "hospital–family" alliance."[10] Shock, however, fissured this alliance.

ψ

Shock is understood as a form of care in both military and humanitarian settings. In clinical settings, shock jump-starts treatment: it is used after other treatments, such as psychopharmaceuticals, have failed to deliver results. For psychiatrists, ECT's efficacy helped inaugurate a more ethical, modern psychiatry by shortening hospitalizations. In other words, they argued, shock moved patients from *zoë*—a life of mere survival, withering away in institutions—to *bios*—a happy and fulfilled life with one's family and community.[11]

Similarly, in military and counterinsurgency doctrines, shock and other forms of torture are justified as ways of keeping the nation-state safe. "Shock"—as in "shock and awe"—is a military strategy aimed at achieving rapid dominance over an adversary using overwhelming force and firepower. Torture is deployed against criminals or suspected terrorists in the name of national security to elicit confessions or enact civic discipline.[12] Despite these specific uses of shock, it is used liberally as a crisis technology in both settings. Shock helps bring medical and military encounters to a close. Such closures mark progress and work completed, critical to both military and medical bureaucracies.

Contrary to the popular narrative that torture appears only exceptionally in modern liberal democracies, scholars have shown that torture is continually implemented to maintain national sovereignty, particularly in policing and security imperatives.[13] Although liberal democratic states have historically hidden or denied using torture, democracies like India and the United States have creatively accommodated these forms of "excess violence" into jurisprudence.[14] A 2002 US Justice Department memo to the White House argued that torturing al Qaeda terrorists in custody "may be justified" if government employees were doing so "in order to prevent further attacks on the United States."[15] Days after his inauguration, Donald Trump publicly extolled the virtues of torture in the war on terror. In the Indian context, state and military officials have also defended torture. For example, after a highly publicized incident in 2017 in which Indian army soldiers tied a Kashmiri man to the front of an army jeep as a human shield, General Bipin Rawat, the head of the Indian army in Jammu and Kashmir, defended the action in an interview. He stated, "This is a proxy war and a proxy war is a dirty war. It is played in a dirty way. That is where innovation comes in. You fight a dirty war with innovations."[16] In carceral settings, torture is proffered as a necessary innovation in a never-ending "dirty" war.

These defenses have been upheld in law. After armed gunmen attacked the Indian parliament in 2001, the Supreme Court of India upheld the right to an "extraordinary" response to combat "terrorism," including removing antitorture safeguards during interrogation.[17] The investigation following the parliament attack implicated Kashmiri Muslims and led to one, Afzal Guru, being secretly executed in an Indian prison.[18] For Kashmiris, these events bolstered conditions of emergency and made Kashmiris living outside the region also subject to extraordinary laws.

Electric shock (also called "magneto" or "magneto torture") has been widely used in torture and interrogation processes in Kashmir and throughout India.[19] In 2012, the Jammu and Kashmir Coalition of Civil Society (JKCCS), a human rights group, conducted the first statewide study of torture, surveying fifty villages and identifying more than two thousand cases of extreme torture.[20] The report found that one in six Kashmiris had experienced torture. In addition, the report identified a torture-scape: more than 150 marked and unmarked torture centers and thousands of unmarked graves were found scattered across Kashmir, many of them unacknowledged by the Indian state. The report also found that most torture victims were not "militants," but relatives or neighbors of suspected militants thought to have information. Others were accused of having sheltered militants, hiding weapons, or engaging in other "antinational" activities. In 2010, diplomatic cables leaked by WikiLeaks revealed that the International Committee of the Red Cross (ICRC) had briefed US officials about the systematic abuse of Kashmiri detainees in Indian prisons, which often took place in the presence of senior officers.[21] However, the report did nothing to stop these practices.

Within torture or interrogation processes, what does shock, or karant, do? According to the torture expert Darius Rejali, torturers are interested "not in confessions to crimes (for that is already taken for granted), but in *information*. They torture to secure a *complete file* on a person's contacts and recruit their victims as informers [emphasis mine]."[22] Shock thus infiltrates and weaponizes a person's social relations. In addition, shock is often used to scale up interrogations when other techniques have failed. The narrative of a nineteen-year-old student named Masroof Sultan shows this use of shock. While Masroof's account is more than twenty-five years old, his narrative exemplifies the experience of those who have undergone military shock.[23]

One Thursday morning in April 1993, the Border Security Force (BSF) arrested Masroof as he was going to university. Despite his persistent objections that he was a chemistry student and not a militant, Masroof was blindfolded and taken to an unknown location. During his custody, Masroof was kept blindfolded and was told several times he would be released in "ten minutes." These false messages, as well as the use of the blindfold, disordered his sense of time and space.[24] When Masroof's blindfold was finally removed, he found himself in a small room with three other civilians and twelve armed officers. The officers wrote down their names and addresses. Then they said: "You are our brothers. Tell us that you are militants and we won't [hurt] you. . . . Admit you are a militant. Tell us about your weapons. Admit that you are a member of Hezb-ul Mujahidin [a pro-Pakistani armed group]. . . . Our officers tell us to hit you if you don't admit to being a militant."[25]

Masroof and the other civilians were presented with a double bind: either they would be tortured until they admitted to being militants or they could admit to being militants, which could incriminate them, possibly leading to death. When Masroof protested that he was not a militant, one of the BSF officers responded: "Everyone in Kashmir is a militant. Even a child is a militant. You are also a militant."[26] Based on this logic, the end point of interrogation—he was a militant—was already known. The question was how to match what was already known.[27] Shock helped make this alignment happen.

After several hours of torture, Masroof was warned that if he refused to admit to being a militant, he would be given electric shocks and taken to "Papa 2"—Kashmir's most notorious secret interrogation center. On hearing this, Masroof described how he felt "pain in my heart. They told me they would release me after ten minutes. I am a student, a college student, I am nothing. What are they doing? What is [the] Indian government doing? This is the rule of the Indian government? A person is going to college and they catch him and interrogate him and kill him?"[28] Masroof refused to confess. At Papa 2, he was given electric shocks for half an hour, during which he was repeatedly told to "give up his gun."[29] Eventually, Masroof was taken to an unknown outdoor location with several others, shot in both legs, and left to die. An hour later, a few policemen found Masroof and took him to a hospital. Somehow, he survived.

The Human Rights Watch report in which Masroof's ordeal is painstakingly described, ends with technical, forensic descriptions of the length and breadth of injuries Masroof received. According to the Danish physician from Physicians for Human Rights who examined him, the marks on Masroof's body confirmed the veracity of his narrative. As is typical of the genre, the report focuses on details of bodily harm and the specificity of events, saying little about how this incident has affected Masroof's life and family.

As Lotte Segal points out, both human rights and psychiatric knowledge tend to see torture as a "discrete event" that affects "singular subjects."[30] However, ethnographic knowledge reveals how shock is a social and relational technology. Beyond the individual person who is tortured, torture has ripple effects. In Kashmir and elsewhere, reports of torture have led to enduring protests, civil society activism, and political subjectivities. The collective awareness among Kashmiris about the political uses of torture explains why patients like Sohaib were extremely reluctant to accept it as care. This overdetermined meaning of shock as torture, not treatment, affected goings-on in the clinic.[31] Ironically, while the punitive meaning of shock constrained psychiatrists, for patients, it enabled some agency over their own treatment.

ψ

One day, while Dr. Abdul and I were chatting in his office in the psychiatric hospital, a patient named Nasir entered.[32] Nasir was suffering from suicidal depression. Based on the lack of pleasantries exchanged between them, I realized I was witnessing—or eavesdropping on—an ongoing negotiation. Without any prompting, Dr. Abdul told Nasir, "Your disease makes you an ideal candidate for ECT." He did not use the word *shock* or the Urdu word *karant*, but the English-language acronym, ECT.

Nasir's face crumpled, tears welling in his eyes. He said, "I know you are doing the best for me. I have no doubt you are doing the best for me. But I don't want ECT." Nasir slipped comfortably between English and Urdu, revealing his upper-middle-class status. His eyes widened when he spoke, his voice was soft but emphatic.

Dr. Abdul had scheduled Nasir for two ECT sessions, the previous Monday and Saturday, but he had missed both appointments. Nasir was trying to explain his absence. He asked Dr. Abdul if he could give his medications more time to work.

"I have a chronic phobia of ECT," Nasir said. "I know what shock has done in Kashmir."

Dr. Abdul continued to negotiate, telling Nasir it would take too much time to determine whether or not his medications were working, time that Nasir could ill afford, given his "suicidal tendencies." ECT could work instantaneously, Dr. Abdul said.[33] During this intense and emotional back and forth, one of the postgraduate psychiatry students, Dr. Gagan, burst into the room. He was wearing latex gloves and had a panicked look on his face.

"Sir, the ECT machine has not been working for the last two patients." Out of breath, he glanced quickly at Nasir and me before continuing: "We haven't been able to generate convulsions."

Dr. Abdul told Dr. Gagan to "stop doing ECT immediately." I could not help but look at Nasir, who was as still as the paperweight on Dr. Abdul's desk. His face, full of expression a minute earlier, was now expressionless. Was he relieved that it was not him on the ECT table, or had his phobia multiplied?

After Dr. Gagan left, Dr. Abdul's tone became more conciliatory. He told Nasir, "Anyway, ECT is not like magic. It won't work if you don't comply with my instructions." He reminded Nasir that he was already on a very high dose of antidepressants. "But," Dr. Abdul said wearily, "it is your right to choose your own treatment."

By relating this vignette of a broken machine, I do not wish to reproduce a familiar narrative of technological failure in a resource-poor setting. Rather, as Alice Street observes, everyday clinical failures in "unstable" places can also tell us something important about enactments of personhood, agency, and the ethics of care in hospitals.[34] Nasir and Dr. Abdul's debate made visible tensions around competing bioethical imperatives—between the principles of beneficence (doing good), the right to treatment (access to care), and autonomy (a patient's right to choose their own treatment), for example. Perhaps surprisingly, machine failure offered Nasir an opening. While Nasir's class, educational background, and posture of deference toward Dr. Abdul may have helped his persuasion, I am not convinced that these were enough in and of themselves. After all, Dr. Abdul only acknowledged Nasir's right to choose his own treatment *after* the ECT machine malfunctioned. The failed ECT machine allowed the ethic of patient autonomy to supersede beneficence, whereas beneficence and the right to treatment generally trumped autonomy.

Beneath the surface of this conversation was an ontological question. What was the clinic? Was it contiguous with, or apart from, the interrogation center? For psychiatrists like Dr. Abdul, the clinic, a humanitarian space, was easily distinguished from the militarized space of the interrogation center. ECT constituted care, not torture. But for patients like Nasir, the presence of shock in both settings undermined a clear demarcation.

In both military and humanitarian settings, shock mitigated (different) crises. In psychiatry, ECT produced rapid improvements when patients were suffering from schizophrenia or severe depression, or when they became unresponsive to psychopharmaceuticals; it offered a meantime treatment if doctors were struggling to diagnose, or it could help psychiatrists arrive at a diagnosis retrospectively; and it was affordable in settings of economic scarcity.[35] Given soaring patient demand and chronic shortages, ECT allowed patients to access care, freed up bed space, and enabled shorter hospitalizations. In other words, ECT was an ideal technology to facilitate a globally accepted and valorized approach to mental health care called "community-based mental health care."

Supported by the World Health Organization (WHO), the Movement for Global Mental Health (MGMH), and other international organizations, community mental health care shifts mental health services out of large, centralized asylums into community settings.[36] The community-based model developed in response to long-standing critiques by psychiatrists about the failures of institutional care:

> Most [institutionalized] patients continue to vegetate in a dehumanized asylum environment, not on account of clinical considerations, but because they have been abandoned by their families. . . . Yet, we continue to prescribe the creation of new mental hospitals as the panacea of all ills. This pernicious philosophy will result in the culpable waste of scarce resources, which can be better utilized to create therapeutically rational as well as more cost-effective community-based mental health care services. While it costs Rs. 500 per day to keep a patient in a mental hospital, the per capita national expenditure on health is only Rs. 200 per year.[37]

Community-based mental health care also reconciled neoliberal and public health goals: not only were shorter hospitalizations and care "in the community" more efficient and cost-effective than institutional care, they were also more humane and "therapeutically rational."[38] For psychiatrists, community-based care addressed the pressing problem of families abandoning mentally ill relatives in psychiatric institutions.[39] In advocating for community-based care over institutional care, psychiatrists reproduced a familiar binary: asylums or institutions were spaces of abandonment, while families and communities offered care and solace. This allowed psychiatrists to avoid attending to asylum conditions while shifting the burden of care onto families. In rare cases when patients were institutionalized, every effort was made to discharge them quickly, ideally within thirty days. This happened even if family members and patients desired more institutional care.[40] While many community-based care goals were laudable, they also had unintended effects. For one, they increased psychiatrists' reliance on ECT. Shock accelerated institutional treatment.

ॐ

Despite psychiatrists' ethical justifications of ECT as facilitating community-based care, ECT use in Indian psychiatry has come under intense public and legal scrutiny. One key area of controversy has been over the pervasive administration of ECT in Indian hospitals without anesthetics, muscle relaxants, or oxygenation. The United Nations Special Rapporteur on Human Rights describes ECT without anesthesia as constituting ill treatment or torture. In 2001, a patient advocacy group filed a petition to the Indian Supreme Court calling for a ban on all unmodified ECT.[41] The petition stated that ECT was overused in clinical settings, was often given to patients and families without proper consent, and when delivered without anesthesia or muscle relaxants, amounted to torture.[42] In other words, the petition argued that ECT's use had made it into a custodial and punitive, not caring or curative, practice.

The ECT petition came on the heels of a nationally reported tragedy involving the deaths of twenty-five mentally ill, institutionalized persons in a fire because they had been chained to their beds. Once again, a national debate around mental health care was sparked. The ECT debate revealed the presence of competing frameworks of bioethics in Indian psychiatry, namely between patient autonomy (choice) and the right to treatment. The petition against unmodified ECT cited patient autonomy—the right to choose—as an ethical value that should trump discussions about access to treatment. Meanwhile, psychiatrists privileged the right to treatment over patient autonomy and choice, arguing that ECT in any form, modified or unmodified, was "appropriate" for under-resourced settings like Indian public hospitals. They argued that restricting ECT to its "modified" form—that is, with anesthesia, muscle relaxants, or oxygenation—increased costs, added potential complications and risks, and greatly restricted it, since anesthesiologists are not available in most public mental health settings. Rather than see modified ECT as an ethical alternative to unmodified ECT, they argued that "a complete ban on unmodified ECT" contradicted the ethical principle of beneficence, because it restricted access to an effective and lifesaving treatment."[43] Psychiatrists also argued that unmodified ECT was a culturally appropriate technology that "fit" India's political economy. The widespread use of ECT responded to "felt needs and ground realities in standards of medical care in developing countries," they argued.[44] In these conditions, "suboptimal practice is better than no intervention."[45]

On the surface, these arguments seem to echo anthropological demands for more context-specific and culturally appropriate biomedical treatments, particularly in the Global South. However, as Adriana Petryna warns, economic and political-economic differences can become justifications for radically different standards of care and protection—what she calls "ethical variability"—for vulnerable populations.[46] The argument that even "suboptimal" ECT was better than "no treatment" reflected this approach. While acknowledging that unmodified ECT was not "the *ideal* form of the procedure," psychiatrists compared it to the necessary use of "suboptimal medical and surgical practice in emergencies."[47]

As in their comparison of ECT to defibrillation, psychiatrists once again analogized their practice to surgery. Rather than see emergencies as exceptional, they saw themselves as embedded in a milieu of emergency, one which justified subverting clinical standards—such as obtaining consent or contending with shortages of personnel and equipment—much like emergency surgeons might do.[48] Yet there were important differences in emergency medicine and ECT use in psychiatry: while emergency conditions, such as war or famine, are supposed to be exceptional and short-term, there was no sign that the chronic resource shortages in Indian public health would disappear anytime soon. Similarly, while ethical shortcuts permissible in emergency settings accommodated situations like patients being unconscious and unable to consent, these were not the conditions of care in the psychiatric hospital. Doctors and patients could communicate with each other; the majority of patients in mental health settings could consent to treatment or not. However, comparing psychiatry with emergency medicine obviated concerns about ethical variability and asserted the moral rectitude and urgency of certain psychiatric interventions.

Eventually, patient advocacy groups prevailed in the ECT debate. In 2013, the Indian government passed a mental health care bill that prohibited the use of ECT without muscle relaxants, anesthesia, and in a number of other situations.[49] Nonetheless, psychiatrists continued to defend ECT as a cornerstone of community-based care and felt morally justified in continuing to administer "suboptimal" ECT despite the prohibition.

Because of the unavailability of anesthesiologists, and because many psychiatrists believed that "suboptimal" ECT was better than no ECT, psychiatrists continued to administer ECT without anesthesia. When I asked about the continued legal violations, Dr. Manzoor and others firmly stated, "Some ECT is better than no ECT." This justification rested on the universal acceptance that the legal subversion was for a greater good—shorter hospitalizations and community-based care.

The model of community care radically reoriented psychiatrists' attention. Whereas the "rebel generation" of doctors had cut their teeth in the closed wards among chronically ill patients, doctors now spent most of their time in the hospital's OPD and the short-term inpatient ward (the family ward). They rarely visited patients in the long-term, "closed" wards unless there was an emergency. Dr. Gagan told me that there was no need to visit the long-term wards because it would be a miracle "if those patients showed any improvement." By contrast, the prefigured temporal horizon of thirty days of inpatient stay in the family ward meant these were spaces of progress and momentum.[50] Ilana Feldman has similarly described the long temporality of humanitarian aid in Palestine, in which emergencies can galvanize and energize experts, whereas chronic conditions can produce feelings of futility and frustration or—as we saw in Dr. Gaga's case—indifference. Psychiatrists did rounds of the family wards at least twice a day and kept meticulous patient records. In contrast to patients in the closed wards, all the patients in the family ward were considered capable of improvement. The family ward was a dynamic space, buzzing with sociality and hope.[51] In the OPD and family ward, doctors, patients, and kin all participated in the therapeutic process. For doctors, the family ward demonstrated how families—rather than the state—were taking responsibility for mentally ill persons, heralding a more modern and humane psychiatry. This represented the overcoming of stigma that had structured psychiatry for so long and had led to patient abandonment.

While the goals of community-based care and shortened inpatient stays are laudable, how were these goals actually achieved? How were faster patient discharges accomplished and to what effect?[52] Meanwhile, what did community care look and feel like from the perspective of families? What were the textures of living with a mentally ill person after institutionalization?

To accomplish a speedy discharge, the trajectory of care was prefigured: patient admitted, patient improved, patient discharged. ECT helped make this goal achievable—and inevitable—within thirty days. Yet, ironically, the reliance on shock to achieve these ends also brought humanitarian psychiatric practices closer to military procedures and practices, since unmodified ECT is widely understood to be analogous to torture. For patients and kin, unmodified ECT produced irreversible harms. That these were disguised as care made them even more egregious. Put differently, the only route to ethical care (returning patients home) was through a thicket of subversions. Was this still care? As Pinto describes, psychiatric care decisions are rarely clear-cut: "In committing a family member to inpatient care, or managing a loved one's medications, or bringing a family member 'home,' or making a new home for oneself when things have come undone, care became—necessarily—indistinguishable from constraint; freedom felt a bit like abandonment. . . . In many situations, [these] spectra operated simultaneously, their terms overlapping, even collapsing in the work of everyday ethics."[53] Similarly, for patients and kin, the use of unmodified ECT upended ready-made distinctions and value judgments in normative psychiatry and anthropology between abandonment (something that happens only in institutions) and care (something that happens primarily in the community). Efforts to establish more ethical care were entangled with modalities of harm. Rather than eliminate abandonment, community care merely shifted its locus from the hospital to the family. The story of a young woman I call Mauna Irshad illustrates these dynamics.

ॐ

girl
with phantoms of fire
in her heart.

Mauna was twenty-two years old when I met her in the family ward in the spring of 2010. I tell Mauna's story from a number of different perspectives, all of which are fragmentary. Collating these pieces does not reveal a whole or complete picture of what happened; rather, it highlights the kaleidoscopic quality of all narratives, including clinical ones.[54] As with Inayat, my journey with Mauna was ambiguous and uncertain. Instead of accumulating information or knowledge through time, I felt myself both gain and lose ground as my relationship with Mauna deepened. I tell this story in a nonlinear fashion, as I experienced it.

I first heard about Mauna from Dr. Farah, one of only two clinical psychologists at the psychiatric hospital. Her name, Mauna, is significant. It means silence.[55] One day, while Dr. Farah and I were eating lunch together—generously buttered, thick slices of toast and chai from the hospital's canteen—she told me about a "difficult case." Mauna, she said, was being treated as an outpatient for obsessive-compulsive disorder (OCD), when she was referred to Dr. Farah for cognitive behavioral therapy (CBT).[56] In their first session together, Mauna spoke incessantly about fire. Whenever she would see a flame, she would put her hand over it and burn herself. Mauna had arrived at one counseling session with a burned nose. According to Dr. Farah, the burned nose was related to Mauna's ongoing delusions.

"Mauna sees herself as a sinner. Maybe she thinks she deserves to be punished for some sins she has committed, sins she thinks are unforgivable," Dr. Farah explained.[57] Dr. Farah began treating Mauna with CBT, to help Mauna see her delusions as "irrational."

Then, Mauna stopped showing up for her appointments. A month passed. A week ago, Dr. Farah had bumped into Mauna's mother on the street. Mauna's mother burst into tears upon seeing her and told her that Mauna had not eaten for the last two weeks. Dr. Farah urged Mauna's mother to have Mauna admitted to the psychiatric hospital's family ward, where Mauna could receive intensive care in the company of her parents. Mauna's mother agreed.

Mauna's intake form included biographic details (Mauna Irshad, daughter of Irshad Mushtaq), age, education (high school graduate), marital status (unmarried), language (Kashmiri, Urdu), occupation (student).[58] Her parents' occupations and educational levels were also noted. Her father is a "metric pass" (studied up to the tenth grade), and he owns a small shop in the Old City; her mother's occupation was listed as "housewife" and her educational status as "nil." After this comes Mauna's case history. As per biomedical norms of expertise, her case history is sparse ("concise," as doctors put it) but also, at times, inaccurate.[59]

[Since 2003]
Complaints of restlessness
Loss of interest in work
Feeling of impending doom
Excessive washing
History of suicidal thoughts and five suicidal attempts. Patient withdrawn medication on his [sic] own since Feb. 10.

During Mauna's psychiatric examination, given to all patients at the time of admission, her "general behavior" was listed as "emaciated, conscious, non-cooperative, depressed. No involuntary movements—dressed appropriately." Her "nonverbal expression of affect" was described as "depressed." Her verbal behavior was characterized by "repetition of sentences." Under the category hallucinations, "none." Under the final category—diagnostic formulations—the resident had written: "Resistant OCD with depressive features and suicidal tendencies."

Because suicide loomed over her case, psychological interventions—including Dr. Farah's—were suspended in lieu of an emergency biomedical response. The next day, on April 1, 2010, Mauna was admitted to Ward 4, the family ward, accompanied by her parents. In addition to oral feeding, she was given a daily regimen of fifteen milligrams of the antidepressant mirtazapine; five milligrams of olanzapine, an atypical antipsychotic; and an injection of lorazepam, a benzodiazepine, to decrease anxiety and help her sleep.

Immediately, the short-term care clock started ticking. The urgency to move Mauna from illness to improvement to discharge became palpable in the way her file was written. Her file told a story of conflict: the clinicians tried to establish a trajectory of improvement, but Mauna's behavior obstructed them.[60] For example, on the third day of her admission, a large and bold "+" sign was made in the file, signaling improvement. Later that same day, however, a note was written in larger letters, "Pt. not improving," followed by a comment that Mauna was refusing to eat and take her medication. "F_{20}?" was written next. F_{20} is the International Classification of Diseases (ICD) symbol for schizophrenia. The F_{20} seemed to be a scaling-up of Mauna's diagnosis. I wondered in my field notebook if the diagnosis was retaliation for Mauna's noncooperation. I had seen other "difficult" patients receive a schizophrenia diagnosis.

On Day 8, Mauna was given a nasogastric tube for feeding and another "+" sign was made in the file. On Day 10, Mauna removed the tube: "Pt. continuing to refuse to take orally," the file said. New handwriting appeared, suggesting more consultations, the hint of a widening crisis.

"F_{20}?" another hand asked, a second query for schizophrenia.

Mauna's refusal to eat signaled a "threat to life," according to her attending doctors. Next, a letter was stapled into Mauna's file. A technological failure forced the hospital to reach out to other departments for help:

To: The Registrar, Department of Anesthesia,
SMHS Hospital, Srinagar

Respected Sir,

Kindly examine and advise us about the pt. admitted with our department for the last 10 days, a c/o [case of] schizo-obsessive disorder with suicidal ideation with five previous attempts of suicide. Pt. is most of the time agitated and not cooperative. Presently, she is not accepting anything orally in order to harm herself for the past five days. Pt. needs ECT therapy but ECT machine is out of order and we have to maintain her on medication till ECT machine starts working. So, kindly help us to start her oral feeding by putting in a Ryle's tube [a stomach tube].

Thank you in advance,
Registrar—Department of Psychiatry

The letter identified ECT as the appropriate crisis technology in Mauna's case, *despite* its unavailability, echoing earlier claims about "some ECT" being better than "no ECT." In fact, Mauna needed to be kept alive so she could receive shock: "we have to maintain her on medication till ECT machine starts working."

On Day 13, the ECT machine started working again, and the rhythm of the file shifted. The written clinical narrative became more and more minimal and shock entered the file to align Mauna with the only possible end point of care: discharge.[61] Mauna also continued a regimen of psychopharmaceuticals: fluvoxamine, to treat OCD and depression; lorazepam, an antianxiety medication; and propranolol, for hypertension, anxiety, and panic. The sparseness of writing helped produce ECT as a treatment that was minimally invasive, noncontroversial, standardized, and effective. Yet all the ECT Mauna was given was without anesthesia, muscle relaxants, or oxygenation.

On Day 16, Mauna received her first round of ECT. The event was noted with a pithy "ECT given." This was followed by a positive development: "Pt. accepting [medication] orally." The file was quick to note the success of the ECT, its immediate, positive effects. However, the next day, there was backpedaling. Mauna was "irritable, verbally arguing." The file noted: "Pt. complaints [resemble] psychotic depression." Despite the possible change in diagnosis, a second ECT was scheduled for four days later.

On Day 21, Mauna received her third round of ECT. After this, the rhythm of the file changed significantly. There was less back and forth between Mauna and the doctors. The trajectory toward discharge became visible.

Day 21: "Pt. doing well."

Day 22: "4th ECT done. Pt. doing well."

Day 25: "5th ECT done. No complications." The underlining captures a sense of confidence as we approach the thirty-day mark.

But then a trace of Mauna's illness reappeared: "Attendants [Mauna's parents] complaining that she doesn't sleep at night and keeps on talking to us and laughs...but is not inappropriate."

Then, from Day 26 on, Mauna's presence in the file diminished even more. There were fewer interruptions, the rhythm steadying:

Day 27: "Pt. doing well; ECT done; symptomatically improved."

Day 29: "7th ECT done. Pt. doing well. Continue same treatment (Rx—CST)."

While doctors did not make the thirty-day deadline, they were close:

Day 32: "Improvement ++ (Rx—Continue Same Treatment)."

Day 36: "8th ECT done. Pt. improving +."

Her provisional diagnosis was changed again: psychotic depression with suicidal ideation, the specter of schizophrenia elsewhere for the time being.

Then, on Day 42: "To be discharged on Friday. Doing well. Continue same treatment."

On the day of discharge, there was no ambulance available to take Mauna and her parents home. She had to remain in the ward for a few more days.

Day 46: "Doing well. Continue same treatment."

Mauna's diagnosis was changed again: "BPAD [bipolar affective disorder]: current episode psychotic depression with OCD." The ambulance became available.

On Day 50: "Pt. to be discharged tomorrow."

While psychiatrists were not able to achieve the thirty-day deadline, for such a "complicated and difficult case as Mauna," as one described it, the fifty-day treatment was still a success in the model of community-based care. Mauna's file indicated significant improvement: the phrase *patient doing well* appeared more frequently as her treatment neared completion. Mauna was made discharge-able.

Mauna's file shows how the clinic's bureaucratic and moral authority is not automatically conferred, but has to be achieved through specific expert techniques.[62] In particular, technologies (shock) and aesthetic practices (writing) countered and eventually dominated Mauna's voice and presence in the file, leading to her discharge. The more Mauna resisted treatment, the more doctors had something to discipline and the more solid their disciplinary power became. As Riles and Jean-Klein have argued, bureaucratic orders are not unsettled by messiness and critique; rather, "this messiness serves as more fodder for further disciplinary projects."[63] The medical record was less significant for the meaning or information it conveyed; rather, it was a "tool in the construction of fixed and shared meaning."[64] Mauna's medical file illustrated that the fixed and only possible outcomes of care were improvement and discharge.

Writing played a critical role not just in signaling, but in producing, an end point of care. The less written, the less there was to be done, the more improved Mauna was, and the closer we were to the bureaucratic end. Matthew Hull has noted that bureaucratic files are often written in the present perfect tense, because bureaucrats often represent themselves not as "experiencing selves," but as "constrained, passive, or uninvolved agents" in the events they document.[65] Similarly, psychiatrists also described Mauna's condition in cool, matter-of-fact, and distant tones ("pt. doing well"). This helped create a sense of reality that was neutral, objective, and external to those documenting it. However, unlike the bureaucratic files Hull examined, in which the future tense was stringently avoided because it committed actors to actions for which they may be held accountable, the regime of community-based care *demanded* the use of the future tense: "pt. to be discharged tomorrow." The future tense delimited care to a specific temporal horizon, established the clinic's humanitarian orientation, and shored up bureaucratic authority because discharge was a sign of successful treatment. Meanwhile, Mauna's presence in the file was minimized and eventually erased.

While doctors found Mauna's case exceptionally difficult to diagnose, the number of shocks she received was not unusual.[66] As in other cases, shock mitigated a "crisis": it prevented Mauna from ending her life and avoid long-term institutionalization, while enabling ethical care in the community. Doctors were not alone in their desire to return Mauna home quickly. Her parents, who had been residing in the hospital for the duration of her treatment, also wanted to return home. However, the ethics of care espoused by psychiatrists—the use of shock to facilitate a quick discharge—created long-term consequences that were difficult to bear for the family.

ψ

When Dr. Farah first told me about Mauna, she had been hospitalized for three weeks. It took me a few more weeks to track the family down. By the time I got access to Mauna's file, it was Day 54 of her inpatient treatment; she was "ready for discharge." That day, I sat in the nurses' station in the hospital, frantically copying Mauna's file. I was not allowed to take photos or to photocopy the file, but I could take notes by hand. Other than these instructions, no one questioned my reasons for looking at her file. Since Mauna was still an inpatient, her file was circulating between the postgraduates, her consulting psychiatrist, and the nurses' station and was easier to access. After patients are discharged, their files are moved to the medical records section, where accessing them requires extra permissions.

It was noisy in the nurses' station. Four middle-aged women sat around a large table with long ledgers between them, reading patient names out, ward by ward. An electric kettle whistled in the corner. An elderly male orderly in a fez cap, Wani Sahib, sorted out colored pills on a steel tray—orange, white, and green—the colors of the Indian flag. Dr. Gagan sat in one corner writing discharge slips. Two of the middle-aged nurses flirted with him mercilessly—he was tall and handsome—in the way only middle-aged women can. He blushed and tried his best to send clever quips back, but he melted under their sizzling wit.

It was not a bad space, this nurses' office. It took me out of the disturbing drama unfolding in Mauna's file, even if just for a moment. I fell into a hypnotic state, the familiar feeling of long hours spent in school copying notes from the blackboard. One of the nurses poured me a cup of tea, despite my half-hearted refusals, and Wani Sahib gave me a *czochworu* (a small sourdough bread with sesame seeds), which was delicious and soft. I didn't even try to refuse.

Seeing Mauna's father pacing anxiously in front of the nurse's office broke my reverie. He occasionally peered into the nurses' office through the mesh doors. I realized he was waiting for Dr. Gagan to finish the necessary documentation for Mauna's discharge. What must we have looked like, drinking chai and having a laugh? I went outside and asked him if everything was okay. He said he had been waiting for the discharge slip since the morning and now it was late afternoon. He reminded me that they had been here, day and night, for almost two months. Every moment of waiting seemed excessive.

Then he asked if I'd like to meet Mauna, who was awake.

ψ

The first time I saw Mauna (though I did not actually meet her until Day 54), she had been in the ward for twenty-seven days and had received six ECTs. She was sitting on the cement floor outside the family ward, on a colorful dhurrie. I happened to pass by on my way somewhere. I saw her licking the remnants of rice and *rajma* (red kidney bean curry) from her fingers, relishing the last textures of her meal. Her mother had cooked for her, as she had done every day since Mauna's admission. Her parents, sitting beside her, watched her eat, a relief after weeks of struggle. I took in the scene: a healthy daughter, two loving parents, golden sunshine. I was eager to talk to the family since Dr. Farah had told me about the case a few days earlier. I told myself I would return soon.

By the time I returned to the family ward, Mauna was taking an afternoon nap. I introduced myself to her parents as a friend of Dr. Farah's who wanted to see how Mauna was doing. Dr. Farah was on vacation, but Mauna's parents seemed happy that someone was checking on them while she was away. Her mother was washing utensils at the communal tap outside the ward and was a little distracted, but warm toward me. Mauna's father took me aside and told me that Mauna had undergone many karants. As he was telling me this, Mauna's mother joined the conversation. She lifted up her gray *pheran* (overcoat) and said she had not bathed or changed her clothes since Mauna's admission almost a month ago. Both Mauna's parents had been sleeping on the floor, in the narrow space on either side of her hospital bed, since she was admitted. The beds in the family ward were full, but so were these in-between spaces, which were taken up by kin. Taking care of her was a full-time job, they said. Though institutions expect families to "share the burden" of care, they make little or no accommodations for them to actually live, sleep, and eat in the hospital. Mauna's parents were both elderly.[67]

Mauna's mother told me Mauna had been stubborn, insisting that both parents remain with her. This meant the family had been without an income—which was already meager—for the last month. From his corner shop in the Old City, Mauna's father's take-home salary was about Rs. 5,000 per month (in purchasing power parity, about US$380). The family owned their home, but had always struggled to make ends meet. The seriousness of Mauna's condition and her insistence that her parents stay by her side had taken a toll. Then her mother said words that stung for a long time afterward: "After the karant, the light has gone out from her eyes." Mauna was alive but this was no bios, just zoë.

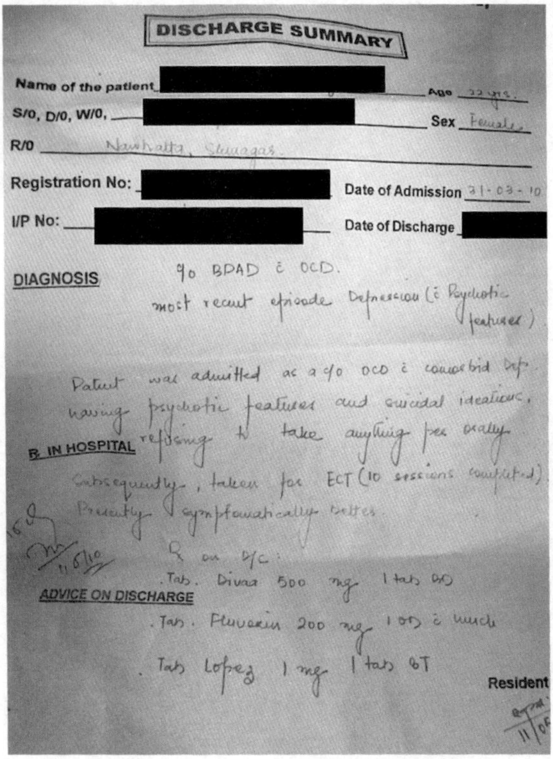

FIGURE 3.1.
Mauna's discharge slip.
Photo by author

∾

For all the talk of community-based care, discharge procedures remained cumbersome because of strained hospital resources. However, Mauna's father's persistence, his pacing outside the perimeter of the nurses' station, finally paid off on Day 54. Dr. Gagan handed over the discharge slip. I left the comfort of the nurse's office to accompany Mauna's father to the family ward.

I felt nervous. How would the "file" Mauna compare with the real person? On entering the ward, Mauna was sitting up, alert, dressed in a pink and purple salwar kameez. Still quite skinny, she was wearing her glasses for the first time in weeks. Her parents introduced me as "Doctor Saiba, Dr. Farah's friend." While her parents gathered their belongings, Mauna and I chatted. I asked what she'd like to do when she got home. She paused, then said, "Some housework, wash my clothes, help my mother with the housework, and then"—she smiled shyly—"maybe watch some TV." The to-do list of a perfect daughter. In this moment, there was a convergence between the file Mauna and the person in front of me. She seemed healthy. *Pt. improved.*

Then, a minute later, the façade came crashing down. Mauna turned to me and asked if I could teach her how to swim. "Will you teach me how to swim? This fear of water, I fear it so much, it's holding me back in life," she said.

Mauna's mother and I exchanged glances. *This talk of water, where was it coming from?* I wrote later in my field notebook. *Why these basic elements of life, water, and fire? Is it their purifying properties? Is it about how they mark life and death?* I never found the answers.

Mauna kept talking frenetically, words flowing out faster than she could keep apace. "Stop talking this way," her mother interjected, speaking in a tone I could not have imagined she possessed, given her otherwise gentle and kind demeanor. Yet I thought I understood why those words needed to be uttered so forcefully. Perhaps Mauna's mother hoped her command, if made powerfully enough, could do things in the world. Perhaps they could stop Mauna's train of thinking and make Mauna better. But as the words left Mauna's mother's lips, so did her strength. I felt she was going to fold into herself, a tight origami flower.

Mauna stopped, looked down at her hands: "I am full of sadness and regret. You can't imagine how bad I feel. My heart is weak; I know it is. I wish I could bear this pain, but I can't."

In locating distress in her heart (*dil*), rather than her brain, Mauna conveyed the limits of psychiatric care and its most valorized treatment, ECT. ECT worked on the brain, but not the heart, the seat of emotions from a Kashmiri perspective.[68] Her statement of having "a weak heart"—one easily susceptible to pain and sadness—after more than fifty days of inpatient care revealed that her treatment was incomplete. Discharge marked an end point to hospital care, but this was not a triumphant return home to her "community." Her face and the faces of her parents were etched with worry.

ψ

Over the next few months, during the summer of 2010, the unrelenting cycle of protests, tear gas, civilian deaths, funerals, and more protests took hold. The streets became battlefields. Middle-class Kashmiris used the English word "turmoil" to describe these conditions—a word that perfectly captures the convergence between the traumatic environment on the streets and upheaval in bodies and psyches.

Among its many effects, turmoil also destroys ethnography. It was not always possible to find an auto-rickshaw to Mauna's neighborhood, located near one of Srinagar's most famous mosques, the austere, amber Jama Masjid, but I tried visiting the family as regularly as I could. The neighborhood sits on one of the city's oldest protest fault lines. Yet whenever I crossed the threshold into Mauna's home—a bright blue door marked by a simply etched "Allah" written on top of the doorframe—I entered a different world.

Mauna did not remember much about her hospitalization. She was surprised to learn that she had had ECT. "How many shocks did I have?" she asked me several times. She looked stunned when I told her. Her memory was fragmented, effects of ECT psychiatrists describe as "unusual" and "temporary."[69] She remembered other things, though. She was studying literature in college before she got sick; Ernest Hemingway's *The Old Man and the Sea* was her favorite novel. I told her I would try to find a copy in one of the bookstores in Lal Chowk. Mauna demurred. She was unsure how much she would remember and if she could pronounce the English words correctly.

I found a copy of the Hemingway and we began reading together. I hoped reading something familiar might help her regain confidence. As we read, she paused frequently and told me that she didn't know this word or that. But she remembered the plot. We read in English first and then together translated into Urdu. During those languid afternoons, Mauna's mother sat beside us, listening, her knees folded near her chest. We moved through the story, sentence by sentence, very slowly. I didn't mind the pace; it was a soothing counterpoint to the fast-paced violence on the streets outside. At one point in the story, the boy tells the old man that he's sorry he left him, but he had to obey his father. Mauna's mother piped up. She reminded Mauna that she, too, should listen to her parents. Mauna responded earnestly that she would try. She "was not doing it—any of it—on purpose," she insisted.

Meanwhile, Mauna still spent most days in bed. She sat up when I came, but sometimes she didn't have the energy. Once or twice, when it was safe and she was feeling up to it, we walked around the neighborhood, Mauna modest in hijab.

ψ

August 21, 2010: *I wanted to visit Mauna today but decided against it. Getting to the Old City was next to impossible, and I was too demoralized (kamzor?) to insist. I spoke to Mauna's father on their landline, the only form of communication that has not been cut. On top of the financial losses incurred by Mauna's illness, he was*

facing months of lagātār bandh—continuous shutdowns—in which all shops, busi-
nesses, schools, and most government offices were closed. Meanwhile, everyone was
awaiting the stomach-churning news of more deaths. During this period of unrest,
shock's other modality—interrogation—reappeared.[70] In addition to more than 100
civilian deaths, more than 5,000 protestors, most of whom were high school or col-
lege students, were arrested and tortured in prison under the emergency Public Safety
Act.[71] This shock certified what the state already knew: that the protests were spon-
sored by Pakistan, that people were protesting only because they had been paid, and
that the protests were not spontaneous but were organized by a terrorist mastermind
somewhere.[72]

ॐ

The next time I went to Mauna's house she was lying on a makeshift bed in the middle of the living room floor, watching the Discovery Channel. She was fascinated by shows about bodily deformities and disfigurements. We watched a program about elephantiasis together. While we were watching, she started asking me questions about swimming again. Could I teach her to swim? Was swimming difficult? Could I show her how to hold her breath under water? She had been practicing holding her breath, diving under the covers until she had to come up for air. My mind raced, thinking of how I could find a swimming pool in Kashmir—the only one I knew was in a five-star hotel. I wondered if swimming lessons might actually help her fear dissipate.

"I really want to learn how to swim. Then this fear of water will go away," Mauna was telling me as her father walked into the room. He looked at her angrily through his glassy blue eyes. "Stop talking like this!" he shouted. "Can't you see how much we are suffering?"

Mauna snapped back: "Can no one understand my helplessness, what I'm going through?!"

"If you don't stop this, we'll put you in the pāgal khānā [asylum], they'll lock you up," he warned.

Mauna yelled back: "Why would I want to hurt myself? You think I'm doing this on purpose?"

I hadn't seen this affective intensity between them before. The threads that bound them were fraying. As Sarah Pinto notes, "mental illness adds vulnerability to the already—and inherently—vulnerable conditions of kinship."[73] This statement reminds us of the burden that mental illnesses, particularly chronic illnesses, place on intimate relations. The effects of both illness and care are not limited to just the "pathological" individual, but are shared.[74] This fact is often represented in community-based models of care as evidence of overcoming stigma and burden sharing, yet it often disguises the difficulties and vulnerabilities that chronic illnesses produce—which may have little or nothing to do with stigma. In Mauna's family's case, I understood her parents' anger not as product of stigma, but as helplessness, a sense of lost agency and an unclear path forward in the aftermath of clinical care. Their anger was not only toward Mauna, but also toward the clinical care that had discharged her without adequately treating her. Her father invoked the hospital as a site of punishment—"we'll send you to the pāgal khānā"—rather than a space of care.

In addition to not curing her, Mauna's parents also felt that doctors had not adequately prepared them for the consequences of ECT. Psychiatrists had insisted that shock would save Mauna's life, and since Mauna was not eating, they were desperate.[75] Initially, after Mauna had regained her appetite, they had felt hopeful. It seemed she was recovering. But her breathless talk, erratic behavior, and inner turmoil continued unabated. Mauna's mother told me she had hoped shock would have provided Mauna a "protective numbing" from the thoughts afflicting her, but ECT had dulled her other senses instead. The effects of the ECT were more than "temporary side effects," as the doctors had described. Since her return home, she had barely left her bed, let alone helped her mother with household chores, as she had dreamed that day in the hospital. They longed for the "old" Mauna to return. They told me this many times: we just want her back as she was before. Her memory loss and the ECT's dulling effects ("the light has gone out from her eyes") made her parents believe shock had unmade Mauna. Mauna's mother feared that without her memory, her daughter was no longer herself. Mauna wasn't her file self, she wasn't her former self, so who was she?

It was not just Mauna's continued illness that was troubling to her parents, but the discrepancy between what doctors had told them and what they were witnessing. By silencing Mauna in the file, shock had produced the illusion of successful, complete treatment that allowed doctors to wash their hands of the case. While Mauna's doctors felt that they had exhausted all options, Mauna's parents felt care had harmed her. Mauna had not received the stability that doctors had promised, the restoration of her former self that they desired, or to be free of pain as Mauna desired. Instead, Mauna's parents found themselves confronting a resurgent illness without help from anyone. It was not that Mauna's family and her doctors had radically different ideas about the outcome of her treatment. Everyone had wanted Mauna to return home. But Mauna's parents realized that the clinicians' priorities, the conditions within which they triaged care, were significantly different from what they wanted.

The lack of trust between Mauna's parents and the hospital indicated a rupture within what Janzen long ago called the "therapy management group," the set of individuals who take charge of treatment with or on behalf of the sufferer.[76] In contrast to the ideals of community-based care, in which institutional abandonment is replaced by care in local and familial settings, the breakdown in the hospital–kin alliance rippled into a breakdown in kin relations. Rather than the scenario feared by mental health experts—an abandoned patient—it was now Mauna's family who was left to deal with the consequences of incomplete care. Far from the "family" or "community" being a site of refuge, they became places riddled with tension. The clinic had infiltrated domestic and intimate spaces, and clinical failures had become embodied as kinship failures.[77]

While mental health experts deny many of the subjective effects of ECT and claim that the difference between modified and unmodified ECT is negligible, Mauna's story conveys a different truth. Perhaps because the aftereffects of ECT are difficult to quantify, or perhaps because those reporting them are not seen as reliable subjects, these experiences are excluded from clinical studies and debates about the technology's "efficacy."

Nonetheless, the effects of unmodified ECT and incomplete clinical care were devastating. ECT alienated Mauna from herself. She expressed this several times: *Do you think I want to be acting like this? Do you think I'm doing this on purpose? My heart is weak.* Mauna highlighted the fragmentation and dissociation wrought by her illness and failed treatment, experiences that are similar to those of torture survivors.[78] In Mauna's case, these dissociations were psychic and social. Mauna felt disconnected from her thoughts and body, but she was also disconnected from her parents, and they from her. Meanwhile, the family was further disconnected from their social world. I worried that these disconnections might result in Mauna's parents turning away from her. I worried her father's threat of returning her to the pāgal khānā would materialize, a strange and tragic boomerang effect of failed community care.

ψ

I didn't hear it, her parents didn't hear it, maybe even Mauna didn't hear it, but a signal was embedded in Mauna's discordant words. A few weeks later, while her mother was bathing, Mauna ran out of the house. She reportedly tried to jump off a bridge into the Jhelum River. Luckily someone stopped her.

A few weeks went by. I went to Delhi, a much-needed breather after months of curfews and shutdowns. The "normal" things felt surreal: I could walk out of the house without seeing bunkers and soldiers, go to a coffee shop, go out after dusk, go to the cinema. The cruelty of withholding these everyday, taken-for-granted aspects of life hit me, how burdensome life becomes when every move, every action, has to be calculated.

When I returned to Kashmir, I visited Mauna's family and learned about another troubling incident that had happened in my absence. After the bridge incident, Mauna had showed small signs of improvement. Since they had been caring for her at home for months now, her parents felt that an outing, a change of scene, might do them some good. A cousin of Mauna's was having an engagement party (*nikāh*) in Batwara, an area outside of Srinagar. The family decided to go.

There, among her extended kin, Mauna felt a "strange" (*ajeeb*) sensation come over her. While hanging out with her cousins, Mauna thought she heard one of them say, referring to her, in English, "She's empty, that's why she makes so much noise." Throughout the day, she heard the phrase come out of the mouths of different relatives, until the voices were unbearable. By evening, Mauna was completely incapacitated, unable to even "drink a cup of tea," her mother said. She begged her parents to return home. They eventually hired a taxi to take them back to Srinagar, arriving home at 1 a.m. Since the conflict began, such late-night travel in Kashmir was rare. Not only was it an extravagant expense for the family, but it also affected her parents' relationships with the extended family, causing more whispers and rumors about Mauna's condition. Later, when Mauna told me about what had transpired, she admitted that the voices she heard had maybe not been real, that they had probably emanated from her mind.

Despite this incident and her parents' occasional threats, they refused to take Mauna back to the hospital. When I asked, they said empathically, "*Nā!* We are done with that place." When I spoke to Dr. Abdul, Mauna's consulting psychiatrist, about Mauna's condition at home, he responded that there were some patients who "simply do not get well, no matter what we try." The statement absolved the hospital of any further responsibility. It also revealed the contradictions inherent in community-based care: Would care mean rehospitalizing Mauna, or would that be a sign of abandonment? When did familial "responsibility" shade into "burden," and who defined those boundaries? Although community-based treatment was designed to shift care into the community, it had led to Mauna and her parents' abandonment. The situation reminds us, once again, of the inadequacy of pregiven moral assumptions about care/abandonment, community/institution, freedom/constraint, and normal/abnormal.[79] Shock had done its work. But what kind of life was Mauna being offered?

ॐ

Women like Mauna who have received copious ECT usually live tucked away in their homes or in closed, dark, institutional settings. By contrast, those who have been tortured with shock often become spectacles. In the novel *The Collaborator*, the author describes how the bodies of torture survivors become sites of public, ritual visitation: "For three weeks, Gul's house became a shrine. Every day somebody came to visit, to see the boy returned from army detention, to see what had happened to him, to check his torture marks, and then to sigh loudly and wish him all the best of health, while also secretly thanking God, I guessed, that it hadn't been their son."[80]

The scene powerfully conveys how shock has permeated the social in Kashmir. Not only does everyone know who has been tortured, but the body of the torture survivor becomes public property, a site for "bearing witness" to state harm, but also for forensic examination. These visitations, however, take their toll. Gul's body is doubly alienated: first through torture, and now by the prurient gazes of neighbors.

What does the aftermath of care look like? Like Mauna, Gul is home, but he is not himself. Like Mauna, his body holds more than just the physical marks of torture; it carries a "stink."[81] While Mauna's body does not become a public memorial in the way Gul's does, her family, too, carries a "stink," the intangible reverberations of shock and incomplete clinical care. While mainstream biological psychiatry locates the effects and efficacy of shock in the individual body, these examples reveal how their effects are social. Both distress and care can sever people's social worlds. Rather than make patients whole, functional, or complete, military or humanitarian care can unmake subjects and kin relatedness.[82]

Shock, a form of clinical care, becomes harmful not only because of its cultural and political associations with torture, but also because of how it is bartered, triaged, and rationed in clinical settings. Harm consists of not only inflicting specific forms of physical violence—such as administering ECT without anesthesia—on patients like Mauna, but also the "layered dissolutions" produced by pragmatic clinical logics (some ECT is better than

FIGURE 3.2.
Ectlectrc Pencil by
James Edward
Deeds Jr.

none).[83] Mauna's case raises troubling questions about the difference between torture in prisons and shock in psychiatric care, and whether the latter is not defined as torture simply because it is done in the name of care.

This tension is not easily fixed by calling for the law to be implemented and for ending the use of unmodified ECT. Rather, at stake is a more fundamental, ontological problem in clinical knowing, one that deprioritizes and delegitimizes the experiences of patients like Nasir and Mauna, and which denies that medical technologies do much more than simply intervene in a person's neurobiological capacities.

ψ

I do not have an ending for Mauna's story, because it has not ended. So I offer something else: a drawing called *Ectlectrc Pencil*. In 1950, when he was twenty-five years old, James Deeds was admitted to State Hospital No. 3, an asylum in Nevada, Missouri, where he was subjected to ECT, once or twice a week, for thirty-seven years.[84] During his institutionalization, Deeds drew prolifically, using the material of asylum authority—pages torn from case files and ledgers—as his canvas.

For years, people assumed that the misspelling of the word *electric* in the drawing's title was an effect of his dyslexia, but later they noticed the misspelling was a cryptogram, ECT rendered twice.[85] Deeds's drawings are palimpsestic, overwriting shock with something else. *Ectlectrc Pencil* shows a young woman, her eyes wide, astonished at the flowers which are blue and orange and yellow. Electric. Deeds's work shows how people reclaim their bodies—after ECT, interrogation, torture, and violence. I hear echoes of Mauna's efforts at reclaiming herself: her objections, her seeking out the source of her pain, her desire to forget, even her desire to escape.

CHAPTER 4

Debrief

> But around her, the air was sad, somehow. And behind the smile in her eyes,
> the Grief was a fresh, shining blue. Because of a calamitous car crash. Because
> of a Joe-shaped hole in the universe.
> —Arundhati Roy, *The God of Small Things*

Care encounters come to a close, sometimes too soon. But how do we know
when humanitarian care meets its stated goals? What counts as care, and
how is care counted? In this chapter, we turn away from the psychiatric
hospital to another site of care—NGOs providing psychosocial care that
have been combating Kashmir's epidemic of trauma since the early 2000s.
Psychosocial care refers to nonbiological and nonpharmacological interventions, such as counseling or psychotherapy, and has become one of the most
popular forms of medical humanitarianism globally.

Humanitarian organizations in Kashmir conceptualize psychosocial care
as distinct from and as counteracting the harms of both public health care
and militarism. As we saw in the public health system in chapter 2, Kashmiris held widespread concerns about how a culture of impunity stemming
from emergency laws had infiltrated medicine, making it less accountable,
ethical, and responsive to patients' needs. By contrast, humanitarian NGOs
stake their ethics of care on demonstrating accountability to their beneficiaries and quantifying the impact of their work.[1] Quantitative data, such
as surveys and censuses, have historically been ways that governments see,
order, and care for their citizenry. Now, these tools are being used to fulfill
new ethical obligations, such as the need for humanitarian organizations to
produce transparent, replicable, efficacious, and culturally appropriate interventions.[2] As humanitarian interventions have become more complex,
expectations from both donors and recipients have shifted, forcing organizations to develop more elaborate procedures for measuring and standardizing
their work. In other words, now, humanitarian NGOs must give equal weight
to treating distress *and* evaluating their treatments.

To "count" care, humanitarian organizations will often interview or survey recipients to determine whether or not the organization and the aid received have positively benefited them. At least theoretically, this means recipients can have a voice in crafting future interventions, because they can provide feedback to the organization as to more or less effective strategies. These postintervention evaluations, sometimes called "debriefings," help subvert long-standing tropes in development and humanitarian practices that aid recipients are hapless, silent victims.[3]

However, like the other technologies we've encountered in this book, debriefing is also a shared military and humanitarian technology. Military debriefings occur after a mission has been completed to determine what information can be released to the public and what must be withheld. Psychosocial organizations and the disciplines of psychology and psychiatry have borrowed the language of debriefing to describe and evaluate the psychological support a community receives after a traumatic experience. However, much like military debriefings, humanitarian debriefings also reveal how processes of knowledge gathering *and* withholding are both central to the work of care.

Though measuring impact has become a necessity for humanitarian organizations, it is a Herculean task. It requires organizations to "[define] impact, specify their goals, translate them into measurable indicators, gather data in unstable emergency settings, establish a baseline to generate a 'before and after' snapshot, control for alternative explanations and variables, and construct reasonable counterfactual scenarios."[4] While these goals are already challenging, they are made even more difficult when applied to psychosocial care, which, as a relatively recent addition to humanitarian aid, lacks the established mechanisms and standards of care in other fields of humanitarian assistance.[5]

For example, although MSF incorporates psychosocial care into more than forty of its projects globally, Kashmir had one of very few programs that were exclusively focused on psychosocial care.[6] Further, unlike other forms of distress, psychiatric distress is not always visually discernible.[7] While wars or epidemics have countable parameters—such as casualties, numbers of vaccines or antiretroviral drugs delivered—psychological distress is often nebulous and a product of slow, longue durée violence (chapter 1). Unlike other cases of mass trauma, where individuals or communities, such as refugees, might be removed from the site of trauma, in Kashmir, organizations had to provide psychosocial care in the midst of long-term conflict. This complicated how and if organizations could set a mental health baseline. For example, what did it mean to be mentally well in a context of long-term conflict?

What was wellness when everyone was kamzor and when claims of illness had political significance and were tied to critiques of occupation?

Nonetheless, many organizations and aid workers welcomed these challenges, as well as the new culture of accountability. Some felt their new, more professional, bureaucratic role helped ground them when chaotic and violent situations erupted.[8] However, these new demands also expanded the meaning and work of care for which humanitarian organizations were responsible. It shifted humanitarian care away from its origins in good intentions, the right ethical orientation, or alleviating suffering in the moment. Instead, care became about proving that the organization had met the needs of recipients, who could, in turn, acknowledge improvement.

While ostensibly done in the name of care—to make organizations more efficient, transparent, and accountable—processes of evaluation produced "tensions in practice" in humanitarian work. These tensions occurred at several different scales: between providing care and accounting, measuring, and enumerating that care; between organizations' commitments to psychosocial care and the needs their recipients recognized and wanted; and between instruments of measurement (such as surveys) and the messy, intersubjective encounters in which those measurements are gathered.

Humanitarian NGOs were ostensibly caught between opposing aims. In her work on migrant care in Italy, Cristiana Giordano usefully distinguishes between two outcomes of state or nonstate interventions: "recognition" and "acknowledgment." She describes recognition as creating techniques or categories—such as "victim of human trafficking" or a PTSD diagnosis—that "make the social world intelligible to the state" and determine who is worthy of care. By contrast, acknowledgment is "the political and ethical act of surrendering the desire to know through already established categories" while embracing "the possibility of not knowing, not understanding, and thus embracing uncertainty."[9] The psychosocial organizations with whom I worked in Kashmir were engaged in practices of recognition through measuring and evaluating their work and surveying their recipients, but they were also committed to acknowledgment. As we saw in chapter 2, many embraced techniques of nonjudgmental listening and withholding diagnosis so as to avoid pathologizing their clients, tools they used to positively distinguish their work from the psychiatry practiced in public health settings.

At other moments, however, humanitarian organizations failed to achieve either recognition or acknowledgment. Despite the efforts of humanitarian organizations to translate the lived experiences of victims of violence into tidy, mobile packages of knowledge, such as numbers and percentages, there were experiences and knowledge of violence that emerged as irreducible and untranslatable. Encounters between aid recipients and aid workers were often sites of layered miscommunications and mistranslations because both had radically different expectations of care and were under different kinds of pressure. While accountability measures, such as surveys, were explicitly designed to bridge this gap, in many ways they widened it. They brought to the surface the tenuous knowledge practices and unpredictable relations that underpin psychosocial care work.

To be clear, in foregrounding these tensions, my aim is not to critique humanitarian organizations for failing to achieve their objectives. Neither is this only a story about how deserving subjects are excluded from care through arbitrary determinations of worthiness. While these have been important contributions to the anthropology of humanitarianism, the tensions of practice and incommensurabilites that I tracked in psychosocial humanitarian work were not because aid organizations were careless, callous, or inattentive to local cultural contexts. Rather, the incommensurabilities reveal the significant relational, epistemological, and methodological challenges of doing and evaluating psychosocial work.

ψ

Humanitarian NGOs—including MSF, Action Aid International, and Kashmir LifeLine—provide nonpharmaceutical psychosocial care to victims of violence in Kashmir, in the form of counseling, nonjudgmental listening, and psychotherapy. While they never directly confronted the Indian military's role in causing mass psychological distress (because doing so would have likely led to their expulsion from the region), these methods were *indirect* ways of critiquing the Indian state's denials of its own history of violence. For example, while the state ignored, dismissed or obscured reports of human rights abuses, psychosocial organizations built trusting relationships with their clients through empathetic listening and painstaking documentation. In other words, the epidemiological surveys, interviews, reports, workshops, camps, radio shows and one-on-one, free counseling they offered were ways of acknowledging, measuring, detailing, and treating the effects of occupation. As vectors of biopower, humanitarian organizations nourished life while state necropower extinguished it.[10]

Humanitarian NGOs also defined the care they offered against public mental health care. As one aid worker put it, public mental health care was "overly pharmaceuticalized," overburdened, and under-resourced. While

FIGURE 4.1. Kashmir LifeLine.
Source: Kashmir LifeLine

psychiatrists employed in the public health system might spend only five minutes with each patient, counselors in humanitarian NGOs scheduled between thirty minutes and an hour for each counseling session. Unlike public health settings, which did not guarantee confidentiality to patients, psychosocial organizations held closed sessions to maintain their clients' privacy. As Kashmir LifeLine (KLL), a humanitarian organization funded through a UK-based charity, describes on its website: "Unfortunately, psychiatrists in Kashmir often experience such an overload of patients that they are unable to spend the time to properly diagnose and ensure continuity of patient care." However, through one-on-one counseling, KLL's counselors could "devote time and energy to fully understanding the stories of our patients."[11] KLL provided care that was "free, confidential and anonymous."

In 2010, KLL inaugurated an anonymous telephone helpline, the first of its kind in Kashmir. The organization argued that the helpline could redress some of the problems patients face in accessing mental health services, such as social stigma in accessing a psychiatric hospital, the difficulty of reaching a clinic during curfews and strikes, and the lack of confidentiality in crowded OPD settings. Although Lisa Stevenson's work on suicide prevention programs by the Canadian state for Inuit communities has shown that anonymity is not always a form of care, in Kashmir, where mentally ill patients generally kept their treatments secret from extended kin and friends, anonymity was crucial.[12]

Further, KLL emphasized how its approach to empathetic listening worked against the culture of surveillance and mistrust perpetuated by the Indian state:

A helpline staffed by highly trained listeners . . . offers anonymity and total confidentiality. This is particularly powerful in a society where it is hard for people to be able to speak in private about the emotional and mental problems that they are facing. This project is also targeting a sector of Kashmiri youth that feels disenfranchised and disempowered by the situation in the state. One of the fundamental issues is that these young people do not feel they are being heard, and therefore in some cases, they resort to violence. . . . A helpline that allows callers to talk, and that guides them towards examining their frustrations and fears, has been proven one of the most effective ways of breaking through this youth sector.[13]

Unlike the Indian state, which characterized protestors and stone throwers in Kashmir as "miscreants" and subjected them to punitive security provisions, organizations like KLL understood their frustration and anger as an effect of their disenfranchisement and disempowerment. They also saw their work as explicitly political: as mediating the mistrust between Kashmir's youth and the Indian state.

There was, however, a major impediment to these efforts to enact psychosocial care. Most Kashmiris were unaccustomed to techniques such as psychotherapy and counseling. In contrast, biomedical and pharmaceutical treatments (*davai*) were extremely popular and widely culturally accepted. For example, whenever I visited people's homes and the conversation turned to illness, the drugs people were consuming would be duly fanned out before me, along with the adage, "Everyone is a patient in Kashmir." Illness was expressed through material things: pills, medical records, tonics, and syrups. Meanwhile, psychosocial care and the theories underpinning it—such as narrating a traumatic experience in order to gain relief from it—were unfamiliar to most Kashmiris. Intimate conversations about loss and pain were generally reserved for kin, and grief was meant to overflow in the quiet inner sanctums of a home, shrine, or mosque, not in a cold institutional setting, in front of someone younger and less experienced (most counselors were in their twenties and thirties).

For humanitarian organizations, the stakes of this misrecognition of psychosocial care were high. Because new measures of accountability meant that aid recipients were required to evaluate the quality of care they received, humanitarian organizations had to make psychosocial care recognizable as therapeutic, appropriate, and effective. This was a laborious task, requiring counselors to take out precious time during one-on-one sessions to explain how counseling and psychotherapy worked. In other words, psychosocial organizations had to "educate" their clients, as they put it. Because client evaluations were so critical to determining their efficacy, organizations began prioritizing "awareness-raising" and "educative" programs over providing treatment. Yet despite these efforts, counseling sessions often ended with clients asking, "Can I have my medications now?"[14] This question revealed how the ideology behind psychotherapy had not displaced preexisting ideas about care. In psychosocial care, clients were meant to feel relief simply through narrating their suffering—a process many found unfamiliar and also, occasionally, ineffective. They were more comfortable with a model of care based on exchange, such as in public health settings and sites of religious healing, where people receive a prescription (*parchī*), pharmaceuticals, medicines, amulets, or blessed food in return for being a patient or client. Lacking these "material embodiments of transaction," talk therapy was unrecognizable as care.[15]

Rather than view psychosocial care within a rich cultural ecology of other care practices, many humanitarian organizations felt clients' misunderstandings about psychosocial care were a result of "superstitious" or "backward" ideas that needed to be changed. Like the Indian military, they too were engaged in changing—and winning—hearts and minds. They developed a range of awareness-raising and educative programs so their clients could better understand the gifts they were receiving *as* gifts. These programs were not in the wheelhouse for many humanitarian organizations; after all, emergency medical relief, such as providing clean drinking water and food, does not require any awareness-raising. These efforts demanded more humanitarian evangelism but offered less moral clarity.[16] Yet, the stakes were incredibly high. The future of their projects depended on it.

ψ

Even organizations like MSF—one of the largest and most well funded medical humanitarian organizations in the world, and one of the most influential NGOs in Kashmir—struggled to balance their goal of treating and alleviating psychological suffering with raising awareness about psychosocial care.

MSF began its project in Kashmir in 2001 with the aim of providing "free, highly quality counseling" to victims of state violence who were experiencing psychological distress. On its website, MSF explained the rationale for its project in Kashmir: "Years of conflict in Jammu and Kashmir have taken a toll on people's mental health in the state. According to a survey conducted by MSF in 2015, nearly 45% of the adult population [about 1.8 million people] in the Kashmir Valley show symptoms of significant mental distress. This is compounded by the stigma associated with mental illness."[17] Just as MSF publicizes the numbers of vaccinations given in its emergency relief projects, it stated on its Kashmir website that it had conducted almost four thousand individual counseling sessions. Here, once again, psychosocial care was firmly situated within the logic of emergency, aid and counseling was given an injection of efficacy in the structural comparison with vaccinations.

Despite its numerical success—the sheer number of clients being treated was, indeed, impressive—organizations like MSF had to address the fact that "mental health is not well known in Kashmir," as one aid worker put it. Another described the organization's work as "breaking the myth," or as undoing the false beliefs, stigma, and superstitions Kashmiris held toward mental illness, including that it is caused by madness, the intrusive presence of malevolent spirits, or somatic symptoms, and requires the intervention of a religious healers (pīrs).[18] To establish their positive impact on the epidemic of trauma in Kashmir, humanitarian organizations could not simply count the number of people served. They had to ensure that psychosocial care was recognizable and legible to recipients, so that those recipients could articulate how and to what extent they had been helped. As one of MSF's project managers described, they had to make psychosocial care a need "that Kashmiris themselves felt."

Humanitarian organizations developed creative strategies to transform how Kashmiris saw and treated mental distress. Some, like Action Aid International, "smuggled" psychosocial care within general health care by offering free community health camps, which included mental health and psychosocial components. MSF had a more expansive strategy. It conducted mental health camps, publicity campaigns, and even developed a radio soap opera about mental health called *Hello, Brother, Hello* (*Alaw Baya Alaw*), which has been on air since 2005. The radio show has examined topics ranging from substance abuse to familial disputes to grief and loss. It is structured around conversations between two characters: a young, educated woman named Yasmin, who is seen as having the "right" and "modern" approach to mental health, and her older male relation, Mir Sahab, who is seen as having the "old" and "backward" approach. In one show about loss, Yasmin and Mir Sahab are sitting on the porch of their house when another man walks past. Mir Sahab comments that the man is walking "strangely, talking to himself, he must be mad [mot]." Yasmin asks why he says this, noting the man has perhaps lost someone in the conflict. "Everyone is affected," she says.[19]

The show displaces indigenous notions of madness in favor of a psychological understanding of the relation between an event (past trauma) and a behavior (talking to oneself). However, in placing Yasmin as having the "right" perspective, it also does much more than this. It reverses social hierarchies and norms of respect based on age; whereas in Kashmiri society, elders are repositories of knowledge and cultural values, here the younger (female) character embodies the more enlightened perspective. The show thus not only introduces audiences to new information about psychosocial distress; it also reconfigures gendered, familial, and cultural norms and subjectivities.

In other words, beyond delivering care, MSF and other psychosocial organizations were selling a worldview: Kashmiris needed to be psychologically and culturally transformed before they could be properly cared for. What was left unsaid was that this transformation was necessary for the organization to demonstrate its efficacy.

&

One of MSF's flagship public awareness-raising events was its annual celebration of World Mental Health Week and World Mental Health Day (October 10). One October morning, on my way to the OPD at the psychiatric hospital, I noticed posters advertising MSF's public events during Mental Health Week.[20] In 2009, World Mental Health Day fell on a Friday (*jummā*), the Day of Assembly for Muslims.

Every Friday in Kashmir, the workday ends after noon, when mosques sound the call to prayer. All across the city, fathers take infant sons by the hand and head toward neighborhood mosques, wearing complementary large and miniature fez caps and salwars, the flapping of large and mini–flip flops an irregular percussion beat. Sometimes the little ones skip along happily; sometimes they squirm. Outside mosques, young and old untie their shoelaces, remove their socks, rinse hands and arms, and partake in *wudu*, the ritualized washing of the most polluted parts of the body, before disappearing inside for prayers. NGOs generally avoided scheduling activities or programs on Fridays because these were days of congregation, prayer, and political protest. Some *imams* were known to make politically charged sermons, and religious assemblies often transfigured into protest assemblies. But because the date of World Mental Health Day was fixed, the incommensurability between the religious and global health calendars stood.

I arrived at MSF's camp in a park in the upper-middle-class neighborhood of Jawahar Nagar in the late afternoon. The juxtaposition between the camp—with its focus on Western techniques of mental health care—and the lilting tones of the weekly sermon (*khutbah*) flowing out of the mosque's loudspeakers was striking. Two very different forms of care, side by side. A giant marquee had been set up, covering nearly the entire park, and MSF's staff—both expatriate and local—strolled among the crowds, standing out in their white coats emblazoned with the organization's fiery logo.[21] The turnout at the camp was good, even though it was a Friday. I walked through the different rooms that had been partitioned. In one, actors performed mini-plays on a makeshift stage, acting out domestic dramas of how people might identify and relate to mentally ill kin. Another room displayed the results of a children's art and poetry competition sponsored by MSF. Some of the pieces had been awarded prizes—blue ribbons for the best work. I wondered what was being rewarded—the most vivid account of suffering or the most vivid account of overcoming it. In the last room, a video of the emergency relief that MSF provided after the 2005 earthquake played on a loop. Clumps of people (mostly men) moved through the exhibition space together. I realized, for the first time, the implicit, individualistic order of art in galleries and museum spaces.

The camp revealed how MSF as an organizational structure—not its recipients—conceptualized its positive impact in Kashmir. Statistics abounded—more than two thousand individual consultations held; 60 percent of first visits were women; and 34 percent of first visits were from people between the ages of twenty and twenty-nine. Through these quantitative tools, the organization reinforced its reach, its success as an access point for care. These statistics were animated by tasteful photos of MSF's counselors (in focus) providing relief to anonymous patients (out of focus). By blurring or concealing patients' faces (to protect their identities) and focusing on the faces of the counselors instead, the photos reinforced MSF's agentive role in healing Kashmir's trauma. By spotlighting experts, the photos and the camp conveyed confidence and hope: a medical crisis had been identified and was being mitigated; mental illnesses were treatable; and people's suffering could be understood and ethically treated. Perhaps less intentionally, these photos also produced a population in need: a large but ill-defined traumatized cohort. Through the camp, Kashmiris were being taught to recognize MSF's gifts. Their reward for doing so? Recognition in the form of counseling, psychotherapy, and new vocabularies of distress.

While humanitarian organizations like MSF are expert at setting up camps like this, this camp was both like and unlike the organization's other educative camps. Like the faux refugee camps that MSF regularly displays to New Yorkers or Parisians that Peter Redfield has described, the camp in Srinagar allowed audiences to gaze at suffering from a distance. The experience of being or living in a humanitarian emergency (in this case, mental illness) was mediated by the organization, its experts, and its unflappable care.[22] However, whereas model refugee camps produce difference—they are usually directed at donors or potential volunteers who marvel or gaze with horror at life in faraway places—the mental health camp in Srinagar produced proximity, since the targets and audience of the camp were one and the same. Instead of being directed toward future aid workers by eliciting feelings of anger, outrage, or compassion, the camp was designed to subjectively transform aid recipients. Kashmiris were being taught about themselves. They were being taught that they were a population in distress and that letting go of their incorrect beliefs and embracing a Western methodology could positively transform their lives, bringing them recognition *and* acknowledgment.

As much as the camp was a carefully curated site of knowledge production, it was also a site of knowledge concealment. MSF did not reveal how it had arrived at these certainties about its own efficacy, its mastery, and containment of violence and suffering. In the camp's dramaturgy, psychosocial care was stripped of all relational thickness and ambiguity. So, how did recipients themselves respond to psychosocial care?

ψ

In addition to awareness-raising programs, to "maximize" their impact, organizations such as MSF and Action Aid International focused on identifying and treating "the most vulnerable" individuals and families in the population. They argued that focusing on those suffering from traumatic and post-traumatic symptoms was the best use of their time and resources.[23] For psychosocial humanitarian organizations, the diagnosis of PTSD was highly useful, both clinically and socially, because it immediately established recipients' degree of vulnerability and need.[24] Further, PTSD victim-survivors belong to a globally recognized, legitimate category. Thus, by limiting their interventions on PTSD victim-survivors, organizations could produce usable and comparative data.

In Kashmir, humanitarian organizations felt those most likely to be suffering from trauma and PTSD symptoms were families of the disappeared, of militants, or others killed in encounters. In other words, there was a large overlap between subjects of humanitarian aid and human rights.[25] In addition to treating these vulnerable populations with psychotherapy and counseling, humanitarian NGOs also targeted them for evaluative surveys and impact assessments, surmising that those most in need would be most likely to reflect positively on the NGO's work.

However, despite organizations' attempts to establish clear parameters of vulnerability and need, they struggled to demonstrate their positive impact and efficacy. This was because there was a profound mismatch between the organization's priorities and recipients' needs. Rather than modes of accumulating knowledge, impact assessment tools became sites of two-way miscommunications and misunderstandings between experts and recipients. They revealed how processes of knowledge gathering—no matter how "scientific" and rational—can be fraught and incomplete. In the end, these tools produced uncertain and unsatisfying outcomes for both aid workers and recipients. Surprisingly, and contrary to most anthropological analyses of humanitarian encounters, they revealed how these tools operated as more significant modes of recognition for aid workers than recipients.[26]

In 2010, Action Aid International was asked by its donor agency, the European Commission Humanitarian Aid Office (ECHO), to evaluate its project and determine whether it should be renewed. A few years earlier, the organization had received a €2 million, multiyear grant to help "the most vulnerable people overcome their traumatic experiences and provide them with better health conditions."[27] The organization's main focus was on providing psychosocial care to victims of violence, but it supplemented this with livelihood support and emergency relief kits when necessary.[28] Like MSF, Action Aid followed what its project administrator, Sohaib, described as a "community-based, decentralized, destigmatized, psychosocial model" of care. Unlike MSF, which hired counselors with graduate and postgraduate degrees in psychology, social work, and related disciplines, Action Aid hired high school graduates, arguing that they were more likely to be embedded in their own communities. This policy gave the organization the reputation of being more "grassroots" than MSF. Also, unlike MSF, which had a two-tiered hierarchy of expatriate and national staff, all of Action Aid's staff was national (Kashmiri). While MSF worked in public hospitals, Action Aid was committed to "establishing coping structures in the community itself," Sohaib told me.

As with many of these evaluations, ECHO asked Action Aid to survey its clients or beneficiaries to gauge the organization's effectiveness. A successful survey, from Action Aid's perspective, had to show that the organization had reached the "most vulnerable," that they felt their health condition had improved, and that they were willing to articulate this positive experience in the survey. Yet the organization also wanted to show there was more work to be done, so that the project—and the livelihoods of Action Aid's staff—could continue. The staff was understandably nervous about achieving all these goals. To maintain neutrality and objectivity, they hired an independent team of journalists to conduct the survey. I was given permission to tag along.

I waited at the central bus stop in Srinagar, the agreed location. It was 9 a.m. on a Thursday morning in April, rainy and cold. I was particular about the time because humanitarian NGOs like Action Aid and MSF abide by European standards of punctuality, which is to say, there was a steep learning curve for the counselors and me, fodder for many jokes shared in Urdu, outside the linguistic capabilities of the organization's expatriate administrators. As expected, the organization's white SUV appeared within two minutes. It was packed with two counselors, five members of the survey team, and the driver. One of the counselors graciously scooted toward the front of the seat and created space out of nothing. I had finally learned how to sit properly in a crowded taxi: someone shuffled to the front of the seat, someone else squeezed in the back, front back, front back, like a jigsaw puzzle.

After a bumpy two-hour ride, we arrived in a picturesque village cradled in a mountain range in Tral district. It was still raining, but less vigorously. Once we disembarked from the SUV, I could hear each raindrop's sound reverberating on the tin roofs of the houses. The paddy fields were verdant and pregnant with muddy water; the narrow alleyways cutting through the village were flooded. Our sandals made squishy sounds as we walked. I followed clumsily behind the team, umbrella in one hand, the other hitching up my salwar just above the ankles so it didn't get soaked. Norms of modesty made me hyperaware of the skin I was revealing above my ankles. Action Aid's "para counselors," as they are officially called, expertly led us through the unfamiliar streets and into the homes of client after client, never knocking on a wrong door.

One of the houses we visited was a large, well-built structure. The client was a woman in her forties named Saleema. After exchanging some brief pleasantries, Saleema, who was accompanied by her teenage daughter and son, took us to a shed at the back of the house. We were all crammed inside the small storage space, filled to capacity with sacks of rice. In times past, when the only connection between the Kashmir Valley and the outside world was a single-carriage road that would get snowed out in the winter months, Kashmiris pickled and stored dried vegetables like eggplant, tur-

FIGURE 4.2. Tral district after the rain. Photo by author

nips, cauliflowers, and gourds (*hokh suin*) in rooms like this. These techniques of storage were repurposed for protracted curfews and strikes, when bazaars could be closed for months on end. "No one will ever starve in Kashmir," people joked. But these sites of agentive resistance were also sites of state violence. Sieges and other counterinsurgency techniques had penetrated intimate domestic spaces. Soldiers with their polished black boots had invaded these spaces, looking for ammunition and militants hidden under piles of dried red chilies, pepper, and black cardamom.

For Saleema and her kin, the storeroom was a more immediate site of loss and violence. Saleema said that this was where her husband was killed in an encounter with paramilitary forces two years earlier. Suddenly, I noticed the walls above us were full of small, perfectly formed round holes; it took me a minute to realize they were bullet holes. One of her daughters said quietly that she didn't like coming in here, where the "wounds" (*zakhm*) were still visible. From a pile of clothes kept neatly folded in the corner, Saleema gingerly took out a *pheran*—a long, woolen coat worn by Kashmiris in the wintertime—which her husband was wearing when he was killed. The pheran was bloodstained and also had round holes in it.[29]

Majid, the head surveyor, began the evaluation. After the initial questions about name, age, members of the family, and income, the survey asked respondents to quantify their trauma—in the form of sleep disturbances, anxiety, direct or indirect experiences of violence—on a scale of one to ten.[30] The questions focused on whether recipients had witnessed or experienced sexual violence, torture, imprisonment, or killings. Had Saleema ever seen someone arrested in the village? Tortured? Killed? Did she have insomnia? How much anxiety had she experienced? How disturbed, on a scale of one to ten, was her sleep?

The survey was printed out in English and was spontaneously translated into Kashmiri by Majid. By now, he had translated the survey several times, but each time he varied the questions slightly. The survey questions were meant to take people's embodied experiences of violence, turn them into psychological symptoms, and then quantify those symptoms according to severity. However, several questions were met with long pauses from Saleema and other clients we interviewed. Rather than enhancing our understanding of Saleema's experiences after her husband's death, each question seemed to enlarge the gap between Majid and Saleema. Rather than gathering information, the survey unraveled it. For example, when asked about sleep disturbances, Saleema responded that she had no complaints of insomnia, although she felt troubled while awake. Majid was unsure how to capture this response in the survey, which had no space for qualitative descriptions. Instead, he went back and changed Saleema's answer to an earlier question about anxiety. When Majid asked again about how anxious or worried she felt on a daily basis, Saleema pointed to her head: "Look," she said, "my hair has turned white."

Majid's pen hovered above the paper; I'm not sure what he wrote, but his hesitation suggested a struggle to translate Saleema's response into a number.

The next section of the survey focused on the organization's work and the quality of care Saleema had received from Action Aid. This was the more critical part of the survey as far as the organization was concerned, since it measured its impact on recipients. Majid asked about the organization's role after her husband's death. Saleema said the organization had given the family an emergency relief kit—a ten-kilogram bag of rice, lentils, and some blankets—soon after he was killed. She did not mention the counseling she received, even though the counselors who had previously visited her were present, and even though the organization's primary focus was psychosocial care. In fact, Majid had to ask Saleema if she had actually received counseling from the two young men standing in the corner.

"Do you know them? They came to talk to you?" Majid asked, waving his pen in the direction of the counselors.

Saleema nodded. When Majid asked Saleema how helpful the counseling was, Saleema did not answer. Instead, she said: "Actually, we would like to receive something." "Thing" was a euphemism for financial assistance.

Majid responded, quickly, "We are not a government agency or anything like that."

It was after we had been in Saleema's storage room for half an hour that Majid finally explained the purpose of the survey to her. He said the team was trying to assess "the damage done" from her husband's death. Majid, of course, meant psychological damage. But Saleema pointed to the bullet-ridden wall behind her.

"See this wall? It is like a sieve," she said. "The question is, do we fix this wall, or do we take care of our children?"

"Thank Allah [Alhamdulillah] you are all right," Majid replied. I had heard this phrase said countless times as a source of comfort, but now it felt dismissive.

Saleema continued, as if she hadn't heard him, "There is no door, there are no windows, nothing is intact."

"You must thank Allah for what you have," Majid said, more forcefully.

The interview ended shortly after this exchange. After declining Saleema's and her mother-in-law's repeated pleas to have nun chai, we shuffled back into the SUV. Once we were all seated, Majid began scolding the counselors.

"Why did you bring us to this house?" he demanded.

"But you wanted to meet our clients," one of the counselors responded, a hesitant question mark hanging at the end of his statement.

Majid said, "Saleema is not needy enough. Her children are studying, look at the condition of her house, it is well built. She's not the kind of victim we are looking for."

ॐ

We go, but the bullet-ridden walls remain.

In contrast to the self-contained world of the camp, or the many accounts we have of "needy" recipients out in the field, it was humanitarian organizations who depended on their recipients for validation. Saleema could not, or would not, convert her embodied experiences of violence into the language of the survey, which was based on PTSD symptomology and a quantification of lived experience. This produced a crisis of fit ("she is not the kind of victim we are looking for") and efficacy for Action Aid. Ironically, evaluation tools meant to help humanitarian NGOs become more effective, responsive, and attentive to their recipients were threatening to undermine these organizations.

Saleema was not alone in her failure—or refusal—to speak in the language of the survey. In other survey interviews I witnessed, many others could also not answer the survey questions. For example, the same day we visited Saleema, we interviewed another woman from a Gujar household whose son, a militant, had been killed. When Majid asked her age, she shrugged and said, "somewhere between sixty and eighty." Majid shot his colleague an amused look and wrote "65" on the survey form. Other questions were even more illegible to interviewees: "On a scale of one to ten, how disturbed is your sleep?" was one that all interviewees failed to answer. Additionally, Majid struggled to translate many of Saleema's complaints—her white hair, the bullet holes, the bloodstained pheran—into numbers and degrees of distress. As the surveyor, not only did Majid have to translate and quantify Saleema's experience; he also had to capture Action Aid in a favorable light.

Majid's frustration erupted in the car. As unsettling as Majid's outburst was, it was also understandable given that establishing need and efficacy from uncertain and messy intersubjective encounters like these was nearly impossible. The perfect aid recipient had to demonstrate their abjection through conforming to PTSD symptomology, but not present themselves as so abject that they were beyond improvement.

While surveys are considered rational instruments of truth and objectivity, the encounter between Saleema and Majid showed that processes of collecting data can be affectively intense and fraught. While we imagine most humanitarian encounters as primarily involving sentiments of pity and compassion, this encounter produced a different emotional constellation. An affective exchange took place, but it included Saleema's frustration and anguish at Action Aid and Majid withholding, not extending, compassion to her, a recognized "victim of violence." Anthropologists have critiqued aid encounters for producing hierarchies between "subjects"—aid workers who represent the suffering of others in front of the world—and "objects"—recipients who are rendered voiceless and helpless victims.[31] Yet Majid and Saleema's encounter did not result in a clearly defined subject/object hierarchy. It produced murkier circumstances in which neither received exactly what they wanted; both were partly defined by each other, but also partly eluded each other.

The miscommunication and misrecognition did not flow one way—it was mutual. Unlike other cases, it was not an effect of a lack of local or cultural knowledge. Both Majid and Saleema are Kashmiri, yet their cultural proximity did not lead to a more empathetic encounter.[32] In fact, Majid used cultural platitudes—such as Alhamdulillah—to *dismiss*, rather than recognize, Saleema's request for financial aid.

This encounter revealed an incommensurability between two ways of counting care and harm. The regime of therapy reached its limit with clients like Saleema. Just as Action Aid was desperate to turn donor euros into an efficacious psychosocial care program with measurable results, recipients like Saleema were also looking for material, quantitative validation in the form of financial assistance to complete repairs. Recipients were not, generally speaking, looking for more opportunities to be counseled for their pain. By refusing her request for financial assistance—"we are not a government agency or anything like that"—Majid communicated that he understood Saleema's request, but he did not (or could not) recognize it as legitimate. Although Saleema was eventually excluded from the survey, she had little investment in its outcome, as the gifts the organization had offered her had done little to suture what her daughter had described as the "wounds" with which the family still lived.

It might be tempting to diagnose Saleema as a victim here—of both state violence and the unintended harms of humanitarian care. But Saleema was not mute or helpless. At the same time, she was not heard in a meaningful way.[33] Her voice ricocheted off the walls of that claustrophobic storeroom but found no place to land. Though Majid understood Saleema, he did not truly hear her, in the sense that Lauren Berlant describes, "of bearing to be changed by what is being said."[34] Being changed by what Saleema had said would require Majid and Action Aid to entirely reconceptualize and reorganize their project: from how they gathered knowledge, the language they used, to the care they offered, the kind of presence they wanted to be. While Action Aid had a very specific, delimited sense of trauma—feelings of anxiety, insomnia, and flashbacks, for example—Saleema showed that trauma was all around her. It had permeated the materials of her life and body. Bullet-ridden walls were more than just the external, material leftovers of a traumatic event. Their haunting presence showed that trauma lives in spaces and atmospheres as much as in bodies. The Argentinian psychoanalyst Juan-David Nasio notes how, in grief and in the poetics of lament, we retrace how our love for a person has attached itself "in very particular places of the wall, in its cracks and crevices," revealing intricately intertwined lives.[35] For Saleema and her family, those walls and bullet holes *were* the wounds, attachments to their lost kin that would not let go. In this imaginary, rebuilding their home and supporting her children's education might be more important for the family's future than reliving the past. Perhaps Saleema was calling for repair in the external world as a way to begin repairing her shattered inner world. Perhaps Saleema did not intend to resist Action Aid's goals, but was asking to heal in her own way. With this in mind, it is difficult to see Saleema *only* as a victim of Action Aid's mismanagement.

Counterintuitively, it was not Saleema, but Action Aid that had more at stake in this encounter.[36] Saleema's failure to demonstrate a traumatized subjectivity and gratitude for care, and Majid's refusal to hear her, endangered the organization more than it did her. Rather than aid recipients becoming subservient to aid workers, I observed a reversed process. The new regime of evaluation made humanitarian NGOs—and more specifically their local or national staff—more needy than their beneficiaries. While beneficiaries received care that was minimal or even illegible to them, the careers of local and national staff—who in many cases constitute more than 90 percent of humanitarian organizations' total human resource strength—depended on recipients saying the "right" thing. Action Aid needed Saleema and its other recipients to enact their new subjectivities—that which they are taken to be by humanitarian organizations—in this case, victim-survivors of PTSD. As Foucault notes, for psychiatric power, it is the patient who makes and shores up psychiatric power by subordinating herself to it.[37] This insight can extend to humanitarian power as well, which is similarly dependent on subjects like Saleema for validation.

While Saleema's life was not significantly changed by this event, Majid and the other national staff felt the weight of their own and the organization's future on their shoulders. If a project was deemed inefficient, not impactful, or culturally inappropriate, the project would close. Expatriate staff would move to another location and another crisis, but national or local staff would lose their jobs. This was a fear among all the Kashmiri staff in humanitarian organizations I met, who worked as administrators, publicity coordinators, counselors, drivers, and cooks, but it was most pronounced among counselors, who had become financially and emotionally invested in techniques of psychosocial care. These pressures made the surveyors determined not only to make the survey work, but to "work" the survey—which meant massaging the results, when possible, in order to show Action Aid in a positive light.[38]

Through these (intentionally and unintentionally) missed moments, the survey encounter exemplified the bumpy, uneven fissures of care work: the incompatibilities between what recipients want and what aid organizations can give and how humanitarian organizations are increasingly beholden to the perspectives of their recipients, without the tools to respond to their needs. Rather than a story of exclusion (escape) or, inversely, a story of medicalization (capture), the survey was a struggle, a "rumbling of battle" between two worldviews, neither triumphant.[39]

♆

Despite the best efforts of humanitarian NGOs to publicize their work, psychosocial care remained marginal and insignificant to victims of violence. If psychosocial care was insignificant as a mode of redressal, then how did people, including "the most vulnerable," redress suffering? How did they remember, mourn, and acknowledge what they had lost in ways meaningful to them? While institutionalized challenges to state violence, whether psychosocial care or human rights claims, are extremely important, attending to how survivors cohabit and contend with loss in their everyday lives is perhaps an even more politically and ethically urgent task.[40]

Despite Saleema's isolation in the survey encounter, she was not alone. There were many more voices that sang out with hers, that shared the same register of grief. As Arundhati Roy describes in *The God of Small Things*, those who are lost leave a "a hole in the universe" in their own form. Those who are disappeared, killed, and whose bodies are buried in unmarked graves leave a trace. The artist Rollie Mukherjee captures the excessive, haunting quality of encounter killings in her painting *Shadows beyond the Ghost Town*, in which a woman, perhaps a half-widow (a woman whose husband is disappeared), works at the edge of a forest brimming with the ghostly traces of war. Those encountered are buried in forests without names. In the painting, the guns and trees merge into hybrid militarized creatures. And yet the woman's expression is serene, almost transcendent. She tends to the forest; it has gone from a wasteland to a garden in her hands. Is she a jinn herself, or has she decided to live among ghosts?

In my experience, survivors like Saleema were less concerned with reversing the losses they had suffered and more concerned with "ethically learning from their irretrievability."[41] Across Kashmir, survivors live their losses through dreams, songs, and reveries. Iffat Fatima's documentary film *Khoon*

FIGURE 4.3. Shadows beyond the ghost town. Courtesy Rollie Mukherjee

diy Baarav (Blood leaves its trail) follows women whose family members have disappeared. Not forgetting is not just a mark of trauma; it is also a way of living in the aftermath of catastrophic loss. Yet, we should not romanticize it. It is not a smooth process; it is not without emotional vicissitudes; it is not apart from everyday life, but unfolds in and through it.

One of the film's central figures is Shamima Bano, a woman whose husband went missing years ago. Shamima describes seeing her disappeared husband in a recurring dream. As Shamima narrates her dream, we hear the soothing acoustics of a *shikārā*'s lapping oar, which transports the listener into a trance-like state. Shamima's husband identifies himself, but Shamima doesn't believe it's him. The dream pivots on this moment of misrecognition. Shamima demands that he do a blood test to prove his identity. She will compare his DNA to his father's and then she will know if it is truly him. Her doubt, and the quivering regret she feels for doubting him, wake her every time.

Psychosocial organizations would categorize Shamima as a "vulnerable person." In addition to being a direct victim of state violence, belonging to the spectral tribe of families of the disappeared, she also exhibits one of the most significant symptoms of PTSD: intrusive, recurring nightmares. Had she been surveyed by Action Aid or another organization, her dream might have been transformed to a number between one and ten; she might have received a high score. But even more violent than converting lived experience into quantification is the erasure of the ontological and epistemological ground on which that translation occurs.

Unlike what psychosocial organizations and PTSD symptomology dictate, Shamima does not call her dream an intrusion or nightmare. She does not want to be rid of it. Instead, her dream offers her a dialogic space—the only remaining place—where she can interact, and do that intimate thing, with her husband. At the same time, Shamima's dream shows how spaces of dream or reverie are not necessarily free from the pain and misunderstandings of real life. Her dream is not a respite, but a vessel for her pain. The dream space foregrounds the vulnerability and tenuous trust characteristic of all intimacies. It retains, rather than voids, the potent traces of militarization, revealing how state violence—its myriad effects of mistrust, fear, and misrecognition—permeates the deepest, innermost layer of thought.

In the dream, loss transfigures into misrecognition, a misrecognition lodged, clandestinely, in a dream. A Kashmiri proverb says *Aadam bastan manz che siv aasan* (Within the skin of humans, there are secrets)—a warning that things might not be as they appear. Though he looks and acts like her husband, Shamima doubts whether it is really him. In making a forensic demand (DNA test), bio-logics—the tyrannical logic of exhumation and scientific evidence as the only truth—reveal their hold on Shamima's imagination. Shamima's fear of misrecognition was birthed in a milieu of fake encounters and disappearances. The misrecognition in the dream replicates misrecognitions on other terrains: Do (fake) encounters make a person someone else? Is a person who dies as someone else still themselves? Do fake identity cards melt with the bodies of those buried? These questions haunt Shamima's dream along the edges. And, at the same time, the dream represents Shamima's attempt to wrestle free of this crisis. She refuses to be fooled by an imposter; she demands certainty in the only way she knows how.

Humanitarian organizations aim to rid people like Shamima of such traumatizing experiences as part of the work of care. Yet these in-between and uncertain dreamscapes have very different meanings for survivors themselves. They allow them to coexist with those whom they have lost in the present rather than relegate them to the past, as psychiatric and psychological models of grief and recovery would mandate. What dreams mean, what work they do, marks another disjuncture between humanitarian and everyday forms of care.

Both humanitarian and militarized care are relations based on reciprocity, in which recipients have to demonstrate gratitude for care received. By contrast, everyday care—such as dreaming, but also hospitality and notions of duty—offer nonreciprocal, nondual, and open-ended relations. Chapter 5 explores these modes of everyday care in more detail.

Gratitude

We're talking about a few hundred people standing up to five million troops.
It might not be a good decision to stand up against the state. It might be a bad
choice. But, sometimes, you have to make a bad choice.
—Kashmiri medical technician, SMHS hospital

On Tuesday, September 1, 2014, as the monsoons dribbled to a stop in much of the Indian subcontinent, it began raining across Kashmir. The region was approaching drought-like conditions, so the rain was a relief at first. The Jammu and Kashmir state weather agency had told residents to expect heavy rain, after which the weather would improve and water levels would decrease.[1] But soon the hard and incessant downpour became troubling. The Jhelum River rose three inches in three hours. By the following day, floods and landslides were reported in the Indian-controlled territories of Jammu, Punjab, and the Kashmir Valley, as well as Pakistani-controlled regions of Azad Jammu and Kashmir and Gilgit-Baltistan. Not for the first time, nature rendered the India–Pakistan border insignificant.

On September 5, several rivers breached their banks. Soon, much of the city of Srinagar was under twelve feet of water. Residents described seeing a "wall of water" gush toward them. The state government's evacuation call came too late; people were already stranded in their homes. Government helplines rang off the hook, without anyone answering them. Soon, all communication systems collapsed and electricity was cut off, allowing fears to unfurl with abandon. Rather than organize rescue operations, the state government—which we later learned was reduced to a few dozen officials armed with a single walkie-talkie set—was itself in need of rescue.[2]

Only much later would the true scale of the damage be known. The flood became the worst natural disaster to hit the region in more than fifty years—more than 280 people were killed; 390 villages completely submerged; frail infrastructure, including bridges and roads, was severely damaged; and the region suffered massive financial losses, an estimated 1 trillion Indian rupees (about US$1.4 billion).

Living in Durham, North Carolina, at the time, I watched news reports of the floods online in the surreal, removed way one does from across the world. Rajbagh, the neighborhood I considered home, built on a reclaimed floodplain, disappeared from view. I could not fully digest what I was seeing.

With the state government stranded, Indian armed forces launched major humanitarian assistance programs called Mission Sahāyatā (Assistance) and Operation Megh Rāhat (Cloud Rescue).[3] Since I couldn't reach friends in Kashmir, I turned to Indian television channels for updates. Thunderous updates and loud graphics signaling the unfolding disaster dominated each hourly news update. Since the local Kashmiri press was paralyzed, the Indian press had total control over the relief narrative, as Indian journalists embedded themselves with the National Disaster Relief Force (NDRF). Dramatic rescue and relief operations set against looming mountains and swollen glacial rivers offered photogenic, ready-made action for the twenty-four-hour news cycle, equally if not more enthralling than the melodramatic soap operas on air every night. Indian journalists dispatched noisy reports from whirring boats and helicopters, interviewed solemn but committed military personnel (the rescuers) and emotional, slightly disoriented, but grateful civilians (the rescued). These reports crystallized images of a brave, magnanimous, efficient, and militarized nation-state saving helpless Kashmiris. One Hindi-language news station described the Indian army as an army of heaven-sent angels.

The first week after the flood, Indian media outlets focused on the scale of aid and relief delivered. The Indian army, air force, and navy committed thirty thousand troops, fifteen engineer task forces, eighty-four aircraft and helicopters, four field hospitals and more than 106 medical detachments to the rescue operations, used social media outlets like Twitter, WhatsApp, and Facebook to post relief updates.[4] One army publicity poster showed an image of people being rescued across a gushing river, captioned: "Last Year Uttarakhand, Today Kashmir . . . Any Weather, Any Place, Any War—Man or Nature, Any Time: The Indian Army Is Always Ready!" The tagline, "any war—man or nature"—connected the political conflict with the flood, both producing Kashmir as a permanent zone of disturbance, while simultaneously depoliticizing the struggle for self-determination. By connecting Kashmir to other Indian states which have also experienced natural disasters in recent years, Kashmir was readily incorporated into the national body politic as an object of militarized care.

While other natural disasters, such as the Haiti earthquake, Hurricane Katrina, and Hurricane Maria, have been used to enact dramatic socioeconomic changes, the Kashmir flood was seen as an opportunity to mark the Indian military's counterinsurgency success.[5] Images of Kashmiris being rescued, receiving aid, and embodying postures of gratitude synecdochally represented their acquiescence to Indian rule. The flood was constructed as a critical turning point in Indian-Kashmiri relations—reorienting Kashmiris away from pro-independence politics to finally accepting Indian rule.[6]

The flood was imbued with supernatural powers. Through its total destruction, it had revealed the true character of Kashmiris. On Twitter and other social media platforms, the hashtag #Kashmirfloods was often accompanied by another hashtag, #KashmirArmyKeSaath"—Kashmir is with the army. Kashmiris were portrayed as politically aligned with Indian armed forces and as fickle and weak (kamzor), ready to abandon their political demands at the first speedbump. For example, one tweet showed two images of the same Kashmiri woman, "Fatima." In the first image, taken in the immediate aftermath of the flood, she stands distressed on the sidelines as another woman pleads for help from Indian soldiers. In the second image, from the past, she throws stones, likely at paramilitary or military forces. The juxtaposition of these images conveys how the flood transformed Fatima from a troublesome stone thrower into a subservient, feminine, proper subject of a militaristic, masculinist Indian state. The tweet's caption, "Ms. Fatima, before and after the flood," captures how Kashmiri civilians are seen as nonideological, misguided, malleable, and corruptible.

Unlike NGO humanitarianism, which often occurs on a terrain of difference—through care enacted "at a distance" toward "suffering strangers"[7]—the militarized post-disaster care emphasized and produced *intimacy* between Indian armed forces and the civilian population. As one media outlet described:

> Over the years the Indian Army has established a *special bond* with the people of Jammu and Kashmir. There would hardly be a soldier who has not served in the state at some point in time during his career span. The people and the soldiers have jointly met the challenge of foreign sponsored terrorism and brought the region back to normality from the brink of disaster. During this journey there have been many instances of calamity towards which the army has *exhibited great sensitivity* and has come to the aid of the people spontaneously as *a friend and a well-wisher* [emphasis mine].[8]

While humanitarian aid is often criticized for reproducing hierarchies and distance between those designated "saviors" and those who are "saved," this report reveals how militarized care operates through a different logic. Drawing from a counterinsurgency imaginary of intimacy between military forces and civilians, the report argued that shared experiences of disaster and terrorism had led Kashmiris and the Indian military to develop a "special bond" as a "friend and well-wisher."[9] In this rosy imaginary, civilians and the military were not only cooperating, but had developed a deep, trusting relationship. Given the state of relations between Kashmiri civilians and Indian security forces, these claims were performative utterances: they were not merely descriptive, but also aspirational, hoping to create the reality they described.

Kashmiris were familiar with these counterinsurgency aspirations. Counterinsurgency's transformative capacities were encoded into the grammar of everyday life under Indian state occupation. Posters and billboards strategically placed along roads and highways all around the Kashmir Valley show Kashmiri civilians and military personnel bound together: sometimes holding hands, with their arms around each other, in relations of codependence. One billboard shows an elderly Kashmiri (Muslim) man bent over, cupping his hands to accept water from the flask of a young Indian (Hindu) soldier. The image reverses age hierarchies in South Asia, as the elderly man is shown in a posture of dependence, while the young soldier is positioned as the benefactor. Sharing water signifies a moral act, since exchanges of body substances (saliva, in this case) are regulated through caste norms. Here, Hindu upper-caste generosity is established while caste hierarchy is carefully maintained—the young soldier expresses his generosity by sharing, and on his part, the elderly man does not drink directly from the flask and therefore does not "pollute" the water. Such acts displayed the ideal sociality of occupation: a robust, benevolent, militarized Indian nation-state can care for an enfeebled Kashmiri body politic, but such care is always mediated by the right amount of proximity and distance.[10]

Yet, as with other forms of Indian state intervention in Kashmir, militarized care was also marked by nervousness.[11] Narratives of counterinsurgency success gave way to narratives of donor anxiety. Attending to the emotional and affective valences of care—their tensions, edginess, and volatility—reminds us that "moods *matter*" in historical and ethnographic interpretation. Care is not always accompanied by compassion or pity, but often coincides with more ambivalent and complex feelings.

A week after the flood, Barkha Dutt, one of India's most famous journalists, hosted a primetime television news special. Instead of celebrating Kashmiri acquiescence to Indian rule, the program questioned Kashmiris' worthiness as recipients of Indian aid. The English-speaking Indian public was no longer in the mood for love. After the show aired, Dutt tweeted: "Army & Air Force are risking their own lives to save lives in #JKfloods. Separatists [pro-independence Kashmiris] who have only abused the *Fauj* [army] should feel chastened now." Dutt's use of the word *abused* was deliberate. When Kashmiris generally use the English-language word *abuse*, it is generally in the context of mass human rights abuses that have been committed by Indian security and paramilitary forces over the last three decades. Instead, Dutt cleverly turned the word's association on its head—"abuse" now referred to Kashmiri critiques of the Indian military, which were irrational and unsubstantiated, like a teenager's tantrum. Dutt felt obliged to tell Kashmiris *how* to feel and behave in relation to militarized care: to be "controlled, chaste, disciplined, and coerced."[12] However, embedded in the word *should* were not just instructions, but doubts. The certainty of the flood's totalizing effects crumbled. Although Kashmiris *should* be grateful and chastened, *would they be? Would* the flood finally bring Kashmiris to their knees? These messages revealed how the future of Indian-Kashmiri relations remained uncertain.

At the same time, the tweet revealed that militarized care was not magnanimous or altruistic, but conditional. There was only one acceptable form of Indian-Kashmiri relationality: the latter's complete deference. Militarized care would not be extended automatically or unconditionally by virtue of the fact that Kashmiris are Indian citizens.[13] Rather, Kashmiris had to demonstrate and perform their worthiness as recipients. Worthiness was defined differently in militarized care and NGO humanitarianism. While recipients of NGO humanitarianism had to demonstrate their worthiness through bureaucratic and quantitative measures (chapter 4), subjects of militarized care were judged on how they embodied particular affects, such as helplessness and supplication, and if they were willing to abandon "anti-national" pro-independence politics.

These public demands for Kashmiris to display gratitude in exchange for aid remind us that humanitarianism, and particularly militarized care, is a mode of governance through affect. Not all victims are equally deserving of aid. Rather, they are judged on their character and behavior—judgments that are, of course, overdetermined by long-standing historical tropes.[14] After Hurricane Katrina, for example, the US media disguised the state's grossly negligent relief efforts in communities of color by perpetuating narratives of anti-blackness. The media consistently focused on how New Orleans's black residents were engaged in criminal activities—raping, murdering, and looting fellow residents—in the storm's aftermath. The governor of Louisiana even ordered soldiers to shoot to kill looters in an effort to restore calm. Inquiries later revealed that almost no crimes had taken place. However, these discourses of black criminality helped justify why poor black and brown people could be left stranded for days and weeks without food, water, or shelter in the wealthiest country in the world without consequence.[15]

Like the poor black residents of New Orleans, Kashmiri recipients of aid were also doomed to fail the test of deservingness. Although post-flood relief was presented as a rational and efficient exercise of state and military power—underscored by a focus on the numbers of those rescued and aid distributed—it was undergirded by nervousness. Long-standing Islamophobic fears about Muslim and Kashmiri betrayal surfaced. The media reported that, in some places, army and NDRF rescuers were being greeted with stones instead of gratitude. One article described a food drop from an air force helicopter. Instead of accepting the grain, recipients tore open the gunny sacks and poured out all the grain. One person had cried out, "We don't want food from India." Instead of thanks, rescue workers received complaints from Kashmiri civilians that they had taken too long.[16] As these stories leaked into social media, the tone of the rescue changed significantly.

Demands for gratitude were replaced with threats: "#KashmirFloods #stonethrowers now call u r [sic] so-called brother #Pakistan 4 help" trended. Another asked: "Wonder where the stonethrowers and their sponsors are now?" The grateful subject of militarized care was gone, replaced by old tropes of Kashmiri Muslims as criminal, seditious troublemakers. Rather than pity or compassion—the paradigmatic qualities associated with clinical or humanitarian care—disgust bubbled up to the surface. Meanwhile, as in Katrina, the prefigured unworthiness of aid recipients allowed the state to justify taking more punitive steps.

ψ

Demands for gratitude pervaded both military and biomedical spaces. While they reached a fever pitch after the flood, demands that Kashmiris show gratitude for militarized care were also present in medical settings, such as the De-Addiction Centre (DDC). Although displays of gratitude and deference are common in public health settings across India, they acquired a different valence in occupied Kashmir. In the police-run DDC, patients had to perform "recovery narratives," in which they had to publicly express gratitude to the clinic's staff and the police establishment for curing them. Here, too, proper affect was read symbolically: as a sign of sobriety *and* evidence of the efficacy of the police's "winning hearts and minds" campaign.

Each of the DDC's inpatients learned to perform "recovery narratives" during group therapy, which occurred every alternate day.[17] Unlike an AA meeting, in which people can speak of their own volition, DDC group therapy was more like a classroom, similar to some of the educative programs conducted by humanitarian NGOs. Patients who were close to being discharged had to tell "recovery narratives" in which they detailed their drug use, abuse, and recovery process.[18] These were highly structured and scripted performances. Recovery narratives always ended with an acknowledgment of deference to the clinicians, the De-Addiction Centre, and the police for providing lifesaving care. More recently admitted patients had to listen carefully and emulate these narratives when it was their turn. Patients' discharge from the clinic was contingent on performing these public acknowledgments of gratitude properly. While these performances were read as a sign of recovery, through them, the police also placed patients in a relation of ongoing indebtedness to the apparatus of militarized care. This fact was not lost on patients themselves.

While patients mostly performed their recovery narratives with aplomb, during one-on-one interviews, I learned their experiences of care were at odds with their public recovery narratives. Many harbored suspicion and mistrust toward the police and feared their public expressions of gratitude could be used to enlist them as police informers or collaborators once their treatment was over. Given the experiences of patients like Inayat, these fears were not unfounded (chapter 1). Contrary to their public statements that the DDC was like "home," many were uncomfortable in the highly surveilled and stigmatized space and were desperate to leave. Patients were careful not to air these critiques openly, knowing that they could invite violence, censure, and prolong their stay. Nonetheless, the gap between recovery narratives and patients' private statements revealed militarized care's failure to produce subjective transformation and unquestioning loyalty in patients.[19]

Whether in routinized spaces such as the DDC, or under exceptional circumstances such as post-flood relief, gratitude was not a spontaneous outpouring of emotion or feeling, but was a "political emotion."[20] Though many Kashmiris had initially played along with the militarized state's demands for gratitude, the renewed mistrust between Indian security forces and recipients led to new ethical and political alignments.

ψ

I returned to Kashmir in the summer of 2016, almost two years after the flood. So much had happened. In the 2014 legislative assembly elections, the National Conference (NC) had suffered a humiliating defeat, which many attributed to its impotence during the flood. The People's Democratic Party (PDP) had won the election, but without an outright majority, leading it to ally with the Hindu nationalist Bharatiya Janata Party (BJP). Many viewed this alliance as a betrayal of the PDP's pro-human rights platform and message. Meanwhile, aid monies for flood relief became sites of new controversy. At one end, there were gross inadequacies, and at the other, gross excesses. Some families who lost their homes reported receiving a check for a paltry Rs. 3,000 from the government (about US$50).[21] As many struggled to re-build their homes, others received siphoned grant money for new business ventures. Guest houses and hotels sprouted up all over the city, reminding Kashmiris that disasters are always economic opportunities for some.

When I arrived in Delhi in early July, en route to Srinagar, my mind was still on the flood. But soon I was swept away by another crisis. The warnings came as they always do, in vague, coded language: *mahaul theek nahin hai*, the situation is not good. Like all flare-ups in violence, it was impossible to know how long this one would last: days, weeks, months? On July 8, 2016, Burhan Wani, a twenty-two-year-old charismatic Kashmiri militant leader, was assassinated by Indian security forces. According to local reports, Wani had joined the militant group Hizb-ul-Mujahideen after Indian security forces had tortured and detained his older brother without cause. Though Burhan, as he is fondly called, lacked military experience, his highly popular social media posts reflected collective frustration toward Indian militarization and offered an alternative to nonviolent civil disobedience, which many felt had been fruitless. Unlike previous generations of militants who had crossed into Pakistan-controlled Kashmir to receive arms and munitions training, Burhan belonged to a new generation whom the state describes as "homegrown terrorists." Burhan and the new generation of armed fighters are Kashmiris who have lived their whole lives in the valley. Though they remain a tiny minority (there are, at most, five hundred active militants in a population of eight million people), they are local celebrities, particularly among the youth.[22] Their social medial profiles have thousands of followers, and people graffiti their names on walls and wear T-shirts with their faces stenciled on them.

After a dramatic three-hour long cordon-and-search operation, Wani was killed in an encounter with police and army. News of his death hit hard, and impassioned, largely nonviolent, pro-independence protests broke out across Kashmir. Though similar in form to other mass protests since 2008, the content of these protests was different. This time, demands for independence were not couched in other issues, such as land rights or the revocation of draconian extrajudicial laws. Rather, calls for āzādī were pervasive, undisguised, and center stage.[23] With the PDP's latest betrayal and the ascent of the BJP, many felt the space for negotiating with the Indian state had disappeared. The mood was freedom or bust.

The protests presented yet another test of the Indian military's commitments to "humanitarian" warfare and the principles of counterinsurgency. After 2010, when Indian security forces killed more than 120 unarmed civilians, the Indian military had changed its policy of using live ammunition in favor of what it described as "nonlethal" or "less lethal" weapons, such as tear gas and rubber pellets. Indian military and paramilitary forces now pledged "maximal restraint" in their approach to crowds and riot control.[24]

However, in the protests following Wani's death, while civilian casualties remained relatively low, the numbers of people injured multiplied.[25] By the end of July, thirty-six Kashmiris had been killed, and over five thousand were injured. "Nonlethal" lead-coated pellets—fired at close range and with hydraulic pump-action guns—blinded hundreds of young Kashmiris in one or both eyes, suggesting a contravention of military and counterinsurgency protocols to minimize harm. The Kashmiri writer Mirza Waheed described the protests as "the world's first mass blinding."[26] The crisis distilled: *pellets and tear gas versus stones and slogans*. As July turned into August, the Indian military and paramilitary forces enacted round-the-clock curfews and shut down telecommunications, including cell phone and mobile internet services. In the absence of any voices from Kashmir, Indian news channels once again controlled the narrative. The familiar figure of the violent and disorderly Kashmiri stone thrower—on whose body any kind of state violence could be justified—reappeared.

At the beginning of August, I decided to take my chances and go to Kashmir, despite the escalating crisis. I was tired of waiting in Delhi, and I told myself I had already seen the worst. A few hours before my flight, there were unusual reports of street clashes and stone throwing on the highly securitized airport road, the main artery into the city. Still, on the plane—the longest one-hour flight in the world—all was faux normal. The strange but predictable combination of passengers—Hindu pilgrims on their way for the annual Amarnath pilgrimage, seemingly oblivious to the crisis brewing on the ground, and reluctant Kashmiri expatriates, well aware of the mess unfolding before them—sat side by side. When we landed in Srinagar that morning, a world away from the smog and blistering heat of Delhi. It happened to be the thirtieth continuous day of curfew.

Over the next few days, as I reconnected with friends and tried to jumpstart new fieldwork, I was surprised to find that people were still keen to discuss the flood, despite being in the midst of another crisis. *Perhaps the flood provides a narrative distraction,* I initially thought, wrongly. After some time, it became clear that the 2014 and 2016 crises were related in other ways.

One day, sitting in the office of a mutual friend, I met Abid, a journalist at *Greater Kashmir,* an English-language daily newspaper. Abid described his experience in the flood:

> The government sounded an alarm, but it came very late. I was watching TV when I heard that the river had breached at Pampore Chowk. It was raining hard. The Jhelum rose as it has never risen before.
>
> It was about 10:30 p.m. I was at home with my parents and two of my sisters. My friend came over and said, "You better leave right now, the water is about to reach you." Just the day before, the elders in the village had told us that the water had never reached this far before. So we felt like we could wait it out. At about midnight, I opened my bedroom window and saw the water coming full speed toward us. We quickly packed whatever we could and left for a safer area. We managed to go to a small hillock near our house, which was dry. The next morning, muddy water was everywhere. We ended up staying on top of that hill for a month.
>
> After about fifteen days, the water started receding. It was smelly—full of dead animals and debris. And in some cases, there were dead bodies too. In south Kashmir, a local graveyard caved in and dead bodies flowed up the river.[27]

I asked Abid about the army's role in the rescue and relief operations. He laughed. "The army airdropped a packet of expired biscuits. It was the joke of the century." He kept the biscuits as a memento.

Unlike the heroic rescue narratives gracing millions of television screens across India, I heard different refrains. Some, like Abid, were sardonic in the face of what they described as the military's propaganda and inefficiency. Others offered more troubling accounts of eking out survival in the absence of militarized care: *We were left alone. We were left to die.* The words *calamity* and *abandoned* were used often. In sharp contrast to the celebratory tone on television, many said, "*Sahlāb os poreh tabāhī ti*" (the flood was utterly calamitous). "The security forces did an excellent job rescuing," another person told me. "But first you must ask: Whom did they rescue?"

Imtiaz, a friend, described how he and two others had waited for days to be rescued from his flooded apartment in Srinagar. Trapped with them was a goat that had floated in through the window, which they named Sultan and which became a symbol of their survival. Imtiaz had what he described as a "first-class view" of the rescue operations. First, he saw the NDRF and air force rescue bureaucrats and government officials. Then, they came for the tourists (mostly Indian Hindu pilgrims). Then they came for the police informers and collaborators. Although Imtiaz and his friends had always suspected who the informers and collaborators in their neighborhood were, now they had confirmation. Then, abruptly, the rescue ended. There was silence.

Yawning gap between the robust rescue shown on television and the sense of abandonment felt on the ground emerged. When I shared these stories with Indian friends and family, many said: *Rubbish. They are lying to you. The security forces rescued everyone.* For a moment, I wondered if I was being fooled. I realized then how my doubt was a product of my social and intellectual conditioning. One legacy—an inherited Hindu majoritarian perspective of not trusting the perspectives of minoritized communities—intersecting with another—an anthropological legacy of doubting our interlocutors, thinking we "know better."[28] Both were traces of colonial knowledge that needed to be exorcized.

Like all critical events—events which produce new subjectivities, ethical and political horizons—the flood splintered into multiple "mythohistories."[29] Contradictory and layered expectations of militarized care emerged. On one side, Kashmiris were configured as ungrateful liars. On the other, the Indian state was deemed incapable of truly caring for Kashmiris. Despite their difficult history with the Indian state, many Kashmiris said they had hoped for some degree of "humanity" (*insāniyat*) in the aftermath of the disaster. While they uniformly rejected the correlation between accepting Indian aid and acquiescing to Indian rule, they had expected the state to perform its basic obligation of rescuing civilians. But this was not the case.[30]

Kashmiris described the floods as a turning point, but not in the way imagined by the Indian military and media. Rather than reorienting them *toward* the state, the flood reoriented people *away* from it. Dr. Abdullah, the surgeon who was kidnapped by militants (related in chapter 2), was also stranded in the flood for more than fifteen days. He too described the event as transformative and articulated the events of 2014 and 2016:

> It *began* in 2014. In the flood. This is when people realized that the government of India and the state government are not interested in them. This is when people *started thinking*. I was stuck in the flood for fifteen days. I saw the NDRF and army once. They came to rescue their own people. There is an army camp near where I live, in Bemina [a suburb of Srinagar]. I saw two helicopters drop food, and while they were doing it, I also saw them video it, to project to the outside world that they are helping a lot!
>
> In Bemina, we got six hours' notice that the flood [*sahlāb*] was coming. It was just enough time for us to move all our necessities upstairs. For the first four days we lived comfortably. After that, things became difficult. But people from the neighborhood helped us a lot. They would throw tomatoes, potatoes, bottled water, whatever they had, into the attic where we were stranded [emphasis mine].[31]

Though Dr. Abdullah and his family were caught in a situation of abjection, for him the flood was not just a paralyzing, traumatic event. It was also a moment when "people started thinking." It offered a political opening.

Dr. Abdullah's narrative offered a powerful counterpoint to dominant representations of victims of traumatic events and to the notion of a humanitarian emergency itself. In the aftermath of emergencies, humanitarian relief efforts often focus on providing basic necessities—food, water, first aid, and psychological counseling—to those in need. However, in so doing, they unintentionally circumscribe meanings and definitions of life to a minimal, immediate scale. For example, as Peter Redfield describes for MSF, the organization provides care that is "better than nothing for the chosen few," but "hardly an ideal basis for a full life."[32] In other words, humanitarian organizations reduce the complex lives and subjectivities of survivors into what is deemed necessary for their biological survival. Whereas the temporality of emergency humanitarian care is usually structured in a linear manner—basic survival first, questions about rights and dignity second—these concerns were intertwined and simultaneous for Dr. Abdullah.[33] Like thousands of others stranded in the flood, Dr. Abdullah was struggling to survive, yet he did not stop thinking about politics and dignity, of what the flood meant for an occupying state and its occupied citizens.

Emergencies can have varied, multiple, and contradictory effects. For Dr. Abdullah, the agony of *being stuck*—the very definition of trauma underpinning the humanitarian imaginary, in which victims are in a state of profound loss and shock, unable to move forward and in urgent need of external assistance[34]—became about movement and transformation, remaking and retelling history, and reclaiming one's life. Dr. Abdullah's statement signaled how crises can be catalysts of social and political upheaval, which can wobble sovereign power, bring communities together, or enact social change.[35] For Dr. Abdullah, the flood revealed the hollowness of militarized care and benevolent Indian rule. His anger and humiliation at watching the army evacuate its own camp crystallized a sense of the Indian state's indifference and callousness vis-à-vis Kashmiris. In its path of destruction, the flood had washed clean the dynamics of occupation.

In Kashmiri popular discourse, these affects of anger and disappointment were combined with expressions of wit, irony, irreverence, and refusal. One person wrote on their Facebook page: "I saw *a* cop the other day." The joke was that in a place crawling with military and paramilitary personnel for the past three decades, suddenly, when one was actually needed, there was no one to be found. Another neighborhood raised a banner mocking the bombastic affect of the televised rescues: "We don't need Indian rescue and relief. Stop the drama of choppers."

A counter-ethic to militarized care also emerged: the sense of being abandoned gave way to people *asking* to be left alone. Stories of refusal—discarded gunny sacks of food aid, bombastic banners, and snide jokes mocking Indian rescue efforts—traveled through the grooves of everyday sociality. These stories of refusal challenge mainstream analytics of biopower and abandonment in anthropology. Scholars writing about the aftermath of disasters or crises have drawn on Michel Foucault's notion of biopower to theorize how state processes render some individuals, communities, and populations useless, disposable, abandoned, or, in Foucault's words, "let die," while others are marked for enhancement, flourishing, and thriving.[36] "Letting die" describes how social, economic, and political abandonment happens to people without their consent. The ironic registers of commentary in the flood's aftermath complicated dichotomies of care (good) versus abandonment (bad) that are conventionally used to evaluate biopower.[37] While analyses of "letting die" are designed to be sympathetic to those left behind or left out, these analyses rarely consider how people can have complicated and contradictory desires.[38] Much like the DDC patients who found themselves caught in an impossible situation between care and collaborating with the police, victims of the flood, too, found themselves confronting two unpalatable options: abandonment came with dignity or rescue with dependency.

On the other hand, the sheer scale of the damage and the lack of preparedness for the flood meant that many people were desperate to be rescued. The discrepancy between what was being shown on television and what was happening on the ground produced a contradiction too painful to bear. "It can make your head explode," one person said. This emotional mix—of needing to be rescued and wanting to refuse the rescue—was not illogical or irrational, but was a product of decades of military and humanitarian overinvestments, which have produced a complex landscape in which calls for the state to fulfill its obligations and calls to refuse aid circulated simultaneously.

ψ

Despite the differing reactions to the flood, one thing was clear: the flood was not *merely* a story of abandonment or ruination. It was also a story of survival, of making do in the absence of militarized care. As with most disasters, the bulk of aid and relief was local, not national or international.[39] I heard quiet stories of bravery: young boys labeled "miscreants" by the Indian state using arms honed through throwing stones and cricket balls to launch water bottles, medicines, and food into attics; people making makeshift boats out of water tanks; wooden coffins and tourist shikārās transformed into life-saving rescue vessels. A man named Rafiq, one of Abid's neighbors, rescued eleven people, two dogs, and a sheep, crossing back and forth across a street swollen with waist-high water for hours, despite not knowing how to swim. Tales of survival were not always about social cohesion, however; old social fault lines also reasserted themselves. Mohamad Junaid describes how, in one water-clogged village, struggles over clean drinking water exacerbated tensions between more powerful village cultivators (*zamindārs*) and less powerful members of the fishing community (*hænz*).[40]

When I asked how people survived in the shadow of militarized care, the overwhelming response was that Kashmiris helped one another. As one retired doctor I interviewed explained: "The way people came together after the flood has to do with the culture of hospitality [mehmān nawāzī] in Kashmir." He cited the Prophet Muhammad: "Let the believer in God and the Day of Judgment honor his guest." He described how hospitality was a moral obligation akin, or even superior to, piousness in Islam.[41] In Islamic theology, hospitality is defined as a constitutional acceptance or receptiveness to others. It is the foundation of social relations necessary to build social solidarity or *ummah* (brotherhood) within Islam.

Hospitality productively contrasts with the gift—that is, militarized or humanitarian care. Unlike the gift, or the notion of charity, which can reinscribe a hierarchical, binary relationship between giver and receiver, in Islam, hospitality is a triangular relation between giver, receiver, and God.[42] It is through acting on the guest and treating them well that one fulfills a duty to God. As Amira Mittermaier points out, hospitality thus makes the host a conduit or mediator, rather than the *source* of divine justice.[43] Second, although given in generosity, gifts are not given freely, whereas hospitality is reversible, egalitarian, and nonreciprocal. Meanwhile, gifts are laden with expectations of return. As Marcel Mauss noted, the failure to return a gift can change its essence—it can become poisonous.[44] In contrast, hospitality, in its ideal form, should be given without expectation. Though hospitality is a duty to God, the doctor reminded me it should be given freely and joyously; "mehmān nawāzī is not just a duty, but a *pleasure*," he emphasized. The burden was on the giver, not the receiver, to generate the right affect and atmosphere. Because hospitality was intimate (classically associated with domestic spaces), lacked calculation (appeared spontaneous but was carefully executed), and nonreciprocal (given without expectation of return), it made the giver, not the receiver, radically vulnerable. Finally, whereas humanitarian care operates through the logic of the exception, hospitality is habitus. It is an ordinary, everyday practice, so deeply ingrained as to be almost unremarkable and universally attainable, regardless of a person's economic status.

Hospitality is not an unchanging or all-encompassing cultural or theological "Islamic" attribute, however.[45] In anthropology and political theory, hospitality has been theorized as a form of morality that operates "beyond politics" or that transcends the existing political and moral systems in which we live.[46] Contrary to these perspectives, hospitality was described to me as an ethical and religious obligation shaped by historical contingencies. People described how Kashmiri hospitality developed alongside trade routes that once connected Kashmir with Tibet, northern Pakistan, Afghanistan, Kyrgyzstan, Uzbekistan, Iran, Iraq, and Syria. Abid the journalist explained: "Before 1947, we had a lot of trade with Central Asian countries and with Iran, very ancient trade routes that would go from Lal Chowk [the city center] all the way to Tehran. When traders, such as carpet traders, used to come, we would receive them and offer them tea and food. Back then, we used to grow our own rice and potatoes. This tradition of hospitality goes back thousands of years. . . . This hospitality, it is *very intact*."[47]

Rather than a cultural essence, Abid described how hospitality was closely intertwined with Kashmir's history of trade, commerce, and local sovereignty.[48] Hospitality was a trace of vibrant histories of cultural and economic exchange *and* economic self-sufficiency. Because of its rich cultural production—from intricately woven woolen shawls to the *Saussurea lappa*, the most lucrative aromatic plant used in herbal medicine—Kashmir was a critical node along transregional trade routes. Abid also referred to how, prior to Indian rule in 1947, Kashmir used to produce its own indigenous variety of paddy called mushkibudij until the grain was replaced by a higher-yielding Chinese hybrid called budij China during the Green Revolution. This evocation of indigenous rice, the staple of the Kashmiri diet (the phrase *have you eaten?* in Kashmiri is literally "have you eaten rice?") mapped a moral and political imaginary beyond occupation and militaristic and humanitarian dependencies, in which Kashmir was both self-sufficient *and* cosmopolitan. In contrast to the region's present as a securitized, partitioned, and enclosed space, Abid charted a cartography of connection, a cartography that was undoubtedly cathartic for him to imagine.[49] These histories, economic practices, and modes of political autonomy had disappeared, but by remembering them, Abid sowed the seeds of a still-possible future.

Although trade routes had dried up, hospitality had not. Yet, since 1947, but particularly after the armed conflict began, notions of hospitality had been transformed. Until the armed conflict, Kashmir's thriving tourist industry saw famous visitors including Lord Mountbatten (the last viceroy of India), George Harrison, and Ravi Shankar. Its success was attributed to Kashmir's history of mehmān nawāzī. Foreign visitors popularized a touristic culture of houseboats, "floating palaces, combining Edwardian English amenity with evocations of Moghul grandeur."[50] However, like other aspects of Kashmir's economy, tourism was decimated by the conflict. Tourism fell from approximately 700,000 visitors a year in the early 1980s to barely ten thousand by the mid-1990s.

In recent years, calls to revive Kashmir's tourist industry have emerged as an explicit "peace-building" policy recommendation.[51] However, as Cabeiri

Robinson astutely points out, efforts to promote tourism in Kashmir do not make these regions safer for the populations who live there. Rather, they "make it possible for Pakistanis" and Indians, especially "the urban middle classes, to imagine Kashmir as a place where a long-standing conflict has ended and where demands for justice, rehabilitation and family reunification are already resolved."[52] Nor do these efforts recognize the effects of more than 30 years of living under a state of emergency on Kashmiris. Many Kashmiris are aware of how tourism is used as a political strategy to show that "normalcy" is "returning."[53] As Deepti Misri notes, these narrative pit "the hospitable Kashmiri" as diametrically opposed to the figure of the Kashmiri male militant or street protestor.[54] While many Kashmiris remain skeptical of appropriations of hospitality and tourism, their precarious economic position leaves them with little choice but to participate.

At the same time, notions of hospitality were not entirely subsumed by the politics of occupation. People continually reminded me that hospitality predates occupation. The examples of how people were rescued and the circuits of care that emerged in the flood's aftermath were nothing new, I was told, but were remnants. Writing about Syrian refugees on Turkey's southern border, Yael Navaro describes remnants as minute forms of generosity in everyday life "which *endure* in the form of attachments, intimacy, sociality out of habit and interdependence across local communities."[55] Similarly, Ana Esther Ceceña describes how spontaneous forms of revolt are, more often than not, "crafted in daily interaction . . . they draw on a tradition that is prior to a situation of oppression and that precedes the immediate causes of a contemporary uprising."[56] Hospitality was like the almond slices you find at the bottom of a cup of *kehwa* that you always knew were there, but had forgotten you were waiting for.

ॐ

I began to see how the events of 2014 and 2016 were connected. In both, Kashmiris confronted not only direct state harm, but also the aporia between the state's injurious effects and its humanitarian claims. In both, hospitality emerged as a bulwark.

Despite the Indian state's commitment to using "nonlethal force" on protestors in 2016, newspapers that summer were filled with gory images of bandaged and wounded Kashmiris, including many children, whose bodies, faces, and eyes were mutilated by rubber and lead-coated pellets.[57] After hundreds of young Kashmiris were blinded, many on the ground felt that the "true" aim of humanitarian warfare was harm, not care.[58] As several people noted, "Pellets are only used on Kashmiris. Elsewhere they are used on animals." As the numbers of injured continued their uptick, Kashmiris waited in vain for the central Indian government to stop the bloodletting. At least previous governments had made statements of regret when Kashmiri civilians were killed, Imtiaz noted. Now, under the right-wing, xenophobic BJP government, even those watered-down, ineffectual statements were missing. The BJP had already proven not only that did it not care about Muslims, but that it would participate in targeted violence against them and other minorities.[59]

As the numbers of people wounded by nonlethal weapons swelled, the state's humanitarian mode of presence—its public health apparatus—came under pressure to bear the weight of its military excesses. The humanitarian apparatus began cracking. After each protest, droves of wounded persons were brought to SMHS with little notice. Rather than maintaining its integrity as a neutral and protected humanitarian space, military logics leaked into the clinic. As one earnest and energetic orthopedic surgeon named Dr. Atif described, "it felt like war had arrived." On July 10, the police fired tear gas shells inside the hospital, targeting the emergency and casualty wards, where most of the injured were being treated.[60] Rather than a refuge, the hospital became an extension of the battlefield. As in other settings of long-term violence, the clinic was not simply a target, but also became a *tactic* of state violence.[61] Biomedical and humanitarian norms of neutrality disappeared. Clinicians expressed their frustration at not being able to guarantee even the most basic protections for their patients while they were receiving treatment. From the government's perspective, pellet marks signified sedition. All injured patients were assumed to be guilty of "antinational" activities and therefore detainable, arrestable, and torturable. The hospital was, as one doctor described, "crawling with police officers in plainclothes" trying to access inpatient admission files. As a result of this intense scrutiny of injured bodies by the state, many of those injured denied that they had been protesting, insisting that they were caught in crossfire, at the wrong place at the wrong time. It was impossible to know who was telling the truth. It did not matter. Under emergency laws, anyone could be detained—without charge—for up to two years.

By the beginning of August, the protests still in full force, SMHS began running out of vital medicines and emergency equipment, including ventilators, critical care ambulances, injectable antibiotics, and catheters. The atmosphere inside the hospital, already tense because of the military infiltration, became even more fraught. Despite hospital administrators' appeals to the state government for more funding and equipment, the Jammu and Kashmir state government, just like the central government, was unresponsive. The resource shortages made doctors once again vulnerable to patients' frustrations: "It's difficult for patients to understand that doctors have no control over hospital supplies," Dr. Atif explained. It was a rare acknowledgment that the gap between doctor and patient apprehensions of public health systems had a legitimate basis.

Given the well-publicized dearth of ambulances, I was surprised to hear that twenty of ninety-seven state-owned ambulances had been attacked either by security forces or protestors.[62] While attacks on ambulances by security forces have been well documented since the 1990s, I was puzzled to hear that protestors were also vandalizing ambulances. That was, until I heard rumors of state officials siphoning ambulances for their own private use.[63] I heard the story of a bureaucrat who had requested an ambulance—which could technically move freely during curfews—to take him on a leisure excursion to Pari Mahal, a seventeenth-century library built by the Mughal king Dara Shikoh, which in the 1990s had been used as an interrogation center and was now a popular, albeit still militarized, tourist destination. The bureaucrat had apparently asked for a "fresh" ambulance—one that wasn't too bloody. This story had circulated widely among protestors, for whom ambulances now represented not only a chronically underfunded public health system, but the state's callousness toward Kashmiri lives. Whether the story was apocryphal or not, it fit preexisting narratives of how the state's humanitarian mode of presence was subservient to its military presence.

In the midst of these heated contestations over medicine, doctors and hospital staff struggled to treat not only the numbers of people injured, but also the *nature* of their injuries. Treating "pellet patients," Dr. Atif explained, "was much more complex than treating bullet injuries. Because when pellets hit, it's like a shower, a pellet shower. The whole surface area of a person is involved." Because pellets do not follow a definite path, identifying if and where they had penetrated the body and ruptured organs required sophisticated imaging technologies, such as MRIs and CT scans, which were scarce.

Rather than acquiesce to the military appropriations of public health, however, doctors, civil society activists, and communities mobilized. Some doctors began allowing patients to use pseudonyms in their patient files to protect their identities or granted early discharge if and when they felt tracked by security agencies. As in previous crises, doctors did not passively watch their neutrality erode. Some used their position as scientific experts

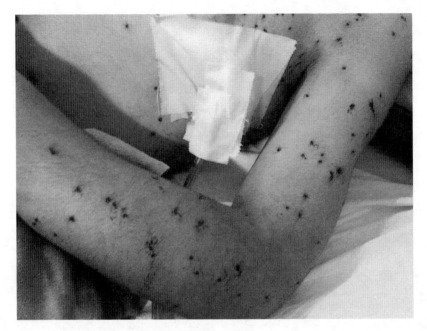

FIGURE 5.1. Pellet shower. Photo by author

to speak out against the systemic violations of counterinsurgency protocols—such as firing pellets above the waist and from short range—which
they had observed while treating injuries. As news about the hospital's depri-
vations reached public outlets, a dozen or so NGOs—some politically affili-
ated, but most not—set up makeshift tents outside SMHS offering a variety
of supplementary services. One organization offered free ambulance services
to patients and their families. Another procured and set up a free landline
telephone. Volunteers cooked giant steel vats of rice, mutton soup, and lentils and served two free meals a day to anyone. At another tent, a constant
stream of chai flowed. Other volunteer groups provided necessities—fresh
clothes, little packets of sterilized needles, bandages, analgesics, antibiotics, eyeglasses, and tissue paper to wipe the involuntary tears that flowed
after ophthalmological surgeries. The outside of the hospital, a barren, concrete parking lot, was transformed into a fairground, full of activity and
energy.

The NGOs also developed a system of triage, acting as buffers between
patients, attendants, and doctors. Unlike biomedicine's model of individu-
alized care, volunteers recognized that patients came with a social network
that also had to be cared for. Dr. Atif explained how, at the beginning of the

protests, he had to perform CPR with "ten people on my back." Echoing the concerns of Heena and Nazima in chapter 2, he described how the presence of an agitated and emotional crowd—doubly motivated by state violence and the pervasive mistrust of medical institutions—impeded doctors' ability to provide care. To alleviate the burden, NGO staff waited at the hospital's entrance. As soon as injured civilians arrived, volunteers separated patients from the dozens of attendants accompanying them and guided them efficiently through the labyrinthine hallways of SMHS to the appropriate department for screening or treatment. Attendants and community members were channeled to the volunteer tents. This system shaved precious minutes off the clock. This "human chain has saved lives," Dr. Atif said. "It's that simple."

As had happened after the flood, something outside militarized care again shimmered into focus. State abandonment offered opportunities for forging—and foraging—ethical and political subjectivities from a medley of existing practices and habits. Hospitality's pliancy once again became evident. It revealed itself as "intact," despite being challenged by centuries of state projects of violent integration, militarization, insecurity, and mistrust. Yet it was also adaptable. Whereas hospitality was traditionally practiced toward strangers, in 2014 and 2016, it was enacted proximately, between fellow Kashmiris. Hospitality became mobile, extending out into community kitchens and mobile clinics, and proved, to borrow a favorite global health concept, scalable. Mosque-based community treasuries (baitul māl) in rural and urban areas became collection centers for distributing food, money, fresh water, and medicine to the injured and their families.[64] In 2014 and 2016, baitul māl were critical vectors of hospitality, demonstrating that not all social life, care, and relationality were colonized by military and humanitarian logics.

The spontaneous emergence of these collective projects reminded Kashmiris that they had not entirely forgotten how to trust and rely on each other. One CT technician at SMHS, a man in his thirties, explained: "After every uprising, something remains in the subconscious. A trace. That's why the next uprising is worse than the previous. This is also why, with each uprising, Kashmiris get more organized." This psychoanalytical perspective reversed many commonsensical claims about trauma, such as that it impedes people's capacities to withstand pain. From his perspective, repeated traumas fostered collective strength. Another hospital worker said, "It would seem as if someone was organizing all this, but no one is. Our past experiences and the repression we have faced have made us into a very cohesive community." This statement—it would seem as if someone was organizing this—was an indi-

FIGURE 5.2. Outside SMHS. Photo by author

rect response to long-standing claims in the public sphere that Kashmiris are puppets in a global Islamist project to destabilize India. In contravention of these discourses, the technician insisted that the spirit of resistance was indigenous, spontaneous, and motivated by Kashmiris themselves. In both 2014 and 2016, hospitality emerged as a "politico-ethical" practice.[65]

ॐ

The collection of volunteers who gathered in response to the crisis of non-lethal weapons were diverse. Their aspirations overlapped with, but also existed in tension with, Kashmiri political aspirations of self-determination. Two volunteers I met—Umar and Altaaf Sahab—embodied these distinctive perspectives.

Umar was a petite, wiry man in his mid-forties who helped me navigate the network of volunteer organizations that had sprung up during the 2016 protests. He owned a business selling medical equipment, and in both 2014 and 2016, he organized medical suppliers all across the state to help with relief efforts. During the flood, he established an NGO and helped deliver medical supplies to flooded areas. In 2016, his NGO was lending medical equipment to SMHS and offering free laboratory tests to those who had been wounded by

FIGURE 5.3. Help Poor volunteers. Photo by author

lead-coated pellets. For Umar, this work was directly related to the movement for Kashmiri independence (tehreek): "Of course these actions are contributing to the tehreek. We are showing the government that even if our hands are empty, we can run things." For Umar, practices of self-help and hospitality served a political purpose. They demonstrated to the state and to fellow Kashmiris that they could take charge of difficult situations efficiently — today it was public health care, perhaps tomorrow it could be a new nation. Umar's volunteer work worked to make a postoccupation future possible.

Altaaf Sahab offered a different explanation. I interviewed him, the cofounder of the NGO Help Poor, during a busy afternoon at the hospital. Altaaf Sahab was also a businessman, but was a generation older than Umar. He was in his sixties and had a gentle, birdlike manner. While we talked in the small, dedicated room that Help Poor had been given by hospital administrators—which spoke to the organization's significant social and political capital—young volunteers bustled all around us, catering to a constant flow of patients and kin in need of bandages, medications, tissues, and other basics. While many organizations like Umar's were relative newcomers to the NGO sector and were operating out of makeshift tents, Help Poor had been working for the past twenty-six years and was well known across Kashmir for providing medical aid and financial assistance to patients.

Altaaf Sahab offered an alternative explanation for the burst of volunteerism since the protests had begun:

> No, there's no connection [between the independence movement and hospitality]. Our work is separate. We're doing this for *humanity*, not for *Kashmiriyat* [an ethos of being Kashmiri]. Even the *yatris* [annual Hindu pilgrims from India] that came to SMHS, we also gave them free treatment.... Couldn't the government do this? We didn't care that yesterday they targeted us with bullets and seven of our children were hit. If anyone comes from any religious background, we help them. If you are a genuine social worker, you don't see the particularities of a person. We don't stop to look—is he Hindu or Muslim?—because then, what will our cause become? Nothing. Our Prophet taught us that if our neighbor is Hindu, or from whatever faith, if they have nothing to do with Islam, we are still responsible for them as much as we are responsible to our own people. Otherwise, what are we? What is the purpose of our work? If a Hindu comes to me and I say, "no, I won't help you, I will only help Muslims," better than this, don't do anything.[66]

Altaaf Sahab described the importance of periods of "turmoil" for practicing worldly ethics. Both he and Umar saw state violence, subjugation, and abandonment as fertile grounds for testing and practicing their ethical and political convictions. But there were also significant differences in their imaginings. Umar's ethical subjectivity was closely tied to being a pro-independence activist and agitating against Indian rule. Altaaf Sahab, in contrast, evoked a humanistic ethics that not only was a response to state violence, but was more encompassing. While Altaaf Sahab delimited the project of Kashmiri self-determination as one for and by Muslims, he insisted that care and hospitality had to be unlimited and undifferentiated.[67] This did not mean that differences—distinctions between Hindu/Muslims and Indians/Kashmiris—were irrelevant. On the contrary, Altaaf Sahab noted these differences—and their ensuing transcendence—as extremely significant.

He described an incident that happened the previous month, in which twenty-three Hindu pilgrims had been injured after their bus collided with a truck. The pilgrims were brought to SMHS for treatment. Altaaf Sahab and other volunteers had stopped all their other work with pellet patients and singularly focused on treating the pilgrims. In so doing, Altaaf Sahab contrasted the care the pilgrims received from Kashmiri Muslims with the treatment Kashmiri Muslims were receiving from the Indian state.

In evoking this moment of hospitality toward the Hindu pilgrims, Altaaf Sahab made several points at once. First, volunteers extended care to the pilgrims *despite* popular anger around the ways Hindu pilgrimages have been promoted by Hindu nationalists to reclaim Kashmir as a primordially "Hindu" landscape and delegitimize Kashmiri Muslim claims over the territory.[68] Further, the injured pilgrims had arrived at SMHS in the heat of war, when hundreds of Kashmiris were being wounded and blinded. Many volunteers perceived the injured pilgrims' arrival at SMHS as the arrival of the Indian state itself—which was now bleeding at their doorstep. Altaaf Sahab described this moment as a test of their ethical fortitude. Unlike Kashmiri protestors, who could not be guaranteed even minimal safety and protection by the Indian state, and who were in fact being directly targeted and harmed, the volunteers prioritized the pilgrims' care and treatment. They *had* to do this, Altaaf Sahab explained. By enacting Kashmiri hospitality and nursing the pilgrims back to health in the face of the state's dehumanization, the volunteers reclaimed their own humanity.

After their discharge from the hospital, several pilgrims recorded messages of gratitude to the volunteers, which were captured on local television stations and circulated on YouTube. Many volunteers at SMHS had saved these videos on their phones and showed them to me proudly. These were rare, public confirmations of their hospitality and ethical fortitude. They also showed how aid relations do not necessarily produce fixed subjects and objects. In this moment of crisis, Kashmiris transformed from recipients to givers, from having to show their gratitude to others, to now having others express gratitude to them.

This example also helped contest popular representations of Kashmiri Muslims as religious extremists. Altaaf Sahab continued:

There was a Jat agitation in Haryana that lasted one whole month [in February 2016].[69] They blocked roads, they stopped trains. . . . Those protestors damaged so much property, and yet no one fired any bullets on them. No one fired any pellets on them. Why? Why did they fire them on people here? Even though they [Jats] set fires, burned cars, burned shops, burned malls.

Here, no one burned any shops. See? Yes, there is a difference. I can take you downtown and you can see everyone is inside, in their homes. No one is doing anything [violent]. *We bear it. We sit quietly and we take it.* But, yes, we want freedom. The people who come to us to get their medicines, we ask them: What do you want? They say, "We want freedom.

Bas [that's it]." When we talk to them [protestors] and ask, "Why do you do this?" They say, "because we want our freedom, that's why" [emphasis mine].

Unlike protestors elsewhere who engaged in destructive and unruly violence, Altaaf Sahab argued that Kashmiris had developed a repertoire of ethical practices, such as patience and forbearance, in response to repeated violations. Restraint was not a passive disposition, but a position requiring immense strength. Similarly, forbearance and patience had to be carefully cultivated as the work of the self and collective, because in addition to moral fortitude, they also required an enduring commitment to a nonreactive politics.[70] For Altaaf Sahab, that Kashmiris had collectively learned to "bear it," "sit quietly," and submit to suffering revealed how they had learned to maintain their dignity in the face of unspeakable violence. These capacities enacted social and ethical difference—they separated Kashmiris from others: Kashmiris from other communities with grievances, such as upper-caste Jats, Kashmiris from the Indian state, and "good" Kashmiris (those who embraced nonviolence) from "bad" ones. While these evaluations were not universally shared across Kashmiri society, they represented Altaaf Sahab's moral map, a framework to think with and act on in the midst of upheaval.[71]

ॐ

In contrast to charity-based humanitarianism, which claims to be ethical but often ends up entangled with politics, or political humanitarianism, which explicitly appropriates humanitarian goals for political ends, the care that mushroomed in 2014 and 2016 was different. It embraced a universal approach to deservingness and harnessed the radical political potential of care, hospitality, and ethics.

But like all moments of collective effervescence, this one too came to an end. It was not just that people's energies had waned. The collective mood had curdled. In September 2016, the police arrested twenty-two volunteers outside SMHS and seized two ambulances belonging to an NGO. On October 2, the police arrived at the hospital at night and told the remaining volunteers to leave the premises within an hour. The volunteer camps outside SMHS were dismantled, and in some cases destroyed. By October, the hospital was back to its spiritless self, its concrete outsides as stark as ever.

When I expressed disappointment at the violent end of the volunteer efforts, Dr. Abdullah pierced through my naivete: "How could you think they would let anything good happen in Kashmir? Did you really think they'd let us be so free?"

I felt flustered. I asked why *he* wasn't disappointed. He laughed disingenuously and then said: "What you saw was passion, madness, insanity [junoon]. The volunteers were caught in the moment. That kind of mad energy is unsustainable."[72] Dr. Abdullah's dismissal of the volunteers as "mad" and "insane" seemed at odds with my experiences with Umar and Altaaf Sahab, and I struggled to understand his meaning. But then his tone softened: "The truth is, as Kashmiris, we don't want to acknowledge when something good is happening, because we are afraid it will be taken away from us."

Dr. Abdullah's evocation of madness and irrationality was not meant to be dismissive. It recognized that acting with passion and embracing "madness" were the only ways forward. His laughter, which I had felt as an attack, I now understood as defensive, a levee against torrential loss that was everywhere. Dr. Abdullah was reflecting on the social reality that every time there was something to be hopeful for in Kashmir—a "true" and uncorrupted freedom fighter, mass street protests, an emergent popular, pro-self-determination leader, or burgeoning civil society organizing—those aspirations, projects, and dreams were systematically destroyed. Rather than see his hope dissolve into disappointment yet again, Dr. Abdullah had refused hope. Nonetheless, his approach unsettled and troubled me. It reminded me of something that Imtiaz had once told me, that living as a Kashmiri meant living "with constant heartbreak. You go to sleep, your heart is broken. Then you wake up the next day, and you try to piece it back together. But it is never the same. You live a life shattered." *To never be whole, but to be less and less whole.*

Dr. Abdullah's reflections also raised questions about whether or not moments of care and hospitality, as ephemeral as they are, can be redemptive. Elizabeth Povinelli states that for social scientists to wish for a redemptive narrative, to seek it, is to wish that social experiments fulfill, rather than upset, given conditions.[73] Did the hospitality and care exercised by the volunteers *fulfill* rather than *upset* militarism? On the one hand, hospitality smoothed out the coarsest edges of state and military violence by providing emergency relief, and in so doing, inadvertently allowed violence to continue. But hospitality also upset the status quo. It reminded besieged Kashmiris that intimacy, self-reliance, and relationality could thrive. As Altaaf Sahab described, to care expansively, demonstrate restraint, and be hospitable were radical gestures not capturable by the politics of the present.

The emergencies of 2014 and 2016 washed away ("upset" in Povinelli's terms) existing scripts of militarized care. Ethical and relational possibilities opened, like portals to other dimensions. Contrary to dominant narratives of Kashmir as a chronically disturbed and dangerous place, hospitality offered a moral imagination and set of relational ethics that was easily and quickly found. Hospitality was *tāqat* (strength), the opposite of kamzorī, in the sense that Shakeela and the women in the closed wards meant (chapter 1). It was a quest for radical self-improvement, a demonstration of a future not yet come, but coming. Hospitality demonstrated a critical, though less commented upon, component of self-determination: the freedom to practice *interdependence* as much as independence.

Through hospitality, Kashmiris exceeded the temporal constraints of an unending occupation. Practices of hospitality were not acts of nostalgia or melancholy, relegated to pastness. Rather, they reimagined the past, and in doing so, dared to imagine a sovereign, cosmopolitan Kashmiri future.[74] They showed Kashmiris that they were already prepared for the next disaster. Like neon-green paddy stalks that light up the earth every spring, these, too, were the products of long histories and intensive labor.

Duty

As the author, I wrote a happy ending, although . . .

I am suspicious of the efficacy of doing so.

But happy endings satisfy the emotions, and I wanted to provide that type of satisfying narrative closure in the hope that it would free the intellect to continue its trajectory beyond the story line, pondering the issues the book raises . . .

In the end, though, it is a tribute to the power of the imagination. You cannot make a better world unless you imagine it so, and the first step toward change depends on the imagination's ability to perform this radical act of faith. I see writing as a similar endeavor.

—Ruth Ozeki, *My Year of Meats*

A sweltering day by Kashmiri standards—temperatures in the low 30s Celsius (low 80s Fahrenheit). A pallid breeze ripples over Dal Lake. India's Independence Day—August 15—is almost here. This is not the cheery, brass-band-sweating-in-cherry-red-uniforms kind of day Indians are used to. In Kashmir, August 15 is a day when the façade of normalcy collapses and the Indian state's nervousness is on full display. The Indian flag can only be unfurled in high security, in a heavily militarized compound, feted by senior government officials. The national anthem sounds off on a televised or radio recording, sovereignty established through dizzying mediations. India's Independence Day takes place under curfew every year in Kashmir, a sign of things being *oh so not normal*. Srinagar's city center, Lal Chowk, has the life sucked out of it. A desiccated river before the monsoon, the streets are emptied of harried vehicles. The white marble clock tower, *ghantā ghar*, looks forlorn. Everyone is at home, "bearing it," as Altaaf Sahab put it. They are trying not to count another year of Indian rule, trying to let it be just another day that passes by, doing housework, a pirated movie on a local cable station buzzing in the background.

August 15, 2016 is different. The usual, passive eeriness is replaced by active clashes. Things have remained unsettled since Burhan Wani died five weeks ago. But because I am only in Kashmir for three weeks, I decide to try doing fieldwork anyway. My destination is SMHS hospital, where people wounded and maimed by pellets are being brought for treatment. The call and echo of a military curfew and shutdown by pro-independence groups is in full effect. I haven't been in Kashmir long enough to be sucked into the temporality of disturbance. The temporality of the United States, the pulse of long working days still in me: *I don't have time.*

Each day, it is a struggle getting to the hospital, which sits on the other end of the city. The irony of traveling thousands of miles only to find that the last five miles are the most difficult hits me. Every day, I am unsure whether I will find an auto-rickshaw to take me to the hospital. Today, as I walk to the rickshaw stand, a lone auto stands there. It waits, like an overdressed bride waiting to be ferried to her new home. The driver, a middle-aged man who has driven me all over the city through several years of fieldwork, to all kinds of dubious locations, greets me. *Salaam alaikum.* Just as I'm rejoicing at my luck in finding him, I imagine he must be thinking of himself as unlucky (*badkismat*), a word Kashmiris also use to describe their collective political fate, ensnared in an impossible conflict.

When I ask him to take me to SMHS, he looks at me with liquid eyes and says, "*Aāpki duty vahī lagī hai?*" [Is that where your duty is?] His voice is thick with feeling. He knows SMHS is the epicenter of the conflict. He knows it is where body and injury counts are being made, where the military's excesses are being witnessed, accounted for, and repressed. He knows the clinic has become part of the battlefield. His empathetic question about duty and the nature of the ongoing emergency assumes I am a medical professional. I don't have the heart to deny it. Yet his question disrupts the purposefulness I felt just a minute earlier.

Is that what this is? A duty? I ask myself.

I can tell he doesn't want to refuse me, though he's worried about getting to SMHS safely during the curfew and even more worried about getting back home. Anyone seen breaking the curfew or the shutdown call faces multiple risks from soldiers and stone throwers. There is an expectation of stillness from both sides, for very different reasons.

Without saying another word, he gets into the driver's seat. His everyday act of hospitality is made extraordinary by these circumstances. As I climb in, someone manually removes the concertina wire blocking the road. The wire is not an impenetrable barrier; its presence is just threatening *enough*.

But by removing it, I feel its affective and psychic force even more strongly. To remove it is an act of defiance. A little bit mad.

Too late now. I am trying to be brave for my rickshaw driver and he is trying to be brave for me. The auto gurgles loudly and off we go.

On the way to the hospital, I cannot get his question out of my mind. *Is that where your duty is?* I think about what it means to approach anthropological work as a "duty." In South Asia, the English word *duty* describes a job (anthropologist reporting for duty, Sir!) but also something more. Duty is an obligation. It marks a social world in which people do what they do, not because they are autonomous, liberal subjects maximizing their individual potential, but because they have obligations and commitments, that which they are *meant* to do. Duty exceeds rationality—we do what we do because we are compelled, not because it makes any sense. Duty conveys something beyond self-interest; duty demands risk. The survey team was doing its duty; so too were the psychiatrists; so too were the stone throwers and the soldiers.

As scholars, to what and to whom do we have duties?[75] Some anthropologists describe our duty as "bearing witness" or "listening." I have never felt comfortable with those confident, moral assertions given the colonial history and present of anthropology, the castles of power in which academics in the Global North are rewarded for telling stories of suffering in the Global South. Instead, I think, maybe we are caught between different meanings of duty—work for the sake of career advancement and work as ethical and political obligation. Maybe we strive to keep them in balance (as if there is a balance). But duty collapses these goals; it is a relation of radical vulnerability. It demands that we be vulnerable for others and others be vulnerable for us. By fulfilling my duty as an ethnographer, I was potentially putting my auto-rickshaw driver at risk. But he was also fulfilling a duty toward me. I was asking him to transport me safely, and he kept my trust. What would it mean to take this sense of responsibility, which is so often wrapped up in risk, away? What would it mean to deny this relationality, the mutual risks and obligations that bind us?

We zip past Rajbagh and the haunted by-lanes of Jawahar Nagar, through the more securitized streets of Lal Chowk, where shop after shop is shuttered and soldiers are lined along the streets, smudges of beige and olive, perfectly spaced ten feet apart from each other. Absent cars and people obstructing it, the rebellious graffiti scrawled all over the city's infrastructure, on walls and ribbed shop shutters, calls out. *World Sleeping?* one sign asks. *Revolution is loading*, reads another. The world may be asleep, but Kashmir is not. Stillness here means deep stirring.

Moving through the city, I feel matter and existence melt away. All that is left is sound. The engine, its deep, throaty roar, meets the sleekness of the road. Every bump sends an electric jolt through my body. Climbing the flyover, we soar over Jehangir Chowk. *Have we left the ground?* Like a twenty-first-century Chitty Chitty Bang Bang, we fly over bright blue skies, over the dull bureaucratic complex of the High Court, past the elegant, dilapidated domiciles of Habba Kadal and Fateh Kadal, perched like birds on a wire along the Jhelum's riverbank, over the austere Pathar Masjid, its stones eaten by ancient moths, past the long-abandoned Hindu temples whose crimson tops still glow in the water, high above the bunkers and gateways out of which peer the tired and alienated eyes of a soldier from Jharkhand or Gujarat or Tamil Nadu. Lost, so far from home. We fly over the city, until it becomes a trapezoid in the distance, a lush, green patch of earth, a valley made from a lake, surrounded by mountains lying in wait, sleeping giants.

֍

The driver asks if he can drop me off at Gole Market, a few blocks away from the hospital. He's too jittery to go on. I pay him several times the normal fare. He is relieved, his duty done. My chariot sputters away. I walk through the narrow neighborhood lanes toward the hospital. The open sewers give off a slightly sweet, rotting smell. The sun blazes down, the gauzy *dupatta* on my head a small savior. A stray dog licks a putrid green puddle of water. On balconies, vegetables are drying upside down—later these will be pickled and jarred for the long winter. More bored-looking soldiers stand around, sweating in their combat fatigues. Dressed for war, stuck in neighborhoods.

At SMHS, I pass the bustling volunteer camps and make my way into the cool, spacious interior of the hospital, which smells strongly of disinfectant, body odor, and metal. Worry and injury olfactorily mingle. The past few days, I've been spending time in the surgery OPD. There are four or five doctors there, attempting to look relaxed while anxiously waiting for the siren signaling another round of injured civilians.

We chat about this and that. Suddenly, we hear a commotion outside. First, there's shouting, several voices at once. It's difficult to make out words. Then we hear footsteps, the sounds of a crowd gathering. One voice calls out sharply, above the others, in Kashmiri. The shouting crescendos, we can't make out what is happening. It's only been a few days since the hospital was teargassed. We hope it's not that.

One of the residents runs to the door and pokes his head outside. After a minute, he tells us: "There's a delegation from India here, including some politicians and journalists. Someone from the PDP [People's Democratic Party] brought them here."

"That PDP guy should not have come here," one of the doctors says bitterly. He and many others are still angry at the PDP's decision to ally with the BJP.

Now we all stick our heads out the door. A huge crowd has assembled in the lobby of the hospital. One of the junior surgeons says some famous Indian politicians and journalists are in the delegation, including Mani Shanker Aiyer and Prem Shankar Jha. The delegation is here to report on the unraveling situation and to take the "temperature" of Kashmiris. These delegations come and go after every cycle of protest, armed with a feeble mandate to "gather information." This cycle has been repeated many times before: a fact-finding team will come, talk to people, take up precious time and resources, and then a few months later will release a report with "recommendations." The recommendations will invariably include some version of the same counterinsurgency doctrine that has been tried and failed for three decades (win hearts and minds using violence and care). After a flashy press conference, the report will gather dust on some bureaucrat's shelf somewhere. Many in Kashmir see these fact-finding teams as a way for the state to defer taking any real action such as demilitarization or holding a plebiscite.

This team has been carefully selected: they represent a sympathetic, benevolent, and liberal Indian public that loves Kashmir but not enough to let it go. They tell the aggravated crowd that they have come to SMHS to "speak to the protestors," the pellet patients lying in the wards with bandaged eyes and meteorite bodies. But before they can move past the lobby, a crowd surrounds them from all sides. In the history of South Asian civil disobedience and labor organizing, this technique of encircling powerful officials and spaces is called *gherao*. Through gherao, communities physically enact the ways in which they feel suffocated and besieged by oppressive laws and practices.

A simmering crowd made up of kin, neighbors, and friends of pellet patients gherao the delegation, making a wall on all sides that is at least ten bodies deep. The air is charged, sizzling with anger. We know, and they know, that anything can happen. This is the point of gherao, to assert the power of the collective. People from the crowd shout, the tones hostile: *"Why are they here?" "Why did they come?" "Who called them?" "Do they know they are not wanted?"* The delegation is locked tightly in the center, within thick, impenetrable, concentric circles of people, holding them in a tight formation.

The specter of violence seems imminent. We hold our breaths. I cannot see the faces of the liberal Indian intellectuals stuck inside but I imagine they must be terrified.

In the end, they are turned away by words.

Chants—*Āa-zā-dī*! Thump, thump. *Āa-zā-dī*! Thump, thump. *Āa-zā-dī*! Thump, thump. Chants and stomps demanding freedom ricochet off the walls of the hospital. The clinic reverberates with the two-step. And the well-meaning delegation is driven away.

LETTER TO NO ONE

1 An Urdu word that means "no one," a poetic reference.
2 August 5, 2019.

INTRODUCTION: CARE

1 IMHANS, henceforth the psychiatric hospital, is a 150-bed facility staffed by psychiatrists, clinical psychologists, postgraduates, interns, residents, and other support staff. Psychiatry was a highly gendered profession during my fieldwork—all psychiatrists were men, although today there are more female postgraduates than male. Psychiatrists attributed the gender disparity to the prevalence of stigma around mental health care.
2 Field notes written in November 2009. Fieldwork for this book was conducted between 2009 and 2011, and during the summers of 2013 and 2016.
3 All names, except those of public figures, are pseudonyms. In the psychiatric hospital and the substance abuse clinic (DDC), the two clinical settings in which I worked, I was given permission to observe and take written notes during OPD hours and group therapy sessions. I sought verbal consent for all interviews.
4 This book focuses on events in the Kashmir Valley (known henceforth as Kashmir), in the Indian-controlled state of Jammu and Kashmir. Jammu and Kashmir is composed of three regions: Jammu, the Kashmir Valley, and Ladakh.
5 The Indian nation-state operates through a federalist political structure, in which authority is shared across national, state, and local governments. When referring to the actions of the federal/union/central government that operates from New Delhi, I use the shorthand "Indian state" or the "central Indian government." When referring to the actions of the state government of Jammu and Kashmir—one of twenty-nine states in India until October 2019—I will refer to the "state government of Jammu and Kashmir." Meanwhile, the military and security apparatuses of the state—which include the Indian army, paramilitary and counterinsurgency forces, and intelligence agencies—are referred to as "Indian armed forces" or the "Indian military." The actions of

the Indian state are not singular or unified. Rather, this book examines the "diversity of its rationalities," including tensions between its militaristic and humanitarian tendencies. Didier Fassin, *At the Heart of the State: The Moral World of Institutions*, translated by Patrick Brown and Didier Fassin (New York: Pluto, 2015), ix.

6 Military occupation is a distinctly illiberal political arrangement, combining colonialism (foreign rule) and a state of emergency (martial law). Haley Duschinski and Mona Bhan, "Introduction: Law Containing Violence: Critical Ethnographies of Occupation and Resistance," *Journal of Legal Pluralism and Unofficial Law* 49, no. 3 (2017): 253–67; Lisa Hajjar, *Courting Conflict: The Israeli Military Court System in the West Bank and Gaza* (Berkeley: University of California Press, 2005). Occupations have traditionally been framed as military actions or control between separate sovereign states. As Benvenisti notes, in the post–World War II period, occupying powers have tended to deny the status of the regions they are occupying as "foreign soil," since this would mean applying international occupation law. As such, legal and political mechanisms of internal colonization, apartheid, emergency, counter-insurgency warfare, and proxy war are used instead. Eyal Benvenisti, *The International Law of Occupation* (Oxford: Oxford University Press, 2013). Haley Duschinski and Shrimoyee Nandini Ghosh, "Constituting the Occupation: Preventive Detention and Permanent Emergency in Kashmir," *Journal of Legal Pluralism and Unofficial Law* 49 (2017): 4. Beyond its legal definition, I understand occupation as a social, spatial, and phenomenological practice of asserting power through borders, jurisdictional claims, and other modes of "atmospheric violence" that create generalized disruptions and chronic crises. Salih Can Aciksoz, "Medical Humanitarianism under Atmospheric Violence: Healthcare Workers in the 2013 Gezi Protests in Turkey," *Culture, Medicine, and Psychiatry* 40, no. 2 (2016): 198–222; Duschinski and Ghosh, "Constituting the Occupation." My use of the terms *occupied* and *occupation* follows pro-independence Kashmiri scholars' uses of the terms. By this definition, Indian- and Pakistani-controlled Kashmir, as well as Aksai Chin (under Chinese control) are currently occupied.

7 These figures are estimates from the Jammu and Kashmir Coalition of Civil Society and are contested by the Indian government, which places the number of casualties at approximately 47,000.

8 M. A. Margoob, A. A. Beg, and K. S. Dutta, "Depressive Disorders in Kashmir; A Changing Sociodemographic and Clinical Profile of Patients over the Past Two Decades," *JK Practitioner* 2 (1993): 22–24.

9 Zafar Ali, Mushtaq Marghoob, M. M. Dar, and Abdul Hussain, "First Report of PTSD in Disturbed Kashmir: Characteristics of a Treatment-Seeking Sample" (paper presented at the 17th Annual Meeting of the International Society for Traumatic Stress Studies, New Orleans, 2001).

10 Médecins sans Frontières, "Kashmir: Violence and Health," November 2006, https://archive.crin.org/en/docs/msf_mental_health.pdf; M. A. Margoob et al., "Community Prevalence of Trauma in South Asia—Experience from Kash-

mir," *JK Practitioner* 13 (Supplement) (2006): S14–S17; Arooj Yaswi and Amber Haque, "Prevalence of PTSD Symptoms and Depression and Level of Coping among the Victims of the Kashmir Conflict," *Journal of Loss and Trauma* 13 (2008): 471–80.

11 For the history and expansion of PTSD as diagnostic, see Joshua Breslau, "Posttraumatic Stress Disorder in International Health," *Culture, Medicine and Psychiatry* 38 (2004): 113–26; Didier Fassin and Richard Rechtman, *The Empire of Trauma: An Inquiry into the Condition of Victimhood*, translated by Rachel Gomme (Princeton, NJ: Princeton University Press, 2009); Allan Young, *The Harmony of Illusions: Inventing Post-Traumatic Stress Disorder* (Princeton, NJ: Princeton University Press, 1995).

12 Sana Altaf, "800,000 Kashmiris Haunted by Horror," *Inter Press Service News*, February 7, 2012.

13 My fieldwork took place in three languages: Kashmiri, Urdu, and English. All conversations with patients and kin took place in Kashmiri and Urdu (I used the help of a translator for Kashmiri), while my conversations with doctors and other professionals took place in Urdu and English.

14 In 2013–14, India's government expenditures on health amounted to 1.15 percent of GDP, which is lower than average for middle-income countries. While in principle government health services are available to all citizens, in reality, bottlenecks and poor services compel households to seek private care. More than 80 percent of all health financing comes from out-of-pocket payments. Meanwhile, because of the poor quality of public health care in many parts of the country, more than 80 percent of all outpatient visits occur in the private sector, which is poorly regulated, with little or no government oversight. David H. Peters and V. R. Muraleedharan, "Regulating India's Health Services: To What End? What Future?," *Social Science and Medicine* 66 (2008): 2133–44. Mental health care has been a particularly low priority in the public health system. India has only thirty thousand inpatient beds and four thousand psychiatrists for a population of 1.2 billion people, and most of these resources are concentrated in urban areas. India's public health system exemplifies tensions between neoliberal fiscal conservatism and social welfare aspirations to create universal health coverage. For more see Abhay Shukla, "National Health Policy Reflects Conflicts between Public Health and Neoliberalism," *The Wire*, March 29, 2017.

15 In 1999, the National Human Rights Commission (NHRC) found systematic, gross human rights violations in most public psychiatric hospitals in India. The report led to banning "prison-like gate enclosures" and "cells" in all public psychiatric hospitals. National Quality Assurance in Mental Health (New Delhi: National Human Rights Commission, 1999).

16 In clinical and everyday settings, the terms *trauma, PTSD,* and increasingly *collective trauma* were used interchangeably to indicate unresolved wounds caused by long-term violence in individual and collective psyches. Following this norm, I use *trauma* to refer to a generalized sense in which the past or a past

event is conceptualized as a painful wrong that is both clinically identifiable and publicly recognizable.

17 Erna Hoch was a well-known Swiss Daseinsanalyst and psychiatrist who worked in India from 1956 to 1980. She transcribed some of Heidegger's seminars for Medard Boss and wrote many articles and books on Daseinsanalysis and Indian thought.

18 Because most of my fieldwork was conducted in bustling, crowded institutional settings, many of the patients I describe in this book appear only briefly (see chapter 3 for an exception). By contrast, psychiatrists and other expert interlocutors reappear throughout the chapters.

19 Buddhism was dominant in Kashmir during the third century BC. Though it subsequently declined in the Kashmir Valley, it remains the dominant religion in Ladakh. Suvir Kaul, *Of Gardens and Graves: Essays on Kashmir* (New Delhi: Three Essays Collective, 2015).

20 Mona Bhan and Nishita Trisal, "Fluid Landscapes, Sovereign Nature: Conservation and Counterinsurgency in Indian-controlled Kashmir," *Critique of Anthropology* 37, no. 1 (2017): 67–92.

21 Chi Huen, "What Is Context? An Ethnophilosophical Account," *Anthropological Theory* 9, no. 2 (2009): 149–69. For ethnography "inside out," see Annelise Riles, *The Network Inside Out* (Ann Arbor: University of Michigan Press, 2000).

22 Feisal Alkazi, *Srinagar: An Architectural Legacy* (New Delhi: Roli, 2014), 56–57.

23 Walter Roper Lawrence, *The Valley of Kashmir* (London: Henry Frowde, 1895), 194.

24 Cf. Frantz Fanon, *A Dying Colonialism*, translated by Haakon Chevalier (New York: Grove, 1965); Nancy Rose Hunt, *A Nervous State: Violence, Remedies and Reverie in Colonial Congo* (Durham, NC: Duke University Press, 2016); David Pederson, *American Value: Migrants, Money and Meaning in El Salvador and the United States* (Chicago: University of Chicago Press, 2013), 295.

25 See also Hunt, *A Nervous State*; Achille Mbembe, "Necropolitics," *Public Culture* 15 (2003): 11–40; Nadera Shalhoub-Kevorkian, *Security Theology, Surveillance and the Politics of Fear* (Cambridge: Cambridge University Press, 2015); Nitzan Shoshan, *The Management of Hate: Nation, Affect, and the Governance of Right-Wing Extremism in Germany* (Princeton, NJ: Princeton University Press, 2016). As Hunt (*A Nervous State*, 5) describes, "we have not thought enough . . . about colonies as nervous places, productive of *nervousness*, a kind of energy, taut and excitable." Nervousness, she notes, is not anxiety: "it suggests being on edge. Its semantics are unsettled, combining vigor, force, and determination with excitation, weakness, timidity. Nervousness yields disorderly, jittery states."

26 Miriam Ticktin, "Where Ethics and Politics Meet: The Violence of Humanitarianism in France," *American Ethnologist* 33, no. 1 (2006): 33–49. In recent years, anthropologists have published many excellent books on humanitarianism. To name just a few: Erica Bornstein, *Disquieting Gifts: Humanitarianism in New Delhi* (Palo Alto, CA: Stanford University Press, 2012); Erica Bornstein and Peter Redfield, eds., *Forces of Compassion: Humanitarianism between Ethics and Politics* (Santa Fe, NM: School of Advanced Research, 2011); Didier Fas-

sin, *Humanitarian Reason: A Moral History of the Present* (Berkeley: University of California Press, 2012); Ilana Feldman, "Looking for Humanitarian Purpose: Endurance and the Value of Lives in a Palestinian Refugee Camp," *Public Culture* 27, no. 3 (2015): 427–47; Ilana Feldman and Miriam Ticktin, eds., *In the Name of Humanity: The Government of Threat and Care* (Durham, NC: Duke University Press, 2010); Erica Caple James, "Ruptures, Rights and Repair: The Political Economy of Trauma in Haiti," *Social Science and Medicine* 70 (2010): 106–13; Erica Caple James, *Democratic Insecurities: Violence, Trauma and Intervention* (Oakland: University of California Press, 2010); Malkki, *The Need to Help*; Peter Redfield, *Life in Crisis: The Ethical Journey of Doctors Without Borders* (Berkeley: University of California Press, 2013); Ticktin, "Where Ethics and Politics Meet." However, these works almost all focus on Euro-American aid givers.

27 James, "Ruptures, Rights and Repair"; James, *Democratic Insecurities*. I borrow Fanon's famous statement: "medicine is one of the most tragic features of the colonial situation" (*A Dying Colonialism*, 121).

28 Didier Fassin and Mariella Pandolfi, eds., *Contemporary States of Emergency: The Politics of Military and Humanitarian Intervention* (New York: Zone, 2010), 16. See also Nitasha Kaul, "Rise of the Political Right in India: Hindutva-Development Mix, Modi Myth and Dualities," *Journal of Labor and Society* 20, no. 4 (2017): 523–48, for the intertwining of nationalism and development in Hindutva politics.

29 Arthur Kleinman, "Care: In Search of a Health Agenda," *The Lancet* 386 (2015): 240–41; Iain Wilkinson and Arthur Kleinman, *A Passion for Society: How We Think about Human Suffering* (Berkeley: University of California Press, 2016). Kleinman ("Care," 240) describes caring as related to "sensibilities of empathy, compassion, respect, and love" and caregiving as "relational and reciprocal."

30 A politics of unsettling challenges conventional affective and nationalist formulations of belonging, inclusion, and healing. See also Sara Ahmed, *The Promise of Happiness* (Durham, NC: Duke University Press, 2010); Sara Ahmed, *The Cultural Politics of Emotions* (New York: Routledge, 2013); Murphy, "Unsettling Care"; Jennifer Terry, *Attachments to War: Biomedical Logics and Violence in Twenty-First-Century America* (Durham, NC: Duke University Press, 2017).

31 See, for example, Veena Das, *Affliction: Health, Disease, Poverty* (New York: Fordham University Press, 2015); Angela Garcia, *The Pastoral Clinic: Addiction and Dispossession along the Rio Grande* (Berkeley: University of California Press, 2010); Julie Livingston, *Improvising Medicine: An African Oncology Ward in an Emerging Cancer Epidemic* (Durham, NC: Duke University Press. 2012); Sarah Pinto, *Daughters of Parvati: Women and Madness in Contemporary India* (Philadelphia: University of Pennsylvania Press, 2014); Lisa Stevenson, *Life beside Itself: Imagining Care in the Canadian Arctic* (Berkeley: University of California Press, 2014); Miriam Ticktin, *Casualties of Care: Immigration and the Politics of Humanitarianism in France* (Berkeley: University of California Press, 2011).

32 Sameena Mulla, *The Violence of Care: Rape Victims, Forensic Nurses and Sexual Assault Intervention* (New York: New York University Press, 2014); Ticktin, *Casu-*

alties of Care; Sarah Willen, "Darfur through a Shoah Lens: Sudanese Asylum Seekers, Unruly Biopolitical Dramas, and the Politics of Humanitarian Compassion in Israel," in *A Reader in Medical Anthropology: Theoretical Trajectories, Emergent Realities*, vol. 15, ed. B. J. Good, M. M. Fischer, S. S. Willen, and M. J. D. Good (New York: Wiley, 2010).

33 Kalindi Vora, *Life Support: Biocapital and the New History of Outsourced Labor* (Minneapolis: University of Minnesota Press, 2015), 1. See also Sara Ahmed, *The Promise of Happiness* (Durham, NC: Duke University Press, 2010); Sarah Dickey, "Permeable Homes: Domestic Service, Household Space and the Vulnerability of Class Boundaries in Urban India," *American Ethnologist* 27 (2000): 462–89; Barbara Ehrenreich and Arlie Russell Hochschild, eds., *Global Woman: Nannies, Maids and Sex Workers in the New Economy* (New York: Henry Holt, 2004); Michelle Murphy, "Unsettling Care: Troubling Transnational Itineraries of Care in Feminist Health Practices," *Social Studies of Science* 45, no. 5 (2015): 717–37.

34 Liisa Malkki, *The Need to Help: The Domestic Arts of International Humanitarianism* (Durham, NC: Duke University Press, 2015).

35 Pinto, *Daughters of Parvati*.

36 As Kaul notes, gendered representations enable, legitimize, and normalize Indian state violence in Kashmir. Nitasha Kaul, "India's Obsession with Kashmir: Democracy, Gender, (Anti-)Nationalism," *Feminist Review* 119 (2018): 127. See also Inshah Malik. "The Muslim Woman's Struggle for Justice," 2013, http://www.india-seminar.com/2013/643/643_inshah_malik.htm; Nadera Shalhoub-Kevorkian, "The Political Economy of Children's Trauma: A Case Study of House Demolition in Palestine," *Feminism and Psychology* 19, no. 3 (2009): 335–42.

37 The origins of modern counterinsurgency are explicitly antinationalist, designed to quash self-determination struggles. Nasser Hussain, "Counterinsurgency's Comeback: Can a Colonialist Strategy Be Reinvented?" *Boston Review*, January 1, 2010, http://bostonreview.net/world/counterinsurgency%E2%80%99s-comeback; David Kilcullen, *Counterinsurgency* (Oxford: Oxford University Press, 2010). The Indian army is one of the most experienced counterinsurgency forces in the world, conducting counterinsurgency against Nagas since 1956, Mizos from 1966 to 1986, Manipur and Tripura in the 1970s, and during the 1980s and 1990s against Sikhs, Tamils (Sri Lankans), and Kashmiris. Rajesh Rajagopalan, "'Restoring Normalcy': The Evolution of the Indian Army's Counterinsurgency Doctrine," *Small Wars and Insurgencies* 11, no. 1 (2000): 44–68. In 2006, the Indian military published a formal counterinsurgency doctrine that emphasized a "humane and people-centric approach, underscor[ing] the need for scrupulous upholding of the laws of the land, deep respect for Human Rights and minimum use of kinetic means, to create a secure environment, without causing any collateral damage." Ministry of Defence, "Doctrine for Sub-Conventional Operations. Headquarters Army Training Command: Shimla, India," 2006, http://indianstrategicknowledge

online.com/web/doctrine%20sub%20conv%20w.pdf, 3. While the payoffs of winning hearts and minds have been questionable in recent conflicts such as in Iraq and Afghanistan, in India, "Winning hearts and minds (WHAM) remains the primary component of CI [counterinsurgency] for the armed forces." Rahul Bhonsle, "Winning Hearts and Minds: Lessons from Jammu and Kashmir," Manekshaw Paper no. 14, Centre for Land Welfare Studies, New Delhi, 2009, 10. As Bhan has described, from 2006 on, the Indian army significantly increased its budget for WHAM projects, including civilian-military engagements, facilitating elections, reviving the tourist industry, and "countering negative propaganda." The military's justification for WHAM was that the absence of economic opportunities could breed future "antinationals." Mona Bhan, *Counterinsurgency, Democracy and the Politics of Identity in India: From Warfare to Welfare?* (London: Routledge, 2013).

38 Nils Gilman, "Militarism and Humanitarianism," *Humanity* 3, no. 2: 173–78, 174.

39 Rajagopalan, "'Restoring Normalcy,'" 51; Terry, *Attachments to War*, 27.

40 Terry, *Attachments to War*, 40.

41 For example, American psychologists played a critical role in developing torture techniques for US counterinsurgency efforts.

42 Ravina Aggarwal and Mona Bhan, "Disarming Violence: Development, Democracy and Security on the Borders of India," *Journal of Asian Studies* 68, no. 2 (2009): 519–42; Nosheen Ali, "Books vs Bombs? Humanitarian Development and the Narrative of Terror in Northern Pakistan," *Third World Quarterly* 31, no. 4 (2010): 541–59; and Bhan, *Counterinsurgency, Democracy and the Politics of Identity in India*, are notable exceptions.

43 Deepti Misri, "Showing Humanity: Violence and Visuality in Kashmir," *Cultural Studies* 33, no. 3 (2019): 527–49; Stefania Pandolfo, "The Knot of the Soul: Postcolonial Conundrums, Madness, and the Imagination," in *Postcolonial Disorders*, ed. Mary-Jo DelVecchio Good, Sandra Teresa Hyde, Sarah Pinto, and Byron J. Good (Berkeley: University of California Press, 2008).

44 Emma Varley and Saiba Varma, "Spectral Lines: Haunted Hospitals across the Line of Control," *Medical Anthropology* 37, no. 6 (2018): 1–15.

45 Ahmed, *The Cultural Politics of Emotions*, 39; William E. Connolly, "The Evangelical-Capitalist Resonance Machine," *Political Theory* 33, no. 6 (2005): 870.

46 Mohamad Junaid argues that many pro-independence activists view themselves as the proper heirs to Kashmiri protestors who died in the first pro-independence agitation against Dogra rule in 1931 (Junaid, "Youth Activists in Kashmir," 153).

47 Haley Duschinski, Mona Bhan, Ather Zia, and Cynthia Mahmood, eds., *Resisting Occupation in Kashmir* (Philadelphia: University of Pennsylvania Press, 2018).

48 Mridu Rai, *Hindu Rulers, Muslim Subjects: Islam, Rights, and the History of Kashmir* (Princeton, NJ: Princeton University Press, 2004).

49   Ananya Jahanara Kabir, *Territory of Desire: Representing the Valley of Kashmir* (Minneapolis: University of Minnesota Press, 2009), 74–75.

50   Chitralekha Zutshi, *Languages of Belonging: Islam, Regional Identity, and the Making of Kashmir* (Oxford: Oxford University Press, 2004), 308–10.

51   On the eve of independence, the Dogra maharaja requested standstill agreements with both India and Pakistan. In September–October 1947, the maharaja led a campaign of genocide, harassment, and violence against Kashmiri Muslims in Jammu, displacing about half a million people and killing up to 200,000. These events led to an all-out rebellion against the maharaja. As the maharaja escaped from Srinagar in October 1947, he sought military help from India and accepted the Indian demand that Kashmir accede to it. Junaid, "Youth Activists in Kashmir," 13–14; Alastair Lamb, *Kashmir: A Disputed Legacy 1846–1990* (Oxford: Oxford University Press, 1991). When it was incorporated into India, Jammu and Kashmir was granted some legal autonomy from the central government (Article 370 of the Indian constitution). Article 370 granted the state a "special autonomous status" within the Indian Union, but this was systematically eroded through a series of presidential orders and Supreme Court judgments. Mona Bhan, Haley Duschinski, and Ather Zia, "Introduction: 'Rebels of the Streets': Violence, Protest and Freedom in Kashmir," in *Resisting Occupation in Kashmir*, ed. Haley Duschinski, Mona Bhan, Ather Zia, and Cynthia Mahmood (Philadelphia: University of Pennsylvania Press, 2018). In August 2019, fulfilling a long-standing election promise, the nationalist BJP government ended Kashmir's autonomous status by presidential decree and divided the state into two union territories, bringing it under greater central government control.

52   Chitralekha Zutshi, "An Ongoing Partition: Histories, Borders and the Politics of Vivisection in Jammu and Kashmir," *Contemporary South Asia* 23, no. 3 (2015): 266–75.

53   The politics of AJK are beyond the scope of this book. Although the Pakistani state often uses people in AJK as a foil against the occupation of Jammu and Kashmir, there has been intense political repression of pro-freedom ideas in Pakistani-controlled Kashmir as well. Anam Zakaria, *Between the Great Divide: A Journey into Pakistan-Administered Kashmir* (Noida: HarperCollins India, 2018), xxv.

54   Bhan, Duschinski, and Zia, "Introduction," 20. The original UN-mediated plebiscite did not recognize the possibility of Kashmiri independence.

55   In 1962, the Indo-Chinese war over Aksai Chin resulted in the creation of another international border, the Line of Actual Control (LAC), codified by India and China in 1993.

56   Relatively little has been written about how Partition affected Kashmir, particularly when compared with the volumes of work on the Bengal and Punjab partitions. Zakaria, *Between the Great Divide* ; Ather Zia, "Postcolonial Nation-Making: Warfare, Jihad, Subjectivity and Compassion in the Region of Kashmir," *India Review* 13, no. 3 (2014): 300–311.

57 Bhan, Duschinski, and Zia, "Introduction," 22; Hafsa Kanjwal, "Build-
    ing a New Kashmir: Bakshi Ghulam Muhammad and the Politics of State-
    Formation in a Disputed Territory (1953–1963)" (PhD dissertation, University
    of Michigan, 2017); Cabeiri deBergh Robinson, *Body of Victim, Body of Warrior:*
    Refugee Families and the Making of Kashmiri Jihadists (Berkeley: University of Cali-
    fornia Press, 2013).

58 Bornstein, *Disquieting Gifts*; Yogesh Joshi, "India, Libya and the Kashmir Para-
    dox," *World Politics Review,* March 11, 2011, https://www.worldpoliticsreview
    .com/articles/8163/india-libya-and-the-kashmir-paradox.

59 A "postcolonial" lens does not sufficiently recognize the dynamics of incom-
    plete decolonization in places such as Kashmir, Palestine, Kurdistan, or on na-
    tive lands in settler colonial societies. In these places, decolonization did not
    mean the end of colonialism, but the transformation of anticolonial struggles
    into neocolonial ones (Ahmad, personal communication, June 28, 2019). See
    also Goldie Osuri, "Imperialism, Colonialism and Sovereignty in the (Post)
    Colony: India and Kashmir," *Third World Quarterly* 38, no. 11 (2017): 2428–43.

60 Kanjwal, "Building a New Kashmir," 89; Sharad Raghavan, "J&K Gets 10% of
    Central Funds with Only 1% of Population," *The Hindu,* July 24, 2016. https://
    www.thehindu.com/news/national/other-states/JampK-gets-10-of-Central
    -funds-with-only-1-of-population/article14506264.ece; Kashmir's much higher
    percentage of received grants in aid as compared with other Indian states is
    combined with significantly low public and private investment in the region —
    particularly in the areas of infrastructure, power, and connectivity. Kashmir
    received only US$5.5 million in foreign direct investment between April 2000
    and March 2019, the lowest among Indian states. Archana Chaudhary and
    Bidhudatta Pradhan, "Modi's Options for Jammu and Kashmir's Economy
    Are Limited," *Economic Times,* August 14, 2019, https://economictimes.india
    times.com/markets/stocks/news/modis-options-for-jammu-and-kashmirs
    -economy-are-limited/articleshow/70675008.cms?from=mdr; Nishita Trisal,
    "In Kashmir, Nehru's Golden Chains That He Hoped Would Bind the State to
    India Have Lost Their Lustre," *Scroll,* November 30, 2015.

61 Siddhartha Prakash, "Political Economy of Kashmir since 1947," *Economic and*
    Political Weekly 35, no. 24 (2000): 2051–60.

62 In a speech given in 1969 to the Plebiscite Front in Muzaffarabad, Bhat ex-
    plained: "If you think that Kashmir's freedom struggle can be fought with
    the help of Pakistani money, Indian money, American money or any other
    country's resources, then you are only deluding yourself. Kashmir's is a war to
    reclaim the home of Kashmiris and it must be run with our own money. We
    cannot fight our war of freedom if we rely on the resources of others." Wajahat
    Ahmad, "'Our War of Liberation Cannot Be Fought by Beggars or by Those
    Who Seek Aid from Others': Maqbool Bhat," *Kashmir Ink,* February 11, 2018.

63 Ghassan Hage, "Hating Israel in the Field: On Ethnography and Political
    Emotions," *Anthropological Theory* 9, no. 1 (2009): 59–79.

64 Kabir, *Territory of Desire.*

65 Ahmed, *The Cultural Politics of Emotions.* Postindependence Indian nationalism inherited British assumptions of Muslims as "foreign invaders" and "oppressors who ultimately ushered in a period of decline." Barbara Metcalf, *Islamic Contestations: Essays on Muslims in India and Pakistan* (New Delhi: Oxford University Press, 2004), 195; Parvis Ghassem-Fachandi, *Pogrom in Gujarat: Hindu Nationalism and Anti-Muslim Violence in India* (Princeton, NJ: Princeton University Press, 2012).

66 Frank B. Wilderson, "'We're Trying to Destroy the World': Anti-Blackness and Police Violence after Ferguson," in *Shifting Corporealities in Contemporary Performance: Danger, Im/Mobility and Politics*, ed. Marina Gržinić and Aneta Stojnić, 45–59 (Cham, Switzerland: Palgrave Macmillan, 2015), 7.

67 Farrukh Faheem, "Interrogating the Ordinary: Everyday Politics and the Struggle for *Azadi* in Kashmir," in *Resisting Occupation in Kashmir*, ed. Mona Bhan, Haley Duschinski, Ather Zia, and Cynthia Mahmood, 230–47 (Philadelphia: University of Pennsylvania Press, 2018).

68 Junaid, "Youth Activists in Kashmir," 20.

69 Seema Kazi, *In Kashmir: Gender, Militarization and the Modern Nation State* (London: South End, 2009), xxv.

70 Sumantra Bose, *Contested Lands: Israel-Palestine, Kashmir, Bosnia, Cyprus and Sri Lanka* (Cambridge, MA: Harvard University Press, 2007). The rise of the Hizb-ul-Mujahideen was due not only to Pakistan's influence, but also due to the popularity of the Jama'at-e-Islami within Kashmir (Kazi, *In Kashmir*, 168).

71 There are multiple meanings and nuances in the call for freedom, or āzādī. At a formal political level, āzādī means independence from Indian rule, "a voluntary separation from a forced union." Mohamad Junaid, "A Letter to Fellow Kashmiris," in *Until My Freedom Has Come: The New Intifada in Kashmir*, ed. Sanjay Kak (New Delhi: Penguin, 2011), 284. In poetic and literary discourse, āzādī also signifies an existential cry for justice. Rashmi Luthra, "Perils of Translation in a Conflict Situation: Lessons from Kashmir," *International Journal of Communication* 10 (2016): 1097–115.

72 Kazi, *In Kashmir*, xv.

73 While India buys most of its arms from Russia and the United States, it purchases drones, electronic fences, and crowd dispersal tactics from Israel and has also conducted joined security trainings with Israeli defense forces.

74 Junaid, "Youth Activists in Kashmir," 29.

75 Kazi, *In Kashmir*, 94; Rai, *Hindu Rulers, Muslim Subjects*, 297. Although the Kashmir Valley is predominantly Muslim (97 percent) and India is predominantly Hindu, the Indian state and Hindu nationalist organizations have exaggerated the religious dimensions of the Kashmir conflict to mark the dispute as driven by radical Islam, rather than a political movement for self-determination.

76 Nishita Trisal, "India Must Stop Weaponizing the Pain of Kashmiri Pandits," *Washington Post*, August 22, 2019.

77 See also Haley Duschinski, "Destiny Effects: Militarization, State Power, and Punitive Containment in Kashmir Valley," *Anthropological Quarterly* 82, no. 3

(2009): 691–717; Haley Duschinski, "Fake Encounters and the Informalization of Everyday Violence in Kashmir Valley," *Cultural Studies* 24, no. 1 (2010): 110–32; Nasser Hussain, "Hyperlegality," *New Criminal Law Review* 10, no. 4 (2007): 514–31; Mohamad Junaid, "Death and Life under Occupation: Space, Violence, and Memory in Kashmir," in *Everyday Occupations: Experiencing Militarism in South Asia and the Middle East*, ed. Kamala Visweswaran (Philadelphia: University of Pennsylvania Press, 2013); Kazi, *In Kashmir*; Kamala Visweswaran, "Introduction: Geographies of Everyday Occupation," in *Everyday Occupations: Experiencing Militarism in South Asia and the Middle East* (Philadelphia: University of Pennsylvania Press, 2013).

78 Sanjay Kak, ed., *Until My Freedom Has Come: The New Intifada in Kashmir* (New Delhi: Penguin, 2011), xv.

79 Junaid, "Youth Activists in Kashmir," 123. Rather than a posture that associates "social movements with social and cultural resistance, and resistance as an end goal," scholars of decolonization emphasize the importance of discourses and theories of decolonization emerging from practice. Silvia Rivera Cusicanqui, *"Ch'ixinakax utxiwa*: A Reflection on the Practices and Discourses of Decolonization," translated by Brenda Baletti, *South Atlantic Quarterly* 111, no. 1 (2012): 95–109.

80 Niharika Mandhana, "Modi Says Kashmiri Youths Should Have Laptops, Not Stones, in Their Hands," *Wall Street Journal*, August 10, 2016.

81 "'We Have to Hug Each Kashmiri, Create New Paradise,' Says Modi at Nashik Rally," *The Wire*, September 19, 2019, https://thewire.in/politics/we-have-to-hug-each-kashmiri-create-new-paradise-says-modi-at-nashik-rally. The decision to revoke Kashmir's autonomy was also articulated as a form of care, as a way to end "violence, terrorism, separatism and corruption."

82 Between April 2018 and May 2019, approximately 160 civilians were killed, the highest number in a decade. Many commentators worry that the excessive force used on unarmed protestors will lead people in Kashmir to return to armed violence. Office of the UN High Commissioner for Human Rights, "Updates of the Situation of Human Rights in Indian-Administered Kashmir and Pakistan-Administered Kashmir from May 2018 to April 2019," United Nations Human Rights Office of the High Commissioner, July 8, 2019, https://www.ohchr.org/Documents/Countries/IN/KashmirUpdateReport_8July2019.pdf.

83 Saiba Varma, "From 'Terrorist' to 'Terrorized': How Trauma Became the Language of Suffering in Kashmir," in *Resisting Occupation in Kashmir*, ed. Haley Duschinski, Mona Bhan, Ather Zia, and Cynthia Mahmood (Philadelphia: University of Pennsylvania Press, 2018). The use of care, medicine, and psychiatry in colonial and imperialistic projects is not new, though it has come to the fore in a post-9/11 context. See Fanon, *A Dying Colonialism*.

84 Puig de la Bellacasa, drawing on Bruno Latour's notion of "matters of concern," argues that "matters of care" amplify the affective entanglements through which things come to matter and draw attention to marginalized, in-

visibilized, and neglected elements, experiences, and relations. I use this term to critically question the state's interest in the mental health and psychic well-being of its occupied subjects. Maria Puig de la Bellacasa, "Matters of Care in Technoscience: Assembling Neglected Things," *Social Studies of Science* 41, no. 1 (2011): 85–106.

85 Aggarwal and Bhan, "Disarming Violence"; Arpita Anant, *Counterinsurgency and "Op Sadhbhavana" in Jammu and Kashmir* (New Delhi: Institute for Defense Studies and Analyses, 2011).

86 Abid Bashir, "Police Use Psychologists to Control Kashmir Streets," *Greater Kashmir*, accessed May 3, 2018, http://m.greaterkashmir.com/news/kashmir/police-use-psychologists-to-control-kashmir-streets/283940.html.

87 Terry, *Attachments to War.*

88 Chetan Bhatt, "Frontlines and Interstices in the Global War on Terror," *Development and Change* 38, no. 6 (2007): 1081.

89 Marla Framke, "Political Humanitarianism in the 1930s: Indian Aid for Republican Spain," *European Review of History* 23, nos. 1–2 (2016): 63–81. "Political humanitarianism" is humanitarianism in which political motivations are always already explicit. Unlike NGO humanitarianism, which is usually done in the name of a universal humanity, political humanitarianism is tied into nationalist ideals of assimilation, power projections, and national security.

90 Aciksoz, "Medical Humanitarianism under Atmospheric Violence"; Adia Benton and Sa'ed Atshan, "'Even War Has Rules': On Medical Neutrality and Legitimate Non-Violence," *Culture, Medicine and Psychiatry* 40 (2016): 151–58; Omar Dewachi, *Ungovernable Life: Mandatory Medicine and Statecraft in Iraq* (Stanford, CA: Stanford University Press, 2017); Sherine Hamdy and Soha Bayoumi, "Egypt's Popular Uprising and the Stakes of Medical Neutrality," *Culture, Medicine and Psychiatry* 40, no. 2 (2016): 223–41; Emma Varley, "Abandonments, Solidarities and Logics of Care: Hospitals as Sites of Sectarian Conflict in Gilgit-Baltistan," *Culture, Medicine and Psychiatry* 40, no. 2 (2016): 159–80; Varley and Varma, "Spectral Lines." Hospitals and medical professionals have directly suffered the effects of violence through bombings, targeted attacks, kidnappings, and killings of patients and providers. Dewachi has also shown how medicine is not just a target, but a *tactic* of war. Omar Dewachi, "Blurred Lines: Warfare and Health Care," *Medical Anthropology Theory* 2, no. 2 (2015): 95–101.

91 Ticktin, "Where Ethics and Politics Meet"; Ticktin, *Casualties of Care.*

92 Benton and Atshan, "'Even War Has Rules.'"

93 Emma Varley, "Against Protocol: The Politics and Perils of Oxytocin (Mis)Use in a Pakistani Labour Room," *Purusārtha* (2019). In chapter 3, I describe the use of electroconvulsive therapy in the clinic in relation to the use of electric shock as a form of torture.

94 Didier Fassin, "Inequality of Lives, Hierarchies of Humanity: Moral Commitments and Ethical Dilemmas of Humanitarianism," in *In the Name of Humanity: The Government of Threat and Care*, ed. Ilana Feldman and Miriam Iris

Ticktin (Durham, NC: Duke University Press, 2010); Ilana Feldman, *Life Lived in Relief: Humanitarian Predicaments and Palestinian Refugee Politics* (Oakland: University of California Press, 2018), 126; Brian Larkin, "The Politics and Poetics of Infrastructure," *Annual Review of Anthropology* 42 (2013): 327–43; Sherine Hamdy, "When the State and Your Kidneys Fail," *American Ethnologist* 35, no. 4 (2008): 553–69; Pinto, *Daughters of Parvati*, 4; Catherine Smith, "Doctors That Harm, Doctors That Heal: Reimagining Medicine in Post-Conflict Aceh, Indonesia," *Ethnos: Journal of Anthropology* 80, no. 2 (2013): 1–20; Alice Street, *Biomedicine in an Unstable Place* (Durham, NC: Duke University Press, 2012); Livia Wick, "Building the Infrastructure, Modeling the Nation: The Case of Birth in Palestine," *Culture, Medicine and Psychiatry* 32 (2008): 328–57; Varley, "Abandonments, Solidarities and Logics of Care."

95 Waltraud Ernst, "Idioms of Madness and Colonial Boundaries: The Case of the European and 'Native' Mentally Ill in Early Nineteenth Century British India," *Comparative Studies in Society and History* 39, no. 1 (1997): 153–81; Waltraud Ernst, "Crossing the Boundaries of 'Colonial Psychiatry': Reflections on the Development of Psychiatry in British India, c. 1870–1940," *Culture, Medicine and Psychiatry* 35 (2011): 536–45.

96 Peter Redfield, "Doctors, Borders, and Life in Crisis," *Cultural Anthropology* 20, no. 3 (2005): 328–61, 344. See also Feldman, "Looking for Humanitarian Purpose"; Feldman, *Life Lived in Relief*; Ramah McKay, *Medicine in the Meantime: The Work of Care in Mozambique* (Durham, NC: Duke University Press, 2018).

97 Feldman, "Looking for Humanitarian Purpose."

98 Brad Evans interviews Lauren Berlant, "Without Exceptions: On the Ordinariness of Violence," *Los Angeles Review of Books*, July 30, 2018.

99 There seems to be a generalized, indirect way of speaking about violence in ongoing conflict. Mahaul and hālāt are like the Spanish word *la situación*, used in war-torn settings in Latin America. Cf. Janis H. Jenkins, "The State Construction of Affect: Political Ethos and Mental Health among Salvadoran Refugees," *Culture, Medicine and Psychiatry* 15 (1991): 139–65; Emma Varley, "'Hallat Kharab'/Tension Times: The Maternal Health Costs of Gilgit's Sunni-Shia Conflict," in *Missing Links in Sustainable Development: South Asian Perspectives* (Islamabad: Sustainable Development Policy Institute, 2008).

100 For example, Metzl shows how schizophrenia—historically a nonthreatening disease that primarily targeted white, middle-class women—became associated with the perceived hostility, rebellion, mistrust, and violence of black men during the civil rights movement. Jonathan M. Metzl, *The Protest Psychosis: How Schizophrenia Became a Black Disease* (Boston: Beacon, 2009).

101 Hamdy, "When the State and Your Kidneys Fail."

102 Fanon, *A Dying Colonialism*, 250–51. In contrast to Foucault, who endowed criminals, but not the mentally ill, with political subjectivities, Fanon articulates an intimate connection between psychic distress and colonialism. For Fanon, colonialism produces existential crises for both the colonizer and colonized.

103 Karina Czyzewski, "Colonialism as a Broader Social Determinant of Health," *International Indigenous Policy Journal* 2, no. 1 (2011): 4; Per Axelsson, Tahu Kukutai, and Rebecca Kippen, "The Field of Indigenous Health and the Role of Colonization and History," *Journal of Population Research* 33, no. 1 (2016): 1–7.

104 Catherine E. Walsh, "The Decolonial *For:* Resurgences, Shifts, and Movements," in *On Decoloniality: Concepts, Analytics, Praxis*, ed. Walter D. Mignolo and Catherine E. Walsh, 15–33 (Durham, NC: Duke University Press, 2018).

105 Elaine Scarry, *The Body in Pain: The Making and the Unmaking of the World* (New York: Oxford University Press, 1987).

106 Berlant, "Without Exceptions: On the Ordinariness of Violence." Similarly, Spivak affirms that the silence or absent voice of the sexed subaltern subject can only be amplified by someone else's attempt to represent her from their own perspective. Gayatri Chakravorty Spivak, "'Draupadi' by Mahasveta Devi," *Critical Inquiry* 8, no. 2 (1981): 381–402.

107 Lawrence Cohen, *No Aging in India* (Berkeley: University of California Press, 1998), 176. See also Kaul, *Of Gardens and Graves*. "Poetry and culture brim with indirection, ambiguity, lacunae, indeed, with downright silence." Kent Maynard, "The Poetic Turn of Culture, or the 'Resistances of Structure,'" *Anthropology and Humanism* 33 (2008): 66–84. See also Kent Maynard and Melisa Cahnmann, "Anthropology at the Edge of Words: Where Poetry and Ethnography Meet," *Anthropology and Humanism* 35 (2010): 2–19; T. Minh-ha Trinh, *Woman/Native/Other* (Bloomington: Indiana University Press, 1989).

CHAPTER 1: SIEGE

1 Doctor (*tabeeb* in the original) refers to a person who cures spiritual diseases.

2 "Gulrez" is a well-known Kashmiri love poem.

3 Field notes written in 2010.

4 According to the Inter-Agency Standing Committee (IASC) guidelines, psychosocial care or psychosocial support refers to "any type of local or outside support that aims to protect or promote psychosocial well-being and/or prevent or treat mental disorders." Inter-Agency Standing Committee, *IASC Guidelines on Mental Health and Psychosocial Support in Emergency Settings* (Geneva: IASC, 2007).

5 Gujars are a pastoral agricultural ethnic group in India, Pakistan, and northeastern Afghanistan. In Jammu and Kashmir, Gujars are Muslims and are classified as Scheduled Tribes (ST) in the Indian constitution. Aparna Rao, "The Many Sources of Identity: An Example of Changing Affiliations in Rural Jammu and Kashmir," *Ethnic and Racial Studies* 22, no. 1 (1999): 56–91.

6 Unani medicine is a system of healing and health maintenance observed in South Asia, particularly, but not exclusively, among Muslim communities. Its origins lie in ancient Greek, Arabic, and Persian humoral medicine. Diseases result from an imbalance of the four humors, the four qualities in the body, and from the external environment. Helen E. Sheehan and S. J. Hussain,

"Unani Tibb: History, Theory and Contemporary Practice in South Asia," *Annals of the American Academy of Political and Social Science* 583 (2002): 122–35. Medical anthropologists of South Asia have argued that the goal of indigenous medicines—such as Unani, Siddha, and Ayurveda—is not merely the restoration of health or the absence of disease and symptoms, but improving health, defined as a manifestation of power, vigor, fitness, and vitality. Joseph Alter, "Heaps of Health, Metaphysical Fitness: Ayurveda and the Ontology of Good Health in Medical Anthropology," *Current Anthropology* 40, no. S1 (1999): S53.

7 Patients combining biomedical and complementary and alternative medicines—what anthropologists have described as "medical pluralism"— are extremely common across South Asia.

8 Lawrence Cohen, *No Aging in India* (Berkeley: University of California Press, 1998); Byron Good, "The Heart of What's the Matter: The Semantics of Illness in Iran," *Culture, Medicine and Psychiatry* 1, no. 1 (1977): 25–58; Angel Martínez-Hernáez, *What's behind the Symptom? On Psychiatric Observation and Anthropological Understanding*, trans. Susan M. DiGiacomo and John Bates (Oxon, UK: Routledge, 2000), 109; Michael Taussig, *The Nervous System* (New York: Routledge, 1992), 83. While kamzorī is particular to South Asia, there are similar forms of chronic fatigue globally: *nervios* in Latin America, neurasthenia in China, *durbal* in Bangladesh, and so on. These modes of expression are also related to social and economic precarity.

9 Margaret Lock and Vinh-Kim Nguyen, eds., *An Anthropology of Biomedicine* (Chichester, UK: Wiley Blackwell, 2010), 159l.

10 Good, "The Heart of What's the Matter." The "interpretive" approach has been critiqued for reading symptoms as "texts," as transparent holders of meaning that represent something else.

11 I use the Urdu version of the word because that was how I primarily encountered it in the field.

12 Cohen, *No Aging in India*, 232.

13 Cohen, *No Aging in India*, 230.

14 Nancy Rose Hunt, *A Nervous State: Violence, Remedies, and Reverie in Colonial Congo* (Durham, NC: Duke University Press, 2016), 2.

15 Scholars argue that identities of body-persons in South Asia are constituted through exchanges of substances and materials—such as between persons, food, land, and bodies—that carry cultural meaning. The notion of a "bio-moral" body conveys how the body's corporeality is inseparable from ideas of personhood and social position. Joseph Alter, *Moral Materialism: Sex and Masculinity in Modern India* (New Delhi: Penguin, 2012); Christopher A. Bayly, *Origins of Nationality in South Asia: Patriotism and Ethical Government in the Making of Modern India* (New Delhi: Oxford University Press, 1998); Cohen, *No Aging in India*; McKim Marriott, "Hindu Transactions: Diversity without Dualism," in *Transaction and Meaning*, ed. Bruce Kapferer (Philadelphia: Institute for the Study of Human Issues, 1978); McKim Marriott and R. Inden, "Towards Ethnosociology of South Asian Caste System," in *The New Wind: Changing Identities*

in South Asia, ed. D. Kavid (The Hague: Mouton, 1977); Valentine E. Daniel, *Fluid Signs: Being a Person the Tamil Way* (Berkeley: University of California Press, 1984); Akio Tanabe, "Cultural Politics of Life: Biomoral Humanosphere and Vernacular Democracy in Rural Orissa, India," Kyoto Working Papers on Area Studies no. 44, Center for Southeast Asian Studies, Kyoto University, 2009. Thanks to Sarah Pinto for this point.

16 Excerpted from *Ghazal* by Ghulam Hassan "Ghamgeen."

17 The exchange (from April 2010) took place in Kashmiri and was translated with the help of a translator.

18 As Michel Foucault has argued, since the nineteenth century, biomedicine has privileged vision as a way of making the body and illness legible; to know symptoms are "real," physicians need to see them in the body. As Buchbinder notes in her work on chronic pain in the United States, attempts by biomedicine to decipher whether or not pain is "real" are also tied to the legacy of mind–body dualism in US biomedicine and Euro-American culture. As she writes, much clinical intervention on pain presumes that pain "must be either mental or physical, but not both." Mara Buchbinder, *All in Your Head: Making Sense of Pediatric Pain* (Berkeley: University of California Press, 2011), 11.

19 Georges Canguilhem, *On the Normal and the Pathological* (New York: Zone, 1991).

20 According to the Diagnostics and Statistical Manual (DSM), PTSD is defined by two major criteria: *an exposure to a traumatic event* and *a set of psychiatric symptoms that occur (or recur) after the event*. Originally framed as applying only to extreme experiences, PTSD has come to be associated with a growing list of relatively commonplace events, from accidents to muggings to sexual harassment to the shock of receiving bad news. Derek Summerfield, "The Invention of Post-Traumatic Stress Disorder and the Social Usefulness of a Psychiatric Category," *British Medical Journal* 322 (2001): 95–98.

21 Edward Shorter, "Chronic Fatigue in Historical Perspective," in *Chronic Fatigue Syndrome*, ed. Gregory R. Bock and Julie Whelan (Chichester, UK: John Wiley, 1993), 19.

22 Edward Shorter, ed., *Bedside Manners: The Troubled History of Doctors and Patients* (New York: Simon and Schuster, 1985); Lesley Jo Weaver, "*Tension* among Women in North India: An Idiom of Distress and a Cultural Syndrome," *Culture, Medicine and Psychiatry* 41, no. 1 (2017): 35–55. Some sympathetic and "culturally sensitive" psychiatrists might read descriptions of kamzori as examples of trauma, and PTSD's localization in Kashmir as a local "idiom of distress." Mark Nichter, "Idioms of Distress: Alternatives in the Expression of Psychosocial Distress: A Case Study from South India," *Cultural Medicine and Psychiatry* 5 (1981): 379–408. However, the tension between trauma/PTSD and kamzori is not only one of scale, of "global" versus "local" knowledge. Kamzori has been documented as a pan-South Asian phenomenon, a diagnostic category relevant to at least one-sixth of the world's population. It also resonates with other fatigue-related disorders, such as neurasthenia and chronic fatigue syndrome, that have been documented cross culturally. Thus, what is at stake in the com-

parison between PTSD and kamzorī is something *more* or other than how a "local" idiom of distress (kamzorī) is being co-opted to fit international public health criteria. Relatedly, I am not arguing that kamzorī is more culturally resonant than PTSD; as we will see in the following section, PTSD has been localized and used to many different political ends in Kashmir. Rather, my argument is that, as clinical complaints, PTSD and kamzorī have different moral and political stakes and each reveals a different ontology of violence, trauma, and personhood.

23 Jocelyn Chua, "The Register of 'Complaint': Psychiatric Diagnosis and the Discourse of Grievance in the South Indian Mental Health Encounter," *Medical Anthropology Quarterly* 26, no. 2 (2012): 221–40.

24 See Veena Das, *Affliction: Health, Disease, Poverty* (New York: Fordham University Press, 2015); Michael Nunley, "Why Psychiatrists in India Prescribe So Many Drugs," *Culture, Medicine and Psychiatry* 20, no. 2 (1996): 165–97.

25 Erica Caple James, "Ruptures, Rights and Repair: The Political Economy of Trauma in Haiti," *Social Science and Medicine* 70 (2010): 106–13.

26 Kaz de Jong, N. Ford, S. Kam, K. Lokuge, S. Fromm, R. van Galen, B. Reilley, and R. Kleber, "Conflict in the Indian Kashmir Valley I: Exposure to Violence," *Conflict and Health* 2 (2008a), 10; Kaz de Jong, S. Kam, N. Ford, K. Lokuge, S. Fromm, R. van Galen, B. Reilley, R. Kleber, "Conflict in the Indian Kashmir Valley II: Psychosocial Impact," *Conflict and Health* 2 (2008b): 11; Tambri Housen, Annick Lenglet, Showkat Shah, Helal Sha, Shabnum Ara, Giovanni Pintaldi, and Alice Richardson, "Trauma in the Kashmir Valley and the Mediating Effects of Stressors of Daily Life on Symptoms of Posttraumatic Stress Disorder, Depression and Anxiety," *Conflict and Health* 13 (2019), 58; M. A. Margoob, M. M. Firdosi, R. Banal, A. Y. Khan, Y. A. Malik, S. A. Ahmad, et al., "Community Prevalence of Trauma in South Asia—Experience from Kashmir," *JK Practitioner* 13 (Supplement) (2006): S14–17; J. I. Khan, "Armed Conflict: Changing Instruments and Health Outcomes, a Study of Urban Households in Kashmir," *International Journal of Physical Social Sciences* 3, no. 7 (2013): 1–14.

27 Judith Matloff and Robert Nickelsberg, "Beyond the Breaking Point," *Dart Center*, April 9, 2009, http://dartcenter.org/content/beyond-breaking-point.

28 Gregory Bistoen, *Trauma, Ethics and the Political beyond PTSD: The Dislocations of the Real* (London: Palgrave Macmillan, 2016), 44.

29 See Saiba Varma, "From 'Terrorist' to 'Terrorized': How Trauma Became the Language of Suffering in Kashmir," in *Resisting Occupation in Kashmir*, ed. Haley Duschinski, Mona Bhan, Ather Zia, and Cynthia Mahmood (Philadelphia: University of Pennsylvania Press, 2018).

30 Wajahat Ahmad, "Appointment with Terror," *Fountain Ink*, June 6, 2012, https://fountainink.in/essay/appointment-with-terror.

31 Basharat Peer, *Curfewed Night* (New Delhi: Penguin, 2008).

32 Ahmad, "Appointment with Terror."

33 Laleh Khalili, *Time in the Shadows: Confinement in Counterinsurgencies* (Palo Alto, CA: Stanford University Press, 2012); Jennifer Terry, *Attachments to War: Bio-*

medical Logics and Violence in Twenty-First-Century America (Durham, NC: Duke University Press, 2017).

34 "Eight-day Village Crackdown Ends in Kashmir," *Kashmir Newz* (February 21, 2008), https://www.kashmirnewz.com/n000297.html.

35 Ahmad, "Appointment with Terror."

36 Ahmad, "Appointment with Terror."

37 Julie Livingston, *Debility and the Moral Imagination in Botswana* (Bloomington: Indiana University Press, 2005), 1.

38 Sherine Hamdy, "When the State and Your Kidneys Fail," *American Ethnologist* 35, no. 4 (2008): 553–69. In her work on patients suffering from renal failure in Egypt, Hamdy describes how Egyptian patients dependent on public health care understand and experience their illness in terms of Egypt's larger social, economic, and political failures, including corrupt institutions, polluted water, mismanagement of toxic waste, and unsafe food.

39 Before biomedicine—or "English medicine," as it is colloquially called in South Asia—came to Kashmir in the late nineteenth century, an elaborate network of *hakīms* (herbal medicine practitioners) and *pīrs* (faith healers) were responsible for the health of the population. Walter Roper Lawrence, *The Valley of Kashmir* (London: Henry Frowde, 1895), 74. While there are virtually no hakīms left in Kashmir today, many Kashmiris retain some herbal knowledge and prescribe household remedies; many doctors also trace their lineages back to hakīms. Pīrs, however, continue to be an important part of the care landscape.

40 Dermot Norris, *Kashmir: The Switzerland of India: A Descriptive Guide with Chapters on Ski-ing and Mountaineering, Large and Small Game Shooting, Fishing, etc.* (Calcutta: Newman, 1925), 7.

41 Eugene Stock, *Beginnings in India* (London: Central Board of Missions, 1917).

42 Stock, *Beginnings in India.*

43 Christopher Snedden, *Understanding Kashmir and Kashmiris* (London: C. Hurst, 2015), 46.

44 Stock, *Beginnings in India.*

45 Arthur Neve, *Thirty Years in Kashmir* (Lucknow: Asian Publications, 1984), 303. Originally published in 1913.

46 Mridu Rai, *Hindu Rulers, Muslim Subjects: Islam, Rights, and the History of Kashmir* (Princeton, NJ: Princeton University Press, 2004), 85; Neve, *Thirty Years in Kashmir,* 33.

47 William Elmslie, *Seedtime in Kashmir: A Memoir of William Jackson Elmslie* (London: J. Nisbet, 1875), 77. The British government bore at least some responsibility for this situation, according to Elmslie: "Yes, disgraceful to *us* English, for we sold, literally sold, the country into the hands of its present possessors; and seeing it, sold it with the flesh and blood of thousands of our fellow creatures,— sold them into perpetual slavery. Disgraceful, too, that it should lie under the shadow of our well-ruled provinces, and yet be so ground down; that the ruler should be a tributary of ours, and yet be allowed so to tyrannize" (202). These complaints went unheeded.

48 Arthur Neve, *Picturesque Kashmir* (London: Sands and Company, 1990), viii. Originally published in 1900.

49 Neve, *Thirty Years in Kashmir*, 30.

50 Walter Roper Lawrence, "Kashmir: Its People and Its Produce," *Pharmaceutical Journal: A Weekly Record of Pharmacy and Allied Sciences* 2 (1896): 275.

51 Khalili, *Time in the Shadows*; Terry, *Attachments to War*.

52 Zahid Maqbool, "Who Manufactured Spurious Tablets?," *Greater Kashmir*, March 15, 2015, http://www.greaterkashmir.com/news/news/who-manufactured-spurious-tablets/143728.html.

53 Gardiner Harris, "Medicines Made in India Set Off Safety Worries," *New York Times*, February 14, 2014, https://www.nytimes.com/2014/02/15/world/asia/medicines-made-in-india-set-off-safety-worries.html.

54 Mazzarella asks how scandals become scandalous when there is no element of surprise. He argues that corruption becomes scandalous in post-liberalization India when it disrupts key markers of socioeconomic progress, namely access to information, transparency, and an efficient corporate managerial vision. However, in Kashmir, many of these foundational elements of democracy were never established. Thus, the amoxicillin scandal registered for different reasons. William Mazzarella, "Internet X-Ray: E-Governance, Transparency and the Politics of Immediation in India," *Public Culture* 18, no. 3 (2006): 473–505.

55 Rakib, "Fake Drugs Scam: Kashmir Shuts in Protest," *Free Press Kashmir*, April 20, 2013, http://archives.freepresskashmir.com/fake-drugs-scam-kashmir-shuts-in-protest/.

56 Rakib, "Fake Drugs Scam."

57 "MEJAF President Dr. Nisar-Hasan Arrested," *Kashmir Observer*, June 26, 2013, https://kashmirobserver.net/2013/06/26/mejaf-president-dr-nisar-ul-hassan-arrested/.

58 "MEJAF President Dr. Nisar-Hasan Arrested."

59 The economic base of the insurgency was complex and transnational, including private foreign donors, *hawala*-based transfers, interstate financing, black money, diaspora funds, the South Asian drugs and arms trade, international aid economies, and illicit and licit cross-border transactions. Chetan Bhatt, "Frontlines and Interstices in the Global War on Terror," *Development and Change* 38, no. 6 (2007): 1085–86. However, in recent years, the transnational smuggling of arms and ammunition has been greatly reduced due to increased surveillance of the Line of Control and transnational economic (hawala) transactions. Aditi Saraf, "Occupying the Frontier" (paper presented at the Annual Meeting on South Asia, Madison, WI, 2016).

60 Gowhar Fazili, "Police Subjectivity in Occupied Kashmir: Reflections on an Account of a Police Officer," in *Resisting Occupation in Kashmir*, ed. Haley Duschinski, Mona Bhan, Ather Zia, and Cynthia Mahmood (Philadelphia: University of Pennsylvania Press, 2018), 203–4.

61 Hasan indirectly referred to Kashmiris recruited as counterinsurgents (ikhwāns) starting in the mid-1990s.

62 Elizabeth A. Povinelli, "Geontologies of the Otherwise," *Fieldsights*, January 13, 2014, https://culanth.org/fieldsights/geontologies-of-the-otherwise.

63 "Dear Media: Stop Projecting Dr Nisar Hassan as DAK President," *Change.org*, https://www.change.org/p/editors-guild-kashmir-dear-media-stop-projecting -dr-nisar-Hasan-as-dak-president.

64 Alain Badiou, *Being and Event* (New York: Continuum, 2005), 371.

65 Cohen, *No Aging in India*, 176.

66 Emily Martin, *Bipolar Expeditions: Mania and Depression in American Culture* (Princeton: Princeton University Press, 2009), 8.

67 At the beginning of the armed conflict in 1990, the Jammu and Kashmir police— which is staffed by locals from the state, except at the most senior level, where they are drawn from a national Indian Police Service (IPS) cadre—was dis- banded and replaced by centrally commissioned military and paramilitary forces and intelligence networks. In the mid- to late 1990s, the J&K police force was resuscitated and rearmed, primarily as a counterinsurgency force. As Fazili ("Police Subjectivity in Occupied Kashmir") describes, since then, the force has continued to negotiate its dual identity as a public service institution on the one hand, and a repressive counterinsurgency mechanism on the other.

68 Tufeel Baba et al., "An Epidemiological Study on Substance Abuse among Col- lege Students of North India (Kashmir Valley)," *International Journal of Medical Science and Public Health* 2, no. 3 (2013): 562–67. Although benzodiazepines and opioids are controlled substances, substance users were able to procure them relatively easily from neighborhood chemist shops.

69 For a fuller account of the DDC, see Saiba Varma, "Love in the Time of Occu- pation: Reveries, Longing and Intoxication in Kashmir," *American Ethnologist* 43, no. 1 (2016): 50–62.

70 Though I am not equating my experiences as a fieldworker with how Kash- miris experience the militarized state, my discomfort allowed me to relate, in some degree, to the ambivalence that Kashmiris feel in being dependent on a state that has harmed them.

71 There were parts of his story that I erased at his request.

72 Sarah Pinto, "The Limits of Diagnosis: Sex, Law and Psychiatry in a Case of Contested Marriage," *Ethos* 40, no. 2 (2012): 119.

73 See Varma, "Love in the Time of Occupation," for the relation between love affairs and narrative etiology in the clinic.

74 Mirza Waheed, *The Collaborator* (New Delhi: Penguin, 2011), 184.

75 Praveen Swami, "India's Forgotten Army," *The Hindu*, September 14, 2003, http:// www.thehindu.com/thehindu/2003/09/14/stories/2003091406170800.htm.

76 Some mukhbirs are suspected militants; others are volunteers who work for money. Some joined the armed forces to avenge the death of a family member at the hands of militants. Peer, *Curfewed Night*.

77 Begoña Aretxaga, "Madness and the Politically Real: Reflections on Violence in Postdictatorial Spain," in *Postcolonial Disorders*, ed. Mary-Jo DelVecchio Good, Sandra Teresa Hyde, Sarah Pinto, and Byron J. Good (Berkeley: Uni-

versity of California Press, 2008), 58–59. As Aretxaga notes, the word *cipayo* comes from the Hindustani word *sipahī*, used to describe Indian soldiers in the British army.

78 The hashish smokers I met in Kashmir mixed hashish and tobacco and smoked it in a cigarette. The mixture of tobacco and hashish helped disguise the fact that they were smoking hashish.

79 Personal communication, July 29, 2011.

80 The SOG used to be called the Special Task Force (STF). See Fazili, "Police Subjectivity in Occupied Kashmir," 194–95.

81 Gregory Bateson, Don D. Jackson, Jay Haley, and John Weakland, *Steps to an Ecology of Mind* (Chicago: University of Chicago Press, 2000), 209–10.

82 Bateson et al., *Steps to an Ecology of Mind*, 211–12.

83 Sarah Pinto, *Daughters of Parvati: Women and Madness in Contemporary India* (Philadelphia: University of Pennsylvania Press, 2014), 260.

84 As Wagner writes: "a fractal person is never a unit standing in relation to an aggregate, or an aggregate standing in relation to a unit, but always an entity with relationship integrally implied." Roy Wagner, *The Anthropology of the Subject: Holographic Worldview in New Guinea and Its Meaning and Significance for the World of Anthropology* (Berkeley: University of California Press, 2001), 163.

85 My thanks to Ellen Corin for helping me articulate this point.

86 Arif Ayaz Parrey in *Until My Freedom Has Come*, ed. Sanjay Kak, 179–89 (New Delhi: Penguin, 2011).

87 Parrey, "A Victorious Campaign."

CHAPTER 2: A DISTURBED AREA

1 Field notes written in October 2009.

2 Iffat Rashid, "Theatrics of a 'Violent State' or 'State of Violence': Mapping Histories and Memories of Partition in Jammu and Kashmir," *South Asia: Journal of South Asian Studies* 44 (2020). Rashid argues that the Kashmir Valley's resistance against invading Pakistani "tribals" was constructed by Indian nationalists as the triumph of an Indian secular nationalist project over Pakistani Muslim nationalism. However, this obscures records of the massacres of Muslims in Jammu in 1947 at the hands of Dogra soldiers, which were the first major displacements in the state, much before the arrival of Pakistani tribals.

3 Andrew Whitehead, *A Mission in Kashmir* (New Delhi: Penguin, 2007), 63.

4 This chapter looks at the effects of disturbance on the public health system and medical providers generally. I indicate when observations are particular to psychiatrists/mental health care and when they relate to the public health system as a whole.

5 Under the Indian constitution, the president of India has the power to impose emergency rule in any or all of the states of India in response to a security threat by war, external aggression, or "internal disturbance or imminent dan-

ger of internal disturbance." The Jammu and Kashmir Disturbed Areas Act (1990) designated six districts of Kashmir and Rajouri and Poonch districts of Jammu as disturbed. In 2001, under Section 3 of AFSPA, the entire state (except Leh and Kargil) was designated as disturbed. While the DAA has expired, Jammu and Kashmir remains "disturbed" through AFSPA. AFSPA protects military and paramilitary officers from "suits, persecutions or other legal proceedings," unless sanctioned by the state government.

6 Globally, states extend emergency powers into nonemergency periods. This "institutionalization" of emergency powers has become "a permanent part of India's democratic experiment." David H. Bayley, *Preventive Detention in India*, cited in Anil Kalhan, Gerald P. Conroy, Mamta Kaushal, and Sam Scott Miller, "Colonial Continuities: Human Rights, Terrorism, and Security Laws in India," *Columbia Journal of Asian Law* 20 (2006): 125; Haley Duschinski and Shrimoyee Nandini Ghosh, "Constituting the Occupation: Preventive Detention and Permanent Emergency in Kashmir," *Journal of Legal Pluralism and Unofficial Law* 49 (2017): 314–37; Duncan McDuie-Ra, "Fifty-Year Disturbance: The Armed Forces Special Power Act and Exceptionalism in a South Asian Periphery," *Contemporary South Asia* 17, no. 3 (2009): 255–70. Despite a 1997 Supreme Court ruling in which the Court declared that the designation of a "disturbed area" should be reviewed every six months, there was no limit placed on the number of times the designation could be renewed. As such, Kashmir saw the seamless renewal of successive disturbed area acts. Though the DAA was meant to be effective for only three years, it was extended for almost ten. Similarly, the Public Safety Act (PSA) can be used to arrest or rearrest anyone, even if they were just released from jail, ad infinitum. From the perspective of human rights activists, the seamless application of emergency laws is one of their most objectionable qualities.

7 Ilana Feldman, "The Humanitarian Condition: Palestinian Refugees and the Politics of Living," *Humanity: An International Journal of Human Rights, Humanitarianism and Development* 3, no. 2 (2012): 155–72; Ilana Feldman, *Life Lived in Relief: Humanitarian Predicaments and Palestinian Refugee Politics* (Oakland: University of California Press, 2018). Calhoun helpfully distinguishes "emergency"—a mode of imagining that emphasizes an event's "apparent unpredictability, abnormality, and brevity"—from "crisis," a more systemic, chronic, or structural failing. Craig Calhoun, "A World of Emergencies: Fear, Intervention, and the Limits of Cosmopolitan Order," *Canadian Review of Sociology* 41, no. 4 (2004): 375. Mental health experts and other humanitarians must simultaneously contend with both emergencies *and* crises.

8 Makiko Kimura, "Protesting the AFSPA in the Indian Periphery: The Anti-Militarization Movement in Northeast India," in *Law and Democracy in Contemporary India*, ed. T. Yamamoto and T. Ueda (Cham, Switzerland: Palgrave Macmillan, 2018), 148.

9 In one of the most egregious acts of violence committed by Indian armed forces in the insurgency's early years, an estimated one hundred unarmed

protestors were gunned down at Gawakadal Bridge in Srinagar. After the incident, rather than face prosecution, Indian armed forces imposed a strict curfew that lasted for months.

10 See Didier Fassin and Mariella Pandolfi, eds., *Contemporary States of Emergency: The Politics of Military and Humanitarian Intervention* (New York: Zone, 2010), 16; Liisa Malkki, "Speechless Emissaries: Refugees, Humanitarianism, and Dehistoricization," *Cultural Anthropology* 11, no. 3 (1996): 377–404; Miriam Ticktin, *Casualties of Care: Immigration and the Politics of Humanitarianism in France* (Berkeley: University of California Press, 2011); Miriam Ticktin, "A World without Innocence," *American Ethnologist* 44, no. 4 (2017): 577–90. For legal exceptionalism in Kashmir, see Haley Duschinski, "Fake Encounters and the Informalization of Everyday Violence in Kashmir Valley," *Cultural Studies* 24, no. 1 (2010): 110–32; Arup Kumar Sen, "Kashmir: A State of Exception," *Economic and Political Weekly* 50, no. 8 (2015); Ather Zia, "Kashmir from Orient to a State of Exception," *Funambulist* 8 (2016). While Indian rule accommodates exceptionalism—namely military humanitarianism and illiberal modes of government, such as emergency powers and occupation—it also departs from the classic Agambian definition. In particular, I note the absence of compassion in favor of more complex, ambivalent uses of political emotions in nationalist projects. Rather than submit Kashmir to an "empirical test" of exceptionalism, I reveal how legal, political, and military structures of disturbance influence people's experiential, moral, and social worlds. Didier Fassin and Maria Vasquez. "Humanitarian Exception as the Rule: The Political Ethology of the 1999 *Tragedia* in Venezuela," *American Ethnologist* 32, no. 3 (2005): 390.

11 Adia Benton and Sa'ed Atshan, "'Even War Has Rules': On Medical Neutrality and Legitimate Non-Violence." *Culture, Medicine and Psychiatry* 40 (2016): 152; Sherine Hamdy and Soha Bayoumi, "Egypt's Popular Uprising and the Stakes of Medical Neutrality," *Culture, Medicine and Psychiatry* 40, no. 2 (2016): 223–41.

12 As Fazili notes, "occupied subjects are constrained by circumstances to exist somewhere on the spectrum defined by resistance and collaboration and marked by a bit of both." Gowhar Fazili, "Police Subjectivity in Occupied Kashmir: Reflections on an Account of a Police Officer," in *Resisting Occupation in Kashmir*, ed. Haley Duschinski, Mona Bhan, Ather Zia, and Cynthia Mahmood (Philadelphia: University of Pennsylvania Press, 2018), 206. For Kashmiris employed by the state, such contradictions are more deeply felt.

13 Rather than critiquing professionals for these shifts or inconsistencies, following Ewing, I understand multiple, inconsistent self-representations as an inevitable part of the work of the self. Katherine P. Ewing, "The Illusion of Wholeness: Culture, Self and the Experience of Inconsistency," *Ethos* 18, no. 3 (1990): 251.

14 Omar Dewachi, "Blurred Lines: Warfare and Health Care," *Medical Anthropology Theory* 2, no. 2 (2015): 95–101; Annie Pfingst and Marsha Rosengarten, "Medicine as a Tactic of War: Palestinian Precarity," *Body and Society* 18, nos. 3–4 (2012): 99–125; Catherine Smith, "Doctors that Harm, Doctors that Heal:

Reimagining Medicine in Post-Conflict Aceh, Indonesia," *Ethnos: Journal of Anthropology* 80, no. 2 (2013): 1–20; Emma Varley and Saiba Varma, "Spectral Lines: Haunted Hospitals across the Line of Control," *Medical Anthropology* 37, no. 6 (2018): 1–15; Emma Varley, "Abandonments, Solidarities and Logics of Care: Hospitals as Sites of Sectarian Conflict in Gilgit-Baltistan," *Culture, Medicine and Psychiatry* 40, no. 2 (2015): 159–80; Livia Wick, "Building the Infrastructure, Modeling the Nation: The Case of Birth in Palestine," *Culture, Medicine and Psychiatry* 32 (2008): 328–57.

15 One of the worst incidents of mass rape took place in the villages of Kunan and Poshpora. In February 1991, more than thirty women were raped during a cordon-and-search operation. See Essar Batool, Ifrah Butt, Samreena Mushtaq, Munaza Rashid, and Natasha Rather, *Do You Remember Kunan Poshpora?* (Delhi: Zubaan, 2016).

16 Nishita Trisal, "Banking on Uncertainty: Debt, Default and Violence in Indian Administered Kashmir," PhD diss., University of Michigan, 2020.

17 Trisal, "Banking on Uncertainty."

18 While many scholars have attended to the *spatial* dimension of colonial occupations, less attention has been given to their *temporal* dimensions. See Iris Jean-Klein, "Nationalism and Resistance: The Two Faces of Everyday Activism in Palestine during the Intifada," *Cultural Anthropology* 16, no. 1 (2001): 83–126.

19 While most ethnographies of humanitarianism focus on aid recipients, not experts, there are some notable exceptions. Vincanne Adams, *Doctors for Democracy: Health Professionals in the Nepal Revolution* (Cambridge: Cambridge University Press, 1998); Omar Dewachi, *Ungovernable Life: Mandatory Medicine and Statecraft in Iraq* (Stanford, CA: Stanford University Press, 2017); Hamdy and Bayoumi, "Egypt's Popular Uprising"; Liisa Malkki, *The Need to Help: The Domestic Arts of International Humanitarianism* (Durham, NC: Duke University Press, 2015); Chika Watanabe, *Becoming One: Religion, Development, and Environmentalism in a Japanese NGO in Myanmar* (Honolulu: University of Hawai'i Press, 2018). Anthropologists have also produced wonderful ethnographies about the everyday clinical dilemmas psychiatrists face. Paul Brodwin, *Everyday Ethics: Voices from the Front Lines of Community Psychiatry* (Berkeley: University of California Press, 2013); Tanya M. Luhrmann, *Of Two Minds: An Anthropologist Looks at American Psychiatry* (New York: Random House, 2000); Sarah Pinto, *Daughters of Parvati: Women and Madness in Contemporary India* (Philadelphia: University of Pennsylvania Press, 2014); Lorna Rhodes, *Emptying Beds: The Work of an Emergency Psychiatric Unit* (Berkeley: University of California Press, 1991).

20 Gulzar Mufti, *Kashmir: In Sickness and in Health* (New Delhi: Penguin, 2013), 1–2.

21 Mufti, *Kashmir*, 2. This mode of coping with trauma is, of course, very different from Western psychotherapeutic models, which emphasize talking and narrating trauma in order to overcome it. Similar modes of strategic forgetting and coping with trauma have also been described elsewhere. Michael Jackson,

"The Prose of Suffering and the Practice of Silence," *Spiritus* 4, no. 1 (2004): 44–59.

22 Mufti, *Kashmir*, 3. In contrast to Mufti's characterization of leather dealers, in *The Night of Broken Glass*, Kashmiri writer Feroz Rather relates the perspective of a low-caste cobbler, who, after the Bijbeyor (Bijbehara) massacre, creates a memorial to the victims by making a garland of their shoes. Feroz Rather, *The Night of Broken Glass* (Noida: HarperCollins India, 2018).

23 A 1996 Human Rights Watch report describes the presence of armed forces and militants in the hospital: "They have been given free rein to patrol major hospitals in Srinagar, particularly the Soura Institute, the Sri Maharaja Hari Singh (SMHS) hospital, and the Bone and Joint Hospital. They have murdered, beaten, and detained hospital staff and removed patients from hospitals; in some cases these abuses have occurred in full view of armed force bunkers or in the presence of armed force officers." "India's Secret Army in Kashmir: New Patterns of Abuse Emerge in the Conflict," *Human Rights Watch* 8, no. 4 (1996), https://www.hrw.org/reports/1996/India2.htm#P53_4784, accessed April 29, 2018.

24 See Dewachi, *Ungovernable Life*, for how the US-led invasion also caused the mass migration of Iraqi medical professionals.

25 Indian commentators attributed this to the JKLF's successful kidnapping of Rubaiya Sayeed, daughter of the Home Minister Mufti Mohammad Sayeed, while she was returning home from duty at Lal Ded Hospital. The JKLF successfully negotiated the release of five prisoners in exchange for Rubaiya, which was seen as a major emotional and psychological victory for the insurgent group against the Indian state.

26 Sumantra Bose, "The Evolution of Kashmiri Resistance," *Al Jazeera*, August 25, 2011, https://www.aljazeera.com/indepth/spotlight/kashmirtheforgotten conflict/2011/07/2011715143415277754.html.

27 My thanks to Wajahat Ahmad for this point.

28 Personal communication, May 21, 2018.

29 This lull occurred after a few years of intense fighting from 1999 to 2002, in which *fidayeen*, or suicide attacks, were carried out against army and paramilitary camps and police headquarters. These attacks were mostly carried out by the Lashkar-e-Toiba (LeT), a Pakistani militant organization. In this period, at least fifty-five fidayeen attacks killed 161 military, paramilitary, and police personnel. Bose, "The Evolution of Kashmiri Resistance."

30 Personal communication, May 21, 2018.

31 Field notes written October 7, 2009.

32 Field notes written July 7, 2011.

33 "Over 45,000 Professionals Unemployed in J&K," *Economic Times*, October 5, 2010, https://economictimes.indiatimes.com/jobs/over-45000-professionals -unemployed-in-jk/articleshow/6692583.cms?intenttarget=no.

34 Sherine Hamdy, "When the State and Your Kidneys Fail," *American Ethnologist* 35, no. 4 (2008): 553–69.

35 For similar dynamics in Haiti, see Rosalind Petchesky, "Biopolitics at the Crossroads of Sexuality and Disaster: The Case of Haiti," Working Paper no. 8, Sexuality Policy Watch, New York, 2012, 15.

36 Mufti, *Kashmir*, 235. The medical college was established during the Jammu and Kashmir state's massive expansion of its public health infrastructure under the Bakshi government. Hafsa Kanjwal, "Building a New Kashmir: Bakshi Ghulam Muhammad and the Politics of State-Formation in a Disputed Territory (1953–1963)" (PhD diss., University of Michigan, 2017).

37 For doctors on strike elsewhere in the Global South, see Ramah McKay, *Medicine in the Meantime: The Work of Care in Mozambique* (Durham, NC: Duke University Press, 2018); Hamdy and Bayoumi, "Egypt's Popular Uprising"; Claire L. Wendland, "Moral Maps and Medical Imaginaries: Clinical Tourism in Malawi's College of Medicine," *American Anthropologist* 114, no. 1 (2012): 108–22.

38 Field notes written October 14, 2009.

39 Pinto, *Daughters of Parvati*, 3.

40 Inshah Malik, *Muslim Women, Agency and Resistance Politics: The Case of Kashmir* (Cham, Switzerland: Palgrave Macmillan, 2013).

41 Cohen argues that senility in India becomes comprehensible or knowable at three different linguistic registers: knowledge of and engagement with and within one's own body is first person; knowledge of some known other is second person; and knowledge of a universal, generalized body is third person. Lawrence Cohen, *No Aging in India* (Berkeley: University of California Press, 1998), 34.

42 Favret-Saada offers an account of "being affected" during fieldwork as a critique of the model of participant observation. Jeanne Favret-Saada, "Being Affected," *Hau: Journal of Ethnographic Theory* 2, no. 1 (2012): 435–45.

43 See also Adams, *Doctors for Democracy*, 6–7.

44 See Saiba Varma, "Disappearing the Asylum: Modernizing Psychiatry and Generating Manpower in India," *Transcultural Psychiatry* 53, no. 6 (2016): 783–803.

45 In addition to the substantial monies received, the grant's prestige also meant the hospital would be upgraded to an institute. Medical institutes in India are highly prestigious, public teaching hospitals with research and training capacities.

46 Mudasir Firdosi, "Personal Reflections of a Doctor Starting Psychiatry Training in Kashmir," 2015, https://www.rcpsych.ac.uk/discoverpsychiatry /overseasblogs/psychiatrytraininginkashmir/personalreflectionsofadoct.aspx, accessed May 15, 2018. For decades, the hospital had existed as a backwater to mainstream biomedicine and to the Government Medical College. Then a devastating fire in 1997 destroyed much of the hospital's infrastructure, which MSF eventually helped rebuild.

47 C. Jason Throop, "Latitudes of Loss: On the Vicissitudes of Empathy," *American Ethnologist* 37, no. 4 (2010): 771.

48 Miriam Ticktin, "Where Ethics and Politics Meet: The Violence of Humanitarianism in France," *American Ethnologist* 33, no. 1 (2006): 33–49.

49 Field notes written December 8, 2009. Action Aid uses the label "mental health worker" instead of "counselor." While many of MSF's counselors have postgraduate degrees in social work or psychology, some of Action Aid's staff had high school diplomas. Mental health experts argued that this base allowed counselors and patients to relate to each other more easily.

50 In using the term *counterhegemonic*, I point to how care sometimes becomes incompatible with biomedical or neoliberal logics. See Tomas Matza, *Shock Therapy: Psychology, Precarity and Well-Being in Postsocialist Russia* (Durham, NC: Duke University Press, 2018), 29.

51 In the DSM-5, complicated grief was renamed "persistent complex bereavement disorder." M. K. Shear et al., "Complicated Grief and Related Bereavement Issues for DSM-5," *Depression and Anxiety* 28, no. 2 (2011): 103–17.

52 Ather Zia, "The Killable Kashmiri Body: The Life and Execution of Afzal Guru," in *Resisting Occupation in Kashmir*, ed. Mona Bhan, Haley Duschinski, Ather Zia, and Cynthia Mahmood (Philadelphia: University of Pennsylvania Press, 2018).

53 As Arthur and Joan Kleinman note, anthropologists claim that psychiatric transformations of suffering re-create human suffering as inhuman disease, thus delegitimizing patients' suffering. However, they note that anthropologists participate in this same process of professional transformation: "nor is it morally superior to anthropologize distress, rather than to medicalize it." Arthur Kleinman and Joan Kleinman, "Suffering and Its Professional Transformation," *Culture, Medicine and Psychiatry* 15, no. 3 (1991): 275–76.

54 The fifth edition of the DSM (the DSM-5), which was unveiled in 2013, includes significant changes to culture-bound syndromes, including the recognition that "all forms of distress are locally shaped, including the DSM disorders." In addition, the notion of "culture-bound syndromes" has been replaced by three concepts: cultural syndromes, cultural idioms of distress, and cultural explanations of distress or perceived causes. American Psychiatric Association, *Diagnostic and Statistical Manual of Mental Disorders*, 5th ed. (Washington, DC: American Psychiatric Association, 2013), 758.

55 See also Sarah Pinto, "'The Tools of Your Chants and Spells': Stories of Madwomen and Indian Practical Healing," *Medical Anthropology* 35, no. 3 (2015): 263–77.

56 Zia, "The Killable Kashmiri Body," 113.

57 Lashkar-e-Toiba (LeT) is one of the most well trained armed organizations fighting against Indian military forces. It pioneered fidayeen operations and instigated systematic massacres of civilians and other spectacular acts of violence within India, such as the Red Fort attack in Delhi in 2010. The LeT was previously engaged in fighting the Soviet occupation in Afghanistan, but after the armed struggle in Kashmir began in the late 1980s, several *mujahideen* groups—funded by the United States, Pakistan, and Saudi Arabia—were

redeployed to Kashmir. See Chetan Bhatt, "Frontlines and Interstices in the Global War on Terror," *Development and Change* 38, no. 6 (2007): 1077–78.

58 Unlike many other militant organizations in Kashmir, LeT's political ideology is intertwined with "the idea of a phantasmatic global jihād that would lead to a planetary *shari'a* system, one which is to be initiated by bringing some ('Muslim') parts and then all India under religious absolutist rule." Hassan Abbas, *Pakistan's Drift into Extremism: Allah, the Army and America's War on Terror* (Armonk, NY: M. E. Sharpe, 2005), 214.

59 This perspective resonates with Sonpar's 2008 qualitative study of ex-militants in Jammu and Kashmir. She found that many former militants embodied characteristics such as good leadership qualities, motivational skills, team work, discipline, and respect for a clear system of authority. Shobna Sonpar, "A Potential Resource? Ex-militants in Jammu and Kashmir," *Intervention* 6, no. 2 (2008): 147–53.

60 As the conflict became dirtier, with greater infighting between different armed groups and more aggressive stories about the ethical actions of militants also dried up. As many people told me, "all the honest and true *shaheed* [martyrs] were killed long ago." Yet, despite the profound loss, memories of the insurgency's pure origins remained.

61 Walter Benjamin, *Illuminations*, ed. Hannah Arendt (New York: Schocken, 1968), 286.

INTERLUDE: THE DISAPPEARED

1 A communist guerrilla fighter.

2 A person belonging to an indigenous community.

3 Gayatri Chakravorty Spivak, "'Draupadi' by Mahasveta Devi," *Critical Inquiry* 8, no. 2 (1981): 381–402.

4 April 2010.

5 Jocelyn Chua, "The Register of 'Complaint': Psychiatric Diagnosis and the Discourse of Grievance in the South Indian Mental Health Encounter," *Medical Anthropology Quarterly* 26, no. 2 (2012): 221–40.

6 "Three Militants Killed as Army Foils Infiltration Bid," *Outlook*, April 30, 2010, http://www.outlookindia.com/newswire/story/three-militants-killed -as-army-foils-infiltration-bid/680686.

7 The LoC is a de facto, not legally recognized, international border created after the Indo-Pakistan war of 1948. For the Indian state, the LoC constitutes a third Partition—along with the Partitions of Bengal and Punjab in 1947–48—that broke up the subcontinent. Pakistan renamed the seized territory Azad (free) Jammu and Kashmir, a title that conveys that Kashmir's proper place, and true freedom, is to be found with Pakistan. The LoC has divided Kashmiris on both sides of the border for generations. Andrew Whitehead, *A Mission in Kashmir* (New Delhi: Penguin, 2007); Anam Zakaria, *Between*

the Great Divide: A Journey into Pakistan-Administered Kashmir (Noida: Harper-Collins India, 2018); Chitralekha Zutshi, "An Ongoing Partition: Histories, Borders and the Politics of Vivisection in Jammu and Kashmir," *Contemporary South Asia* 23, no. 3 (2015): 266–75.

8 Cynthia Keppley Mahmood, "Dynamics of Terror in Punjab and Kashmir," in *Death Squad: The Anthropology of State Terror*, ed. Jeffrey A. Sluka (Philadelphia: University of Pennsylvania Press, 2000), 74.

9 Iftikar Gilani, "Harsh Weather Likely to Damage LoC Fencing," *Daily Times*, September 30, 2007.

10 Zutshi, "An Ongoing Partition," 2.

11 In the regions of India deemed "disturbed" through emergency laws such as AFSPA and the DAA, disappearances become even more powerful tools of warfare because the National Human Rights Commission (NHRC) does not have jurisdiction. As such, the onerous work of identifying graves and counting missing or dead bodies is often left to local civil society or human rights groups. See Ashok Agrwaal, *In Search of Vanished Blood: The Writ of Habeas Corpus in Jammu and Kashmir: 1990–2004* (Kathmandu: South Asia Forum for Human Rights, 2008); International People's Tribunal on Human Rights and Justice in Kashmir, "Structures of Violence: The Indian State in Jammu and Kashmir," 2015, https://jkccs.wordpress.com/2017/05/04/structures-of-violence/; "Submission by the Association of Parents of Disappeared Persons to the Universal Periodic Review of India, United Nations Human Rights Council," https://www.upr-info.org/sites/default/files/ . . . 27 . . . /apdp_upr27_ind_e_main.pdf, accessed June 28, 2018; Ather Zia, *Resisting Disappearance: Military Occupation and Women's Activism in Kashmir* (Seattle: University of Washington Press, 2019).

12 The Indian state has alleged that most of the "missing" are people who crossed the LoC and are now living in Pakistan. Indian state accounts refuse to use the language of "disappearance," which they view as politically charged, instead preferring the neutral "missing."

13 Haley Duschinski, "Fake Encounters and the Informalization of Everyday Violence in Kashmir Valley," *Cultural Studies* 24, no. 1 (2010): 112.

14 As Duschinski writes: "state agents who kill civilians in order to receive bounties and stars are acting, not outside the law, but rather inside of its interstices and folds, within a system that effectively legitimizes violence and terror against and among Kashmiris in the name of the national effort to protect public safety and public order." Haley Duschinski, "Destiny Effects: Militarization, State Power, and Punitive Containment in Kashmir Valley," *Anthropological Quarterly* 82, no. 3 (2009): 125.

15 Feldman argues that enforced disappearances operate through a structure of disavowal, wherein states accidentalize, randomize, render acausal disappearances, and then also erase the conditions under which someone disappeared (in Machil, by burying the three at the scene of the encounter). This produces

an effect he describes as "the disappearance of disappearance." Allen Feldman, *Archives of the Insensible: Of War, Photo Politics and Dead Memory* (Chicago: University of Chicago Press, 2015).

16 Kashmir's high courts have an exceedingly large backlog of habeas corpus petitions: in 2006, there were sixty thousand habeas corpus petitions filed by individuals since 1990 and eight thousand cases of enforced disappearance. Human Rights Watch, "'Everyone Lives in Fear': Patterns of Impunity in Jammu and Kashmir," 18, no. 11(C) (2006); Seema Kazi, "Law, Governance and Gender in Indian-Administered Kashmir," Working Paper no. 20, Center for the Study of Law and Governance, New Delhi, 2012, 13.

17 Baba Umar, "The Dilemma of Kashmir's Half Widows," *Al Jazeera*, October 12, 2013, http://www.aljazeera.com/news/asia/2013/09/dilemma-kashmir-half -widows-201392715575877378.html.

18 On May 10, the families of the three disappeared men filed a first information report at the Panzulla police station. The families initially suspected that a local counterinsurgent, Bashir Ahmad Lone, had kidnapped their sons. But the police investigation ultimately led to an army camp in Kalaroos. See Muzamil Jaleel, "Fake Encounter at LOC: 3 Arrested, Probe Ordered," *Indian Express*, November 24, 2011, http://archive.indianexpress.com/news/fake-encounter-at -loc-3-arrested-probe-ordered/626105/, accessed April 4, 2018.

19 All newspaper articles about ongoing investigations in Kashmir include a gray-scaled text box labeled "Police Version." This box recognizes the presence of multiple ontologies and truths in Kashmir. In the newspaper, at least, the delimited box attempts to contain the state's counterreality.

20 Zia, *Resisting Disappearance*.

21 Mick Taussig, "Terror as Usual: Walter Benjamin's Theory of History as a State of Siege," *Social Text* 23 (1989): 3–20, esp. 14–15.

22 In the words of one Indian army general, winning hearts and minds measures were seen as necessary to "instill confidence in the minds of the Kashmiris and wean youth away from the patronage of fundamentalist jihadi organization[s]." Y. N. Bammi, *War against Insurgency and Terrorism in Kashmir* (Dehradun, India: Natraj, 2007), 259–60.

23 Mir Ehsan and Pranav Kulkarni, "Machil Fake Encounter Case: Army Confirms Life Sentences for Its Six Army Personnel," *Indian Express*, September 8, 2015, http://indianexpress.com/article/india/india-others/machil-fake -encounter-case-life-sentences-of-six-army-personnel-confirmed; "Machil Fake Encounter: They Were Wearing Pathan Suits, Which Are Worn by Terrorists, Says Tribunal," *Free Press Kashmir*, July 29, 2017, http://freepresskashmir .com/2017/07/29/machil-fake-encounter-they-were-wearing-pathan-suits -which-is-worn-by-terrorists-says-tribunal/. This episode also has chilling resonances with Prime Minister Modi's statements in late 2019 about "antinational" protestors against the Citizenship Amendment Act, whom he alleged could be identified "by their clothing."

24 Sanjay Kak, ed., *Until My Freedom Has Come: The New Intifada in Kashmir* (New Delhi: Penguin, 2011), x. By the end of the protests in 2010, 118 youths had been killed and 4,000 security personnel injured.

25 Judith Butler, *Frames of War: When Is Life Grievable?* (London: Verso, 2009); Yen Espiritu, *Body Counts: The Vietnam War and Militarized Refugees* (Berkeley: University of California Press, 2014).

26 Taussig, *Terror as Usual*, 11.

27 Blanket and indefinite suspensions of telecommunications networks not only affect the ability of people in Kashmir to seek, receive, and impart information, they also violate a range of other human rights, including freedom of expression and the right to life. Amnesty International, "Communications Blackout in Kashmir Undermines Human Rights," 2016, https://amnesty.org.in/news-update/communications-blackout-kashmir-undermines-human-rights/, accessed July 17, 2018.

28 Worries about my safety reinforced the gulf between Kashmir and India. My friends and family perhaps imagined me being kidnapped or hurt by armed militants—and such incidents did happen back in the 1990s—but they had yet to acknowledge that the main perpetrator of violence in Kashmir was the Indian state and its target was protestors.

CHAPTER 3: SHOCK

1 Field notes written on March 22, 2010.

2 During ECT, a small electrical current is passed through the brain via electrodes applied to the scalp. The current stimulates the brain and elicits a generalized seizure. This has two elements: the central seizure, manifested as characteristic EEG activity, and the peripheral seizure or convulsion. Chittaranjan J. Andrade, "Unmodified ECT: Ethical Issues," *Issues in Medical Ethics* 11, no. 1 (2003): 9.

3 For ethnographic accounts of laughter in other unlikely places, see Julie Livingston, *Improvising Medicine: An African Oncology Ward in an Emerging Cancer Epidemic* (Durham, NC: Duke University Press, 2012) (cancer ward); Adam Reed, *Papua New Guinea's Last Place: Experiences of Constraint in a Postcolonial Prison* (New York: Berghahn, 2003) (prison).

4 Mark Nichter, "Pharmaceuticals, the Commodification of Health, and the Health Care–Medicine Use Transition," in *Anthropology and International Health: Asian Case Studies*, ed. Mark Nichter and Mimi Nichter (Newark, NJ: Gordon and Breach, 1996); Saiba Varma, "Where There Are Only Doctors: Counselors as Psychiatrists in Indian Administered Kashmir," *Ethos* 40, no. 4 (2012): 517–35.

5 Unlike psychopharmaceuticals, which usually do not require extensive explanations, ECT required extensive rhetorical work. Renu Addlakha, *Deconstructing Mental Illness: An Ethnography of Psychiatry, Women and the Family* (New Delhi: Zubaan, 2008); Jocelyn Chua, *In Pursuit of the Good Life: Aspiration and Suicide in*

Globalizing South India (Berkeley: University of California Press, 2014); Sumeet Jain and Sushrut Jadhav, "Pills That Swallow Policy: Clinical Ethnography of a Community Mental Health Program in Northern India," *Transcultural Psychiatry* 46, no. 1 (2009): 60–85; Jocelyn Marrow and Tanya Marie Luhrmann, "The Zone of Social Abandonment in Cultural Geography: On the Street in the United States, Inside the Family in India," *Culture, Medicine and Psychiatry* 36 (2012): 493–513; Michael Nunley, "Why Psychiatrists in India Prescribe So Many Drugs," *Culture, Medicine and Psychiatry* 20, no. 2 (1996): 165–97; Jim Wilce, "'I Can't Tell You All My Troubles': Conflict, Resistance, and Metacommunication in Bangladeshi Illness Interactions," *American Ethnologist* 22, no. 4 (1995): 927–52. Rhetorical work is a two-way process that, to be successful, requires a combination of intellectual and affective persuasive techniques. Aftab Singh Jassal, "Divine Politicking: A Rhetorical Approach to Possession," *Religions* 7 (2016): 117–35.

6   Debates about renaming shock therapy have also occurred in English. For example, Nobel laureate and neurobiologist Paul Greengard has argued that electroshock therapy should be renamed "electrocortical therapy." Benjamin J. Sadock, Virginia A. Sadock, and Pedro Ruiz, *Clinical Psychiatry: Derived from Kaplan and Sadock's Synopsis of Psychiatry*, 11th ed. (Philadelphia: Wolters Kluwer, 2017).

7   Ethnographic evidence from South Asia suggests that Kashmiri patients may be unique in their aversion to ECT. As Marrow writes, in the Indian state of Uttar Pradesh, ECT is used often, and sometimes quite early in the treatment process, with little resistance from patients and their families. Jocelyn Marrow, "Hot Brains and Knotted Nerves: Electroconvulsive Therapy in North India," paper presented at the American Anthropological Association Annual Meeting, 2010.

8   The term *shock therapy* is used metaphorically to describe rapid neoliberal economic transformations following periods of unrest or instability. Vincanne Adams, *Markets of Sorrow, Labors of Faith: New Orleans in the Wake of Katrina* (Durham, NC: Duke University Press, 2013); Naomi Klein, *The Shock Doctrine: The Rise of Disaster Capitalism* (New York: Henry Holt, 2007); Tomas Matza, *Shock Therapy: Psychology, Precarity, and Well-Being in Postsocialist Russia* (Durham, NC: Duke University Press, 2018). While Naomi Klein notes in passing the resonances between different types of shock in crisis situations, I offer a more sustained analysis of how clinical and carceral shock are related. However, there are some important differences too. In clinical contexts, shock is a therapeutic, sometimes lifesaving technology. In carceral contexts, shock is always punitive. These shocks are enacted on different bodies. I did not hear of any one person who had received shock in both the clinic and in the interrogation center, though such cases have happened in other colonial contexts. More women than men are shocked in clinical settings and more men than women in interrogation settings. See Frantz Fanon, *A Dying Colonialism*, trans. Haakon Chevalier (New York: Grove, 1965), 138. Addlakha, *Deconstructing Mental Illness*;

Amita Dhanda, D. S. Goel, and R. K. Chadda, "Law and Mental Health: Common Concerns and Varied Perspectives," in *Mental Health: An Indian Perspective, 1946–2003*, ed. S. P. Agarwal et al. (New Delhi: Elsevier, 2004), 179.

9   William E. Connolly, "The Evangelical-Capitalist Resonance Machine," *Political Theory* 33, no. 6 (2005): 870. If causality is defined as a relation of dependence between different factors, resonance is "energized complexities of mutual imbrication and interinvolvement, in which heretofore unconnected or loosely associated elements *fold, bend, blend*, emulsify, *and dissolve into each* other, forging a qualitative assemblage resistant to classical models of explanation."

10 Addlakha, *Deconstructing Mental Illness*, 97; Jocelyn Chua, "The Register of 'Complaint': Psychiatric Diagnosis and the Discourse of Grievance in the South Indian Mental Health Encounter," *Medical Anthropology Quarterly* 26, no. 2 (2012): 221–40; Claire E. Edington, *Beyond the Asylum: Mental Illness in French Colonial Vietnam* (Ithaca, NY: Cornell University Press, 2018). See also Michel Foucault, *Society Must Be Defended: Lectures at the Collège de France 1975–1976* (New York: Picador, 2003), chapters 5 and 8.

11 Drawing on Hannah Arendt to understand the work of Doctors Without Borders, Redfield argues that there are at least two different meanings and values of "life" operating within contemporary humanitarianism: zoë and bios. Zoë, he argues, implies a state of mere survival and physical existence. By contrast, in bios, a form of elaborated human experience, the value of life is associated with dignity and quality. Peter Redfield, *Life in Crisis: The Ethical Journey of Doctors Without Borders* (Berkeley: University of California Press, 2013).

12 The UN Convention against Torture and Other Cruel, Inhuman, or Degrading Treatment or Punishment (1984) defines torture as "any act by which severe pain or suffering, whether physical or mental, is *intentionally* inflicted on a person for such purposes as obtaining from him or a third person information or a confession, punishing him for an act he or a third person has committed or is suspected of having committed, or intimidating or coercing him or a third person, or for any reason based on discrimination of any kind, when such pain or suffering is inflicted by or at the instigation of or with the consent or acquiescence of a public official or other person acting in an official capacity. It does not include pain or suffering arising only from, inherent in or incidental to lawful sanctions." India signed the Convention against Torture but has not ratified it. India has not adopted the convention's definition of torture in its jurisprudence on interrogation (neither has the United States). Jinee Lokaneeta, *Transnational Torture: Law, Violence and State Power in the United States and India* (New York: New York University Press, 2011), 137–38.

13 Talal Asad, "On Torture, or Cruel, Inhuman and Degrading Treatment," *Social Research* 63, no. 4 (1996): 1081–109; Lokaneeta, *Transnational Torture*; Darius Rejali, *Torture and Democracy* (Princeton, NJ: Princeton University Press, 2009), 22. Electric shock has occurred primarily in democracies engaged in ongoing guerrilla war (Spain, Israel, Turkey, India, and Sri Lanka), societies

transitioning from authoritarian to democratic contexts (Spain, Russia, Brazil, the Philippines), and in democracies with sharp racial and ethnic divisions (United States, Venezuela, South Africa) (Rejali, *Torture and Democracy*, 179).

14 Lokaneeta, *Transnational Torture*, 198.

15 Dana Priest and R. Jeffrey Smith. "Memo Offered Justification for Use of Torture," *Washington Post*, June 8, 2004, http://www.washingtonpost.com /wp-dyn/articles/A23373-2004Jun7.html. The Indian state and military have historically denied the veracity of human rights reports of torture, insisting that they were "two-faced," designed to dupe the international community and Kashmiris into thinking that Indian rule in Kashmir was something other than fair, humanitarian, and democratic. Diane Nelson, "Means and End/s of Clandestine Life," Hemispheric Institute, https://hemisphericinstitute .org/en/emisferica-72/7-2-essays/means-and-ends-of-clandestine-life.html.

16 Justin Rowlatt, "Why Indian Army Defended Kashmir 'Human Shield' Officer," *BBC News*, May 31, 2017, http://www.bbc.com/news/world-asia -india-40103673.

17 Lokaneeta, *Transnational Torture*, 170. The Indian state passed a new anti-terrorism law, known as the Prevention of Terrorism Act (POTA), a law similar to the US Patriot Act. Jayanth K. Krishnan, "India's 'Patriot Act': POTA and the Impact on Civil Liberties in the World's Largest Democracy," *Law and Equity: A Journal of Theory and Practice* 22 (2004): 265–300; Lokaneeta, *Transnational Torture*, 166. Although POTA was repealed in 2004, new regional extraordinary laws were introduced and existing laws were amended.

18 Days after the Indian parliament attacks, four Kashmiris were arrested. The High Court found the evidence against two inadequate and acquitted them, one was given a death sentence and another's sentence was commuted to ten years. As Lokaneeta argues, while the two acquittals demonstrated the power of human rights groups in India, the case "chillingly reflects the impossibility of standing up to extraordinary laws on an individual level, especially in the face of the erosion of traditional safeguards" (*Transnational Torture*, 185). Further, the attack also allowed the ruling BJP government to link the global war on terror with its "proxy war" against Pakistan in Kashmir. As this book was going to press, new reports emerged raising questions about the role of torture in implicating Afzal Guru and the "deep" Indian state's involvement in the Parliament attacks (V. Venkatesan, "Afzal Guru and Davinder Singh: The Missing Link," *Frontline*, February 14, 2020).

19 The electrotorture techniques used in Kashmir were perfected during the Khalistan movement in Punjab during the 1970s and 1980s (Rejali, *Torture and Democracy*, 182).

20 See also Asia Watch, *The Human Rights Crisis in Kashmir: A Pattern of Impunity* (New York: Human Rights Watch, 1993); the documentary *Torture in Kashmir*; and a BBC series called *Kashmir's Torture Trail*; Jean Drèze, "A Never-Ending Nightmare in Kashmir," https://thewire.in/politics/torture-testimonies -detained-youth-kashmir, accessed July 17, 2018.

21 Jason Burke, "WikiLeaks Cables: India Accused of Systematic Use of Torture in Kashmir," *Guardian*, December 16, 2010, http://www.theguardian.com /world/2010/dec/16/wikileaks-cables-indian-torture-kashmir; Lokaneeta, *Transnational Torture*. This finding contradicts the state's position that torture is a function of rogue subordinate officials.

22 Rejali, *Torture and Democracy*, 49.

23 See Asia Watch, *The Human Rights Crisis in Kashmir,* for a full description of Masroof's ordeal. I have chosen not to reproduce the original human rights account, following Riles and Jean-Klein, in order to maintain a productive friction between ethnographic and human rights practices. Whereas human rights documentation can have the unintentional effect of "naturalizing a certain Western neoliberal model of individualism . . . [in which] understanding is located in the tortured or abused individual body," this book foregrounds the relational tissue between different regimes (humanitarianism and militarism) that constitute occupation. Rather than reifying the individual body, my analysis focuses on the forms of sociality produced by conflict and state violence. Annelise Riles and Iris Jean-Klein, "Introducing Discipline: Anthropology and Human Rights Administrations," *Political and Legal Anthropology Review* 28, no. 2 (2005): 179.

24 Nidhi Suresh, "Former Kashmir Torture Chamber Turns Venue for Peace Talks," *News Laundry*, November 15, 2017, https://www.newslaundry .com/2017/11/15/kashmir-torture-chamber-hari-niwas-dineshwar-sharma, accessed August 30, 2018.

25 Asia Watch, *The Human Rights Crisis in Kashmir*, 43.

26 Asia Watch, *The Human Rights Crisis in Kashmir*, 43.

27 For similar testimonies of already-known truths, see "Structures of Violence: The Indian State in Jammu and Kashmir," 2015, https://jkccs.wordpress.com /2017/05/04/structures-of-violence/.

28 Asia Watch, *The Human Rights Crisis in Kashmir*, 43–44.

29 Asia Watch, *The Human Rights Crisis in Kashmir*, 44.

30 Lotte Buch Segal, "Tattered Textures of Kinship: The Effects of Torture among Iraqi Families in Denmark," *Medical Anthropology* 37, no. 7 (2018): 553–67.

31 As Sunder Rajan notes, overdetermination is a relation of contextuality, not causality: "even if a particular set of political economic formations do not in any direct and simplistic way lead to particular epistemic emergences, they could still disproportionately set the stage within which the latter take shape in particular ways and, further, appear to do so to various actors." Kaushik Sunder Rajan, ed., *Lively Capital: Biotechnologies, Ethics and Governance in Global Markets* (Durham, NC: Duke University Press, 2012), 10.

32 Field notes written on February 24, 2010.

33 The specific mechanisms by which ECT works and causes changes in the brain are not known. However, neuroimaging techniques show that ECT changes and reregulates neuronal circuits that are disregulated during depression.

There is also some evidence that ECT is neurotrophic—it releases chemicals in the brain that stimulate nerve growth—and neurogenic—it stimulates the growth of new neurons.

34 Alice Street, *Biomedicine in an Unstable Place* (Durham, NC: Duke University Press, 2014).

35 ECT is a technology of "not knowing" (Street, *Biomedicine in an Unstable Place*, 259). Street describes medical practices of "not knowing" as ways of keeping open a range of possibilities for treatment.

36 Community psychiatry in India has a much longer history than in the Global North, beginning in the 1950s. Ratna L. Kapur, "The Story of Community Mental Health in India," in *Mental Health: An Indian Perspective 1946–2003*, ed. S. P. Agarwal et al. (New Delhi: Elsevier, 2004), 93. In the 1960s, the availability of antipsychotic drugs enabled the establishment of general hospital psychiatric units (GPHUs) and facilitated outpatient care. In 1975, India's premier mental health institute, NIMHANS, launched the first community-based mental health program. Saiba Varma, "Disappearing the Asylum: Modernizing Psychiatry and Generating Manpower in India," *Transcultural Psychiatry* 53, no. 6 (2016): 783–803. While in 1999, all 100 beds in Kashmir's psychiatric hospital were in "closed" (long-term) wards, by 2008, thirty beds had been moved into short-term, "open" wards. There have been many important critiques of community-based mental health care in India. Jain and Jadhav, "Pills That Swallow Policy."

37 D. S. Goel, S. P. Agarwal, R. L. Ichhpujani, and S. Shrivastava, "Mental Health 2003: The Indian Scene," in *Mental Health: An Indian Perspective 1946–2003*, ed. S. P. Agarwal et al. (New Delhi: Elsevier, 2013), 4.

38 Goel et al., "Mental Health 2003," 3. As Amita Dhanda points out, admission to a psychiatric institution raises a number of civil rights challenges. A person can be deprived of the right to contract, get married or stay married, dispose of property, or hold public office. For women in particular, an examination of matrimonial law shows that institutionalization is often used as a mode of getting rid of an inconvenient wife (Dhanda et al., "Law and Mental Health," 180).

39 Goel et al., "Mental Health 2003," 3–16; T. Murali and Kiran Rao, "Psychiatric Rehabilitation in India: Issues and Challenges," in *Mental Health: An Indian Perspective, 1946–2003*, ed. S. P. Agarwal et al. (New Delhi: Elsevier, 2004), 155. Advocates of community-based care argue that, with the advent of new antipsychotic drugs, the vast majority of patients, including those suffering from acute psychotic illness or severe depression, can be "safely and swiftly treated at home with oral medication."

40 See Sarah Pinto, *Daughters of Parvati: Women and Madness in Contemporary India* (Philadelphia: University of Pennsylvania Press, 2014), especially chapter 1.

41 *Saarthak Registered Society versus Union of India*, Writ Petition (Civil) No. 562 of 2001. The petition asked the court to "forthwith ban the use of unmodified/direct ECT" in both public and private institutions, to require patient's con-

sent, or, if recommended, to require the consent of one medical practitioner, one social worker, and one member of an NGO. Amita Dhanda, "The Right to Treatment of Persons with Psychosocial Disabilities and the Role of the Courts," *International Journal of Law and Psychiatry* 28 (2005): 166. In response, the Indian Psychiatric Society, the All India Association of Private Psychiatrists, and the Delhi Psychiatric Society presented expert opinions to establish that all ECT is efficacious and safe for mental illnesses. The legal debate narrowly focused on efficacy.

42 A survey of teaching hospitals in India from 2001 to 2002 found that, on average, a single psychiatrist (*n* = 316) treated sixty-two patients per year with ECT, with each psychiatrist administering 361 instances of ECT. Worrawat Chanpattana, Girish Kunigiri, B. A. Kramer, and B. N. Gangadhar, "Survey of the Practice of Electroconvulsive Therapy in Teaching Hospitals in India," *Journal of Electroconvulsive Therapy* 21, no. 2 (2005): 100–104.

43 Harish Thippeswamy, Kausik Goswami, and Santosh Chaturvedi, "Ethical Aspects of Public Health Legislation: The Mental Healthcare Bill, 2011," *Indian Journal of Medical Ethics* 11, no. 1 (2012): 47.

44 Worrawat Chanpattana et al., "A Survey of the Practice of Electroconvulsive Therapy in Asia," *Journal of Electroconvulsive Therapy* 26, no. 1 (2010): 5.

45 Chittaranjan Andrade et al., "Position Statement and Guidelines on Unmodified Electroconvulsive Therapy," *Indian Journal of Psychiatry* 54 (2012): 119–33.

46 Adriana Petryna, "Ethical Variability: Drug Development and Globalizing Clinical Trials," *American Ethnologist* 32, no. 2 (2005): 183–97.

47 Thippeswamy et al., "Ethical Aspects of Public Health Legislation," 47. For more on pragmatism in Indian psychiatry, see Sarah Pinto, "'The Tools of Your Chants and Spells': Stories of Madwomen and Indian Practical Healing," *Medical Anthropology* 35, no. 3 (2015): 263–77.

48 According to a British Medical Association's manual, these difficult ethical decisions must be made by determining whether "the intervention is likely to deliver an overall benefit to the patient." British Medical Association, *Doctors Working in Conflicts and Emergencies—An Ethical Toolkit* (London: British Medical Association, 2017), 18.

49 The Indian Supreme Court banned the use of ECT as an "emergency treatment" and in the case of minors (under eighteen years of age) without prior consent of a patient's guardian and approval from a professional board.

50 Varma, "Disappearing the Asylum."

51 Allen Feldman, *Archives of the Insensible: Of War, Photo Politics and Dead Memory* (Chicago: University of Chicago Press, 2015); see also Liisa Malkki, *The Need to Help: The Domestic Arts of International Humanitarianism* (Durham, NC: Duke University Press, 2015).

52 While I focus on what happens to a person *after* they are discharged, the process of discharge is also less than ideal. Patient and human rights advocates have called for reforms to the Mental Health Act to allow people to be dis-

charged under the supervision of a psychiatric nurse or social worker and to create institutions that exist in between the hospital and family (Dhanda et al., "Law and Mental Health").

53 Pinto, *Daughters of Parvati*, 3.

54 See Sarah Pinto, "The Limits of Diagnosis: Sex, Law and Psychiatry in a Case of Contested Marriage," *Ethos* 40, no. 2 (2012): 119–41, for similar narrative challenges.

55 I have chosen a pseudonym that conveys the meaning of Mauna's real name.

56 Cognitive behavioral therapy (CBT) is a form of psychotherapy that treats problems by modifying dysfunctional emotions, behaviors, and thoughts. CBT is solution-focused, encouraging patients to change distorted cognitions and destructive patterns of behavior through a limited number of sessions; it has become hegemonic in the United States because of its compatibility with health insurance ideologies.

57 Mauna's delusions were never investigated psychoanalytically, though I wondered if they were related to an experience of childhood or sexual trauma. Since Indian independence, nonpharmacological treatments, including psychoanalysis, have been limited to very few private practitioners in urban areas, accessed mainly by elites. Interest in psychoanalysis among Indian psychiatrists has been declining since the 1960s. Sarah Pinto, *The Doctor and Mrs. A.: Ethics and Counter-Ethics in an Indian Dream Analysis* (New York: Fordham University Press, 2019).

58 Field notes written on May 11, 2010.

59 Learning how to take a concise case history is a key marker of biomedical expertise. As Good notes, "learning to write up a patient correctly is crucial" to the process of learning medicine. Byron Good, *Medicine, Rationality, and Experience: An Anthropological Perspective* (Cambridge: Cambridge University Press, 1994), 77–78.

60 I did not observe interactions between doctors and Mauna; thus, I largely rely on the case's entextualization in the file to capture the biomedical perspective.

61 See Lorna Rhodes, *Emptying Beds: The Work of an Emergency Psychiatric Unit* (Berkeley: University of California Press, 1991).

62 Matthew S. Hull, "Documents and Bureaucracy," *Annual Review of Anthropology* 41 (2012): 251–67; Akhil Gupta, *Red Tape: Bureaucracy, Structural Violence and Poverty in India* (Durham, NC: Duke University Press, 2012).

63 Riles and Jean-Klein, "Introducing Discipline," 186.

64 Cited in Hull, "Documents and Bureaucracy," 256.

65 Matthew S. Hull, "The File: Agency, Authority and Autography in an Islamabad Bureaucracy," *Language and Communication* 23 (2003): 304.

66 According to a survey of ECT use in 334 psychiatric institutions across Asia, patients received a mean of 7.1 ECT treatments (Chanpattana et al., "A Survey of the Practice of Electroconvulsive Therapy in Asia").

67 I later learned that Mauna was adopted. Very unusually in Kashmir, she was an only child.

68 Mauna's use of the word *heart* (dil) here signifies not the physical organ but what we would call a person's constitution. As Marsden has argued in his work on Muslim religious experience in northwestern Pakistan, the locus of a person's genuine thought is the heart, and not the mind (*zehn*) or brain (*dimagh*). Magnus Marsden, *Muslim Religious Experience in Pakistan's North-West Frontier* (Cambridge: Cambridge University Press, 2005), 88.

69 Two recent studies on subjective memory worsening (SMW) among patients who have received (modified) ECT argued that SMW a week after ECT "occurs only in a minority of patients (26 percent, in one Swedish study) and is probably not correlated with objective cognitive impairment. The study found that SMW was more common among women and in younger patients." Ole Brus et al., "Subjective Memory Immediately Following Electroconvulsive Therapy," *Journal of Electroconvulsive Therapy* 33 (2017): 96–103. It is important to point out the radically different conditions in which ECT is administered in Sweden versus India, however. I was unable to find any studies comparing cognitive impairment and memory loss in unmodified versus modified ECT. Carolina Oremus et al., "Effects of Electroconvulsive Therapy on Cognitive Functioning in Patients with Depression: Protocol for a Systematic Review and Meta-Analysis," *BMJ Open* 5, no. 3 (2015).

70 As Hillyard has argued for Northern Ireland, shock as interrogation is reserved for places "where large sections of communities which are perceived as distinct threats to the existing status quo" and require regular and systematic surveillance. Paddy Hillyard, "Law and Order," in *Northern Ireland: The Background to the Conflict*, ed. John Darby (Belfast: Apple Tree, 1983), 46.

71 Although the majority of those arrested under the PSA were later released, they faced surveillance and the strain of prolonged court cases. According to Amnesty International, between eight thousand and twenty thousand people have been detained under the Public Safety Act in Kashmir in the past two decades. "A 'Lawless Law': Detentions under the Jammu and Kashmir Public Safety Act," https://www.amnestyusa.org/files/asa20001201ien_11.pdf, accessed July 17, 2018.

72 These are examples of fake news stories circulated by the Indian state and military to justify a brutal military response to protests after every major uprising. "Pakistan behind Violent Protests in Kashmir: India," *Huffington Post*, November 7, 2016, https://www.huffingtonpost.in/2016/07/11/pakistan-behind-violent-protests-in-kashmir-india_a_21429799/. Many stone throwers either deny reports that they are paid protestors, or in cases when they receive compensation (a few hundred rupees), they see it as analogous to renumeration for other forms of activism. Azizur Rahman, "Kashmir's 'Champion Stone Throwers' Get Paid to Protest," *South China Morning Post*, July 14, 2009, https://www.scmp.com/article/686770/kashmirs-champion-stone-throwers-get-paid-protest.

73 Pinto, *Daughters of Parvati*, 30; Segal, "Tattered Textures of Kinship."

74 Veena Das, *Affliction: Health, Disease, Poverty* (New York: Fordham University Press, 2015).

75 One of the few qualitative studies of patient perspectives on ECT in India (conducted in Kerala) suggests that Mauna's parents' experiences are not unusual. Anto P. Rajkumar, B. Saravanan, and K. S. Jacob, "Perspectives of Patients and Relatives about Electroconvulsive Therapy: A Qualitative Study from Vellore, India," *Journal of Electroconvulsive Therapy* 22, no. 4 (2006): 253–58. Seventy-five percent of patients who have undergone ECT felt they had not been given adequate information about ECT, 60 percent of kin said that memory problems were an adverse effect of ECT, 60 percent of patients weren't sure what the consequences of refusing ECT would be, and 74 percent of kin felt that the patients would have been given ECT by force even after they had refused. Only 12 percent of patients were willing to accept ECT as a treatment for future relapses. "Even the patients who signed consent forms were unable to recall the details about the consent process" (Rajkumar et al., "Perspectives of Patients and Relatives," 255).

76 John M. Janzen, "Therapy Management: Concept, Reality, Process," *Medical Anthropology Quarterly* 1, no. 1 (1987): 68–84.

77 A number of ethnographies powerfully show how kinship enters the clinic (Chua, "The Register of 'Complaint'"; Pinto, *Daughters of Parvati*). Mauna's story tells us the opposite: how the clinic infiltrates kin relations and the space of domesticity.

78 Allen Feldman, *Formations of Violence: The Narrative of the Body and Political Terror in Northern Ireland* (Chicago: University of Chicago Press, 1991), 137.

79 Pinto, *Daughters of Parvati*.

80 Mirza Waheed, "The Collaborator," *The Caravan*, January 31, 2011, https://caravanmagazine.in/fiction/collaborator-2.

81 Waheed, "The Collaborator." "There was a stink to him, or to the mattress, or to the whole room," the narrator notes.

82 Segal, "Tattered Textures of Kinship."

83 Pinto, *Daughters of Parvati*, 260.

84 Although State Hospital No. 3 was established as a Kirkbride asylum—which advocated and practiced a progressive form of care, including outdoor space, activities, and airy Victorian architecture—by the mid-twentieth century, the asylum was overcrowded and ECT use was in its heyday in American psychiatry. The hospital closed in 1991. Brynnan K. Light-Lewis, "The Deeds of Outsider Art" (master's thesis, Sotheby's Institute of Art, 2012).

85 Light-Lewis, "The Deeds of Outsider Art."

CHAPTER 4: DEBRIEF

1 The demand for organizations to demonstrate greater efficacy, transparency, and accountability emerged in response to several key developments: the end of the Cold War and the exponential growth of humanitarian organizations,

a lack of coordination between different agencies, and massive aid failures such as the Rwandan genocide, in which NGOs unintentionally exacerbated the conflict by aiding the architects of the genocide in refugee camps in Zaire. Fiona Terry, *Condemned to Repeat?* (Ithaca, NY: Cornell University Press, 2002). After Rwanda, NGO humanitarianism underwent extensive bureaucratic and institutional transformation, developed mechanisms to measure and evaluate humanitarianism, standardized codes of conduct, produced manuals and guides for the delivery of health and other services in emergency contexts, and calculated the consequences of particular actions. The field became more professionalized as aid organizations developed doctrines, specialized areas of training, and specific career paths. See Michael N. Barnett, "Humanitarianism Transformed," *Perspective on Politics* 3, no. 4 (2005): 723–40.

2 Surveys fulfill what Michel Foucault describes as the biopolitical function of governance: counting, categorizing, and measuring the health of individuals and populations in the name of better management and care. Practices of classification and categorization were central to processes of colonial rule, but within contemporary global health and humanitarian regimes, numbers have gained even more legitimacy. Crystal Biruk, "Seeing like a Research Project: Producing 'High-Quality Data' in AIDS Research in Malawi," *Medical Anthropology* 31, no. 4 (2012): 347–66; Ian Hacking, "Biopower and the Avalanche of Printed Numbers," *Humanities in Society* 5 (1982): 279–95; Thurka Sangaramoorthy and Adia Benton, "Enumeration, Identity, and Health," *Medical Anthropology* 31, no. 4 (2012): 287–91.

3 Efforts from within the humanitarian industry aim to transform existing practices of representing aid recipients and giving them more agency. In 1989, the General Assembly of European NGOs adopted a "Code of Conduct on Images Related to the Third World," which provided standard guidelines in response to critiques that humanitarian organizations were profiting from sensationalistic and graphic images of Third World suffering. Sanaa Nissinen, "Dilemmas of Ethical Practice in the Production of Contemporary Humanitarian Photography," in *Humanitarian Photography: A History*, ed. Heide Fehrenbach and Davide Rodogno (Cambridge: Cambridge University Press, 2015), 298–99.

4 Michael N. Barnett, *The International Humanitarian Order* (London: Routledge, 2010), 186; Humanitarian Policy Group, "Measuring the Impact of Humanitarian Aid: A Review of Current Practices," HPG Research Report no. 17, Overseas Development Institute, London, 2004; James Darcy, "Acts of Faith? Thoughts on the Effectiveness of Humanitarian Action," Social Science Research Council, http://www.ssrc.org/programs/emergencies/publications/Darcy.pdf.

5 Psychosocial care was introduced after reports of mass sexual violence and rape during the Balkans conflict in the early 1990s. There are different models of humanitarian psychological interventions, including: debriefing, which encourages victims to talk about their experiences of violence in order to allevi-

ate PTSD and other symptoms of trauma; psychological support programs and psychological first aid, which are preventive programs for emergencies and conflicts; mental health gap, designed by the WHO to reduce the gap between needs and availability of resources and involve organizations and governments in developing mental health services; the clinical model, which use Euro-American schools of psychology and psychiatry such as the DSM; the psycho-social model, which targets the personal resilience of individual survivors of conflict and community rehabilitation as a whole and includes approaches such as education and awareness programs; and the Inter-Agency Standing Committee (IASC) guidelines for mental health, which help coordinate multiple responses for treating mental health in emergency settings. Lamia M. Moghnie, "Humanitarian Psychology in War and Postwar Lebanon: Violence, Therapy and Suffering" (PhD dissertation, University of Michigan, 2016), 57.

6 MSF started mental health and psychosocial interventions in 1990 in Gaza. Most of its mental health programming takes place in acute or chronic settings of mass conflict. Kaz de Jong, *Psychosocial and Mental Health Interventions in Areas of Mass Violence: A Community-Based Approach*, 2nd ed. (Amsterdam: Rozenberg, 2011); Ilana Feldman, *Life Lived in Relief: Humanitarian Predicaments and Palestinian Refugee Politics* (Oakland: University of California Press, 2018), 119. In Kashmir, MSF began its first mental health project in Ganderbal district in 2001. "MSF Initiates a Mental Health Project in the Ganderbal District, Kashmir." MSF, 2001, http://www.msf.org/article/msf-initiates -mental-health-pilot-project-ganderbal-district-kashmir.

7 See Vincanne Adams, *Metrics: What Counts in Global Health* (Durham, NC: Duke University Press, 2016); Peter Redfield, *Life in Crisis: The Ethical Journey of Doctors Without Borders* (Berkeley: University of California Press), 2013; China Scherz, *Having People, Having Heart: Charity, Sustainable Development and Problems of Dependence in Central Uganda* (Chicago: University of Chicago Press, 2014).

8 Liisa Malkki, *The Need to Help: The Domestic Arts of International Humanitarianism* (Durham, NC: Duke University Press, 2015), 29.

9 Cristiana Giordano, *Migrants in Translation: Caring and the Logics of Difference in Contemporary Italy* (Oakland: University of California Press, 2014), 8–9.

10 Mbembe describes necropower as the technologies of control through which *life is strategically subjugated to the power of death*. Achille Mbembe, "Necropolitics," *Public Culture* 15 (2003): 11–40.

11 *Kasmir LifeLine: What We Do*. Accessed July 20, 2020, http://www.healing mindsfoundation.org/what-we-do/.

12 See Lisa Stevenson, *Life beside Itself: Imagining Care in the Canadian Arctic* (Berkeley: University of California Press, 2014), 86.

13 *Kasmir LifeLine: Our History*. Accessed July 20, 2020, http://www.healing mindsfoundation.org/our-history/.

14 For more, see Saiba Varma, "Where There Are Only Doctors: Counselors as Psychiatrists in Indian Administered Kashmir," *Ethos* 40, no. 4 (2012): 517–35.

15 Veena Das, *Affliction: Health, Disease, Poverty* (New York: Fordham University Press, 2015), 23.

16 My thanks to Peter Redfield for this framing.

17 Although Médecins sans Frontières (MSF-Holland) tried to work in Kashmir in 1995, the organization was only allowed a permanent presence in 2000 when they agreed to collaborate with a state health agency. As of 2018, MSF was running eleven counseling centers in four districts—Baramulla, Bandipora, Pulwama, and Srinagar. In addition to its counseling centers, MSF also assisted in reconstructing and upgrading the psychiatric hospital after several parts of the hospital were destroyed in a fire in the late 1990s.

18 For more on biomedical and nonbiomedical healing in northern India, see Das, *Affliction*, chapter 6; Stefan Ecks, *Eating Drugs: Psychopharmaceutical Pluralism in India* (New York: New York University Press, 2013).

19 "MSF's Kashmir Radio Soap Opera," *MSF Frontline Reports* podcast no. 64, October 19, 2010, https://www.youtube.com/watch?v=EHcSBvKahwo.

20 These field notes were written in October 2009.

21 MSF's administrators and project managers are expatriates who rotate through MSF's different projects around the world. All its local staff, including its counselors, are Kashmiris who do not enjoy the benefits of mobility and the "sans frontiers" philosophy of the organization. See Didier Fassin, "Humanitarianism as a Politics of Life," *Public Culture* 19, no. 3 (2007): 499–520; Peter Redfield, "The Unbearable Lightness of Ex-Pats: Double Binds of Humanitarian Mobility," *Cultural Anthropology* 27, no. 2 (2012): 358–82.

22 Peter Redfield, "Doctors, Borders, and Life in Crisis," *Cultural Anthropology* 20, no. 3 (2005): 328–61.

23 Early research on PTSD focused on displaced populations. The underlying assumption of these studies was that there is a universal human response to violence and that, cross-culturally, people exhibit similar traumatic symptoms. As Fassin and Rechtman have pointed out, these interventions linked diverse experiences such as rape, physical injuries, hearing gunfire or bombs, or losing a loved one in a natural disaster, under the singular sign of a "traumatic event." In places where PTSD has not been well established, the first and most important task facing humanitarian organizations is to develop a local version of a research interview, usually a fully structured questionnaire that will allow researchers to diagnose the disorder in the target population. Following DSM criteria, the interview should include questions about the specific psychiatric symptoms that make up the syndrome—such as reexperiencing, hyperarousal, and withdrawal. These techniques—such as research interviews and surveys—help make the disorder visible, measurable, and commensurate with global scientific discourses. Joshua Breslau, "Posttraumatic Stress Disorder in International Health," *Culture, Medicine and Psychiatry* 38 (2004): 117; see also Didier Fassin and Richard Rechtman, *The Empire of Trauma: An Inquiry into the Condition of Victimhood*, trans. Rachel Gomme (Princeton, NJ: Princeton University Press, 2009); Derek Summerfield, "The Invention of Post-Traumatic Stress

Disorder and the Social Usefulness of a Psychiatric Category," *British Medical Journal* 322 (2001): 95–98; Saiba Varma, "From 'Terrorist' to 'Terrorized': How Trauma Became the Language of Suffering in Kashmir," in *Resisting Occupation in Kashmir*, ed. Haley Duschinski, Mona Bhan, Ather Zia, and Cynthia Mahmood (Philadelphia: University of Pennsylvania Press, 2018).

24 Because a PTSD diagnosis is seen as having causes external to the subject, it is unique among psychiatric diagnoses for conferring "innocence on its victims, dissociating them from the taint of other psychiatric disorders." As Breslau argues, "the narrative connection between events in the world and suffering inside individuals gives this disorder [PTSD] a special ability to stand as hard evidence of suffering backed with the credibility of medical science" (Breslau, "Posttraumatic Stress Disorder," 117–18).

25 Many humanitarian organizations have begun adopting rights-based language. However, as Michael Barnett ("Humanitarianism Transformed") notes, the convergence of human rights and humanitarian logics—one in the idiom of rights and the other in the idiom of relief—are not without frictions. While the logic of relief and the logic of rights both place the human citizen at the fore, use the language of empowerment, and question power, they are different in that relief (humanitarianism) privileges survival over freedom, while the rights perspective views relief as a benefit that is negotiable.

26 See also Malkki, *The Need to Help*.

27 "India: Humanitarian Aid for the Most Vulnerable People of India Affected by the Conflict in Jammu and Kashmir," Report from the European Commission's Directorate-General for European Civil Protection and Humanitarian Aid Operations, July 20, 2004, https://reliefweb.int/report/india/india-humanitarian -aid-most-vulnerable-people-india-affected-conflict-jammu-and-kashmir.

28 An emergency relief kit from Action Aid consisted of cooking oil, lentils, rice, blankets, and other essentials, while livelihood support included providing livestock (one or two goats or cows) to families in need.

29 This gesture reminded me of Veena Das's encounter with women survivors in Sultanpuri in the immediate aftermath of the anti-Sikh riots in 1984, who refused to clean their huts or wash and bathe themselves, to remain close to the horrific violence and to those whom they had lost. See Veena Das, *Life and Words: Violence and the Descent into the Ordinary* (Berkeley: University of California Press, 2007), 155.

30 The survey closely followed the Everstine Trauma Response Index–Adapted (ETRI), which has thirty-five items on two self-rating scales and assesses previous traumatic events and PTSD symptoms along with the duration of the symptoms. Arooj Yaswi and Amber Haque, "Prevalence of PTSD Symptoms and Depression and Level of Coping among the Victims of the Kashmir Conflict," *Journal of Loss and Trauma* 13 (2008): 471–80.

31 Fassin, "Humanitarianism as a Politics of Life," 211; Ilana Feldman, "Looking for Humanitarian Purpose: Endurance and the Value of Lives in a Palestinian Refugee Camp," *Public Culture* 27, no. 3 (2015): 427–47; Miriam Tick-

tin, "Where Ethics and Politics Meet: The Violence of Humanitarianism in France," *American Ethnologist* 33, no. 1 (2006): 34.

32 See Chika Watanabe, "Intimacy beyond Love: The History and Politics of Inter-Asian Development Aid," *Anthropological Quarterly* 92, no. 1 (2019): 59–84, on cultural proximity in aid encounters.

33 See Gayatri Chakravorty Spivak, "Can the Subaltern Speak?," in *Marxism and the Interpretation of Culture*, ed. C. Nelson and L. Grossberg (Basingstoke, UK: Macmillan Education, 1988). In her canonical essay, Spivak asserts that "there is no space from which the sexed subaltern can speak" (307). Spivak affirms that the silence or absent voice of the sexed subaltern subject can only be amplified by someone else's attempt to represent her (in this case, the anthropologist).

34 Lauren Berlant, "Without Exception: On the Ordinariness of Violence: Interview with Brad Evans," *Los Angeles Review of Books*, July 30, 2018, https://lareviewofbooks.org/article/without-exception-on-the-ordinariness-of-violence/.

35 Cited in Charles Briggs, "'Dear Dr. Freud,'" *Cultural Anthropology* 29, no. 2 (2014): 312–43.

36 These dynamics could have been different had the organization offered Saleema a form of "lifesaving" care, such as citizenship or residency permits, as has been documented in the anthropology of humanitarianism (see the introduction).

37 Michel Foucault, *Psychiatric Power: Lectures at the Collège de France 1973–1974*, trans. Graham Burchell (New York: Picador, 2008).

38 Petryna describes the malleability of ethical guidelines in the context of clinical trials. Here, aid workers struggled to produce a "script" that was predetermined but not codified. Adriana Petryna, "Ethical Variability: Drug Development and Globalizing Clinical Trials," *American Ethnologist* 32, no. 2 (2005): 183–97; Mara Buchbinder and Dragana Lassiter, "Script," November 17, 2014, http://somatosphere.net/2014/11/script.html; Summerson E. Carr, *Scripting Addiction: The Politics of Therapeutic Talk and American Sobriety* (Princeton, NJ: Princeton University Press, 2010).

39 Michel Foucault, *Society Must Be Defended: Lectures at the Collège de France 1975–1976* (New York: Picador, 2003), xvii.

40 Kashmiri scholars have produced excellent work on mourning and martyrdom. Mohamad Junaid, "Epitaphs as Counterhistories: Martyrdom, Commemoration, and the Work of Graveyards in Kashmir," in *Resisting Occupation in Kashmir*, ed. Haley Duschinski, Mona Bhan, Ather Zia, and Cynthia Mahmood (Philadelphia: University of Pennsylvania Press, 2018); Inshah Malik, "Gendered Politics of Funerary Processions: Contesting Indian Sovereignty in Kashmir," *Economic and Political Weekly* 53, no. 47 (2018): 63–66; Ather Zia, *Resisting Disappearance: Military Occupation and Women's Activism in Kashmir* (Seattle: University of Washington Press, 2019).

41 Allen Feldman, *Archives of the Insensible: Of War, Photo Politics and Dead Memory* (Chicago: University of Chicago Press, 2015).

1 Basharat Masood, "Srinagar: People Trapped, City Submerged, Administration Missing," *Indian Express*, September 7, 2014, https://indianexpress.com/article/india/india-others/jk-floods-people-trapped-city-submerged-adminstration-missing/.

2 As Junaid astutely notes, the flood brought to the surface the spatiality of occupation, but "almost magically," it also "made the 'state' disappear." He notes how the devastation laid bare the "innards of major military bases and defenses," while revealing the dysfunction of the civil state authority—"no ministers, legislators, bureaucrats, soldiers, police, judges, or even low-level clerks were seen for days." Mohamad Junaid, "Youth Activists in Kashmir: State Violence, Tehreek and the Formation of Political Subjectivity" (PhD dissertation, City University of New York, 2017), 204.

3 Given the Indian military's huge presence in the region—and the fact that its own infrastructure was severely damaged—it is not surprising that Indian armed forces were the first to respond. However, such militarized responses also reflect how disasters are increasingly deemed to be "security" crises. Rosalind Petchesky, "Biopolitics at the Crossroads of Sexuality and Disaster: The Case of Haiti," Working Paper no. 8, Sexuality Policy Watch, New York, 2012, 12.

4 Nida Najar and Ellen Barry, "Embrace of Social Media Aids Flood Victims in Kashmir," *New York Times*, September 12, 2014, https://www.nytimes.com/2014/09/13/world/asia/embrace-of-social-media-aids-flood-victims-in-kashmir.html.

5 Vincanne Adams, *Markets of Sorrow, Labors of Faith: New Orleans in the Wake of Katrina* (Durham, NC: Duke University Press, 2013); Naomi Klein, *The Shock Doctrine: The Rise of Disaster Capitalism* (New York: Henry Holt, 2007).

6 The use of this disaster contrasts sharply with *La Tragedia*—devastating floods in Venezuela that killed thousands. As Fassin and Vasquez argue, in that context, a "humanitarian state of exception" was not feared, but rather was *desired* by victims on the ground. Didier Fassin and Maria Vasquez, "Humanitarian Exception as the Rule: The Political Ethology of the 1999 *Tragedia* in Venezuela," *American Ethnologist* 32, no. 3 (2005): 391.

7 Luc Boltanski, *Distant Suffering: Morality, Media and Politics*, trans. Graham Burchell (Cambridge: Cambridge University Press, 1999).

8 "Remembering Operation Megh Rahat: How the Human Spirit Prevailed," *Business Standard*, September 7, 2015, https://www.business-standard.com/article/news-ani/remembering-operation-megh-rahat-how-the-human-spirit-prevailed-115090700609_1.html.

9 See also Chika Watanabe, *Becoming One: Religion, Development, and Environmentalism in a Japanese NGO in Myanmar* (Honolulu: University of Hawai'i Press, 2018); Chika Watanabe, "Intimacy beyond Love: The History and Politics of Inter-Asian Development Aid," *Anthropological Quarterly* 92, no. 1 (2019): 59–84.

10 Chika Watanabe, "Muddy Labor: A Japanese Aid Ethic of Collective Intimacy in Myanmar," *Cultural Anthropology* 29, no. 4 (2014): 648–71.

11 Nancy Rose Hunt, *A Nervous State: Violence, Remedies, and Reverie in Colonial Congo* (Durham, NC: Duke University Press, 2016), 6.

12 Nitasha Kaul, "India's Obsession with Kashmir: Democracy, Gender, (Anti) Nationalism," *Feminist Review* 119 (2018): 128.

13 Pandey notes how nationalism rests on demands of loyalty, particularly from minoritized populations. As Pandey notes, during Partition and Indian independence, Hindu loyalty to India was seen as unquestioned, since, unlike Muslims, Hindus had no other country that they could claim as theirs (whereas Muslims could choose Pakistan). As Pandey writes, "the test of loyalty is . . . required only of those who are not 'real,' 'natural' citizens." Gayanendra Pandey, *Memory, History and the Question of Violence* (Calcutta: K. P. Bagchi 1999), 611.

14 Many anthropologists and feminist scholars have connected empire, domesticity, intimacy, and affect. Sara Ahmed, *Willful Subjects* (Durham, NC: Duke University Press, 2014); Durba Ghosh, *Sex and the Family in Colonial India* (Cambridge: Cambridge University Press, 2006); Michael Di Gregorio and Jessica L. Merolli, "Introduction: Affective Citizenship and the Politics of Identity, Control, Resistance," *Citizenship Studies* 20, no. 8 (2016): 933–42; Ann L. Stoler, *Carnal Knowledge and Imperial Power: Race and the Intimate in Colonial Rule* (Berkeley: University of California Press, 2010), to name just a few. The affective complexities of humanitarianism are heightened in places like Puerto Rico, Haiti, or Kashmir, where continuing colonial and neocolonial dynamics render impossible "engaging in disaster assistance or defense of human rights in purely 'neutral' terms" (Petchesky "Biopolitics at the Crossroads of Sexuality and Disaster," 5).

15 Henry A. Giroux, "Reading Hurricane Katrina: Race, Class, and the Biopolitics of Disposability," *College Literature* 33, no. 3 (2006): 171–96.

16 Betwa Sharma and Nida Najar, "Kashmiris Cope with Flooding, and Resentment of India," *New York Times*, September 15, 2014, https://www.nytimes.com/2014/09/16/world/asia/kashmiris-cope-with-flooding-and-resentment-of-india.html.

17 Medical anthropologists working in a variety of contexts have shown how group therapy has been globalized and vernacularized. See Sandra Hyde, "'Spending My Own Money, Harming My Own Body': Addiction Care in a Chinese Therapeutic Community," *Medical Anthropology* 36, no. 1 (2016): 61–76; Vinh-Kim Nguyen, *The Republic of Therapy: Triage and Sovereignty in West Africa's Time of AIDS* (Durham, NC: Duke University Press, 2010).

18 Bonnie N. Kaiser et al., "Eliciting Recovery Narratives in Global Mental Health: Benefits and Potential Harms in Service User Participation," *Psychiatric Rehabilitation Journal*, doi: 10.1037/prj0000384; Saiba Varma, "Love in the Time of Occupation: Reveries, Longing and Intoxication in Kashmir," *American Ethnologist* 43, no. 1 (2016): 50–62.

19 For more tactics of resisting militarized care in the DDC, see Varma, "Love in the Time of Occupation."

20 Ghassan Hage, "Hating Israel in the Field: On Ethnography and Political Emotions," *Anthropological Theory* 9, no. 1 (2009): 59–79.

21 Junaid, "Youth Activists in Kashmir," 241.

22 Since 2010, Indian security agencies have identified approximately 467 youths, most of whom come from southern Kashmir, who have taken up arms. They identified a surge in recruitment after Wani's killing. Muzamil Jaleel, "Since 2010, 467 Local Youth from 354 Villages across Jammu–Kashmir Have Become Militants," *Indian Express,* June 12, 2018, https://indianexpress.com/article/india/since-2010-a-militant-or-more-in-every-village-in-jammu-and-kashmir-hizbul-mujahideen-burhan-wani-death-5213627/.

23 Prem Shankar Jha, "Kashmir Is in Danger of Spinning Out of Control," 2016, http://www.premshankarjha.com/2016/08/01/kashmir-is-in-danger-of-spinning-out-of-control/.

24 "CRPF Chief Justifies Use of Pellet Guns on Protesting Kashmiris," *Dunya News,* July 26, 2016, http://dunyanews.tv/en/Pakistan/346464-CRPF-chief-justifies-use-of-pellet-guns-on-protest.

25 Azad Essa and Showkat Shafi, "Kashmiri Doctors Lament Injuries by Pellets in Protests," *Al Jazeera,* July 13, 2016, https://www.aljazeera.com/news/2016/07/kashmiri-doctors-lament-injuries-pellets-protests-160712201432612.html, accessed July 29, 2018. By November 2016, more than seventeen thousand Kashmiri adults and children were wounded by pellets, and almost half of those injured were hit in the eye.

26 Mirza Waheed, "India's Crackdown in Kashmir: Is This the World's First Mass Blinding?," *Guardian,* November 8, 2016, https://www.theguardian.com/world/2016/nov/08/india-crackdown-in-kashmir-is-this-worlds-first-mass-blinding.

27 Field notes, August 11, 2016.

28 Liisa Malkki, *The Need to Help: The Domestic Arts of International Humanitarianism* (Durham, NC: Duke University Press, 2015).

29 Liisa Malkki, "Speechless Emissaries: Refugees, Humanitarianism, and Dehistoricization," *Cultural Anthropology* 11, no. 3 (1996): 377–404.

30 Junaid, "Youth Activists in Kashmir," 231.

31 Field notes, August 20, 2016.

32 Peter Redfield, *Life in Crisis: The Ethical Journey of Doctors Without Borders* (Berkeley: University of California Press, 2013), 16–19.

33 Redfield, *Life in Crisis,* 19.

34 Klein, *The Shock Doctrine.*

35 Rebecca Solnit, *A Paradise Built in Hell: The Extraordinary Communities That Arise in Disaster* (New York: Penguin, 2009), 6. As Solnit eloquently puts it, "disasters provide an extraordinary window into social desire and possibility, and what manifests there matters elsewhere, in ordinary times and in extraordinary times."

36 The concept of "letting die" has been used to describe a range of situations in which state indifference or neglect has devastating consequences for particular vulnerable populations, such as Palestinians living in the occupied territories; poor, black, and elderly residents of New Orleans post-Katrina; and chronically mentally ill persons in Brazil, India, and the United States. João Biehl, *Vita: Life in a Zone of Social Abandonment* (Berkeley: University of California Press, 2015); Giroux, "Reading Hurricane Katrina"; Jocelyn Marrow and Tanya Marie Luhrmann, "The Zone of Social Abandonment in Cultural Geography: On the Street in the United States, Inside the Family in India," *Culture, Medicine and Psychiatry* 36 (2012): 493–513; Jasbir Puar, "The 'Right' to Maim: Disablement and Inhumanist Biopolitics in Palestine," *Borderlands* 14, no. 1 (2015): 1–27.

37 See Sarah Pinto, *Daughters of Parvati: Women and Madness in Contemporary India* (Philadelphia: University of Pennsylvania Press, 2014).

38 Cf. Katherine P. Ewing, "The Illusion of Wholeness: Culture, Self and the Experience of Inconsistency," *Ethos* 18, no. 3 (1990): 251–78.

39 Solnit, *A Paradise Built in Hell*.

40 Junaid, "Youth Activists in Kashmir," 243.

41 See also Magnus Marsden, "Fatal Embrace: Trading in Hospitality on the Frontiers of South and Central Asia," *Journal of the Royal Anthropological Institute* 18, no. 1 (2012): S117–S130; Andrew Shryock, "Thinking about Hospitality, with Derrida, Kant, and the Balga Bedouin," *Anthropos* 103 (2008): 405–21, 406.

42 Amira Mittermaier, "Beyond Compassion: Islamic Voluntarism in Egypt," *American Ethnologist* 41, no. 3 (2014): 518–31. As Mittermaier points out, Islamic traditions of volunteering cannot be fully subsumed within a liberal, humanitarian language of compassion or a political language of citizenship (521).

43 Mittermaier, "Beyond Compassion"; Amira Mittermaier, "Bread, Freedom, Social Justice: The Egyptian Uprising and a Sufi Khidma," *Cultural Anthropology* 29, no. 1 (2014): 54–79.

44 Marcel Mauss, *The Gift: The Form and Reason for Exchange in Archaic Societies* (London: Routledge, 1990), 81. Unlike the discourses of state generosity and magnanimity that proliferated on social media, later reports revealed that the Indian military charged the state government of Jammu and Kashmir 650 crore rupees (about US$106.2 million) for rescue and relief. As per the logic of militarized care, the gift "had to be forcibly repaid." Nishita Trisal, "In Kashmir, Nehru's Golden Chains That He Hoped Would Bind the State to India Have Lost Their Lustre," *Scroll,* November 30, 2015, https://scroll.in/article/772211/in-kashmir-nehrus-golden-chains-that-he-hoped-would-bind-the-state-to-india-have-lost-their-lustre.

45 Rana Sobh and Russell Belk, "Domains of Privacy and Hospitality in Arab Gulf Homes," *Journal of Islamic Marketing* 2, no. 2 (2011): 125–37. There has been much work on the secularization of hospitality in Islamic contexts. Rana Sobh, Russell W. Belk, and Jonathan A. J. Wilson, "Islamic Arab Hospitality and Multiculturalism," *Marketing Theory* 13, no. 4 (2013): 443–63.

46 Marsden, "Fatal Embrace"; Shryock, "Thinking about Hospitality," 46.

47 Field notes, August 11, 2016.

48 See also Shryock, "Thinking about Hospitality," who describes how members of Balga tribes used hospitality to resist and refashion Ottoman, British, and Hashemite ideas of centralized state authority by subjecting them to logics of guest and host.

49 Here I draw inspiration from Elliott Fukui's notion of cathartic cartographies.

50 A. F. Robertson, "The Dal Lake: Reflections on an Anthropological Consultancy in Kashmir," *Anthropology Today* 3, no. 2 (1987): 7.

51 P. R. Chari, D. Suba Chandran, and Shaheen Akhtar, "Tourism and Peacebuilding in Jammu and Kashmir," Special Report no. 281, United States Institute for Peace, 2011; Pankaj Mishra, "Promoting Kashmir," *Travel and Leisure*, May 8, 2009, http://www.travelandleisure.com/articles/paradise-regained.

52 Cabeiri Robinson, "The Dangerous Allure of Tourism Promotion as a Post-Conflict Policy in Disputed Azad Jammu and Kashmir," *JSIS Correspondence*, May 20, 2014, https://depts.washington.edu/know/wordpress/the-dangerous-allure-of-tourism-promotion-as-a-post-conflict-policy-in-disputed-azad-jammu-and-kashmir/.

53 Nasser Hussain, "Hyperlegality," *New Criminal Law Review* 10, no. 4 (2017): 514–31.

54 Deepti Misri, "Showing Humanity: Violence and Visuality in Kashmir," *Cultural Studies* 33, no. 3 (2019): 3.

55 Yael Navaro, "Diversifying Affect," *Cultural Anthropology* 32, no. 2 (2017): 212.

56 Ana Esther Ceceña, "On the Complex Relation between Knowledges and Emancipations," trans. Brenda Baletti, *South Atlantic Quarterly* 111, no. 1 (2012): 115–16.

57 Since 2010, fourteen people in Kashmir have died from the use of pellet guns. What Indian forces call "pellet guns" are in fact pump-action shotguns, which fire up to five hundred lead pellets at once.

58 For similar dynamics in Palestine, see Puar, "The 'Right' to Maim"; Jasbir Puar, *The Right to Maim: Debility, Capacity, Disability* (Durham, NC: Duke University Press, 2017).

59 In 2002, the state government of Gujarat, under the watch of Narendra Modi, oversaw the genocide of two thousand Muslims. More recently, state governments and BJP officials have been complicit in acts of lynching and mob violence against Christians, Muslims, Dalits, and other low-caste persons and communities. Shakuntala Banaji, "Vigilante Publics: Orientalism, Modernity and Hindutva Fascism in India," *Javnost—The Public* 25, no. 4 (2018): 333–50; Parvis Ghassem-Fachandi, *Pogrom in Gujarat: Hindu Nationalism and Anti-Muslim Violence in India* (Princeton, NJ: Princeton University Press, 2012).

60 Shabir Yusuf and Mukeet Akmali, "Cops Fired Teargas Shells inside Hospital: SMHS Medicos," *Greater Kashmir*, July 11, 2016, https://www.greaterkashmir.com/news/kashmir/cops-fired-teargas-shells-inside-hospital-smhs-medicos/.

61 Omar Dewachi, "Blurred Lines: Warfare and Health Care," *Medical Anthropology Theory* 2, no. 2 (2015): 95–101.

62 Mir Ehsan, "How Doctors across Valley Are Tending to Injured," *Indian Express*, July 27, 2016, http://indianexpress.com/article/india/india-news -india/kashmir-unrest-how-doctors-across-valley-are-tending-to-injured -2938290/.

63 This justification helped maintain the moral integrity of stone throwers and other protestors, who are maligned in the Indian press and among sections of Kashmiri society as "miscreants."

64 *Bayt-al Maal* in Arabic, or "House of Money" or "House of Wealth," was the financial institution in the early Islamic Caliphate, serving as the royal treasury and also distributing *zakat* (charity) for public works. See Anne Marie Baylouny, "Creating Kin: New Family Associations as Welfare Providers in Liberalizing Jordan," *International Journal of Middle East Studies* 38 (2006): 349–68, on charitable and family associations as alternatives to state-funded social welfare networks. During the 2010 protests, baitul māls also provided essential goods when security forces blocked the only highway connecting Kashmir to India. As Abid said, "In 2010, they emerged as very strong institutions."

65 Tomas Matza, *Shock Therapy: Psychology, Precarity, and Well-Being in Postsocialist Russia* (Durham NC: Duke University Press, 2018), 131.

66 Field notes written on August 12, 2016.

67 At stake in their different interpretations were fault lines within Kashmiri society about who should belong to a future Kashmiri nation. While Altaaf Sahab saw the movement for self-determination as one by and for Muslims, many Kashmiris I spoke with argued for a multicultural, multiethnic, and multireligious Kashmir.

68 Mona Bhan, "'In Search of the Aryan Seed': Race, Religion and Sexuality in Indian-Occupied Kashmir," in *Resisting Occupation in Kashmir*, ed. Haley Duschinski, Mona Bhan, Ather Zia, and Cynthia Mahmood (Philadelphia: University of Pennsylvania Press, 2018). Despite long-standing efforts to politicize and communalize these pilgrimages, Kashmiri Muslims were proud of the fact that, for over sixteen years, the Amarnath pilgrimage—which sees more than a million visitors annually—had not seen any violence. Rather, in contradiction to the state's narrative of them as "Islamic radicals," Kashmiri Muslims had facilitated the pilgrimage by serving as porters, drivers, and extending other forms of hospitality. They pointed to these examples as demonstrating their unfailing commitment to hospitality.

69 In February 2016, Jats—a dominant farming community in northern India— staged agitations demanding inclusion into the Indian government's affirmative action reservation system (created for low-caste communities). The protestors blocked highway and railway lines to Delhi for days and set fire to cars, shops, and private property.

70 See also Sherine Hamdy, "Islam, Fatalism, and Medical Intervention: Lessons from Egypt on the Cultivation of Forbearance (*Sabr*) and Reliance on God (*Tawakkul*)," *Anthropological Quarterly* 82, no. 1 (2009): 173–96.

71 Claire L. Wendland, "Moral Maps and Medical Imaginaries: Clinical Tourism in Malawi's College of Medicine," *American Anthropologist* 114, no. 1 (2012): 108–22.

72 Humanitarian aid workers also have to contend with the frenzied, accelerated temporality of emergencies marked by slow, sometimes boring, periods of crisis. Mark Snelling, "The Impact of Emergency Aid Work on Personal Relationships: A Psychodynamic Study," *Journal of International Humanitarian Action* 3 (2018): 14–29.

73 Elizabeth Povinelli, *Empire of Love: Toward a Theory of Intimacy, Genealogy, and Carnality* (Durham, NC: Duke University Press, 2006), 25.

74 This resonates with what Cusicanqui calls a "principle of hope" or "anticipatory consciousness" that both discerns and realizes decolonization at the same time. Silvia Rivera Cusicanqui, "*Ch'ixinakax utxiwa*: A Reflection on the Practices and Discourses of Decolonization," trans. Brenda Baletti, *South Atlantic Quarterly* 111, no. 1 (2012): 96.

75 See Annelise Riles and Iris Jean-Klein, "Introducing Discipline: Anthropology and Human Rights Administrations," *Political and Legal Anthropology Review* 28, no. 2 (2005): 173–202.

Abbas, Hassan. *Pakistan's Drift into Extremism: Allah, the Army and America's War on Terror.* Armonk, NY: M. E. Sharpe, 2005.

Abramowitz, Sharon A. "Trauma and Humanitarian Translation in Liberia: The Tale of Open Mole." *Culture, Medicine and Psychiatry* 34 (2010): 353–79.

Aciksoz, Salih Can. "Medical Humanitarianism under Atmospheric Violence: Healthcare Workers in the 2013 Gezi Protests in Turkey." *Culture, Medicine, and Psychiatry* 40, no. 2 (2016): 198–222.

Adams, Vincanne. *Doctors for Democracy: Health Professionals in the Nepal Revolution.* Cambridge: Cambridge University Press, 1998.

Adams, Vincanne. *Markets of Sorrow, Labors of Faith: New Orleans in the Wake of Katrina.* Durham, NC: Duke University Press, 2013.

Adams, Vincanne. *Metrics: What Counts in Global Health.* Durham, NC: Duke University Press, 2016.

Addlakha, Renu. *Deconstructing Mental Illness: An Ethnography of Psychiatry, Women and the Family.* New Delhi: Zubaan, 2008.

Aggarwal, Ravina, and Mona Bhan. "Disarming Violence: Development, Democracy and Security on the Borders of India." *Journal of Asian Studies* 68, no. 2 (2009): 519–42.

Agrwaal, Ashok. *In Search of Vanished Blood: The Writ of Habeas Corpus in Jammu and Kashmir: 1990–2004.* Kathmandu: South Asia Forum for Human Rights, 2008.

Ahmad, Wajahat, "Appointment with Terror." *Fountain Ink,* June 6, 2012. https://fountainink.in/essay/appointment-with-terror.

Ahmad, Wajahat. "'Our War of Liberation Cannot be Fought by Beggars or by Those Who Seek Aid from Others': Maqbool Bhat." *Kashmir Ink,* February 11, 2018.

Ahmed, Sara. *The Cultural Politics of Emotions.* New York: Routledge, 2004.

Ahmed, Sara. *The Promise of Happiness.* Durham, NC: Duke University Press, 2010.

Ahmed, Sara. *Willful Subjects.* Durham, NC: Duke University Press, 2014.

Ali, Nosheen. "Books vs Bombs? Humanitarian Development and the Narrative of Terror in Northern Pakistan." *Third World Quarterly* 31, no. 4 (2010): 541–59.

Ali, Zafar, Mushtaq Marghoob, M. M. Dar, and Abdul Hussain. "First Report of PTSD in Disturbed Kashmir: Characteristics of a Treatment-Seeking Sample." Paper presented at the 17th Annual Meeting of the International Society for Traumatic Stress Studies, New Orleans, 2001.

Alkazi, Feisal. *Srinagar: An Architectural Legacy*. New Delhi: Roli, 2014.

Alter, Joseph. "Heaps of Health, Metaphysical Fitness: Ayurveda and the Ontology of Good Health in Medical Anthropology." *Current Anthropology* 40, no. S1 (1999): S43–S66.

Alter, Joseph. *Moral Materialism: Sex and Masculinity in Modern India*. New Delhi: Penguin, 2012.

American Psychiatric Association. *Diagnostic and Statistical Manual of Mental Disorders*, 3rd ed. Washington, DC: American Psychiatric Association, 2000.

Anant, Arpita. *Counterinsurgency and "Op Sadhbhavana" in Jammu and Kashmir*. New Delhi: Institute for Defense Studies and Analyses, 2011.

Andrade, Chittaranjan J. "Molecular Mechanisms underlying Electroconvulsive Therapy-Induced Amnestic Deficits: A Decade of Research." *Indian Journal of Psychiatry* 50, no. 4 (2008): 244–52.

Andrade, Chittaranjan J. "Unmodified ECT: Ethical Issues." *Issues in Medical Ethics* 11, no. 1 (2003): 9–10.

Andrade, Chittaranjan, N. Shah, P. Tharyan, M. S. Reddy, M. Thirunavukarasu, R. A. Kallivayalil, N. Nagpal, N. K. Bohra, A. Sharma, and E. Mohandas. "Position Statement and Guidelines on Unmodified Electroconvulsive Therapy." *Indian Journal of Psychiatry* 54 (2012): 119–33.

Aretxaga, Begoña. "Madness and the Politically Real: Reflections on Violence in Postdictatorial Spain." In *Postcolonial Disorders*, edited by Mary-Jo DelVecchio Good, Sandra Teresa Hyde, Sarah Pinto, and Byron J. Good, 43–61. Berkeley: University of California Press, 2008.

Asad, Talal. "On Torture, or Cruel, Inhuman and Degrading Treatment." *Social Research* 63, no. 4 (1996): 1081–109.

Asia Watch. *The Human Rights Crisis in Kashmir: A Pattern of Impunity*. New York: Human Rights Watch, 1993.

Axelsson, Per, Tahu Kukutai, and Rebecca Kippen. "The Field of Indigenous Health and the Role of Colonization and History." *Journal of Population Research* 33, no. 1 (2016): 1–7.

Baba, Tufeel, Abdul Ganai, Syed Qadri, Mushtaq Margoob, Qazi Iqbal, and Zahid Khan. "An Epidemiological Study on Substance Abuse among College Students of North India (Kashmir Valley)." *International Journal of Medical Science and Public Health* 2, no. 3 (2013): 562–67.

Badiou, Alain. *Being and Event*. New York: Continuum, 2005.

Bagcchi, Sanjeet. "Rethinking India's Psychiatric Care." *The Lancet Psychiatry* 1 (2014): 503–4.

Bammi, Y. N. *War against Insurgency and Terrorism in Kashmir*. Dehradun, India: Natraj, 2007.

Banaji, Shakuntala. "Vigilante Publics: Orientalism, Modernity and Hindutva Fascism in India." *Javnost—The Public* 25, no. 4 (2018): 333–50.

Barnett, Michael N. "Humanitarianism Transformed." *Perspective on Politics* 3, no. 4 (2005): 723–40.

Barnett, Michael N. *The International Humanitarian Order*. London: Routledge, 2010.

Bateson, Gregory, Don D. Jackson, Jay Haley, and John Weakland. *Steps to an Ecology of Mind*. Chicago: University of Chicago Press, 2000.

Batool, Essar, Ifrah Butt, Samreena Mushtaq, Munaza Rashid, and Natasha Rather. *Do You Remember Kunan Poshpora?* Delhi: Zubaan, 2016.

Bayley, David H. *Preventive Detention in India*. Calcutta: K. L. Mukhopadhyay, 1962.

Baylouny, Anne Marie. "Creating Kin: New Family Associations as Welfare Providers in Liberalizing Jordan." *International Journal of Middle East Studies* 38 (2006): 349–68.

Bayly, Christopher A. *Origins of Nationality in South Asia: Patriotism and Ethical Government in the Making of Modern India*. New Delhi: Oxford University Press, 1998.

Benjamin, Walter. *Illuminations*. Edited by Hannah Arendt. New York: Schocken, 1968.

Benton, Adia, and Sa'ed Atshan. "'Even War Has Rules': On Medical Neutrality and Legitimate Non-Violence." *Culture, Medicine and Psychiatry* 40 (2016): 151–58.

Benvenisti, Eyal. *The International Law of Occupation*. Oxford: Oxford University Press, 2013.

Bhan, Mona. *Counterinsurgency, Democracy and the Politics of Identity in India: From Warfare to Welfare?* London: Routledge, 2013.

Bhan, Mona. "'In Search of the Aryan Seed': Race, Religion and Sexuality in Indian-Occupied Kashmir." In *Resisting Occupation in Kashmir*, edited by Haley Duschinski, Mona Bhan, Ather Zia, and Cynthia Mahmood, 74–102. Philadelphia: University of Pennsylvania Press, 2018.

Bhan, Mona, Haley Duschinski, and Ather Zia. "'Rebels of the Streets': Violence, Protest and Freedom in Kashmir." In *Resisting Occupation in Kashmir*, edited by Haley Duschinski, Mona Bhan, Ather Zia, and Cynthia Mahmood, 1–41. Philadelphia: University of Pennsylvania Press, 2018.

Bhan, Mona, and Nishita Trisal. "Fluid Landscapes, Sovereign Nature: Conservation and Counterinsurgency in Indian-controlled Kashmir." *Critique of Anthropology* 37, no. 1 (2017): 67–92.

Bhatt, Chetan. "Frontlines and Interstices in the Global War on Terror." *Development and Change* 38, no. 6 (2007): 1073–93.

Bhattacharjee, Kishalay. *Blood on My Hands: Confessions of Staged Encounters*. Delhi: HarperCollins, 2015.

Bhonsle, Rahul. "Winning Hearts and Minds: Lessons from Jammu and Kashmir." Manekshaw Paper no. 14, Centre for Land Welfare Studies, New Delhi, 2009.

Biehl, João. *Vita: Life in a Zone of Social Abandonment*. Berkeley: University of California Press, 2015.

Biruk, Crystal. "Seeing like a Research Project: Producing 'High-Quality Data' in AIDS Research in Malawi." *Medical Anthropology* 31, no. 4 (2012): 347–66.

Bistoen, Gregory. *Trauma, Ethics and the Political beyond PTSD: The Dislocations of the Real*. London: Palgrave Macmillan, 2016.

Bock, Gregory R., and Julie Whelan, eds. *Chronic Fatigue Syndrome*. Chichester, UK: John Wiley, 1993.

Boltanski, Luc. *Distant Suffering: Morality, Media and Politics*. Translated by Graham Burchell. Cambridge: Cambridge University Press, 1999.

Bornstein, Erica. *Disquieting Gifts: Humanitarianism in New Delhi*. Palo Alto, CA: Stanford University Press, 2012.

Bornstein, Erica, and Peter Redfield, eds. *Forces of Compassion: Humanitarianism between Ethics and Politics*. Santa Fe, NM: School of Advanced Research, 2011.

Bose, Sumantra. *Contested Lands: Israel-Palestine, Kashmir, Bosnia, Cyprus and Sri Lanka*. Cambridge, MA: Harvard University Press, 2007.

Bose, Tapan, Dinesh Mohan, Gautam Navlakha, and Sumanta Banerjee. "India's 'Kashmir War.'" *Economic and Political Weekly* 25, no. 13 (1990): 650–52.

Breslau, Joshua. "Posttraumatic Stress Disorder in International Health." *Culture, Medicine and Psychiatry* 38 (2004): 113–26.

Briggs, Charles. "'Dear Dr. Freud.'" *Cultural Anthropology* 29, no. 2 (2014): 312–43.

British Medical Association. *Doctors Working in Conflicts and Emergencies—An Ethical Toolkit*. London: British Medical Association, 2017.

Brodwin, Paul. *Everyday Ethics: Voices from the Front Lines of Community Psychiatry*. Berkeley: University of California Press, 2013.

Brus, Ole, Pia Nordanskog, Ullvi Båve, Yang Cao, Åsa Hammar, Mikael Landén, Johan Lundberg, and Axel Nordenskjöld. "Subjective Memory Immediately Following Electroconvulsive Therapy." *Journal of Electroconvulsive Therapy* 33 (2017): 96–103.

Buchbinder, Mara. *All in Your Head: Making Sense of Pediatric Pain*. Berkeley: University of California Press, 2011.

Butler, Judith. *Frames of War: When Is Life Grievable?* London: Verso, 2009.

Butler, Judith. "Giving an Account of Oneself." *Diacritics* 31, no. 4 (2001): 22–40.

Calhoun, Craig. "A World of Emergencies: Fear, Intervention, and the Limits of Cosmopolitan Order." *Canadian Review of Sociology* 41, no. 4 (2004): 373–95.

Canguilhem, Georges. *On the Normal and the Pathological*. New York: Zone, 1991.

Carr, Summerson E. *Scripting Addiction: The Politics of Therapeutic Talk and American Sobriety*. Princeton, NJ: Princeton University Press, 2010.

Ceceña, Ana Esther. "On the Complex Relation between Knowledges and Emancipations." Translated by Brenda Baletti. *South Atlantic Quarterly* 111, no. 1 (2012): 111–32.

Chanpattana, Worrawat, Barry Alan Kramer, Girish Kunigiri, B. N. Gangadhar, Rungrueng Kitphati, and Chittaranjan Andrade. "A Survey of the Practice of Electroconvulsive Therapy in Asia." *Journal of Electroconvulsive Therapy* 26, no. 1 (2010): 5–10.

Chanpattana, Worrawat, Girish Kunigiri, B. A. Kramer, and B. N. Gangadhar. "Survey of the Practice of Electroconvulsive Therapy in Teaching Hospitals in India." *Journal of Electroconvulsive Therapy* 21, no. 2 (2005): 100–104.

Chari, P. R., D. Suba Chandran, and Shaheen Akhtar. "Tourism and Peacebuilding in Jammu and Kashmir." Special Report no. 281, United States Institute for Peace, 2011.

Chua, Jocelyn. *In Pursuit of the Good Life: Aspiration and Suicide in Globalizing South India*. Berkeley: University of California Press, 2014.

Chua, Jocelyn. "The Register of 'Complaint': Psychiatric Diagnosis and the Discourse of Grievance in the South Indian Mental Health Encounter." *Medical Anthropology Quarterly* 26, no. 2 (2012): 221–40.

Cohen, Lawrence. *No Aging in India*. Berkeley: University of California Press, 1998.

Connolly, William E. "The Evangelical-Capitalist Resonance Machine." *Political Theory* 33, no. 6 (2005): 869–86.

Cusicanqui, Silvia Rivera. *"Ch'ixinakax utxiwa*: A Reflection on the Practices and Discourses of Decolonization." Translated by Brenda Baletti. *South Atlantic Quarterly* 111, no. 1 (2012): 95–109.

Czyzewski, Karina. "Colonialism as a Broader Social Determinant of Health." *International Indigenous Policy Journal* 2, no. 1 (2011).

Daniel, Valentine E. *Fluid Signs: Being a Person the Tamil Way*. Berkeley: University of California Press, 1984,

Das, Veena. *Affliction: Health, Disease, Poverty*. New York: Fordham University Press, 2015.

Das, Veena. *Critical Events: An Anthropological Perspective on Contemporary India*. Delhi: Oxford University Press, 1996.

Das, Veena. *Life and Words: Violence and the Descent into the Ordinary*. Berkeley: University of California Press, 2007.

De Jong, Kaz. *Psychosocial and Mental Health Interventions in Areas of Mass Violence: A Community-Based Approach*, 2nd ed. Amsterdam: Rozenberg, 2011.

de Jong, Kaz, N. Ford, S. Kam, K. Lokuge, S. Fromm, R. van Galen, B. Reilley, and R. Kleber. "Conflict in the Indian Kashmir Valley I: Exposure to Violence." *Conflict and Health* 2 (2008).

de Jong, Kaz, S. Kam, N. Ford, K. Lokuge, S. Fromm, R. van Galen, B. Reilley, and R. Kleber. "Conflict in the Indian Kashmir Valley II: Psychosocial Impact." *Conflict and Health* 2 (2008).

Derges, Jane. "Eloquent Bodies: Conflict and Ritual in Northern Sri Lanka." *Anthropology and Medicine* 16, no. 1 (2008): 27–36.

Dewachi, Omar. "Blurred Lines: Warfare and Health Care." *Medical Anthropology Theory* 2, no. 2 (2015): 95–101.

Dewachi, Omar. *Ungovernable Life: Mandatory Medicine and Statecraft in Iraq*. Stanford, CA: Stanford University Press, 2017.

Dhanda, Amita. "The Right to Treatment of Persons with Psychosocial Disabilities and the Role of the Courts." *International Journal of Law and Psychiatry* 28 (2005): 155–70.

Dhanda, Amita, D. S. Goel, and R. K. Chadda. "Law and Mental Health: Common Concerns and Varied Perspectives." In *Mental Health: An Indian Perspective, 1946–2003*, edited by S. P. Agarwal et al., 170–88. New Delhi: Elsevier, 2004.

Dickey, Sarah. "Permeable Homes: Domestic Service, Household Space and the Vulnerability of Class Boundaries in Urban India." *American Ethnologist* 27 (2000): 462–89.

Di Gregorio, Michael, and Jessica L. Merolli. "Introduction: Affective Citizenship and the Politics of Identity, Control, Resistance." *Citizenship Studies* 20, no. 8 (2016): 933–42.

Duschinski, Haley. "Destiny Effects: Militarization, State Power, and Punitive Containment in Kashmir Valley." *Anthropological Quarterly* 82, no. 3 (2009): 691–717.

Duschinski, Haley. "Fake Encounters and the Informalization of Everyday Violence in Kashmir Valley." *Cultural Studies* 24, no. 1 (2010): 110–32.

Duschinski, Haley, and Mona Bhan. "Introduction: Law Containing Violence: Critical Ethnographies of Occupation and Resistance." *Journal of Legal Pluralism and Unofficial Law* 49, no. 3 (2017): 253–67.

Duschinski, Haley, Mona Bhan, Ather Zia, and Cynthia Mahmood, eds. *Resisting Occupation in Kashmir*. Philadelphia: University of Pennsylvania Press, 2018.

Duschinski, Haley, and Shrimoyee Nandini Ghosh. "Constituting the Occupation: Preventive Detention and Permanent Emergency in Kashmir." *Journal of Legal Pluralism and Unofficial Law* 49 (2017): 314–37.

Ecks, Stefan. *Eating Drugs: Psychopharmaceutical Pluralism in India*. New York: New York University Press, 2013.

Edington, Claire E. *Beyond the Asylum: Mental Illness in French Colonial Vietnam*. Ithaca, NY: Cornell University Press, 2018.

Ehrenreich, Barbara, and Arlie Russell Hochschild, eds. *Global Woman: Nannies, Maids and Sex Workers in the New Economy*. New York: Henry Holt, 2004.

Elmslie, William. *Seedtime in Kashmir: A Memoir of William Jackson Elmslie*. London: J. Nisbet, 1875.

Ernst, Waltraud. "Crossing the Boundaries of 'Colonial Psychiatry': Reflections on the Development of Psychiatry in British India, c. 1870–1940." *Culture, Medicine and Psychiatry* 35 (2011): 536–45.

Ernst, Waltraud. "Idioms of Madness and Colonial Boundaries: The Case of the European and 'Native' Mentally Ill in Early Nineteenth Century British India." *Comparative Studies in Society and History* 39, no. 1 (1997): 153–81.

Espiritu, Yen. *Body Counts: The Vietnam War and Militarized Refugees*. Berkeley: University of California Press, 2014.

Ewing, Katherine P. "The Illusion of Wholeness: Culture, Self and the Experience of Inconsistency." *Ethos* 18, no. 3 (1990): 251–78.

Faheem, Farrukh. "Interrogating the Ordinary: Everyday Politics and the Struggle for *Azadi* in Kashmir." In *Resisting Occupation in Kashmir*, edited by Mona Bhan, Haley Duschinski, Ather Zia, and Cynthia Mahmood, 230–47. Philadelphia: University of Pennsylvania Press, 2018.

Fanon, Frantz. *A Dying Colonialism*. Translated by Haakon Chevalier. New York: Grove, 1965.

Fassin, Didier. *At the Heart of the State: The Moral World of Institutions*. Translated by Patrick Brown and Didier Fassin. New York: Pluto, 2015.

Fassin, Didier. *Humanitarian Reason: A Moral History of the Present*. Berkeley: University of California Press, 2012.

Fassin, Didier. "Humanitarianism as a Politics of Life." *Public Culture* 19, no. 3 (2007): 499–520.

Fassin, Didier. "Inequality of Lives, Hierarchies of Humanity: Moral Commitments and Ethical Dilemmas of Humanitarianism." In *In the Name of Humanity: The Government of Threat and Care*, edited by Ilana Feldman and Miriam Iris Ticktin. Durham, NC: Duke University Press, 2010.

Fassin, Didier, and Mariella Pandolfi, eds. *Contemporary States of Emergency: The Politics of Military and Humanitarian Intervention*. New York: Zone, 2010.

Fassin, Didier, and Richard Rechtman. *The Empire of Trauma: An Inquiry into the Condition of Victimhood*. Translated by Rachel Gomme. Princeton, NJ: Princeton University Press, 2009.

Fassin, Didier, and Maria Vasquez. "Humanitarian Exception as the Rule: The Political Ethology of the 1999 *Tragedia* in Venezuela." *American Ethnologist* 32, no. 3 (2005): 389–405.

Favret-Saada, Jeanne. "Being Affected." *Hau: Journal of Ethnographic Theory* 2, no. 1 (2012): 435–45.

Fazili, Gowhar. "Police Subjectivity in Occupied Kashmir: Reflections on an Account of a Police Officer." In *Resisting Occupation in Kashmir*, edited by Haley Duschinski, Mona Bhan, Ather Zia, and Cynthia Mahmood, 184–210. Philadelphia: University of Pennsylvania Press, 2018.

Feldman, Allen. *Archives of the Insensible: Of War, Photo Politics and Dead Memory*. Chicago: University of Chicago Press, 2015.

Feldman, Allen. *Formations of Violence: The Narrative of the Body and Political Terror in Northern Ireland*. Chicago: University of Chicago Press, 1991.

Feldman, Ilana. "The Humanitarian Condition: Palestinian Refugees and the Politics of Living." *Humanity: An International Journal of Human Rights, Humanitarianism and Development* 3, no. 2 (2012): 155–72.

Feldman, Ilana. *Life Lived in Relief: Humanitarian Predicaments and Palestinian Refugee Politics*. Oakland: University of California Press, 2018.

Feldman, Ilana. "Looking for Humanitarian Purpose: Endurance and the Value of Lives in a Palestinian Refugee Camp." *Public Culture* 27, no. 3 (2015): 427–47.

Feldman, Ilana, and Miriam Ticktin, eds. *In the Name of Humanity: The Government of Threat and Care*. Durham, NC: Duke University Press, 2010.

Foucault, Michel. *Psychiatric Power: Lectures at the Collège de France 1973–1974*. Translated by Graham Burchell. New York: Picador, 2008.

Foucault, Michel. *Society Must Be Defended: Lectures at the Collège de France 1975–1976*. New York: Picador, 2003.

Framke, Marla. "Political Humanitarianism in the 1930s: Indian Aid for Republican Spain." *European Review of History* 23, nos. 1–2 (2016): 63–81.

Galeano, Eduardo. *Days and Nights of Love and War*. Translated by Judith Brister. London: Pluto, 1983.

Garcia, Angela. *The Pastoral Clinic: Addiction and Dispossession along the Rio Grande*. Berkeley: University of California Press, 2010.

Ghassem-Fachandi, Parvis. *Pogrom in Gujarat: Hindu Nationalism and Anti-Muslim Violence in India*. Princeton, NJ: Princeton University Press, 2012.

Ghosh, Durba. *Sex and the Family in Colonial India*. Cambridge: Cambridge University Press, 2006.

Gilman, Nils. "Militarism and Humanitarianism." *Humanity* 3, no. 2 (2012): 173–78.

Giordano, Cristiana. *Migrants in Translation: Caring and the Logics of Difference in Contemporary Italy*. Oakland: University of California Press, 2014.

Giroux, Henry A. "Reading Hurricane Katrina: Race, Class, and the Biopolitics of Disposability." *College Literature* 33, no. 3 (2006): 171–96.

Goel, D. S., S. P. Agarwal, R. L. Ichhpujani, and S. Shrivastava. "Mental Health 2003: The Indian Scene." In *Mental Health: An Indian Perspective 1946–2003*, edited by S. P. Agarwal et al. New Delhi: Elsevier, 2013.

Good, Byron. "The Heart of What's the Matter: The Semantics of Illness in Iran." *Culture, Medicine and Psychiatry* 1, no. 1 (1977): 25–58.

Good, Byron. *Medicine, Rationality, and Experience: An Anthropological Perspective*. Cambridge: Cambridge University Press, 1994.

Gupta, Akhil. *Red Tape: Bureaucracy, Structural Violence and Poverty in India*. Durham, NC: Duke University Press, 2012.

Hacking, Ian. "Biopower and the Avalanche of Printed Numbers." *Humanities in Society* 5 (1982): 279–95.

Hage, Ghassan. "Hating Israel in the Field: On Ethnography and Political Emotions." *Anthropological Theory* 9, no. 1 (2009): 59–79.

Hajjar, Lisa. *Courting Conflict: The Israeli Military Court System in the West Bank and Gaza*. Berkeley: University of California Press, 2005.

Hamdy, Sherine. "Islam, Fatalism, and Medical Intervention: Lessons from Egypt on the Cultivation of Forbearance (*Sabr*) and Reliance on God (*Tawakkul*)." *Anthropological Quarterly* 82, no. 1 (2009): 173–96.

Hamdy, Sherine. "When the State and Your Kidneys Fail." *American Ethnologist* 35, no. 4 (2008): 553–69.

Hamdy, Sherine, and Soha Bayoumi. "Egypt's Popular Uprising and the Stakes of Medical Neutrality." *Culture, Medicine and Psychiatry* 40, no. 2 (2016): 223–41.

Hillyard, Paddy. "Law and Order." In *Northern Ireland: The Background to the Conflict*, edited by John Darby, 32–60. Belfast: Apple Tree, 1983.

Housen, Tambri, Annick Lenglet, Showkat Shah, Helal Sha, Shabnum Ara, Giovanni Pintaldi, and Alice Richardson. "Trauma in the Kashmir Valley and the Mediating Effects of Stressors of Daily Life on Symptoms of Posttraumatic Stress Disorder, Depression and Anxiety." *Conflict and Health* 13 (2019): 58.

Huen, Chi. "What Is Context? An Ethnophilosophical Account." *Anthropological Theory* 9, no. 2 (2009): 149–69.

Hull, Matthew S. "Documents and Bureaucracy." *Annual Review of Anthropology* 41 (2012): 251–67.

Hull, Matthew S. "The File: Agency, Authority and Autography in an Islamabad Bureaucracy." *Language and Communication* 23 (2003): 287–314.

Humanitarian Policy Group. "Measuring the Impact of Humanitarian Aid: A Review of Current Practices." HPG Research Report no. 17, Overseas Development Institute, London, 2004.

Human Rights Watch. "'Everyone Lives in Fear': Patterns of Impunity in Jammu and Kashmir," vol. 18, no. 11(C), 2006.

Hunt, Nancy Rose. *A Nervous State: Violence, Remedies and Reverie in Colonial Congo.* Durham, NC: Duke University Press, 2016.

Hussain, Nasser. "Hyperlegality." *New Criminal Law Review* 10, no. 4 (2007): 514–31.

Hyde, Sandra. "'Spending My Own Money, Harming My Own Body': Addiction Care in a Chinese Therapeutic Community." *Medical Anthropology* 36, no. 1 (2016): 61–76.

Inter-Agency Standing Committee. *IASC Guidelines on Mental Health and Psychosocial Support in Emergency Settings.* Geneva: IASC, 2007.

International People's Tribunal on Human Rights and Justice in Indian-Administered Kashmir. *Buried Evidence: Unknown, Unmarked and Mass Graves in Indian-Administered Kashmir.* Srinagar: IPTK, 2009.

Jackson, Michael. "The Prose of Suffering and the Practice of Silence." *Spiritus* 4, no. 1 (2004): 44–59.

Jain, Sumeet, and Sushrut Jadhav. "Pills That Swallow Policy: Clinical Ethnography of a Community Mental Health Program in Northern India." *Transcultural Psychiatry* 46, no. 1 (2009): 60–85.

James, Erica Caple. *Democratic Insecurities: Violence, Trauma and Intervention.* Oakland: University of California Press, 2010.

James, Erica Caple. "Ruptures, Rights and Repair: The Political Economy of Trauma in Haiti." *Social Science and Medicine* 70 (2010): 106–13.

Janzen, John M. "Therapy Management: Concept, Reality, Process." *Medical Anthropology Quarterly* 1, no. 1 (1987): 68–84.

Jassal, Aftab Singh. "Divine Politicking: A Rhetorical Approach to Possession." *Religions* 7 (2016): 117–35.

Jean-Klein, Iris. "Nationalism and Resistance: The Two Faces of Everyday Activism in Palestine during the Intifada." *Cultural Anthropology* 16, no. 1 (2001): 83–126.

Jenkins, Janis H. "The State Construction of Affect: Political Ethos and Mental Health among Salvadoran Refugees." *Culture, Medicine and Psychiatry* 15 (1991): 139–65.

Joshi, Manoj. *Lost Rebellion: Kashmir in the Nineties.* New Delhi: Penguin, 1999.

Junaid, Mohamad. "Death and Life under Occupation: Space, Violence, and Memory in Kashmir." In *Everyday Occupations: Experiencing Militarism in South Asia and the Middle East*, edited by Kamala Visweswaran, 158–274. Philadelphia: University of Pennsylvania Press, 2013.

Junaid, Mohamad. "Epitaphs as Counterhistories: Martyrdom, Commemoration, and the Work of Graveyards in Kashmir." In *Resisting Occupation in Kashmir*, edited by Haley Duschinski, Mona Bhan, Ather Zia, and Cynthia Mahmood, 248–77. Philadelphia: University of Pennsylvania Press, 2018.

Junaid, Mohamad. "A Letter to Fellow Kashmiris." In *Until My Freedom Has Come: The New Intifada in Kashmir,* edited by Sanjay Kak, 279–88. New Delhi: Penguin, 2011.

Junaid, Mohamad. "Youth Activists in Kashmir: State Violence, Tehreek and the Formation of Political Subjectivity." PhD dissertation, City University of New York, 2017.

Kabir, Ananya Jahanara. *Territory of Desire: Representing the Valley of Kashmir.* Minneapolis: University of Minnesota Press, 2009.

Kaiser, Bonnie N., Saiba Varma, Elizabeth Carpenter-Song, Rebecca Sareff, Sauharda Rai, and Brandon A. Kohrt. "Eliciting Recovery Narratives in Global Mental Health: Benefits and Potential Harms in Service User Participation." *Psychiatric Rehabilitation Journal* (July 29, 2019). doi: 10.1037/prj0000384.

Kak, Sanjay, ed. *Until My Freedom Has Come: The New Intifada in Kashmir.* New Delhi: Penguin, 2011.

Kalhan, Anil, Gerald P. Conroy, Mamta Kaushal, and Sam Scott Miller. "Colonial Continuities: Human Rights, Terrorism, and Security Laws in India." *Columbia Journal of Asian Law* 20 (2006): 93–234.

Kanjwal, Hafsa. "Building a New Kashmir: Bakshi Ghulam Muhammad and the Politics of State-Formation in a Disputed Territory (1953–1963)." PhD dissertation, University of Michigan, 2017.

Kapur, Ratna L. "The Story of Community Mental Health in India." In *Mental Health: An Indian Perspective 1946–2003,* edited by S. P. Agarwal et al., 92–100. New Delhi: Elsevier, 2004.

Kaul, Nitasha. "India's Obsession with Kashmir: Democracy, Gender, (Anti-)Nationalism." *Feminist Review* 119 (2018): 126–43.

Kaul, Nitasha. "Rise of the Political Right in India: Hindutva-Development Mix, Modi Myth and Dualities." *Journal of Labor and Society* 20, no. 4 (2017): 523–48.

Kaul, Suvir. "'An' You Will Fight, till the Death of It. . . .': Past and Present in the Challenge of Kashmir." *Social Research* 78, no. 1 (2011): 173–202.

Kaul, Suvir. *Of Gardens and Graves: Essays on Kashmir.* New Delhi: Three Essays Collective, 2015.

Kazi, Seema. *In Kashmir: Gender, Militarization and the Modern Nation State.* London: South End, 2009.

Kazi, Seema. "Law, Governance and Gender in Indian-Administered Kashmir." Working Paper no. 20, Center for the Study of Law and Governance, New Delhi, 2012.

Khalili, Laleh. *Time in the Shadows: Confinement in Counterinsurgencies.* Palo Alto, CA: Stanford University Press, 2012.

Khan, J. I. "Armed Conflict: Changing Instruments and Health Outcomes: A Study of Urban Households in Kashmir." *International Journal of Physical Social Sciences* 3, no. 7 (2013): 1–14.

Kilcullen, David. *Counterinsurgency.* Oxford: Oxford University Press, 2010.

Kimura, Makiko. "Protesting the AFSPA in the Indian Periphery: The Anti-Militarization Movement in Northeast India." In *Law and Democracy in Contem-*

porary India, edited by T. Yamamoto and T. Ueda, 147–68. Cham, Switzerland: Palgrave Macmillan, 2018.

Klein, Naomi. *The Shock Doctrine: The Rise of Disaster Capitalism.* New York: Henry Holt, 2007.

Kleinman, Arthur. "Care: In Search of a Health Agenda." *The Lancet* 386 (2015): 240–41.

Kleinman, Arthur, and Joan Kleinman. "The Appeal of Experience: The Dismay of Images: Cultural Appropriations of Suffering in Our Times." *Daedalus* 125, no. 1 (1996): 1–23.

Kleinman, Arthur, and Joan Kleinman. "Suffering and Its Professional Transformation." *Culture, Medicine and Psychiatry* 15, no. 3 (1991): 275–301.

Krishnan, Jayanth K. "India's 'Patriot Act': POTA and the Impact on Civil Liberties in the World's Largest Democracy." *Law and Equity: A Journal of Theory and Practice* 22 (2004): 265–300.

Lamb, Alastair. *Kashmir: A Disputed Legacy 1846–1990.* Oxford: Oxford University Press, 1991.

Larkin, Brian. "The Politics and Poetics of Infrastructure." *Annual Review of Anthropology* 42 (2013): 327–43.

Lawrence, Walter Roper. "Kashmir: Its People and Its Produce." *Pharmaceutical Journal: A Weekly Record of Pharmacy and Allied Sciences* 2 (1896): 275–76.

Lawrence, Walter Roper. *The Valley of Kashmir.* London: Henry Frowde, 1895.

Light-Lewis, Brynnan K. "The Deeds of Outsider Art." Master's thesis, Sotheby's Institute of Art, 2012.

Livingston, Julie. *Debility and the Moral Imagination in Botswana.* Bloomington: Indiana University Press, 2005.

Livingston, Julie. *Improvising Medicine: An African Oncology Ward in an Emerging Cancer Epidemic.* Durham, NC: Duke University Press, 2012.

Lock, Margaret, and Vinh-Kim Nguyen, eds. *An Anthropology of Biomedicine.* Chichester, UK: Wiley Blackwell, 2010.

Lokaneeta, Jinee. *Transnational Torture: Law, Violence and State Power in the United States and India.* New York: New York University Press, 2011.

Lokaneeta, Jinee, and Amar Jesani. "India." In *Does Torture Prevention Work?*, edited by Richard Carver and Lisa Handley, 501–48. Liverpool: Liverpool University Press, 2016.

Luhrmann, Tanya M. *Of Two Minds: An Anthropologist Looks at American Psychiatry.* New York: Random House, 2000.

Luthra, Rashmi. "Perils of Translation in a Conflict Situation: Lessons from Kashmir." *International Journal of Communication* 10 (2016): 1097–115.

Mahmood, Cynthia Keppley. "Dynamics of Terror in Punjab and Kashmir." In *Death Squad: The Anthropology of State Terror,* edited by Jeffrey A. Sluka, 70–90. Philadelphia: University of Pennsylvania Press, 2000.

Malik, Inshah. "Gendered Politics of Funerary Processions: Contesting Indian Sovereignty in Kashmir." *Economic and Political Weekly* 53, no. 47 (2018): 63–66.

Malik, Inshah. *Muslim Women, Agency and Resistance Politics: The Case of Kashmir.* Cham, Switzerland: Palgrave Macmillan, 2013.

Malkki, Liisa. *The Need to Help: The Domestic Arts of International Humanitarianism.* Durham, NC: Duke University Press, 2015.

Malkki, Liisa. "Speechless Emissaries: Refugees, Humanitarianism, and Dehistoricization." *Cultural Anthropology* 11, no. 3 (1996): 377–404.

Margoob, M. A., A. A. Beg, and K. S. Dutta. "Depressive Disorders in Kashmir: A Changing Sociodemographic and Clinical Profile of Patients over the Past Two Decades." *JK Practitioner* 2 (1993): 22–24.

Margoob, M. A., M. M. Firdosi, R. Banal, A. Y. Khan, Y. A. Malik, S. A. Ahmad, et al. "Community Prevalence of Trauma in South Asia—Experience from Kashmir." *JK Practitioner* 13 (Supplement) (2006): S14–17.

Marriott, McKim. "Hindu Transactions: Diversity without Dualism." In *Transaction and Meaning*, edited by Bruce Kapferer. Philadelphia: Institute for the Study of Human Issues, 1978.

Marriott, McKim, and R. Inden. "Towards Ethnosociology of South Asian Caste System." In *The New Wind: Changing Identities in South Asia*, edited by D. Kavid. The Hague: Mouton, 1977.

Marrow, Jocelyn. "Hot Brains and Knotted Nerves: Electroconvulsive Therapy in North India." Paper presented at the American Anthropological Association Annual Meeting, 2010.

Marrow, Jocelyn, and Tanya Marie Luhrmann. "The Zone of Social Abandonment in Cultural Geography: On the Street in the United States, Inside the Family in India." *Culture, Medicine and Psychiatry* 36 (2012): 493–513.

Marsden, Magnus. "Fatal Embrace: Trading in Hospitality on the Frontiers of South and Central Asia." *Journal of the Royal Anthropological Institute* 18, no. 1 (2012): S117–S130.

Marsden, Magnus. *Muslim Religious Experience in Pakistan's North-West Frontier.* Cambridge: Cambridge University Press, 2005.

Martin, Emily. *Bipolar Expeditions: Mania and Depression in American Culture.* Princeton, NJ: Princeton University Press, 2009.

Martínez-Hernáez, Angel. *What's behind the Symptom? On Psychiatric Observation and Anthropological Understanding.* Translated by Susan M. DiGiacomo and John Bates. Oxon, UK: Routledge, 2000.

Matza, Tomas. *Shock Therapy: Psychology, Precarity and Well-Being in Postsocialist Russia.* Durham, NC: Duke University Press, 2018.

Mauss, Marcel. *The Gift: The Form and Reason for Exchange in Archaic Societies.* London: Routledge, 1990.

Maynard, Kent. "The Poetic Turn of Culture, or the 'Resistances of Structure.'" *Anthropology and Humanism* 33 (2008): 66–84.

Maynard, Kent, and Melisa Cahnmann. "Anthropology at the Edge of Words: Where Poetry and Ethnography Meet." *Anthropology and Humanism* 35 (2010): 2–19.

Mazzarella, William. "Internet X-Ray: E-Governance, Transparency and the Politics of Immediation in India." *Public Culture* 18, no. 3 (2006): 473–505.

Mbembe, Achille. "Necropolitics." *Public Culture* 15 (2003): 11–40.

McDuie-Ra, Duncan. "Fifty-Year Disturbance: The Armed Forces Special Power Act and Exceptionalism in a South Asian Periphery." *Contemporary South Asia* 17, no. 3 (2009): 255–70.

McKay, Ramah. *Medicine in the Meantime: The Work of Care in Mozambique*. Durham, NC: Duke University Press, 2018.

Metcalf, Barbara. *Islamic Contestations: Essays on Muslims in India and Pakistan*. New Delhi: Oxford University Press, 2004.

Metzl, Jonathan M. *The Protest Psychosis: How Schizophrenia Became a Black Disease*. Boston: Beacon, 2009.

Misri, Deepti. "Showing Humanity: Violence and Visuality in Kashmir." *Cultural Studies* 33, no. 3 (2019): 527–49.

Mittermaier, Amira. "Beyond Compassion: Islamic Voluntarism in Egypt." *American Ethnologist* 41, no. 3 (2014): 518–31.

Mittermaier, Amira. "Bread, Freedom, Social Justice: The Egyptian Uprising and a Sufi Khidma." *Cultural Anthropology* 29, no. 1 (2014): 54–79.

Moghnie, Lamia M. "Humanitarian Psychology in War and Postwar Lebanon: Violence, Therapy and Suffering." PhD dissertation, University of Michigan, 2016.

Mufti, Gulzar. *Kashmir: In Sickness and in Health*. New Delhi: Penguin, 2013.

Mulla, Sameena. *The Violence of Care: Rape Victims, Forensic Nurses and Sexual Assault Intervention*. New York: New York University Press, 2014.

Murali, T., and Kiran Rao. "Psychiatric Rehabilitation in India: Issues and Challenges." In *Mental Health: An Indian Perspective, 1946–2003*, edited by S. P. Agarwal et al., 152–60. New Delhi: Elsevier, 2004.

Murphy, Michelle. "Unsettling Care: Troubling Transnational Itineraries of Care in Feminist Health Practices." *Social Studies of Science* 45, no. 5 (2015): 717–37.

Murthy, H. N. "Effects of Electroconvulsive Treatment on Memory and Intelligence in Schizophrenics." *Indian Journal of Psychiatry* 8 (1966): 138–42.

National Human Rights Commission. "Quality Assurance in Mental Health." New Delhi: National Human Rights Commission, 1999.

Navaro, Yael. "Diversifying Affect." *Cultural Anthropology* 32, no. 2 (2017): 209–14.

Neve, Arthur. *Picturesque Kashmir*. London: Sands and Company, 1990.

Neve, Arthur. *Thirty Years in Kashmir*. Lucknow: Asian Publications, 1984.

Nguyen, Vinh-Kim. *The Republic of Therapy: Triage and Sovereignty in West Africa's Time of AIDS*. Durham, NC: Duke University Press, 2010.

Nichter, Mark. "Idioms of Distress: Alternatives in the Expression of Psychosocial Distress: A Case Study from South India." *Cultural Medicine and Psychiatry* 5 (1981): 379–408.

Nichter, Mark. "Pharmaceuticals, the Commodification of Health, and the Health Care–Medicine Use Transition." In *Anthropology and International Health: Asian Case Studies*, edited by Mark Nichter and Mimi Nichter, 265–326. Newark, NJ: Gordon and Breach, 1996.

Nissinen, Sanaa. "Dilemmas of Ethical Practice in the Production of Contemporary Humanitarian Photography." In *Humanitarian Photography: A History*, edited by Heide Fehrenbach and Davide Rodogno, 297–321. Cambridge: Cambridge University Press, 2015.

Norris, Dermot. *Kashmir: The Switzerland of India: A Descriptive Guide with Chapters on Ski-ing and Mountaineering, Large and Small Game Shooting, Fishing, etc.* Calcutta: Newman, 1925.

Nunley, Michael. "Why Psychiatrists in India Prescribe So Many Drugs." *Culture, Medicine and Psychiatry* 20, no. 2 (1996): 165–97.

Oremus, Carolina, Mark Oremus, Heather McNeely, Bruno Losier, Melissa Parlar, Matthew King, Gary Hasey, Gagan Fervaha, Allyson C. Graham, Caitlin Gregory, Lindsay Hanford, Anthony Nazarov, Maria Restivo, Erica Tatham, Wanda Truong, Geoffrey B. C. Hall, Ruth Lanius, and Margaret McKinnon. "Effects of Electroconvulsive Therapy on Cognitive Functioning in Patients with Depression: Protocol for a Systematic Review and Meta-Analysis." *BMJ Open* 5, no. 3 (2015).

Osuri, Goldie. "Imperialism, Colonialism and Sovereignty in the (Post)Colony: India and Kashmir." *Third World Quarterly* 38, no. 11 (2017): 2428–43.

Pandey, Gayanendra. *Memory, History and the Question of Violence.* Calcutta: K. P. Bagchi, 1999.

Pandolfo, Stefania. "The Knot of the Soul: Postcolonial Conundrums, Madness, and the Imagination." In *Postcolonial Disorders*, edited by Mary-Jo DelVecchio Good, Sandra Teresa Hyde, Sarah Pinto, and Byron J. Good, 329–58. Berkeley: University of California Press, 2008.

Parrey, Arif Ayaz. "A Victorious Campaign." In *Until My Freedom Has Come*, edited by Sanjay Kak, 179–89. New Delhi: Penguin, 2011.

Pederson, David. *American Value: Migrants, Money and Meaning in El Salvador and the United States.* Chicago: University of Chicago Press, 2013.

Peer, Basharat. *Curfewed Night.* New Delhi: Penguin, 2008.

Petchesky, Rosalind. "Biopolitics at the Crossroads of Sexuality and Disaster: The Case of Haiti." Working Paper no. 8, Sexuality Policy Watch, New York, 2012.

Peters, David H., and V. R. Muraleedharan. "Regulating India's Health Services: To What End? What Future?" *Social Science and Medicine* 66 (2008): 2133–44.

Petryna, Adriana. "Ethical Variability: Drug Development and Globalizing Clinical Trials." *American Ethnologist* 32, no. 2 (2005): 183–97.

Pfingst, Annie, and Marsha Rosengarten. "Medicine as a Tactic of War: Palestinian Precarity." *Body and Society* 18, nos. 3–4 (2012): 99–125.

Pinto, Sarah. *Daughters of Parvati: Women and Madness in Contemporary India.* Philadelphia: University of Pennsylvania Press, 2014.

Pinto, Sarah. *The Doctor and Mrs. A.: Ethics and Counter-Ethics in an Indian Dream Analysis.* New York: Fordham University Press, 2019.

Pinto, Sarah. "The Limits of Diagnosis: Sex, Law and Psychiatry in a Case of Contested Marriage." *Ethos* 40, no. 2 (2012): 119–41.

Pinto, Sarah. "'The Tools of Your Chants and Spells': Stories of Madwomen and Indian Practical Healing." *Medical Anthropology* 35, no. 3 (2015): 263–77.

Povinelli, Elizabeth. *Empire of Love: Toward a Theory of Intimacy, Genealogy, and Carnality*. Durham, NC: Duke University Press, 2006.

Prakash, Siddhartha. "Political Economy of Kashmir since 1947." *Economic and Political Weekly* 35, no. 24 (2000): 2051–60.

Puar, Jasbir. *The Right to Maim: Debility, Capacity, Disability*. Durham, NC: Duke University Press, 2017.

Puar, Jasbir. "The 'Right' to Maim: Disablement and Inhumanist Biopolitics in Palestine." *Borderlands* 14, no. 1 (2015): 1–27.

Puig de la Bellacasa, Maria. "Matters of Care in Technoscience: Assembling Neglected Things." *Social Studies of Science* 41, no. 1 (2011): 85–106.

Rai, Mridu. *Hindu Rulers, Muslim Subjects: Islam, Rights, and the History of Kashmir*. Princeton, NJ: Princeton University Press, 2004.

Rajagopalan, Rajesh. "'Restoring Normalcy': The Evolution of the Indian Army's Counterinsurgency Doctrine." *Small Wars and Insurgencies* 11, no. 1 (2000): 44–68.

Rajkumar, Anto P., B. Saravanan, and K. S. Jacob. "Perspectives of Patients and Relatives about Electroconvulsive Therapy: A Qualitative Study from Vellore, India." *Journal of Electroconvulsive Therapy* 22, no. 4 (2006): 253–58.

Rao, Aparna. "The Many Sources of Identity: An Example of Changing Affiliations in Rural Jammu and Kashmir." *Ethnic and Racial Studies* 22, no. 1 (1999): 56–91.

Rashid, Iffat. "Theatrics of a 'Violent State' or 'State of Violence': Mapping Histories and Memories of Partition in Jammu and Kashmir. *South Asia: Journal of South Asian Studies* 44 (2020).

Rather, Feroz. *The Night of Broken Glass*. Noida: HarperCollins India, 2018.

Redfield, Peter. "Doctors, Borders, and Life in Crisis." *Cultural Anthropology* 20, no. 3 (2005): 328–61.

Redfield, Peter. *Life in Crisis: The Ethical Journey of Doctors Without Borders*. Berkeley: University of California Press, 2013.

Redfield, Peter. "The Unbearable Lightness of Ex-Pats: Double Binds of Humanitarian Mobility." *Cultural Anthropology* 27, no. 2 (2012): 358–82.

Reed, Adam. *Papua New Guinea's Last Place: Experiences of Constraint in a Postcolonial Prison*. New York: Berghahn, 2003.

Rejali, Darius. *Torture and Democracy*. Princeton, NJ: Princeton University Press, 2009.

Rhodes, Lorna. *Emptying Beds: The Work of an Emergency Psychiatric Unit*. Berkeley: University of California Press, 1991.

Riles, Annelise. *The Network Inside Out*. Ann Arbor: University of Michigan Press, 2000.

Riles, Annelise, and Iris Jean-Klein. "Introducing Discipline: Anthropology and Human Rights Administrations." *Political and Legal Anthropology Review* 28, no. 2 (2005): 173–202.

Robertson, A. F. "The Dal Lake: Reflections on an Anthropological Consultancy in Kashmir." *Anthropology Today* 3, no. 2 (1987): 7–13.

Robinson, Cabeiri deBergh. *Body of Victim, Body of Warrior: Refugee Families and the Making of Kashmiri Jihadists*. Berkeley: University of California Press, 2013.

Roy, Arundhati. *The God of Small Things*. New York: Random House, 1997.

Sadock, Benjamin J., Virginia A. Sadock, and Pedro Ruiz. *Clinical Psychiatry: Derived from Kaplan and Sadock's Synopsis of Psychiatry*, 11th ed. Philadelphia: Wolters Kluwer, 2017.

Sangaramoorthy, Thurka, and Adia Benton. "Enumeration, Identity, and Health." *Medical Anthropology* 31, no. 4 (2012): 287–91.

Saraf, Aditi. "Occupying the Frontier." Paper presented at the Annual Meeting on South Asia, Madison, WI, 2016.

Scarry, Elaine. *The Body in Pain: The Making and the Unmaking of the World*. New York: Oxford University Press, 1987.

Scherz, China. *Having People, Having Heart: Charity, Sustainable Development and Problems of Dependence in Central Uganda*. Chicago: University of Chicago Press, 2014.

Segal, Lotte Buch. "Tattered Textures of Kinship: The Effects of Torture among Iraqi Families in Denmark." *Medical Anthropology* 37, no. 7 (2018): 553–67.

Sen, Arup Kumar. "Kashmir: A State of Exception." *Economic and Political Weekly* 50, no. 8 (2015).

Shalhoub-Kevorkian, Nadera. "The Political Economy of Children's Trauma: A Case Study of House Demolition in Palestine." *Feminism and Psychology* 19, no. 3 (2009): 335–42.

Shalhoub-Kevorkian, Nadera. *Security Theology, Surveillance and the Politics of Fear*. Cambridge: Cambridge University Press, 2015.

Shear, M. K., N. Simon, M. Wall, S. Zisook, R. Neimeyer, N. Duan, and C. Reynolds. "Complicated Grief and Related Bereavement Issues for DSM-5." *Depression and Anxiety* 28, no. 2 (2011): 103–17.

Sheehan, Helen E., and S. J. Hussain. "Unani Tibb: History, Theory and Contemporary Practice in South Asia." *Annals of the American Academy of Political and Social Science* 583 (2002): 122–35.

Shorter, Edward, ed. *Bedside Manners: The Troubled History of Doctors and Patients*. New York: Simon and Schuster, 1985.

Shorter, Edward. "Chronic Fatigue in Historical Perspective." In *Chronic Fatigue Syndrome*, edited by Gregory R. Bock and Julie Whelan, 6–16. Chichester, UK: John Wiley, 1993.

Shoshan, Nitzan. *The Management of Hate: Nation, Affect, and the Governance of Right-Wing Extremism in Germany*. Princeton, NJ: Princeton University Press, 2016.

Shryock, Andrew. "Thinking about Hospitality, with Derrida, Kant, and the Balga Bedouin." *Anthropos* 103 (2008): 405–21.

Smith, Catherine. "Doctors That Harm, Doctors That Heal: Reimagining Medicine in Post-Conflict Aceh, Indonesia." *Ethnos: Journal of Anthropology* 80, no. 2 (2013): 1–20.

Snedden, Christopher. *Understanding Kashmir and Kashmiris*. London: C. Hurst, 2015.

Snelling, Mark. "The Impact of Emergency Aid Work on Personal Relationships: A Psychodynamic Study." *Journal of International Humanitarian Action* 3 (2018): 14–29.

Sobh, Rana, and Russell Belk. "Domains of Privacy and Hospitality in Arab Gulf Homes." *Journal of Islamic Marketing* 2, no. 2 (2011): 125–37.

Sobh, Rana, Russell W. Belk, and Jonathan A. J. Wilson. "Islamic Arab Hospitality and Multiculturalism." *Marketing Theory* 13, no. 4 (2013): 443–63.

Solnit, Rebecca. *A Paradise Built in Hell: The Extraordinary Communities That Arise in Disaster.* New York: Penguin, 2009.

Sonpar, Shobna. "A Potential Resource? Ex-militants in Jammu and Kashmir." *Intervention* 6, no. 2 (2008): 147–53.

Spivak, Gayatri Chakravorty. "Can the Subaltern Speak?" In *Marxism and the Interpretation of Culture,* edited by C. Nelson and L. Grossberg, 271–313. Basingstoke, UK: Macmillan Education, 1988.

Spivak, Gayatri Chakravorty. "'Draupadi' by Mahasveta Devi." *Critical Inquiry* 8, no. 2 (1981): 381–402.

Stevenson, Lisa. *Life beside Itself: Imagining Care in the Canadian Arctic.* Berkeley: University of California Press, 2014.

Stock, Eugene. *Beginnings in India.* London: Central Board of Missions, 1917.

Stoler, Ann L. *Carnal Knowledge and Imperial Power: Race and the Intimate in Colonial Rule.* Berkeley: University of California Press, 2010.

Strathern, Marilyn. *Partial Connections.* Walnut Creek, CA: Altamira, 1999.

Street, Alice. *Biomedicine in an Unstable Place.* Durham, NC: Duke University Press, 2014.

Summerfield, Derek. "The Invention of Post-Traumatic Stress Disorder and the Social Usefulness of a Psychiatric Category." *British Medical Journal* 322 (2001): 95–98.

Sunder Rajan, Kaushik, ed. *Lively Capital: Biotechnologies, Ethics and Governance in Global Markets.* Durham, NC: Duke University Press, 2012.

Szasz, Thomas. *The Myth of Psychotherapy: Mental Healing as Religion, Rhetoric and Repression.* Garden City, NY: Anchor, 1978.

Tanabe, Akio. "Cultural Politics of Life: Biomoral Humanosphere and Vernacular Democracy in Rural Orissa, India." Kyoto Working Papers on Area Studies no. 44, Center for Southeast Asian Studies, Kyoto University, 2009.

Taussig, Michael. "Culture of Terror, Space of Death: Roger Casement's Putumayo Report and the Explanation of Torture." *Comparative Studies in Society and History* 26, no. 3 (1984), 467–97.

Taussig, Michael. *The Nervous System.* New York: Routledge, 1992.

Taussig, Mick. "Terror as Usual: Walter Benjamin's Theory of History as a State of Siege." *Social Text* 23 (1989): 3–20.

Terry, Fiona. *Condemned to Repeat?* Ithaca, NY: Cornell University Press, 2002.

Terry, Jennifer. *Attachments to War: Biomedical Logics and Violence in Twenty-First-Century America.* Durham, NC: Duke University Press, 2017.

Thippeswamy, Harish, Kausik Goswami, and Santosh Chaturvedi. "Ethical Aspects of Public Health Legislation: The Mental Healthcare Bill, 2011." *Indian Journal of Medical Ethics* 11, no. 1 (2012): 46–49.

Throop, C. Jason. "Latitudes of Loss: On the Vicissitudes of Empathy." *American Ethnologist* 37, no. 4 (2010): 771–82.

Ticktin, Miriam. *Casualties of Care: Immigration and the Politics of Humanitarianism in France.* Berkeley: University of California Press, 2011.

Ticktin, Miriam. "Where Ethics and Politics Meet: The Violence of Humanitarianism in France." *American Ethnologist* 33, no. 1 (2006): 33–49.

Ticktin, Miriam. "A World without Innocence." *American Ethnologist* 44, no. 4 (2017): 577–90.

Trinh, T. Minh-ha. *Woman/Native/Other.* Bloomington: Indiana University Press, 1989.

Trisal, Nishita. "Banking on Uncertainty: Debt, Default and Violence in Indian Administered Kashmir." PhD dissertation, University of Michigan, 2020.

Varley, Emma. "Abandonments, Solidarities and Logics of Care: Hospitals as Sites of Sectarian Conflict in Gilgit-Baltistan." *Culture, Medicine and Psychiatry* 40, no. 2 (2015): 159–80.

Varley, Emma. "Against Protocol: The Politics and Perils of Oxytocin (Mis)Use in a Pakistani Labour Room." *Purusārtha* (2019).

Varley, Emma. "'Hallat Kharab'/Tension Times: The Maternal Health Costs of Gilgit's Sunni-Shia Conflict." In *Missing Links in Sustainable Development: South Asian Perspectives*, 53–80. Islamabad: Sustainable Development Policy Institute, 2008.

Varley, Emma, and Saiba Varma. "Spectral Lines: Haunted Hospitals across the Line of Control." *Medical Anthropology* 37, no. 6 (2018): 1–15.

Varma, Saiba. "Disappearing the Asylum: Modernizing Psychiatry and Generating Manpower in India." *Transcultural Psychiatry* 53, no. 6 (2016): 783–803.

Varma, Saiba. "From 'Terrorist' to 'Terrorized': How Trauma Became the Language of Suffering in Kashmir." In *Resisting Occupation in Kashmir*, edited by Haley Duschinski, Mona Bhan, Ather Zia, and Cynthia Mahmood, 129–52. Philadelphia: University of Pennsylvania Press, 2018.

Varma, Saiba. "Love in the Time of Occupation: Reveries, Longing and Intoxication in Kashmir." *American Ethnologist* 43, no. 1 (2016): 50–62.

Varma, Saiba. "Where There Are Only Doctors: Counselors as Psychiatrists in Indian Administered Kashmir." *Ethos* 40, no. 4 (2012): 517–35.

Visweswaran, Kamala, ed. *Everyday Occupations: Experiencing Militarism in South Asia and the Middle East.* Philadelphia: University of Pennsylvania Press, 2013.

Vora, Kalindi. *Life Support: Biocapital and the New History of Outsourced Labor.* Minneapolis: University of Minnesota Press, 2015.

Wagner, Roy. *The Anthropology of the Subject: Holographic Worldview in New Guinea and Its Meaning and Significance for the World of Anthropology.* Berkeley: University of California Press, 2001.

Waheed, Mirza. *The Collaborator.* New Delhi: Penguin, 2011.

Walsh, Catherine E. "The Decolonial *For:* Resurgences, Shifts, and Movements." In *On Decoloniality: Concepts, Analytics, Praxis,* edited by Walter D. Mignolo and Catherine E. Walsh, 15–33. Durham, NC: Duke University Press, 2018.

Watanabe, Chika. *Becoming One: Religion, Development, and Environmentalism in a Japanese NGO in Myanmar.* Honolulu: University of Hawai'i Press, 2018.

Watanabe, Chika. "Intimacy beyond Love: The History and Politics of Inter-Asian Development Aid." *Anthropological Quarterly* 92, no. 1 (2019): 59–84.

Watanabe, Chika. "Muddy Labor: A Japanese Aid Ethic of Collective Intimacy in Myanmar." *Cultural Anthropology* 29, no. 4 (2014): 648–71.

Weaver, Lesly Jo. "*Tension* among Women in North India: An Idiom of Distress and a Cultural Syndrome." *Culture, Medicine and Psychiatry* 41, no. 1 (2017): 35–55.

Wendland, Claire L. "Moral Maps and Medical Imaginaries: Clinical Tourism in Malawi's College of Medicine." *American Anthropologist* 114, no. 1 (2012): 108–22.

Whitehead, Andrew. *A Mission in Kashmir.* New Delhi: Penguin, 2007.

Wick, Livia. "Building the Infrastructure, Modeling the Nation: The Case of Birth in Palestine." *Culture, Medicine and Psychiatry* 32 (2008): 328–57.

Wilce, Jim. "'I Can't Tell You All My Troubles': Conflict, Resistance, and Metacommunication in Bangladeshi Illness Interactions." *American Ethnologist* 22, no. 4 (1995): 927–52.

Wilderson, Frank B. "'We're Trying to Destroy the World': Anti-Blackness and Police Violence after Ferguson." In *Shifting Corporealities in Contemporary Performance: Danger, Im/Mobility and Politics,* edited by Marina Gržinić and Aneta Stojnić, 45–59. Cham, Switzerland: Palgrave Macmillan, 2015.

Wilkinson, Iain, and Arthur Kleinman. *A Passion for Society: How We Think about Human Suffering.* Berkeley: University of California Press, 2016.

Willen, Sarah. "Darfur through a Shoah Lens: Sudanese Asylum Seekers, Unruly Biopolitical Dramas, and the Politics of Humanitarian Compassion in Israel." In *A Reader in Medical Anthropology: Theoretical Trajectories, Emergent Realities,* vol. 15, edited by B. J. Good, M. M. Fischer, S. S. Willen, and M. J. D. Good, 505–21. New York: Wiley, 2010.

Yaswi, Arooj, and Amber Haque. "Prevalence of PTSD Symptoms and Depression and Level of Coping among the Victims of the Kashmir Conflict." *Journal of Loss and Trauma* 13 (2008): 471–80.

Young, Allan. *The Harmony of Illusions: Inventing Post-Traumatic Stress Disorder.* Princeton, NJ: Princeton University Press, 1995.

Zakaria, Anam. *Between the Great Divide: A Journey into Pakistan-Administered Kashmir.* Noida: HarperCollins India, 2018.

Zia, Ather. "Kashmir from Orient to a State of Exception." *Funambulist* 8 (2016).

Zia, Ather. "The Killable Kashmiri Body: The Life and Execution of Afzal Guru." In *Resisting Occupation in Kashmir,* edited by Mona Bhan, Haley Duschinski, Ather Zia, and Cynthia Mahmood, 103–28. Philadelphia: University of Pennsylvania Press, 2018.

Zia, Ather. "Postcolonial Nation-Making: Warfare, Jihad, Subjectivity and Compassion in the Region of Kashmir." *India Review* 13, no. 3 (2014): 300–311.

Zia, Ather. *Resisting Disappearance: Military Occupation and Women's Activism in Kashmir.* Seattle: University of Washington Press, 2019.

Zutshi, Chitralekha. *Languages of Belonging: Islam, Regional Identity, and the Making of Kashmir.* Oxford: Oxford University Press, 2004.

Zutshi, Chitralekha. "An Ongoing Partition: Histories, Borders and the Politics of Vivisection in Jammu and Kashmir." *Contemporary South Asia* 23, no. 3 (2015): 266–75.

border: Kashmir and, 17–18, 104, 106–7, 167; militarization of, 21, 23, 105. *See also* cross-border terrorism; Line of Control (LoC)

Border Security Force (BSF), 21, 22, 61, 99, 119. *See also* security forces

care: affects of, 12, 26, 30, 45–46, 104, 116, 160, 170, 171; affective labor and, 13, 39, 26–27, 71, 133, 145, 147, 181; aftermath of, 138–41, 144; colonialism and, xvi, 15, 20, 23–24, 29, 42, 50, 100, 170, 198, 211n83; contestations over, 28, 35, 71, 75, 81, 86, 113, 120–21, 124, 163; theorizations of, xx, 9, 11–14, 25–26, 30, 56, 63–64, 125–26, 150, 180, 190, 192–93, 205n29. *See also* everyday care; humanitarianism; militarized care; psychosocial care; treatment

Cargo detention center, 61

Ceceña, Ana Esther, 183

Central Reserve Police Force (CRPF), 7, 21–22, 108–9. *See also* security forces

Centre of Excellence, 89–90, 92, 95–96

Chua, Jocelyn Lim, 39, 240n77

civil disobedience, xviii, 2, 23, 72, 174. *See also* strike: protest and

clinic: disturbances in, 27, 43, 46, 56, 68, 70–71, 74–77, 88–92, 98, 109, 112–13, 115, 184, 198; ethnographic object as, 8–9; failures of, 138–39, 141; interactions in, 4, 6, 8, 28, 37–38, 40, 56–57, 78, 86, 120–21; knowing in, 11, 30, 142; miscommunications in, 15, 38, 71, 147, 155, 161; theorizations of, 11, 13–14, 25–28, 35, 100, 116, 121, 184. *See also* IMHAN; public health; SMHS

clinical care. *See* psychiatry; public health

clinical narrative, 126–31. *See also* recovery narrative

cognitive behavioral therapy (CBT), 127, 238n56

Cohen, Lawrence, 36, 53

collaboration: counterinsurgency and, 42–43, 57–59, 177; fears of, 53, 56, 87,

173, 180, 223n12; *mukhbir* and, 59, 61, 63–64; network of, 13, 15, 55, 97; psychiatric distress and, 62, 64. *See also* counterinsurgency; īkhwan

The Collaborator, 106, 141

colonialism: British rule, 16, 18–19, 28, 45, 47, 52, 72; Dogra rule, 15–16, 19, 45–47, 54, 67; history of, xix, 2, 9, 10, 13–14, 21, 25, 29, 41, 50–51; Indian neocolonialism and, 18, 20, 24, 209; love and, 10, 13, 19–20, 198; medicine and, 28–29; settler colonialism, xvii–xviii; Sikh rule, xix, 15, 16. *See also* occupation

communication blackout, xvi–xvii, 15, 17, 19, 23, 112, 231n27

community-based mental health care: incompleteness of, 137–39; rationales for, 122–25; temporalities of, 128–31; tensions in, 133–35. *See also* asylum; IMHANS; psychiatry

contextualization, 8–9, 147, 235

continue same treatment (CST), 3, 130

coping. *See* everyday care; trauma: coping and

Corin, Ellen, 63

corruption: activism against, 49–53, 85–87; Kashmir and, 8, 15, 27, 45, 75, 77, 81, 83–85, 98, 169, 193; medicine and, 15, 23, 27, 48–50, 77–78, 81. *See also* pharmaceuticals: scandal of

counterinsurgency: effects of, 15, 26–27, 36, 44, 56, 64, 71, 157; gender and, 14; history of, 201n5, 206–7n37; imaginaries of, 9, 12–13, 41–44, 58, 71–72, 117, 157, 170; military doctrine and, 54, 70, 175, 186, 198; police and, 61–62, 169–70, 186, 220n67; remains of, 7, 43. *See also* ikhwān; militarized care; winning hearts and minds

crisis: Kashmir and, 15, 28, 68, 77, 175–76, 188; mental health, 3, 24, 29, 35, 40, 91, 115, 160; public health, 74, 81, 84; technologies of, 117, 129, 131; temporality of, 69, 72, 125, 178–79, 222n7, 252n72

cross-border terrorism, 2, 20–21. *See also* border; Line of Control (LoC)

Fanon, Frantz, 29, 205n27, 211n83, 213n102

Fatima, Iffat, 163–64

Favret-Saada, Jeanne, 87

Fazili, Gowhar, 220n67, 223n12

Feldman, Ilana, 69, 125

fieldwork: disturbance and, 68, 73, 88, 109; process of, 1, 3, 8, 12–13, 87, 103–4, 176, 201n2, 203n13, 204n18, 220n70, 226n42; temporality and, xix, 194–95

flood: counterinsurgency and, 169, 171; destruction and, 167–68; narratives of, 168, 170, 175, 177–78; rescue and relief, 168, 172

Foucault, Michel, 162, 179, 213n102, 216n18, 241n2

gender: activism and, 84–85, 107; care and, 12, 32, 36–37, 49, 83, 87, 104, 107, 152; counterinsurgency and, 13–14; diagnosis and, 35, 39, 194, 213n100; psychiatry and, 104, 201n1, 232n8, 236n38; state violence and, 41–42, 67, 72, 74, 96, 164, 206n36, 224n15

Ghosh, Shrimoyee Nandini, 202n6

gift: hospitality vs., 181, 249n44; psychosocial care as, 28, 150, 153, 161. See also Mauss, Marcel

Gilgit-Baltistan, 16, 17, 167

Giordano, Cristiana, 146

Government Medical College (GMC), 82, 83, 226n36. See also SMHS (Sri Maharaja Hari Singh) hospital

Gujar, 34, 160, 214n5

habitus. See occupation: habitus and

Hamdy, Sherine, 218n38

hearing: politics of, 30–31, 53, 54, 65

Hindutva, 205n28. See also Bharatiya Janata Party (BJP); Modi, Narendra

Hizbul Mujahideen (HM), 20, 174, 210n70, 248n22. See also insurgency; Wani, Burhan

hospitality: economic as, 183, 251; Islamic notions of, 181–82, 191; politico-ethical practice and, 12, 30, 73, 112, 166,

187–90, 192–94, 195. See also everyday care; gift: hospitality vs.

humanitarianism: dependency and, 21, 51, 182; militarism and, 9–11, 14, 17, 26, 56, 62, 85, 113, 116, 117, 121–22, 126, 141, 183–85; nationalism and, 11, 25; organizations and, 3, 12, 40, 45, 79, 93, 144, 148–49, 153, 156; theories of, 13, 15, 26–30, 69, 81, 125, 145, 147, 150, 155, 159, 165–66, 170–72, 178–79, 181, 192, 202n5; transformations in, 146, 151, 160, 162–63. See also Action Aid International; Kashmir LifeLine; Médecins sans Frontières (MSF); political humanitarianism; psychosocial care

human rights: advocacy and, 40, 58, 75, 163, 230n, 234, 235, 237; organizations, 118, 154; violations of, 22–23, 58, 62, 99, 106, 119–20, 123, 171, 203n15, 206n37, 211n82, 222n6, 225n23, 229n14, 230n16, 231n27, 234n15. See also Jammu and Kashmir Coalition of Civil Society (JKCCS)

humor, xv, 71, 78–79, 80, 81, 93, 114–15, 193, 231n3

Hunt, Nancy Rose, 204n25

ikhwān, 5, 22, 58–59, 77, 92. See also collaboration; counterinsurgency

IMHANS (Institute of Mental Health and Neuro Sciences), 90, 201n1. See also asylum; community-based mental health care; psychiatry

impact. See humanitarianism: transformations in

imperialism. See colonialism

impunity: emergency laws and, 8, 69–70, 230n16; public health and, 14–15, 23, 79, 87, 144–45; security forces and, 68, 74

independence. See āzādī; pro-independence movement

Indian state: Kashmir strategies, xvii, 13, 18, 19, 20, 22, 25, 41, 50–51, 57–58, 68, 72, 74, 105, 106, 147, 149, 168–69, 179, 183, 201n5; nervousness and, 11, 78, 170,

vulnerability: determinations of, 154–55; mental illness and, 137; relations of, 165, 196

Waheed, Mirza, 58, 106, 175
Wani, Burhan, 174–75, 185, 193–94, 198, 248n22. *See also* Hizbul Mujahideen; insurgency; pro-independence movement; protest

winning hearts and minds, 10–11, 13, 54, 99, 107, 150, 173, 175, 198, 206–7n37. *See also* counterinsurgency; militarized care

World Health Organization (WHO), 89, 122

Zia, Ather, 107
zoë, 117, 133; *bios* vs., 233n11